Marking God's Word
Understanding Jesus

Phillip A. Ross

Marietta, Ohio

©2007 Phillip A. Ross
Edition: 2020.11.24

ISBN: 978-0-6151-7603-1

Published by
Pilgrim Platform
149 E. Spring St.
Marietta, Ohio 45750
www.pilgrim-platform.org

Unless otherwise noted Scripture quotations in this publication are from the Modern King James Bible. Copyright (c) 1962, 1990, 1993, Jay Green, Sr., Published by Sovereign Grace Trust Fund, Lafayette, Indiana, USA, 47903.

Printed in the United States of America

to my wife, Stephanie,
for her perseverance

BOOKS BY PHILLIP A. ROSS

The Work At Zion—A Reckoning, Two-volume set, 772 pages, 1996.

Practically Christian—Applying James Today, 135 pages, 2006.

The Wisdom of Jesus Christ in the Book of Proverbs, 414 pages, 2006.

Marking God's Word—Understanding Jesus, 324 pages, 2006.

Acts of Faith—Kingdom Advancement, 326 pages, 2007.

Informal Christianity—Refining Christ's Church, 136 pages, 2007.

Engagement—Establishing Relationship in Christ, 104 pages, 1996, 2008.

It's About Time! — The Time Is Now, 40 pages. 2008.

The Big Ten—A Study of the Ten Commandments, 105 pages, 2001, 2008.

Arsy Varsy—Reclaiming The Gospel in First Corinthians, 406 pages, 2008.

Varsy Arsy—Proclaiming The Gospel in Second Corinthians, 356 pages, 2009.

Colossians—Christos Singularis, 278 pages, 2010.

Rock Mountain Creed—The Sermon on the Mount, 310 pages, 2011.

The True Mystery of the Mystical Presence, 355 pages, 2011.

Peter's Vision of Christ's Purpose in First Peter, 340 pages, 2011.

Peter's Vision of The End in Second Peter, 184 pages, 2012.

The Religious History of Nineteenth Century Marietta, Thomas Jefferson Summers, 124 pages, 1903, 2012 (editor).

Conflict of Ages—The Great Debate of the Moral Relations of God and Man, Edward Beecher, 489 pages, 1853, 2012 (editor).

Concord Of Ages—The Individual And Organic Harmony Of God And Man, Edward Beecher, D. D., 524 pages, 1860, 2013 (editor).

Ephesians—Recovering the Vision of a Sustainable Church in Christ, 417 pages, 2013.

Galatians: Backstory/Christory, 315 pages, 2015.

Poet Tree—Root, Branch & Sap, 72 pages, 2013.

Inside Out Woman—Collected Poetry, Doris M. Ross, 195 pages, 2014 (editor).

God's Great Plan for the World, 305 pages, 2019.

John's Miracles—Seeing Beyond Our Expectations, 210 pages, 2019.

TABLE OF CONTENTS

INTRODUCTION

I decided to preach through the Gospel of Mark to see if Mark—and Jesus—addressed the fact that people misunderstand the Gospel. So much of what calls itself Christianity today appears to misunderstand, misinterpret, and misappropriate the Gospel that I wondered if this trend was new. It's not. People have been misunderstanding the God's Word since week two—the Fall.

People ought to see the real truths of Scripture in the life and from the lips of Jesus, not just from Paul and the Apostles, or the Protestant Reformers. Understanding that the biblical teachings about God's grace come from the life and teachings of Jesus should provide them with more credibility among contemporary Christians. People brush off the idea that there is biblical truth with the notion that anything anyone says about the Bible is just their opinion. Well, our thoughts and ideas ought to conform to the truth, but such conformity does not mean that biblical truth is merely a matter of personal opinion.

As Jesus began His ministry He was met with much misunderstanding and disbelief. No one seemed to know what He was doing or talking about. His friends and family misunderstood Him. Even the twelve disciples failed to understand the gospel until Jesus returned in His resurrected form to explain it to them. We find story after story of Jesus being misunderstood or attempting to correct many popular misunderstandings that were in circulation at the time. Those stories and misunderstandings centered on the miracles and wonders that seemed to accompany Jesus wherever He went. People were tempted to make Him into a sort of magician. Crowds came, not to hear His preaching, but to see wonders and receive miracles. They came for what they could get for themselves or for their families.

The disciples, like most everyone else in Mark's gospel, were focused on themselves and what they could get from Jesus. In exasperation Jesus finally contradicted their self-centeredness with a clear expression of His intent.

> "Whoever desires to come after Me, let him deny himself, and take up his cross, and follow Me" (Mark 8:34).

The disciples had been in it for own their glory, Christ was in it for the cross and God's glory.

My faithful assistants on this Markan journey have been John Calvin (*Commentaries*, Baker Books, reprint 1993) and J.C. Ryle (*Mark*, Banner of Truth, reprint 1994). They have been helpful allies. Although I have received much instruction from them, I have not bound myself to them. Rather, I have tried to expose the gospel in a way that is both practical and instructive, particularly in regard to correcting and/or challenging aberrant Christian beliefs afoot in our day. I pray the result is both edifying to genuine faith, and challenging to faith that is less than genuine.

Special thanks are also due to Putnam Congregational Church, Marietta, Ohio, for persevering through this series. The chapters were first presented as a sermon series over the course of my ministry at Putnam (1996-1999). It was not one long series, but was broken up over several years, and represents the general character of my preaching there. I pray that the Lord will find it faithful and useful for His purposes.

Phillip A. Ross
Marietta, Ohio

1. PREPARATION

The beginning of the gospel of Jesus Christ, the Son of God. As it is written in the Prophets: 'Behold, I send My messenger before Your face, Who will prepare Your way before You. The voice of one crying in the wilderness: "Prepare the way of the LORD; Make His paths straight."' John came baptizing in the wilderness and preaching a baptism of repentance for the remission of sins. Then all the land of Judea, and those from Jerusalem, went out to him and were all baptized by him in the Jordan River, confessing their sins. Now John was clothed with camel's hair and with a leather belt around his waist, and he ate locusts and wild honey. And he preached, saying, 'There comes One after me who is mightier than I, whose sandal strap I am not worthy to stoop down and loose. I indeed baptized you with water, but He will baptize you with the Holy Spirit.' It came to pass in those days that Jesus came from Nazareth of Galilee, and was baptized by John in the Jordan. And immediately, coming up from the water, He saw the heavens parting and the Spirit descending upon Him like a dove. Then a voice came from heaven, 'You are My beloved Son, in whom I am well pleased' Immediately the Spirit drove Him into the wilderness. And He was there in the wilderness forty days, tempted by Satan, and was with the wild beasts; and the angels ministered to Him. —Mark 1:1-13

Mark begins his story with John the Baptist in order to indicate that the story of the gospel of Jesus Christ actually began in the Old Testament. Jesus Christ is the fulfillment of the Old Testament messianic promises, and to fail to understand this will obscure the fact that the two Testaments belong to a single story. According to Mark, John's voice crying out in the wilderness of a bankrupt religious system provided the prophetic hinge between the Old and New Testaments. In the old days heralds would run ahead of an approaching king to announce his immanent arrival so that people could prepare for him. In the same way, John announced the coming of King Jesus.

1

But note also that the Old Testament taught that God Himself through His messengers would prepare the hearts and minds of His people to receive His Son as Lord and Savior. How? By sending John, His messenger. The Greek word is *aggelos* and means a messenger, envoy, or one who is sent. It is often translated as *angel,* to suggest a messenger from God. God's grace is not only the grace of salvation, it is the grace of preparation. How can sinners prepare for a salvation that is entirely foreign to them? Only by the grace of God preveniently anticipating before He intervenes.

Jesus Christ broke into human history uninvited. Jesus was not replying to an invitation to provide salvation for lost men. Rather, He was sent by His Father to provide a salvation that was beyond the reach of both the desires and abilities of men to provide, or even to ask. But not beyond hope.

John came "preaching a baptism of repentance" (v. 4). Baptism among the Old Testament Jews was reserved for non-Jews who converted to the Jewish faith. They did not baptize infants, they circumcised infants as a sign that God's covenant had been imposed upon them by God's law. Infants did not ask to be circumcised. Baptism was a sign and seal of conversion—not merely entry into the faith, but a complete change of mind and heart. It signaled the complete letting go of one life, with all the beliefs, values, and relationships that attended it, and the conscious, intentional taking up of another life that comprised a completely different set of beliefs, values, and relationships.

John didn't simply offer this baptism of repentance, he proclaimed it. John didn't bring an offer of the gospel of Christ to all who would accept it. John announced that God had decreed it. God didn't do any feasibility studies. He didn't survey the locals to see if they might respond to the salvation of Jesus Christ. God, said John, declared it because He willed it, not because people might want to participate. The salvation that John announced was the fiat of God.

Yet, the baptism that John preached was not an unconscious change of mind and heart. John preached the baptism of repentance. John called for a return to something prior, not merely a change to something new. To repent means to think again about something. It, too, signifies a change, and more specifically repentance as John used it called for a return to a previous relationship with God. John called for a return to biblical values, and therefore, a return to the gospel of grace that had been long abandoned by the Pharisees of his time.

The Pharisees, men of position in the temple and among the Jews during John's day, had abandoned the gospel of grace for a feigned obedience to the law. The Pharisees represented a legalism of the most stringent kind. They had fallen from an understanding that God's law was a goad for the gospel of grace, to a belief that they could—and must—obey God perfectly. For a variety of reasons the Old Testament gospel of grace had been abandoned.

That often happens when church administration becomes the dominant church motif. Administration is an effort of control and order, which are certainly necessary, but not primary. The problem comes when we view control and order as our responsibility rather than God's. We get into trouble when we attempt to control God's church. We usually end up imposing our own thoughts, desires, and efforts upon the teaching of God's Word. Rather than reading God's will out of Scripture, we too easily read our own will into it. Rather than hearing what it says, we make it say what we want to hear.

John proclaimed a return to the old ways of grace and dependence upon God. In this, John struck a sympathetic chord among the people. Mark notes that

> "all the land of Judea, and those from Jerusalem, went out to him
> and were all baptized by him in the Jordan River, confessing
> their sins" (v. 5).

Does that mean that there was not a single Jew who did not receive John's baptism? No, it doesn't. The Pharisees, for instance, did not. Is Scripture then inaccurate? No.

The best way to understand John's use of the word *all* here is to think of your teenage son or daughter, who says to you, "But dad, *all* the kids are going to the party!" Are *all* of the children in the neighborhood or school really going to the party? No, they aren't. Your teenager simply means that *most* of the people that are important to him or her will be there. Similarly, Mark indicates that John's preaching marked a significant movement among the people. Their response to his preaching constituted a major social movement.

John also makes a categorical differentiation between his baptism of repentance and the Lord's baptism "with the Holy Spirit" (v. 8). There are many differences that we can make between these two baptisms, but suffice it to say that John's baptism was symbolic while Christ's is real. Baptism with the Holy Spirit amounts to an actual, spiritual initiation into God's kingdom or Christ's Church. As such, neither the kingdom nor the Church are coterminous with any human organization, but overlap earthly institutions with the reality of the invading kingdom of God. John's baptism was a temporal ordinance, while Christ's baptism is a divine ordinance. One happens in time, the other in eternity. Sometimes they are coterminous, but not always.

In an amazing demonstration of humility Jesus submitted to John's baptism of repentance. As Christ submitted to John for baptism, He brought eternity and history together through the incarnate flesh of the Lord of glory. The other gospel writers add more details to the story. Mark simply notes that it happened.

The issue of reading our own expectations into Scripture looms large in the story of Jesus' baptism. For instance, many people assume that Jesus was immersed in the Jordan, but the truth of the matter is that there simply isn't enough information given to determine how the baptism was done.

If we assume that John's baptism was by immersion, then that's what we see. But if we assume it was by pouring or sprinkling, we can see just as much evidence to support it. All that Mark tells us is that Jesus came "up from (or out of) the water" (v. 10). An immersion assumption reads that He emerged from being completely immersed under the water of the river, where a pouring or sprinkling assumption reads that He came up from (or out of) the river, having been baptized in water that may not have been deep enough for immersion. Mark doesn't spell out the mode of baptism, probably because it was so common as to be assumed. There was no question about the mode of baptism when it was written.

With Jesus' baptism the Holy Spirit descended upon Him. Jesus saw it and John the Baptist witnessed it (John 1:32). Again, the presence of the Holy Spirit coming upon Jesus reveals a harmony between the Old and New Testaments. Mark quoted Isaiah 40:3 when he previously identified John as the precursor of Christ. John, he said, prepared the way for the Suffering Servant as described in Isaiah 53. Isaiah also prophesied that the Spirit of God would fall upon the Messiah.

> "Behold! My Servant whom I uphold, My Elect One in whom
> My soul delights! I have put My Spirit upon Him; He will bring
> forth justice to the Gentiles" (Isaiah 42:1).

Indeed, Jesus would bring the gospel to the Gentiles.

Mark tells us that no sooner was Jesus baptized than he was sent into the wilderness for forty days of temptation. It is natural to assume that

Satan brought Him to the dessert to tempt Him. But that's not what Mark said. Mark said that "the Spirit *drove* Him into the wilderness" (v. 12—italics added). Like Job, Jesus was brought into temptation by the will of God.

We often pray that the Lord will keep us from temptation, yet once we find ourselves in the midst of it we must necessarily conclude that we are there as a function of God's sovereign providence. Rather than simply blaming God for our misfortunes, such a belief will provide us with the assurance that because God brought us into temptation, God will see us through it. Even in the midst of temptation, we are not beyond the protection and care of the Lord. And what is even more awesome, we must conclude that we are in the midst of trials and temptations for our own good, to strengthen or purify us.

As "the angels ministered to Him" (v. 13), so the Lord will minister to us in our difficulties. But it is also true that just as God brought Jesus into the wilderness to be tempted, God may also test us in the kilns of temptation as well. Yet because Jesus was not abandoned in the wilderness, neither will His people be abandoned to temptation.

Two things happened to Jesus in the wilderness of temptation. Jesus engaged the protection of God's Word by quoting Scripture in the midst of temptation, and the Lord sent ministering angels. Thus, Scripture is always our best defense against the storms of temptation.

2. Fishin' With Jesus

Now after John was put in prison, Jesus came to Galilee, preaching the gospel of the kingdom of God, and saying, 'The time is fulfilled, and the kingdom of God is at hand. Repent, and believe in the gospel.' And as He walked by the Sea of Galilee, He saw Simon and Andrew his brother casting a net into the sea; for they were fishermen. Then Jesus said to them, 'Follow Me, and I will make you become fishers of men.' They immediately left their nets and followed Him. When He had gone a little farther from there, He saw James the son of Zebedee, and John his brother, who also were in the boat mending their nets. And immediately He called them, and they left their father Zebedee in the boat with the hired servants, and went after Him. —Mark 1:14-20

The instructive events of Christ's childhood and maturity into manhood—as valuable as they are—are ignored by Mark. The earliest and briefest of the gospel writers, Mark pressed immediately and relentlessly to the primary purpose of Christ's advent. Jesus Christ came to earth to save His people from aimlessness and sin. Mark was not concerned with looking back at Jesus' birth, but with the importance of the Lord's presence among people. The sense of immediacy that pervades Mark's gospel cuts right to Jesus' public ministry.

Briefly noting that John the Baptist set the stage for Jesus, Mark began his gospel record with Jesus' public ministry. John's ministry served as a preparation for the ministry of the Lord. John's ministry was so important that Jesus submitted to him for baptism. By submitting to John's baptism, Jesus acknowledged His debt to the Old Testament prophets, of whom John was one.

John's preaching message was simple, "Repent, for the kingdom of heaven is at hand!" (Matthew 3:2). John's message was essentially the same as all of the Old Testament prophets from Noah to Malachi. Fallen humanity desperately needs to abandon their sinful ways. Jesus, as the Messiah, was the fulfillment of this Old Testament teaching.

Jesus was not baptized by John because He needed to repent. Christ, the only sinless man to ever live, had nothing to repent of. Jesus' baptism was a different sort of baptism. There is much evidence that the baptism of Jesus served as a kind of ceremonial entry into His priesthood, or public ministry. It was an ordination, if not officially, then substantially. Attaining the age of thirty was the last priestly requirement for Jesus to fulfill. He had studied at a synagogue as a boy—and had astonished some teachers in the Temple one day with His understanding of the things of God (Luke 2:46-47), and had attended all the requisite religious festivals. John's baptism, which began Jesus' public ministry, served as a kind of ordination or commissioning service.[1]

Jesus picked up John's message,

> "The time is fulfilled, and the kingdom of God is at hand.
> Repent, and believe in the gospel" (v. 15).

Repentance and belief was the same message that John the Baptist had been preaching. One might say that Jesus and John were in the same tradition, preaching the same message. John even began to preach Christ crucified—"Behold, the Lamb of God" (John 1:29). By calling Jesus the Lamb of God, he prophetically pointed to Jesus' impending crucifixion.

Like John, Jesus also preached repentance. While repentance is not a condition that must be met prior to the reception of God's grace, it is a necessary fruit of regeneration. Personal repentance will always accompany genuine belief. And where personal repentance is not present, faithfulness must be in doubt.

Faithful Christians always stand ready to testify about their repentance. People who don't know what particular sins they have renounced, don't yet know the saving forgiveness of Christ. Faithful preaching of the gospel, from time immemorial, from the Old Testament to the New, has always been about faith and repentance. Real repentance always involves a real change—a change of attitude, a change of understanding, and a change of behavior. Sometimes the change is sudden, sometimes it's gradual, but it's always real. And because it is real, faithful Christians can testify to the difference Christ has made in their lives.

Mark says that

---

1   See Adams, Jay. *The Meaning and Mode of Baptism*, P&R Publishing, Philipsburg, NJ, 1975, p. 9-ff.

> "as (Jesus) walked by the Sea of Galilee, He saw Simon and
> Andrew his brother casting a net into the sea; for they were
> fishermen. Then Jesus said to them, 'Follow Me, and I will make
> you become fishers of men.' They immediately left their nets and
> followed Him" (vs. 16-18).

Have you ever wondered how these men could respond to Christ's call so promptly, when so many of the rest of us struggle with it for so long?

As we look at those who respond to the gospel of Christ, we can always trace their response to some prior activity or action by the Lord. Before people respond to God's grace we find that the Lord has prepared the way for their response. Scripture establishes this fact because Jesus had crossed Simon's path earlier.

The calling of Simon Peter is told in the fifth chapter of Luke in greater detail, as if Luke had been answering questions about how the first disciples came to be disciples. Luke tells us that Jesus had been teaching in Galilee.

> "When He had stopped speaking, He said to Simon, 'Launch out
> into the deep and let down your nets for a catch.' But Simon
> answered and said to Him, 'Master, we have toiled all night and
> caught nothing; nevertheless at Your word I will let down the
> net.' And when they had done this, they caught a great number
> of fish, and their net was breaking. So they signaled to their
> partners in the other boat to come and help them. And they came
> and filled both the boats, so that they began to sink. When
> Simon Peter saw it, he fell down at Jesus' knees, saying, 'Depart
> from me, for I am a sinful man, O Lord!' For he and all who were
> with him were astonished at the catch of fish which they had
> taken; and so also were James and John, the sons of Zebedee,
> who were partners with Simon. And Jesus said to Simon, 'Do not
> be afraid. From now on you will catch men.' So when they had
> brought their boats to land, they forsook all and followed Him"
> (Luke 5:4-11).

Here we see some of Luke's evidence regarding the process of Peter's conversion. However, prior to this experience Luke recorded that Jesus had visited Simon Peter's home. It seems that Peter's mother-in-law had been ill and Jesus "stood over her and rebuked the fever, and it left her" (Luke 4:39). Jesus had been working in Peter's life preparing him for faithfulness before He issued a formal call for Peter to follow and become a disciple. When we ask how Peter was able to follow Christ, we find that Christ had been working earlier in Peter's life to set up the conditions that would bring him to choose to follow the Lord.

For instance, when Andrew discovered Jesus he went directly to Simon (Peter) with the news. Why? God had paved the way for them both to come to faith. The story of Peter's conversion traverses over a long and rocky road, with many ups and downs. Peter's was a two-steps-forward-and-one-step-back conversion. But the Lord was always working in the background.

It is sometimes called prevenient grace. The word *prevenient*, from *prevent*, means to act before or in anticipation of something. To prevent forest fires you must do something about them before they start. Thus, prevenient grace is the grace that goes before God's calling that insures that the faithful will respond accordingly. Because God is all-powerful and all knowing, there is no question that the people He calls will come. They must come because God makes no mistakes.

This is a great comfort to the saints because they can rest assured that when they discern God's call upon them they have the assurance that God will complete what He began, and see them through to the end. That is the promise of the gospel! The gospel promise is not that God might save some people if they respond properly, but that God will save all of the people He calls. All those whom God calls will be saved (1 Timothy 2:4), none will be lost (John 6:37).

The idea of *prevenient grace* originated with Augustine and is used differently by Protestants and Catholics. Protestants understand it to be God's secret, preparatory work in the heart of a sinner before he actually believes. Whereas the Roman Catholic Church teaches that prevenient grace is imparted by baptism and works secretly in the hearts of the baptized to bring about faith. I don't want to get tied up with these differences, but only mention them to show that the biblical teaching of prevenient grace goes way back, and that it sets up a never-ending recession of causes that reach forever back in time.

When seeking the ultimate cause of something, questions can always be formed that lead to previous causes. But in order to establish a foundation of knowledge or experience an ultimate or first cause must be established. The argument of the First Cause is one of the classical proofs of the existence of God. Something had to get everything started, therefore God exists as the First Cause. This line of thinking is biblical in origin. It finds its origin in God's plan established before time itself.

> "Declaring the end from the beginning, And from ancient times things that are not yet done, Saying, 'My counsel shall stand, And I will do all My pleasure'" (Isaiah 46:10).

Deuteronomy 7:6 also testifies to the fact that God did the choosing:

> "...the Lord your God has chosen you to be a people for Himself,
> a special treasure above all the peoples on the face of the earth."

God chose Israel. And from Ephesians 1:4-5 we learn that

> "He chose us in Him before the foundation of the world, that we
> should be holy and without blame before Him in love, having
> predestined us to adoption...."

God chooses whom to save. The Old Testament teaches that He chose Israel, not because they were better, but for His own purposes. The New Testament teaches that God gave to Christ particular individuals who would be saved, again, not because they were better, but for His own purposes. Christ brought salvation, not only to Israel, but is bringing salvation to the whole world. People from every nation will be saved in Christ Jesus.

When we skirt this issue by saying that God chooses those who choose Him, we give the power of salvation to the person being saved and take it away from God. If I am saved because I choose to follow Jesus, then my decision for Christ determines my salvation. But Jesus said that not all who thought themselves saved would actually be saved.

> "Not everyone who says to Me, 'Lord, Lord,' shall enter the
> kingdom of heaven" (Matthew 7:21).

It's not our decision in time that saves us, it's God's decision in eternity. Our decision only confirms what God has already done. And because God determines who will be saved—and because God is all-powerful, all-knowing, and doesn't make mistakes, His salvation is assured. That is great news and a great comfort to the elect.

But for those who spurn the Lord by their words or their actions, it is neither good nor comforting. Paul said that

> "we are to God the fragrance of Christ among those who are
> being saved and among those who are perishing. To the one we
> are the aroma of death leading to death, and to the other the
> aroma of life leading to life. And who is sufficient for these
> things?" (2 Corinthians 2:15-16).

The same aroma, the same teaching, the same gospel is understood differently by these two groups.

However, God's prevenient grace does not eliminate the human responsibility to choose to follow Christ. Only those who intentionally and willingly choose and persevere in following Christ are finally saved. God's election does not turn human beings into mindless robots. God employs the means of grace for the salvation of the elect. God works preveniently to cause His people to choose Christ and to persevere in following Him. Salvation is neither automatic nor entirely mysterious. The elect must choose Christ and follow Him to the end.

Yet, choosing and following Christ require God's presence and power to bring about the decision and commitment to salvation. We cannot of our own will or strength make such decisions in this sinful world, nor do we have the strength in ourselves to carry out our decisions once we make them. We are dependent upon God's Holy Spirit at every stage of the process.

We can sum up God's election like this: the human decision to choose and follow Christ is necessary, but not sufficient for salvation. It is necessary to bait the hook to catch a fish—or to throw in the net if you are net fishing. But it is neither the bait nor the net that causes any particular fish to be caught. What causes a particular fish to bite on a specific hook or to get caught in a specific net is beyond our ability to know or to anticipate, much less to plan. It is in the realm of God's providence. Yet, only a fool would fish without bating the hook or casting in the net.

Christ suffered and died for the remission of sin. He has secured the salvation of the faithful beyond any doubt. Yet, only those who believe and who persevere in actually following Christ will be saved. What about you? Do you believe? Have you decided to follow Jesus?

3. UNCLEAN SPIRIT

Then they went into Capernaum, and immediately on the Sabbath He entered the synagogue and taught. And they were astonished at His teaching, for He taught them as one having authority, and not as the scribes. Now there was a man in their synagogue with an unclean spirit. And he cried out, saying, 'Let us alone! What have we to do with You, Jesus of Nazareth? Did You come to destroy us? I know who You are—the Holy One of God!' But Jesus rebuked him, saying, 'Be quiet, and come out of him!' And when the unclean spirit had convulsed him and cried out with a loud voice, he came out of him. Then they were all amazed, so that they questioned among themselves, saying, 'What is this? What new doctrine is this? For with authority He commands even the unclean spirits, and they obey Him.' And immediately His fame spread throughout all the region around Galilee. —Mark 1:21-28

Having been rejected in his home town of Nazareth, Jesus traveled east over a mountain range to the Sea of Galilee. Jesus, of course, was not born in Nazareth, but He was raised there. Mark tells us that it was on this, His first preaching tour, that He called the fishermen, Simon, Andrew, James, and John. "They" (v. 21) then together continued on to Capernaum, a bustling sea port on the Northwest coast of the Sea of Galilee.

We will notice as we go along that Mark was generous in his use of the word *immediately*. He uses the word seventeen times in his short gospel. We can assume that Mark means that Jesus wasted no time, but as soon as He landed (or as soon as possible, without delay) He went to the synagogue. He went, of course, on the Sabbath because that was when people were there. He didn't go to listen, but to teach, "He entered the synagogue and taught" (v. 21).

We usually assume that Jesus was an excellent teacher—clear, organized, interesting, to the point, etc. And, no doubt, He was. However, we find that the people responded to His teaching with *ekplesso*—astonishment. The Greek word means to strike out, expel by a blow, drive out or drive away; to cast off by a blow; commonly, to strike with panic, shock, astonishment. The word carries the sense of an offense, as in an attack. They were offended by what Jesus taught, and by his sense of authority.

There is a force in the definition of this word that is both attractive and repelling. The astonishment that people felt in the presence of Jesus' teaching provided a startling blow to the values they held dear. They were in the vernacular "blown out of the water" by Christ's teaching. They were stunned, struck dumb with fear, terror, surprise, and wonder. They were amazed. Such are the English epithets of the word *astonish*.

The point is that Jesus' teaching was not only unlike that of the Pharisees, but the content of His teaching was unlike anything they had ever heard. That in itself is a tragedy because of the doctrinal consistency of the Old and New Testaments. Jesus didn't teach anything new or different from the Old Testament prophets. Rather, He extended and fulfilled their teaching. The tragedy was that the people hadn't ever heard the teaching of the prophets during their lifetimes.

Even when Jesus said, as for instance in the Beatitudes,

> "You have heard that it was said to those of old...But I say to
> you..." (Matthew 5:21-22),

He was not teaching new principles. He was refreshing and refining the Old Testament teaching. He taught the same principles that are found in the Old Testament, but He raised the standard of compliance to God's Word from actions to attitudes. He criticized, not the Scriptures, but the Pharisees' interpretation of Scripture.

So, we shouldn't be surprised when Scripture challenges our beliefs and values—even if we have been raised in the church. Those people in the synagogue, where Jesus taught, had also been raised in the church (synagogue). They also had been raised on Scripture and Jewish tradition. Yet, they were astonished. Why? Because they had been misled by the teaching of the errant Pharisees and Saducees. Just as many are misled by errant teachings in our own day.

There is nothing more dangerous to God's truth than to believe that all religious teachings lead to God, or even that all teaching that calls itself Christian honors the truth of Scripture. Matthew 7:21 tells us that not everyone who thinks himself a Christian really is. Jesus said that while many self-confessed Christians would find themselves excluded from God's kingdom, no true Christians will be excluded. Thus, the

Master Himself suggested that people can be mistaken in their beliefs and in their professions.

Verse 23 tells us that there was a man in the synagogue who had an "unclean spirit." This is a most distressing insight by Mark. Apparently there was a member of this synagogue who was possessed by an unclean spirit, possessed by an untruth, like a chronic liar who finally believes the web of deceit he spins to maintain his lies. The implication is that the man with the unclean spirit was a regular attendee of the synagogue. Yet, his attendance did not keep him from being possessed by an unclean spirit.

Even though there were strict rules and regulations that forbade sinners and the unclean from participation in the faithful Jewish community, "there was a man in their synagogue with an unclean spirit" (v. 23). He shouldn't have been there. The rules, regulations and practices of the synagogue forbade his presence. He didn't belong there. Yet, there he was.

Most of what the unclean spirit said to Jesus revealed an orthodox understanding of the faith. The unclean spirit was able to correctly identify Jesus. He knew that Jesus was "the Holy One of God" (v. 24). And he knew that Jesus had come for him. Jesus was after hearts and souls, and the unclean spirit knew it. However, he didn't favor the idea. He didn't like it. He was afraid. In that regard he was like the Pharisees and so many others who saw Jesus as a threat.

And, to a certain extent, Jesus actually was a threat to the status quo, inasmuch as the status quo was not in line with Scripture. Jesus came to save people from their sin, but many people don't want to be saved from their sin. The idea of getting saved is okay, but they want their sin to be saved with them. They like their sin. It is familiar. *Salvation is fine,* they say, *just let me take this one sin with me.* Whatever particular sin they covet is not important, except to Jesus. It may be a little thing, and if it is, they should have no trouble giving it up. But often, our favorite sins are most difficult to part with.

The man with the unclean spirit cried out to Jesus, *What are you trying to do with that teaching? We're all fine just like we are. Leave us alone! What are you trying to do, ruin the church? Teaching like that will surely bring us to ruin?*

We tend to think that everybody flocked to Jesus, to hear His teaching. And people did flock to Him! They flocked to hear Him initially, but it wasn't long before the great crowds left Him. They didn't like what He taught. Many people came for the miracles and the food, but when Jesus got down to brass tacks—teaching faith and repentance, they left. The five thousand quickly became twelve (John 6:66-67). His teaching didn't appeal to felt needs. He didn't tell people what they wanted to hear. He told them what they needed to hear.

Jesus rebuked the unclean spirit. To rebuke is to address with sharp and severe disapproval. Imagine the scene. Jesus was on His first preaching tour with His new disciples, when someone in the synagogue complained against His preaching: *You can't teach that kind of thing here!*

How did Jesus respond? *Shut up!* He said it with sharp and severe disapproval. *Shut up and come out of him!* The "shut up" part isn't difficult to understand, but what did Jesus mean by "come out of him" (v. 25)?

Jesus recognized that the man was possessed by an unclean spirit. The man lacked spiritual purity, and because of that lack he misunderstood Jesus' teaching. God's truth is spiritually discerned, and without the requisite spiritual discernment, God's truth is either not understood or misunderstood.

Spiritual discernment is developed by practicing the precepts of God's Word. It grows through practice. Spiritual discernment is given by grace, but it grows through practice. And the practice of God's Word promotes personal purity. Morality or purity is not required for salvation, but once God's grace is received it issues forth in moral improvement, an increase in spiritual purity.

That's what the man lacked. He was dominated by uncleanness. Jesus dealt with him by separating him from his uncleanness, from the unclean spirit. *Come out of him,* Jesus commanded. *Separate yourself from filth and moral depravity.*

Cleanliness is a matter of removing the dirt. When the dirt or filth is removed, a thing is said to be clean. Normally, dirty things are made clean by washing them. So, Jesus may have made an allusion to baptism here.

Paul counseled Christians

> "to speak evil of no one…for we ourselves were also once foolish, disobedient, deceived, serving various lusts and pleasures, living in malice and envy, hateful and hating one another. But when the kindness and the love of God our Savior toward man appeared, not by works of righteousness which we have done, but according to His mercy He saved us, through the washing of regeneration and renewing of the Holy Spirit, whom He poured out on us abundantly through Jesus Christ our Savior, that

having been justified by His grace we should become heirs
according to the hope of eternal life" (Titus 3:2-7).

The "washing of regeneration" is the baptism of the Holy Spirit
(Acts 11:16). Mark said that

"when the unclean spirit had convulsed him and cried out with a
loud voice, he came out of him" (v. 26).

The man was "convulsed," not by the Holy Spirit, but by the unclean
spirit. The Greek word is *sparasso*, translated by the KJV as *torn*, by the
NKJV as *convulsed*. The NIV says, "The evil spirit shook the man violently...."

The point is that what we know as being slain in the spirit, where
people fall down as if dead or exhibit other sorts of contortions at religious rallies is here identified by Mark as the activity of unclean spirits.
Where many people see such behavior as evidence of the Holy Spirit,
Mark says that it is evidence of an unclean spirit. Mark says that as the
unclean spirit left, the man was thrown into convulsions, as if the separation of the unclean spirit from the person causes a ripping apart that
results in a kind of seizure.

Not only did the man convulse, but he "cried out with a *loud voice*"
(v. 26—italics added). The sense of the word is *hollered*. Jesus told the
man to keep quiet, and the man hollered back in defiance. There must
have been some whoopin' and hollerin' goin' on at church that day!
Somehow at the conclusion of this event, the people were aware that an
unclean spirit had been chased out of the man. And they were amazed.

This time the amazement is different. It comes from a different
Greek word—*thambeo*. When Jesus began teaching they were astonished. Now at the conclusion of this purification they are amazed, as in
dumbfounded. Here they are not so much offended as they were earlier,
they are now thoroughly perplexed. They "questioned among themselves" (v. 27) because they didn't know what to think.

Mark makes it clear that what happened was not simply a charismatic experience. The other men in the synagogue were clear that doctrine was at the heart of it. They understood that the source of whatever
happened was the doctrine that Jesus taught. The NIV reads, "What is
this? A new *teaching*—and with *authority*" (v. 27—italics added). But the
Greek word is *didache* and it means doctrine or that which is taught.
Doctrine—what Jesus actually taught—was at the heart of their offense
and of their bewilderment.

Nonetheless, they observed that He taught with authority, and that even the unclean spirits obeyed Him. They heard things that made them very uncomfortable. And they saw things that bewildered them. But what they heard and what they saw were filled with a power that was undeniable. They didn't like what Jesus said, and they didn't understand what He did, but that didn't keep them from talking. "His fame spread throughout all the region around Galilee" (v. 28). People everywhere were talking about what He said and what he did.

Jesus Christ died on the cross for the remission of sin. Who can understand it? But, who can deny it? Those who believe in Christ will be saved! Believe and repent! Christ has come to change our minds, and to change our hearts. Repent and believe!

4. HEALING

Now as soon as they had come out of the synagogue, they entered the house of Simon and Andrew, with James and John. But Simon's wife's mother lay sick with a fever, and they told Him about her at once. So He came and took her by the hand and lifted her up, and immediately the fever left her. And she served them. At evening, when the sun had set, they brought to Him all who were sick and those who were demon-possessed. And the whole city was gathered together at the door. Then He healed many who were sick with various diseases, and cast out many demons; and He did not allow the demons to speak, because they knew Him. —Mark 1:29-34

We come now to a subject of much interest and misunderstanding. The healings of Jesus were miracles of a particular kind. The subject of healing must first be taken up under the broader heading of miracles. In this way the various types of miracles can be better understood in relationship to their general purpose.

The healing of Peter's mother-in-law was plain and simple. She was in bed with a fever, but when Jesus touched her she arose and served Him. It is a simple story about the healing power of the touch of God.

Mark places the story just after the calling of the four fishermen, as does Matthew. But Luke places it before the calling of the disciples. Our challenge regarding the placement of the story is to hold to the truth that all Scripture is true and does not contradict itself. However, in order to maintain the veracity of Scripture we must occasionally probe beyond the simple facts related in the story to the deeper truth that is symbolized. That in itself is a lesson about how to read Scripture. We must always assume first the simplest and most literal reading. But if that reading calls any other biblical principle into question, then we must yield the literal interpretation to the symbolic in order to apprehend its meaning. Yet, we must realize that the most simple and straightforward reading is the most likely to be true.

Here we find that the setting of Jesus' healing of Peter's mother-in-law leads to an apparent difficulty between Luke and Mark/Matthew re-

18

garding the placement of the story. Was it before or after He called the disciples? Calvin said that there was reason to conjecture that Matthew did not put this story in its proper order. The dual placement of the story suggests further consideration is necessary. Therefore, we will explore the symbolic meaning of the event, with the assurance that the Lord has given us this difficulty on purpose. He wants us to probe deeper into the nature and meaning of Christ's healing miracles.[2]

A miracle results when God works in a special way. Miracles are always part of God's self-revelation to man. Some miracles appear to contradict the laws of nature, other miracles are simple extensions of those laws. Normally, a young boy's lunch will not feed five thousand people. Lame people do not normally get up and dance, nor do people normally walk on water, etc.

Miracles are not magic because the whole idea of magic is either an illusion or imaginary and unreal. But miracles are real. They are supernatural events, where supernatural means above or beyond what is our natural (or ordinary) understanding. God can direct and use natural events. He can also speed up or slow down time itself. Events become supernatural when God intervenes in the natural process. For instance, God is able to use a particular virus or bacteria to accomplish His purposes, some of which cause illness and others bring healing. Or God can act directly, effectively bypassing natural causes altogether. God can simply will a thing to be, and it is.

There are three Greek words used in New Testament to describe God's miracles. *Dunamis* (Mark 5:30, 6:2, 6:5, 6:14, 9:1, 9:39, 12:24, 13:25, 13:26, 14:62) means a powerful act. God's actions are mighty indeed. He may command a storm to stop, or start. He may command the dead to rise, etc. These are among the mighty acts of God.

Another word for miracle is *teras* (Mark 13:22), which means wonder. God's mighty acts cause wonder in the hearts of men. We don't understand them. We wonder about them. Their purpose is to displace our reliance upon our own understanding, and cause us to lean on God's understanding, even when we don't fully understand.

The third word is *semeion* (Mark 8:11, 8:12, 13:4, 13:22, 16:17, 16:20), translated as *signs* or *miracles*, and indicates that God's miracles always point to something greater, to a higher or deeper reality behind the mere event. God does not work miracles for their own sake. He is not out to impress us with His power. Rather, His miracles point to

---

2   See *John's Miracles—Seeing Beyond Our Expectations*, Phillip A. Ross, Pilgrim Platform, 2019.

something He wants to say, something that can be communicated symbolically to anyone no matter what language they may speak.

Christ's signs or miracles point to the fact that He is the promised
Messiah, the Son of God. Notice in Scripture that the words *signs* and
wonders often appear together. God's miracles tell us about God. They
are His self-revealing wonders.

However, not all miracles are of God. God's enemies are also able to
work miracles.

> "Pharaoh also called the wise men and the sorcerers; so the
> magicians of Egypt, they also did in like manner with their
> enchantments" (Exodus 7:11).

> "Many will say to Me in that day, 'Lord, Lord, have we not
> prophesied in Your name, cast out demons in Your name, and
> done many wonders in Your name?'" (Matthew 7:22).

The beast of Revelation also

> "performs great signs, so that he even makes fire come down
> from heaven on the earth in the sight of men" (Revelation 13:13).

As with everything else, we must test miracles to see if they confirm
God's Word (Deuteronomy 13:1-5). The point is that the mere presence
of a miracle signifies nothing.

God's message given through the miracle is always directed to the
faithful. Only the faithful can properly discern it. The miracle will encourage the faithful, no matter how little one's faith may be. But the unfaithful will often be discouraged by miracles. Witnessing a miracle will
not lead people to faith. Quite the contrary, it will harden the unfaithful
against God (Exodus 8:32; John 12:37). The unbelieving will always try
to find some natural reason to explain the event. They will resist supernatural explanations because they reject God and His power over nature
(Mark 3:22).

That's why Jesus did so few miracles in Nazareth (Matthew 14:58).
The unbelief of those in Nazareth did not make Jesus unable to heal, it
simply made miracles the wrong thing for Jesus to do in that situation.
Without the requisite faith, Jesus' miracles would have been meaningless. They would point to a reality that was denied by the people. Miracles in such a situation would only harden hearts against the gospel.

God's miracles always point to His central purpose of redemption.
When that connection is discerned by the faithful, miracles are seen as
answers to prayer that confirm God's Word. They are received thank-

fully by faith. They are understood to be acts of God's grace, but not as part of the normal program of the church. Churches are not expected to perform miracles in response to God's gift of salvation. Rather, God performs miracles as He chooses. So, we must not expect them to be part of God's ordinary ways of working with people. To expect miracles involves the sin of presumption (Deuteronomy 17:12, 2 Peter 2:10).

In the primitive ignorance of olden times, people equated miracles and magic. Indeed, people held a magical understanding of the universe. They saw spirits everywhere animating nature. They had no understanding of the laws of nature, and believed that spirits caused things to happen. They were not aware of God's order in the universe.

In those days God performed various miracles to gain attention and demonstrate the authority of His message. God's message then served to raise people above such superstitious beliefs. But superstition has always had a way of creeping back into vogue. It did so during the Middle Ages as the Roman Catholic church pandered to various false but popular beliefs, and then retained them as part of church doctrine. The purchase of indulgences, paying penance for the sins of dead relatives, is an example of such a superstition that arose extra-biblically and was retained in official Roman Catholic doctrine.

Over time the pagan beliefs that supernatural powers were inherent in particular individuals, shrines, streams, rocks, trees, etc., replaced the biblical belief that men have direct access to a God who hears and answers prayer. Throughout history various superstitions have tended to creep back into the belief structure of the church.

The Protestant Reformation reasserted the older biblical truth of God's Word against a rising tide of pagan superstition. That's why the Reformed churches taught that signs and wonders had ceased. They didn't mean that God no longer had the ability to work miracles. Rather, they argued that God was weaning people away from a childish and immature dependence upon them. Certainly, anything is possible with God. God can perform any miracles He chooses whenever and however He chooses. But the Protestant Reformers believed that God wanted people to increasingly rely upon His ordinary means of grace, and not to depend upon a steady diet of miraculous intervention.

It's a parental thing. The parent is able and willing to help the child. But as the child grows, the parent wants him to do things for himself—not to relinquish or outgrow his love for the parent, but to take increasing responsibility for the things that the parent previously provided.

God can do whatever He wants, but He has given the church the ordinary means of grace as a way of increasing our responsibility for the stewardship of His earth. By relying upon the ordinary means of grace, God has thrown much responsibility back upon the church, as if to say, *Yes, you must depend upon Me alone, of course. But in depending upon Me, you must then do as I have said, and take personal responsibility for the means of grace I have provided.*

The Reformation emphasized that, although all things are possible with God, and though people could and should pray directly to God trusting in His providence, after the Apostolic Age the role and purpose that God's miracles played shifted to the means of grace. Miracles decreased and the exercise of the means of grace increased. The place or role of visible miracles as seals of the Word has been taken by the ordinary means of grace—Word and Sacrament.

In one sense miracles will never cease, God is always free and above nature. But with the completion of the writing of the Bible, God tethered the miraculous to the exercise of the ordinary means of grace. He has hidden the reality of the miraculous in the exercise of Word and Sacrament. In obedience to God, then, we must no longer chase after or depend upon miracles, but we must take responsibility for the exercise of God's ordinary means of grace. We must submit ourselves to the preaching of the Word and the breaking of the bread.

Yet today, at the height of modern scientific and technological development we see the same old thing beginning to happen again. We are in the midst of a reassertion of superstition into modern thinking. Much of the New Age Movement, which is very much a part of many churches and certainly well-entrenched in modern society, is nothing more than the classic, pagan superstitions reemerging in modern garb. There is nothing new about the New Age Movement except its rising popularity.

The quest for signs and wonders today is no different than it was during Jesus' day. What did He say about it then?

> "An evil and adulterous generation seeks after a sign (*semeion*),
> and no sign will be given to it except the sign of the prophet
> Jonah" (Matthew 12:39).

He made the only acceptable sign (or miracle) to be the resurrection (prefigured in the story of Jonah). And the power of the resurrection is given to the church through the exercise and administration of Word and Sacrament.

It seems that Jesus continued to heal many people after the Sabbath sunset that day.

"They brought to Him *all* who were sick and those who were demon-possessed" (v. 32—italics added).

But did He heal them all? No, "He healed many..." (v. 34—italics added). And He "cast out many demons" (v. 34). After the shouting match with the unclean spirit, he forbade the demons to speak in His presence.

Do demons speak today? You bet they do. Can Jesus cast them out? Of course He can. And He does! Do you have a demon that needs to be cast out and silenced? Are you in need of spiritual healing? Come to Jesus, He will complete the work He has begun in you. He will bring all of His people into salvation, and break the yoke of the Evil One. Come, Lord Jesus!

5. PREACHING

*Now in the morning, having risen a long while before day-
light, He went out and departed to a solitary place; and there
He prayed. And Simon and those who were with Him searched
for Him. When they found Him, they said to Him, 'Everyone
is looking for You.' But He said to them, 'Let us go into the
next towns, that I may preach there also, because for this purpose I have come forth.' And He was preaching in their synagogues throughout all Galilee, and casting out demons. Now a
leper came to Him, imploring Him, kneeling down to Him
and saying to Him, 'If You are willing, You can make me
clean.' Then Jesus, moved with compassion, stretched out His
hand and touched him, and said to him, 'I am willing; be
cleansed.' As soon as He had spoken, immediately the leprosy
left him, and he was cleansed. And He strictly warned him and
sent him away at once, and said to him, 'See that you say nothing to anyone; but go your way, show yourself to the priest,
and offer for your cleansing those things which Moses commanded, as a testimony to them.' However, he went out and
began to proclaim it freely, and to spread the matter, so that Jesus could no longer openly enter the city, but was outside in
deserted places; and they came to Him from every direction.*
—Mark 1:35-45

Jesus was up early, before his disciples, "a long while before daylight"
(v. 35). He got up so He could be by Himself to pray. The application is obvious. The early morning, when your mind is fresh—not
necessarily fully awake, but fresh—is a good time to interact with the
Lord. Defenses are down in the grogginess of the early morning, and
we are more receptive to God's guidance and influence. The fact that
we are not fully awake or that we don't like to get up early cannot be
used as excuses, because the lack of our normal waking defenses and the
discipline of ignoring our own preferences are the very vehicles that
God often employs for our spiritual growth.

The disciples got up and searched for the Lord. No matter when we get up we find that the Lord is already up and working on our behalf. Nonetheless, we are to get up and seek the Lord. The same pattern is evidenced in the behavior of the disciples. We, then, should follow suit.

> "When they found Him, they said to Him, 'Everyone is looking for You'" (v. 37).

Did they mean everyone in the world? Yes and no. At this point in His ministry, Jesus was unknown to many people, so there is a sense in which those seeking God were not looking for Jesus the man. They had never heard of Him. But it is also true that everyone in the world is seeking the Lord—rightly or wrongly, consciously or unconsciously. We all seek the love and grace that Christ affords. Such seeking is a primary human motivation that God hard-wired into us at creation.

To understand what Jesus said at that point we must look again at the context. According to Luke He had just healed Peter's mother-in-law. The same day

> "they brought to Him all who were sick and demon-possessed... He healed many who were sick with various diseases, and cast out many demons" (vs. 32-33).

Jesus wasn't interested in staying in each town to heal everyone who was ill. Rather, he told the disciples that His purpose was preaching, not healing—that's what He said (v. 38).

Yes, He healed many, but He did so in order to gain a hearing. The purpose of His miracles was to establish His authority in the eyes of the people. His miracles served as calling cards, to point to His divine authority. But once He had established His authority and gained the ear of the people, His main task was to preach the gospel of the kingdom of God. He came to proclaim the gospel, the good news of God's salvation. He came to enact the sacrifice that would satisfy God and thus open the way for the salvation of the world. But that was in God's hands because His "hour had not yet come" (John 7:30). For now, His primary task was to get the news out, to preach.

When you hear the word *preach*, what comes to mind? Proclaim, moralize, advocate, urge, advise, indoctrinate, declare, exhort are among the possibilities. One dictionary tells us that to preach is to discourse on moral or religious topics, especially in a tiresome manner. Contemporary usage of the word suggests that people don't like preaching. The word has a decidedly negative connotation.

Preaching has a negative sense to it because it is usually used against things. Preachers preach against this or that sin. When someone preaches to you they are opposed to you or to your behavior or thinking. They disagree with something you are doing, and, therefore, they preach to you. Isn't that usually the case? Preachers preach against sin and against the world. It seems that preachers are forever against everything!

People get tired of being against everything. It's not very good for one's popularity. If you are always preaching against things, you don't get invited out much. People would rather be for things. Rather than always preaching against sin, why can't we preach for righteousness? And, indeed we can—and we must. Rather than being against the world, we ought to be for Jesus. And, indeed, Christians are for Jesus! Yet, Jesus Himself is against the world, against worldliness.

It's really a matter of emphasis, isn't it. What we choose to emphasize is what we know today as spin. To put the right spin on something requires the right emphasis. But as Christians—and particularly as preachers, we are not free to choose what to emphasize. Rather, we must follow Jesus' lead. We must stick to the emphasis of Scripture, and not overemphasize one thing for the sake of another. Rather, we must maintain the biblical emphasis.

The fact that Jesus was killed shows us that preaching is characteristically received by the world as a negative activity. It was Jesus' preaching that got Him killed. Had He just performed miracles and healed people, He wouldn't have upset the status quo to the point that they felt obliged to have Him killed. Had Jesus simply gone around telling moralistic stories, lifting up the hearts of the down-trodden, making people feel good about themselves, and contributing to their gradual spiritual improvement, He would not have died on the cross.

But the nature of His message—His gospel—deeply disturbed people. People don't like to face up to their sin. They don't like to be preached against. They don't like to have it pointed out where they are wrong in their thinking or behavior. But that's just what Jesus did! That's what He came to do, and that's what He commissions faithful preachers to do today.

Mark tells us that He did this in their synagogues. He was in their face!

> "He was preaching in their synagogues throughout all Galilee,
> and casting out demons" (v. 39).

The reference to casting out demons takes us back to His encounter with the unclean spirit at Capernaum. Apparently, those kinds of encounters continued to accompany His preaching. Yet His popularity rose. People were curious.

In part, the story of the healing of the leper explains the rise in popularity of Jesus. The leper came to Jesus kneeling. The fact that he came on his knees indicates that he revered Jesus. It doesn't mean that the leper had a correct understanding of Jesus as the Son of God. But it does indicate the correct posture or attitude in which to approach Jesus—with humility and supplication.

The leper also knew Jesus' power to heal was not merely by His touch, but also, and more importantly, by His will. The leper said, "If you are willing, You can make me clean" (v. 40). It wasn't a matter of saying the right prayer, or Jesus' touch, or anything else. Healing was accomplished by the will of the Master. Healing is a matter of God's will.

And the good news of the gospel is that God is willing! Christ came not to condemn the world, but to save it. God is willing! Jesus said, "I am willing, be cleansed" (v. 41). The Greek word *katharizo* means clean in the physical sense—free from dirt and pollution. It also means morally pure as in a clean conscience. And it also means to pronounce clean, as in the Levitical or ceremonial sense. All of these meanings of clean and pure are captured in the word *katharizo*.

Katharizo happened immediately. Jesus spoke it and it was. The leprosy left immediately and the leper was physically, morally, and ceremonially clean. But the story is not over.

Jesus "strictly warned him" (v. 43), *embrimaomai* literally means to snort with anger. Jesus gave a strong warning to him, Don't tell anyone about this! Except the priest. Go show the priest and give the required offering for healing. But don't tell anyone on the way!

What is this all about? Why was Jesus so angry? Why couldn't He just have told the man without the stern warning? And why didn't He want anyone to know? The whole scene is very curious. The questions are all answered in the next two verses.

The man disobeyed Jesus and told everyone except the priests, and the people went ballistic. They sought Jesus out in increasing numbers everywhere He went. Soon He couldn't go anywhere without people flocking to Him. And do you think they came to hear Him preach? No, they came seeking miraculous healings. Their own selfish concerns about their own health brought them to Jesus for their own healing.

They didn't care about His preaching or His gospel. They just wanted to feel better.

Jesus knew that if word got out about His ability to heal, He would be inundated with requests and, therefore, unable to preach. "Jesus could no longer openly enter the city" (v. 45). His fame as a healer interfered with His mission as a preacher. It wasn't that His enemies were out to get Him, not at this point. The problem was that people demanded miracles over gospel.

The disobedience of the leper brought people to Jesus "from every direction" (v. 45). They brought the lame and infirm—brothers, sisters, aunts, uncles, etc.—all in terrible health, seeking relief. Jesus' purpose was to preach, but now He was overwhelmed by people too sick to listen.

The pressing needs of the people were medical. So, He began to treat them. He couldn't ignore them, nor was it His will to heal them all. So Jesus, the Master at dealing with the various situations that were presented to Him, began to heal and to teach. He would preach later, when people were more disposed to hear Him. For now He would heal the sick and teach them as He did so. But His primary purpose—preaching, as He Himself had said—would have to wait.

Are you able to hear the preaching of Christ? Or are you too ill and distracted by your ailments? Can you put aside your own concerns, and focus on Christ's primary purpose? The leper's healing did not result in obedience. We all want to be healed, but the Lord wants obedience. Can you receive the preaching of the Lord with humility and submission, even when He rebukes you?

Jesus can heal your illnesses. He can make you feel better. But His real purpose is to preach to your soul. While His miracles might heal your infirmities, His Word will heal your soul.

6. Paralyzed

And again He entered Capernaum after some days, and it was heard that He was in the house. Immediately many gathered together, so that there was no longer room to receive them, not even near the door. And He preached the word to them. Then they came to Him, bringing a paralytic who was carried by four men. And when they could not come near Him because of the crowd, they uncovered the roof where He was. So when they had broken through, they let down the bed on which the paralytic was lying. When Jesus saw their faith, He said to the paralytic, 'Son, your sins are forgiven you.' And some of the scribes were sitting there and reasoning in their hearts, 'Why does this Man speak blasphemies like this? Who can forgive sins but God alone?' But immediately, when Jesus perceived in His spirit that they reasoned thus within themselves, He said to them, 'Why do you reason about these things in your hearts? Which is easier, to say to the paralytic, "Your sins are forgiven you," or to say, "Arise, take up your bed and walk"? But that you may know that the Son of Man has power on earth to forgive sins—He said to the paralytic, 'I say to you, arise, take up your bed, and go to your house.' Immediately he arose, took up the bed, and went out in the presence of them all, so that all were amazed and glorified God, saying, 'We never saw anything like this!'　　　　　　　　　　　　　　　　—Mark 2:1-12

Jesus was chased all around Galilee by the crowds that came to him from every direction. He fled to Capernaum, perhaps to Simon Peter's home, or perhaps His family had moved there. We really don't know. Nonetheless, He had been in Capernaum before and would now use it as a base of operations.

Word got out that He had taken refuge "in the house" or home—either Peter's house or His family's—in Capernaum. As soon as the crowds heard where He had gone, they followed after Him. Having found Him they so crowded into the house that there was no more room, not even standing room in the doorway. Imagine them overflowing out into the yard.

"And (Jesus) preached the word to them" (v. 2). Those who sought healing and who followed Him to Capernaum were subjected to the preaching of Jesus. Don't you wonder what His preaching was like? What did He say to them? You'd think that whatever Jesus said was important, and that it would have been a major part of Mark's story. But the content of His preaching at Peter's house is missing. We don't know what He said.

I suspect that it is missing because those who heard it weren't really interested. They hadn't come for His preaching, but for healing. Jesus knew why they had come. He had been inundated by those seeking healing in Galilee, and many of those same people now sought Him out in Capernaum. They came for healing, and He preached the Word to them. Because nothing is recorded about what He said, let's try to figure out what He probably said based on what He had previously preached.

We are only at the second chapter of Mark. When Jesus began His ministry He preached,

> "The time is fulfilled, and the kingdom of God is at hand.
> Repent, and believe in the gospel" (Mark 1:15).

That's the only preaching recorded up to this point by Mark, so that is likely what He preached at Peter's house. "Repent, and believe!" At the conclusion of His preaching at Peter's house, some of them came to faith. Luke notes that there were Pharisees and doctors of the law (lawyers) present (Luke 5:17).

A paralytic was brought to Jesus. We don't know if it was his own idea to come or someone else's. All we know is that they brought the paralytic to Jesus, and that there were so many people present that they could only reach Jesus by climbing up on the roof of the house, and lowering the paralytic down on ropes. What a scene!

Here was Jesus preaching to the people, doing what He came to do —preaching the gospel of salvation by grace alone. And in the middle of His sermon, the roof of the house opened up and a man was lowered in front of Him. Imagine what a disruption that would have been. Imagine poor Peter—or Peter's mother-in-law, thinking, w*hat's that boy gotten himself into this time!*

So much for remembering what Jesus was preaching about!

Surely there was some commotion. Nonetheless, "Jesus saw their faith" (v. 5). He was, no doubt, preaching faith and repentance, so He made an example of the paralytic. The gospel message is that "by grace you have been saved through faith" (Ephesians 2:8). Salvation is freely given by God's grace, and faith is the means of grace. The faith of these men was not a passive mental assent, but an active seeking after God. Faith for them was not just a verbal thing, not just a hoping for an unseen reality, but it involved them in an active striving after the gift of salvation—not as a way of securing it, but in response to the preaching of the Lord.

He preached faith and repentance, and those who were healthy brought a paralyzed man to be healed. Many people were involved in the faith that Jesus "saw" (v. 5). The paralyzed man would not have been able to present himself before Jesus. He required the help of the others.

Jesus was preaching faith and repentance, when the people brought Him a paralyzed man. The Greek word is *paralutikos*, which the King James translated as *palsy*. He was weak or paralyzed—unable to get around. I think that the point was that his healing involved the community of faith. Surely, that was part of the faith that Jesus saw.

The relationship between the paralyzed man and Jesus' forgiveness of his sin originated in Jesus' preaching, not in the thoughts of the paralyzed man. It seems odd that Jesus would forgive the sins of a paralyzed man, as if his sin was the source of his paralysis. Yet, the connection between the man's sin and his paralysis seems to be Jesus' preaching of repentance, turning from sin.

The connection is repentance. Jesus preached repentance, and to illustrate the connection between faith and repentance, He healed the paralytic. The healing made the connection. His healing demonstrated the real-world connection by revealing Christ's authority and power to both heal and forgive sins. The healing served the glory of God, which is the dominate theme of all the healings in the Scriptures. Healings were always for the glory of God. Jesus healed not only the man's physical paralysis, but He healed His sin-sick soul as well. In fact, the healing of the soul is the greater miracle.

At this point Mark brings in the reaction of the Scribes and Pharisees to this healing. They thought that Jesus spoke blasphemy because only God could forgive sin. The truth is that they had been lying in wait for Jesus to say something that they disagreed with. They hadn't come expecting to hear Him speak the truth. They had come expecting Him to speak lies and blasphemy. They came with their minds already made up. They were looking for a deed or statement that they could use against Jesus.

However, their concern about blasphemy has come down to us in the Scriptures as evidence that they accurately assessed that Jesus acted as only God could act. They didn't deny the healing, nor did they deny that Jesus did it. In this case the testimony of Jesus' enemies is of great interest because we know that they would not try to embellish the situation in Jesus' favor. So, when they recognized that He acted as God, they added their testimony to the divinity of Christ.

Somehow Jesus knew what they were up to. I don't know if He read their thoughts, but He certainly knew what they were thinking. So, He engaged them in conversation.

Jesus went straight to the point. He didn't hem and haw, trying to establish a relationship with them. I suppose that He knew that a saving relationship was not likely. At any rate, He dealt directly with their suspicion.

Why don't you believe Me? Which is easier, He asked, *to heal the man's physical ailments or to forgive his sin?*

He didn't wait for an answer because He went on to say that His purpose was not to simply save and restore the man to a proper relationship with God, but to establish the power and authority of the Son of Man in His own Person as having come into the world.

Jesus knew that healing the man's sin was the greater miracle, and frankly, told them so. Then He told them why He did it—so

> "that you may know that the Son of Man has power on earth to forgive sins" (v. 11).

Again, in case they didn't understand Jesus' divinity, He spelled it out for them. He pointed out the miracle, and what it meant. It pointed to or authorized Christ's power and authority on earth. The lawyers (Scribes and Pharisees) were concerned about Jesus' blasphemy. And Jesus helped them out as well. He told them that they had understood the miracle correctly—that it was indeed a miracle, but that it didn't point to His blasphemy, but to the truth of His divinity.

All of this was done in public, in the midst of a great crowd of people. They were all witnesses of the miracle and of the response of the Scribes and Pharisees. Jesus did it all out in the open as if to publicly challenge them and their faulty interpretations of Scripture. He was in their face, and they didn't like it.

The paralyzed man got up upon hearing the command of Jesus, and walked out. He had been carried in, but he walked out by himself "in the presence of them all, so that all were amazed and glorified God, saying, 'We never saw anything like this!'" (v. 12).

At least three things were going on: 1) Jesus preached the gospel of salvation by grace, 2) He performed a healing miracle in order to establish His authority, 3) He sought to correct the faulty biblical understanding of the religious establishment.

Those three things are the continuing mission of the Holy Spirit and of Christ's church: 1) to preach the gospel, 2) to establish Christ's authority, and 3) to teach orthodoxy—the truth of Scripture,

"the faith which was once for all delivered to the saints" (Jude 1:3).

7. Sinners

Then He went out again by the sea; and all the multitude came to Him, and He taught them. As He passed by, He saw Levi the son of Alphaeus sitting at the tax office. And He said to him, 'Follow Me.' So he arose and followed Him. Now it happened, as He was dining in Levi's house, that many tax collectors and sinners also sat together with Jesus and His disciples; for there were many, and they followed Him. And when the scribes and Pharisees saw Him eating with the tax collectors and sinners, they said to His disciples, 'How is it that He eats and drinks with tax collectors and sinners?' When Jesus heard it, He said to them, 'Those who are well have no need of a physician, but those who are sick. I did not come to call the righteous, but sinners, to repentance.' —Mark 2:13-17

Matthew was a successful man by the world's standards. He had a good job, it paid well. Most people respected his authority in the community, if not his person. Sure there were abuses in the system, bribes and extortion abounded. Palms were greased in order to facilitate business. But such anomalies were figured into the cost of doing business.

We can assume that Matthew had left behind any Jewish values that may have accumulated during his upbringing. He was a Jew by name—Levi, but a Gentile by occupation—Matthew. No committed Jew would serve either the pagan Roman state, nor his own self-interest by submitting himself to the spiritual and moral abuses involved with being a tax collector. Yet, in spite of his outward abandonment of biblical values, some residue of God's purpose remained in him. He was in a tough situation.[3]

Those who sought to befriend Matthew were people of like persuasions. Upstanding Jewish fathers would have had no reason to seek favors from Matthew. They just paid their taxes and husbanded their fam-

---

3   And yet the Temple itself provided a tax revenue to Rome. See: *God's Great Plan for the World*, Phillip A. Ross, Pilgrim Platform, Marietta, Ohio, 2019.

ilies. But the greedy—the rich who paid for influence and favors, and the poor who did the dirty work, who provided the muscle for extortion, who were prostitutes, and thieves—found themselves connected through the authority and influence of Matthew's position. Being engaged in sleaze himself, Matthew knew a lot of sleazy people.

Jesus continued to flee the press of the crowds who sought Him. He escaped them and "went out again by the sea" (v. 13). But they continued to follow Him. He had proved His ability to heal, and the suffering mass of humanity continually pressed Him into service. Yet, it is important to note that Jesus was not in the habit of giving people what they wanted. Rather, He sought to fulfill His primary purpose at every possible opportunity, "He taught them" (v. 13). Again, there is no indication in Mark's account about the nature of His teaching here.

Mark tells us that Jesus noticed Levi (Matthew) sitting in the tax office "as He passed by" (v. 14). It appears that Jesus did not premeditate about the benefits of having a tax collector as a disciple, and then inquire as to where He might find such a person. It is more likely that Jesus simply relied upon God's providence, wandering about teaching and healing freely, when He happened upon Levi. Upon seeing him, Jesus seemed to have had access to his family history. He knew his Jewish name—Levi, and his father—Alphaeus. Somehow Jesus was able to see the truth of this man who had taken a Gentile name for his own protection. Tax collectors were hated by the Jews, and the fact that one of their own people served in such a capacity could mean trouble. So Levi tried to hide his Jewish identity under a false name.

Likely there were more words between Matthew and Jesus than, "Follow me" (v. 14), but they have not been preserved. The result of the conversation was that Jesus called Matthew into discipleship. And here we see the amazing grace of God at work. Matthew was a long way from spiritual purity. He had abandoned his personal faith and his family heritage. And he was working for the enemy—Rome!

We may wonder why Jesus called such a man, not only into personal relationship with Him, but into apostleship. More than likely, Jesus foresaw Matthew's role in the writing of Scripture and called him for that purpose. Being a tax collector, Matthew could read and write, and knew about record keeping. Moreover, being a backslidden Jew, his conversion would be an example to many. And being friends with so many other "tax collectors and sinners" (v. 16), the effects of his conversion would reach into those ranks as well.

Had faithful Jews followed Jesus, people would have paid Him little attention. He would have appeared to be no more than another good Rabbi. If the Zealots had followed Him, He would have appeared to be a political leader. But when tax collectors and other hard core sinners were publicly converted, there could be no denial that something extraordinary was at hand.

The fact that Jesus called Matthew, a despised tax collector and known sinner, provided a clear lesson about God's grace. Neither sin nor public opinion has any bearing upon the administration of grace. The gospel invitation is given to any and all who will respond to it. It was not offered in vain to Matthew, because Scripture says that as soon as Jesus called him, "he arose and followed" (v. 14). Matthew's sins were many and well known, but they could not prevent him from entering the kingdom of grace.

The lesson for us bears repeating. No sinner is ever too far gone, no public slander, nor poor reputation can prevent the effectiveness of God's grace. Christ calls all sinners to repentance and salvation. Again, this doesn't mean them alone—not just someone else, not just other people, not just the people downtown, or in some other city. It means you and me!

"Now it happened..." said Mark. Earlier he said, "As it happened...." Both phrases communicate the same thing. Jesus was not executing some premeditated master evangelism strategy. He was doing evangelism in the midst of His daily activities. Relying on the providence of God, He reached out to those who happened to cross His path. He made examples of situations that presented themselves. His example for the practice of evangelism here is important.

As He was doing what He did, as He was going where He was going, He called people into Christian service. He taught people on the spot. He healed them on the spot. He challenged them on the spot. He didn't let an opportunity go by, but He did it all within the natural flow of life. Jesus' evangelism was not artificial—no canned speeches, no four spiritual laws, none of the evangelistic accouterments that we have grown so used to. Just talk about God in the ordinary circumstances of life.

He ended up at Matthew's house for dinner. By the time He got there it had become a big dinner party. A lot of people were there, and they were not the cream of the crop. They were tax collectors, prostitutes, thugs, and bums. And there was Jesus in the middle of them! Had He no shame? Didn't He understand that these were bad people to hang out with? It was not only against the strict Jewish laws of kosher fellow-ship, but everyone knew that it was just a bad idea. A person could get hurt or corrupted around that kind of people. Nonetheless, there He was, Him and His disciples—at this point, Simon, Andrew, James, and John.

There is speculation that the dinner party was called by Matthew in order to announce that he had become or was planning to become a fol-lower of Jesus. It may have been a kind of going away party. But it also served to announce Jesus' ministry, and as a way to establish contacts, and to recruit other potential disciples. It provided the perfect opportu-nity to reach out to those most in need. There were also Scribes and Pharisees there who made note of the kind of people Jesus was seen with.

How is it that He eats with such rabble?, they inquired. Again, they didn't ask the question because they wanted an answer. They asked the question as a way to stir up gossip that would challenge and undermine Jesus' ministry.

It reminds me of the question: have you stopped beating your wife? This is a great question to ask someone you don't like, but you have to ask it loudly and in public. If he answers *yes*, which would be a good thing, he admits to having beaten his wife in the past. And if he answers *no*, he admits to beating her still. If he says nothing, people will think he is hiding something. If he gets mad, people will think that he is guilty. Anything he does implicates him deeper in the accusation that was never stated, but which underlies the question.

The lawyers and Pharisees were intent on wrecking Jesus' ministry from the very beginning. They began to question the disciples, who couldn't deny breaking the Jewish fellowship laws. Any defense they gave would be either a lie or an admission of guilt. No doubt, they were having a difficult time with the questions. But Jesus overheard them. Maybe He was across the room or whatever, but He heard the question and saw the pickle His disciples were in. They didn't know how to de-fend what He was doing. So, He moseyed on over and found His way into the conversation.

If it ain't broke, He said, *I don't fix it. I didn't come to fix what isn't broken. I came to fix what's broken.* Or as Scripture recorded it,

> "Those who are well have no need of a physician, but those who are sick. I did not come to call the righteous, but sinners, to repentance" (v. 17).

What an insight!

When we use that phrase about not fixing things that aren't broken we usually mean that whatever we're talking about is working fine, so leave it alone. But that's not what Jesus meant. He meant to say that we are all broken-down sinners in desperate need of God's help. But even when we don't see our own brokenness or sense our own sin or our need for salvation, we certainly can see the sins of others—especially the crowd at Matthew's party! It should have been pretty obvious that *those* people were in need of special help. Jesus had gone to where the need was greatest, because there at least the need could be seen.

Jesus' answer pointed out the blindness of those who thought they were fine just as they were. It addresses those who say, *Yeah, Christianity is fine for you—if you need that kind of crutch. But I don't need it.* The problem isn't that such people don't need Christ, the problem is that they are blind to their own deepest need.

Jesus' answer justified His presence at Matthew's party, and it invited those who could see their need to receive the salvation He offered. At the same time, it revealed the spiritual blindness of those who were supposed to be spiritual leaders.

What about you? Do you see your real need? Do you need the healing that Jesus offers? Are you willing to engage the changes in your personal life that such healing will bring? Or are you content the way you are?

Jesus didn't use the word *salvation* in this situation. He didn't talk about salvation, but about sin and repentance—the stumbling blocks of salvation. We all want salvation. But we are not so willing to admit our own sin. It's embarrassing. It's a sign of weakness. So we don't talk about it. We try to cover it up, to hide it. But hiding it is exactly the opposite of what we really need to do. We must recognize and admit our own sin before we will see our need for Jesus. And as difficult as that is, it is still not enough. We must also repent of it. We must change our thinking and behavior.

The job of a preacher is to help people become more aware of their sin, so that they repent of it. Just because you don't see a problem doesn't mean that it's not there. Just because you don't think you are broken or in need of renewal doesn't mean you aren't. How long will we pretend that we aren't broken—individually and culturally? How long, O Lord, how long?

8. Wineskins

*The disciples of John and of the Pharisees were fasting. Then
they came and said to Him, 'Why do the disciples of John and
of the Pharisees fast, but Your disciples do not fast?' And Jesus
said to them, 'Can the friends of the bridegroom fast while the
bridegroom is with them? As long as they have the bridegroom
with them they cannot fast. But the days will come when the
bridegroom will be taken away from them, and then they will
fast in those days. No one sews a piece of unshrunk cloth on an
old garment; or else the new piece pulls away from the old, and
the tear is made worse. And no one puts new wine into old
wineskins; or else the new wine bursts the wineskins, the wine
is spilled, and the wineskins are ruined. But new wine must be
put into new wineskins.'*   —Mark 2:18-22

The religion of the Pharisees was a religion of works. Over time
various disciplines had been developed to augment and clarify
the Ten Commandments. The process of that development was
quite natural. Particular questions about genuine issues required clarification about exactly how to obey them.

For instance, the Sabbath Commandment forbade work on the Sabbath, specifying that no work was to be done by anyone, including
slaves, laborers, and animals. But, as we know, there are some life func-
tions that must continue every day. Accidents and situations arise that
must be tended to. So, over time the Pharisees established various clarifications about exactly how much could be done on the Sabbath to meet
such needs. A person could only walk so far, or only carry certain kinds
of loads, etc. However, such clarifications were not the Word of God,
but the decisions of men which became traditions over time.[4]

Another example might be the giving of the tithe. The determination of exactly what must be tithed is more complex that we might first
think. It is easier for us to understand the issues if we use a contemporary example. Are we to calculate our tithe before taxes or after? Do we

---

4   Yes, they are recorded in the Bible. But they are still traditions of men!

include only our wages? Or do we include interest and investments as well? Do we include gifts and inheritance in figuring our tithe? These are all pertinent questions. The Pharisees sought to help their people answer such questions, and developed a system that turned out to be short on grace and long on works.

We are not going to address all these issues here. Suffice it to say that the Sabbath means that one day in seven is to be wholly dedicated to the Lord. The Sabbath Commandment means doing certain things—worship, study, prayer, works of mercy, etc., more than not doing certain things. One day in seven ought to be given to the study of the Word and service to the Lord. The intent of the Sabbath is to keep people from becoming consumed with the concerns of the world and neglecting the concerns of the Lord.

God instituted the tithe to fund His work in the world. It is not necessary to lay down rules about whether the tithe is calculated before or after taxes, etc. Rather, each individual must make those determinations based upon his own study of Scripture and the leading of the Spirit. The difficulty comes when people don't take Scripture seriously enough to commit to the principle of tithing. We should trust that the faithful can work out the details, and that God's Word provides sufficient guidance.

But we must also remember that Scripture tells us that support for God's work includes tithes and offerings, which means that the tithe should not determine our maximum level of support of God's work, but our minimum. If Christians today took Scripture seriously, church support worldwide would increase four- or five-fold.

I have read that American Christians on the average contribute about two percent of their incomes to their various churches. I don't know if that figure includes support of parachurch ministries or not. But I doubt that Christians give three or four times more to parachurch ministries than they do to their own local churches. The obvious conclusion is that contemporary Christians are derelict in their duties, perhaps deficient in understanding, and even insincere in their commitment to Scripture.

Fasting was another discipline that had been clarified by the Pharisees. There were certain feast days and fast days. The Pharisees wanted people to make their fasting obvious, perhaps to encourage others. However, the Pharisees expected more of the Jews than Scripture commanded.

Scripture notes that both John the Baptist's disciples and the Pharisees fasted regularly, but Jesus' disciples did not. The Pharisees brought this anomaly to Jesus' attention asking why His disciples didn't fast as the more spiritual Jews did. In answer to that question, Jesus spoke about the bridegroom, patching of old cloth with new, and putting new wine in old skins.

Christians often use the story of the wineskins to justify church splits and the creation of new denominations, as if it teaches that you can't teach an old dog new tricks. But as true as that may be, is it the intended teaching of these stories? Bible scholars tell us it is not. God can teach old dogs new tricks! Jesus' teaching on new wineskins does not justify the development of new factions and sects, but has a more important and honorable meaning.

Let's begin with the story of the bridegroom. In essence, Jesus said that fasting was inappropriate behavior for a wedding. The obvious question to ask is, What wedding? Why did Jesus talk about a wedding?

Allowing Scripture to interpret itself we find that Scripture refers to Jesus as the Bridegroom and to His Church as the bride of Christ (Revelation 21:2). With this in mind, the reference to the bridegroom suggests that His ministry was a time of celebration and a kind of wedding or covenant ceremony as He enacted the final sacrifice on the cross for the atonement of sin. The analogy suggests that having an actual marriage proposal in hand is different than hoping to get married some day. What was appropriate prior to His presence on earth was no longer appropriate in His presence, particularly because Jesus came to put an end to the Old Testament ceremonial law.

The point was that the Old Testament ceremonies—the feasts and fasts—would not carry over into the New Testament period. So, it was wrong for the Pharisees to try to mix the old with the new. Each of the examples—the bridegroom, the patch, and the wineskins—pointed to the error of mixing the gospel of Jesus Christ with something else.

> "No one sews a piece of unshrunk cloth on an old garment; or
> else the new piece pulls away from the old, and the tear is made
> worse" (v. 21).

The point of this example was not that the old garment was old and worn out—as true as that might have been, but rather that the new cloth had not been washed. And washing suggests baptism.

His new disciples were just that—*new*. They were new to the faith, and because of that they were green—inexperienced. They were raw recruits, as yet untrained and undisciplined. What could be expected of experienced soldiers, could not be expected of new recruits. The mature disciplines of the faith, like fasting, tithing, and Sabbath observance, were beyond the spiritual maturity of these new disciples.

The solution to the problem of using a piece of new cloth to patch an old garment is not a matter of throwing the old garment out, but of washing and shrinking the patch before it is applied. The same understanding applies to the new wine/old wine parable.

> "And no one puts new wine into old wineskins; or else the new wine bursts the wineskins, the wine is spilled, and the wineskins are ruined. But new wine must be put into new wineskins" (v. 22).

The story is not about what to do with old wine, but what to do with new wine. If you know anything about wine, you know that it improves with age. There was nothing wrong with leaving the old wine in the old skins. They weren't leaking. The problem was what to do with the new wine—the new recruits.

Jesus' disciples were new spiritual recruits, who were filled with the Spirit of the New Testament. The Holy Spirit was the same except that Christ's incarnation began a new or different administration of God's grace. To mix new wine and old wine would ruin both. Jesus was not suggesting such a mix. The point was that even if He took the old wine out of the skins, the new wine would ruin the old skins. Again, the result would be a greater ruin.

Jesus was not so much suggesting the overthrow of the old, as the inauguration of the new. In God's wine cellar the old and the new could coexist. The problem was mixing the new with the old. Such an effort would surely spoil both.

The church at Galatia tried to mix the new teachings of Jesus with the Old Testament and had nothing but trouble. The Galatian church attempted to reconcile Judaism and Christianity.

> "They endeavored to keep alive the law of ceremonies and ordinances, and to place it side by side with the Gospel of Christ".[5]

They tried to both circumcise and baptize. But the Old Covenant was a covenant of works and the New Covenant was a covenant of grace. They tried to mix the theology of works and the theology of

---

5   Ryle, J.C. *Expository Thoughts on Mark*,Banner of Truth Trust, reprint 1994.

grace in the same church (wineskin). The effort produced serious error which Paul then tried to correct.

In fact, that same error has plagued the entire Christian church since its beginning. In the first centuries of the church there were many efforts to mix the gospel with Greek philosophy and Roman paganism. We all know of the efforts of the early Church to try to make Christianity more acceptable to heathen people. It borrowed heathen forms of worship—processions, vestments, and various other practices. It borrowed heathen holy days and tried to Christianize them. In essence, it mixed Christianity with pagan religion. And the errors of those efforts still haunt us today.

These stories of Jesus—the bridegroom, patch, and wineskins—are about the errors of mixing the pure gospel of Jesus Christ (grace) with anything else (works). So much of Christendom has misunderstood and misapplied these important lessons. Christianity today is dominated by the spirit of mixing Christianity with modern worldliness.

People want to claim the Christian faith, without giving up attachments to worldly values. Popular Christianity today is filled with aberrations of the gospel: the prosperity gospel—God wants Christians to be wealthy and here's how to do it; the fulfillment gospel—God wants people to be happy with themselves and here's how to do it; etc. Christian education and counseling too often import the techniques and values of Dewey and Freud, while neglecting the sufficiency of Scripture. Age-based education has replaced family-based training. Students of the Bible in Sunday Schools and seminaries spend much more time with curriculum than with the Bible. The values of fulfillment and self-esteem have supplanted the older values of personal sacrifice and self-discipline. There is very little teaching of God's pure grace in the churches today.

The usual interpretation of these stories of Jesus serves to justify novelty and schism, as if Jesus Himself was the author of a new and schismatic doctrine! Jesus' intent was not to break away from a wrong-headed and aberrant church, but to fulfill Scripture in order to make the church what God wanted it to be from the very beginning.

The lesson before us today is that the pure gospel of Jesus Christ must stand alone in pristine purity—grace alone through faith alone in Christ alone through Scripture alone to the glory of God alone, or suffer the consequences of these parables. The effort to patch up an ailing church by adding members who are not washed in the pure grace of the gospel, or with the teachings of self-improvement and works righteousness is an invitation to disaster. The one will tear the other apart. The mixing of new teaching with old teaching will burst the seams and spoil the whole lot.

It would be difficult to look at the history of modern Christianity with the multiplication of denominations, competing factions, divisive sects, and the overall deterioration of the church's role in society, and not conclude that the modern Christian era has given history a negative example of how to be faithful.

The cure for us today, of course, is the same as the cure has always been. Repent! Return to the old paths, the tried and true teachings of those whose faith has been proven in the kilns of history. Return to the hope that dominated when Christianity waxed strong. Of course, we cannot return to any past age. Rather, we must embrace God's future by leaning into the hope we find in God's Word. The good old days were never actually that good. We must be future faced, not pining for what cannot return.

But the truth is that we will not repent until we discover that *we* have lost our way, lost our bearings.

Lord, open our eyes.

9. Lord of the Sabbath

Now it happened that He went through the grainfields on the Sabbath; and as they went His disciples began to pluck the heads of grain. And the Pharisees said to Him, 'Look, why do they do what is not lawful on the Sabbath?' But He said to them, 'Have you never read what David did when he was in need and hungry, he and those with him: how he went into the house of God in the days of Abiathar the high priest, and ate the showbread, which is not lawful to eat, except for the priests, and also gave some to those who were with him?' And He said to them, 'The Sabbath was made for man, and not man for the Sabbath. Therefore the Son of Man is also Lord of the Sabbath.'
—Mark 2:23-28

The lesson on Sabbath observance was given "as they went" (v. 23). Earlier we noted that this language suggests that Christ did not so much set out to teach various things like an instructor of a class will do. But He taught lessons and used examples as He encountered them amidst ordinary life. In this way Christ's teaching was integrated with living. Learning and living were not treated artificially as separate categories, but held together in the unity of experience.

The issue was that Jesus' disciples picked corn to eat on the Sabbath. There appeared to be no concern that they took something that belonged to someone else, perhaps because of the gleaning laws. When a field was harvested, some of the crop was intentionally left for the poor, who could simply have it for the picking. If the corn was in ear and edible, it was near harvest time, so the gleaning practice may have been in effect. However, it was the Sabbath.

The Pharisees focused on that particular violation. No work was to be done, and picking corn was considered work. Being aware that the Pharisees were hypocrites, we should note how the concerns of hypocrites tend to focus on the particulars of outward behavior (or obedience) and ignore the concerns of inner belief, attitude, and the heart-felt desire to conform to the intentions of Scripture. Hypocrites are forever harping on particulars, and neglecting the greater purpose of spiritual discipline.

Because the Pharisees accused the disciples of doing "what is not lawful on the Sabbath" (v. 24), the issue was about the purpose and practice of Sabbath law. It is critical for us to understand what happened here because Jesus both corrected and changed the Old Testament Sabbath practices. He offered several arguments in defense of His disciples.

First He referred the matter to Scripture, a most important lesson. He cited David's violation of the Jewish showbread, which was used in the ancient worship rituals (Leviticus 24:5-9). The point that Jesus made was that the practice of the priest's exclusive right to the showbread was a man-made custom and not the Word of God. The Levites had developed a practice that went beyond Scripture. Nonetheless, we must remember that Christ came to put an end to that code of ceremonies and sacrifices. The point was that even David was able to understand that ceremonial practices required a certain flexibility.

God instituted the Sabbath as a blessing. And to keep it a blessing, it should not be made into a hard and fast rule by which people were oppressed. It was a blessing, not a weapon. The only reason for keeping the Sabbath was that the people, by sanctifying themselves to God, might worship in truth and in spirit, and not get distracted by the interests and concerns of the world and the flesh. In addition, being free from worldly concerns, they would be free to attend the synagogue and do the disciplines of the people of God—worship, study, prayer, and service.

While meetings and disciplines cannot save people, they are a great blessing to those who are saved. The meetings and disciplines are aides to spiritual growth—sanctification. They further spiritual maturity, which makes for more fully developed and, therefore, happier and more productive Christians. One of the fallacies operating today is that increased production is more a function of 24-hour operation, than of the spiritual maturity and personal development of the workers. The fallacy is that increasing busy-ness does not necessarily increase production.

Because God's wisdom works best, the time will come again when businesses will discover the value and benefits of providing appropriate time for their employees to pursue spiritual maturity and personal development—genuine Sabbath rest. But the point isn't to reinstitute Sunday or Sabbath laws. That would simply reintroduce the error of the Pharisees. The point is the reintegration of God's Sabbath purpose within the lives and work schedules of individuals. Just as the Pharisees could not force Sabbath observance, neither can we—nor should we try. The idea is not to impose it, but to allow and encourage it.

By pleading the example of David—that David's necessity excused him from strict Sabbath obedience, Jesus argued that real necessities could suspend normal Sabbath observance for particular individuals in particular situations. The Lord provided room for those real life contingencies that come up. Upon this argument the Savoy Declaration (the original Congregational statement of faith) and the Westminster Confession allowed for Sabbath variances based on necessity.

However, necessity should not be used as an excuse to neglect the Sabbath, but can be used to cover those circumstances of genuine need that do come up. Anything can be abused, including Christ's Sabbath variance based upon necessity. As with all of Christ's teachings, what is highlighted is not the outward practice, but the inner intent of the heart.

Jesus also taught here that it is lawful to do the things required by Scripture for the worship of God on the Sabbath—going to church, preparing and receiving communion, teaching, Bible study, fellowshipping with the saints—including sharing a meal together, visitation, and other acts of mercy. Sabbath observance does not interfere with worship or the exercise of faithfulness, it enhances it.

The purpose of Sabbath observance is to create a space in our schedules for worship and a desire in our heart for godliness. The tendency is for the concerns of the world—family, work, recreation, etc.—to dominate our schedules, leaving little or no time for God's concerns. And isn't that what happens! Without an intentional effort to the contrary, we schedule church—worship, Bible study, prayer, etc.—out of our lives. I'm sure the number one excuse people give for not attending worship or reading their Bibles is that they just don't have time.

Jesus said,

> "The Sabbath was made for man, and not man for the Sabbath"
> (v. 27).

He meant that people who use God's law as a weapon of destruction misunderstand and abuse it. All of God's law was given as a blessing. It was intended to benefit people, to provide for the increase of their faith, not to destroy it. Any of God's blessings can be abused. Any of God's teachings can be misunderstood and misapplied. Just as Scripture can be quoted out of context, the doctrines of grace can be applied out of context. When Scripture becomes a club to keep people in line, it has gone beyond its intended purpose.

I'm reminded of the misunderstanding and abuse of the doctrine of predestination. It, too, is susceptible to abuse. It was intended to be a great comfort to the saints, in the sense that it teaches that God's absolute care and protection extend from cradle to grave. Understanding that God's calling and care cannot be withdrawn gives believers an unshakable assurance of faith and courage to face the difficulties of life. Such assurance is a great blessing and encouragement to

> "hold fast the confession of our hope without wavering, for He
> who promised is faithful" (Hebrews 10:23).

But thinking that it is no use to pray or go to church because God has already decided who will be saved and who will be damned is a classic misunderstanding and misuse of the doctrine of predestination, just as insisting on absolute Sabbath adherence is an abuse of the Sabbath. Such thoughts are unscriptural. They are products of human error that are not sufficiently grounded in Scripture. Scripture allows some slack in the Sabbath law, just as Scripture allows for what might sometimes seem to sinners to be logical inconsistencies according to our limited perspective and understanding regarding God's predestination.

According to Scripture God's predestination applies first and foremost to the saints. It is a positive teaching that provides comfort and assurance to believers. But when it is used as a weapon to cut people off from the grace of God, it has exceeded its purpose. No one is cut off from the grace of God unless they personally reject it themselves. While all movement toward God is caused by God, all movement away from God is the result of the personal choices of individuals. People go to hell because they choose to, or because they reject God's offer to go to heaven. But in either case it is the failure of people themselves to respond to God that is responsible for their damnation.

Similarly, to say that man was not made for the Sabbath did not mean that Jesus canceled the obligations of Sabbath observance. He did not abolish the Sabbath, He corrected it. By the same token we cannot simply ignore the doctrine of predestination because it does not appear to be universally applicable. Just because we don't understand how it applies in all cases doesn't mean that it doesn't apply in all cases. Discernment is required, and discernment entails the presence and help of the Holy Spirit.

When Christ said that "the Son of Man is Lord even of the Sabbath" (v. 28) He declared that He has the authority to exempt His followers from strict observance of the Sabbath as taught in the Old Testament or by the Pharisees. Again, we know that Christ brought an end to the Old Testament ceremonial law. No doubt the Pharisees were irritated by his open profession of divine authority. But He didn't use it to irritate them, He used it to establish some necessary Sabbath changes. Their irritation was a matter of their own choosing.

Jesus died so that you and I could have the freedom to worship in spirit and in truth, so that we can observe His Sabbath—not because we must, but because we may. He died so that we can grow in grace, so that we can personally *want* to be of service to Him and to His cause, so that we can be saved, and contribute positively to the salvation of others. His death on the cross was sufficient for all this. His atonement for our sin has opened the door.

So, come to Christ! Receive Christ's salvation! Don't neglect the abundant blessings of Christ and His church that are yours through serving Him in His church.

10. STEP FORWARD

And He entered the synagogue again, and a man was there
who had a withered hand. So they watched Him closely,
whether He would heal him on the Sabbath, so that they might
accuse Him. And He said to the man who had the withered
hand, 'Step forward.' Then He said to them, 'Is it lawful on the
Sabbath to do good or to do evil, to save life or to kill?' But
they kept silent. And when He had looked around at them with
anger, being grieved by the hardness of their hearts, He said to
the man, 'Stretch out your hand.' And he stretched it out, and
his hand was restored as whole as the other. Then the Pharisees
went out and immediately plotted with the Herodians against
Him, how they might destroy Him. But Jesus withdrew with
His disciples to the sea. And a great multitude from Galilee fol-
lowed Him, and from Judea and Jerusalem and Idumea and be-
yond the Jordan; and those from Tyre and Sidon, a great multi-
tude, when they heard how many things He was doing, came
to Him. So He told His disciples that a small boat should be
kept ready for Him because of the multitude, lest they should
crush Him. For He healed many, so that as many as had afflic-
tions pressed about Him to touch Him. And the unclean spirits,
whenever they saw Him, fell down before Him and cried out,
saying, 'You are the Son of God.' But He sternly warned them
that they should not make Him known.　　　—Mark 3:1-12

Jesus encountered the man with the withered hand in the synagogue.
Luke tells us that the man's "*right hand* was withered" (Luke 6:6, italics added). First, let me say that this was a real situation. There actually was a man with a withered hand. This story was not made-up to illustrate a point, but was an actual event which God in His providence
provided, and which has great symbolic meaning.

By the providence of God this man's affliction provided another
teaching example for Jesus. The man's withered hand—his right hand—
is a biblical symbol of weakness. His withered hand affected his ability to
provide for his family, to work. The fact that it was withered suggests

that the cause was internal to the man. It hadn't been damaged by an accident, but something within the man reduced or eliminated his ability to provide, to work.

There are various allusions to the right hand in Scripture. The saints of old used their right hand to bless their children. It signified the power of God's blessing (Genesis 48). The Scriptures speak of the right hand of God as a means of protection and blessing. The right hand signifies integrity and honor when, for instance, a woman gives her right hand to a man in marriage. The phrase "right hand" is used 148 times in Scripture, most often with the above symbolic meanings. It is a term familiar to Scripture and therefore, needs to be interpreted scripturally.

Because the man was in the synagogue, the symbolism suggests the withered power of the Jewish faith, the inability of Phariseeism to provide for God's people. The man exemplified Judaism. Jesus was aware that the Jewish church of his day was a spiritually withered institution.

Mark tells us that "they watched Him closely" (v. 2). Well before Jesus did anything to the man, the Pharisees were watching Him, plotting against him, waiting for Him to make a mistake. They weren't just watching to see what He would do. They were watching for an opportunity to trip Him up. They weren't watching out of curiosity, but out of spite. They were watching for opportunities to do Him harm. And Jesus knew it. He knew they were watching Him, and why.

Knowing that they were watching Him, Jesus then called the man forward. Notice that it was not the man's idea to get healed. He didn't volunteer. He didn't ask for healing. Perhaps He didn't believe it was possible. Perhaps He didn't know who Jesus was at that time. Or perhaps he was just minding his own business, trying to "go along to get along" at the synagogue when Jesus called him forward.

If we were to apply this story in a symbolic way to the church, we would say that the church didn't desire to be healed of its withered condition. And isn't that true! So many withered churches are content to just go along to get along. The people aren't particularly unhappy. People learn to live with their withered spirits, and just go through the motions.

But the Lord commands us to step forward! Jesus said,

> "You did not choose Me, but I chose you and appointed you that
> you should go and bear fruit…" (John 15:16).

Here was a man who was not bearing fruit, or by analogy a church that was not fruitful. However, the man was not condemned for his inability, he was healed. Not everyone Jesus came across was healed, but this man was healed because of the Lord's compassion for him. But the story also serves to illustrate a greater truth about His love and grace.

Has God chosen you? Has He singled you out and called you to follow Him? Has He healed you of your withered spirit? That is the application of this Scripture. It is another example of God's wonderful mercy and grace. God reaches out to heal the withered and to reclaim the lost. There is no other way to come to Christ, but to be called by Him. Have you been called by the Master? Have you been healed for service?

Jesus was aware that there were men in that synagogue who were plotting to kill Him. He knew of their schemes. He had run into unclean spirits before. And so as He asked about the Sabbath law, whether it was

> "lawful on the Sabbath to do good or to do evil, to save life or to kill?" (v. 4),

He was pointing out the fact that He would use the Sabbath to benefit life while they used it to plot His death. He directed the question to them—to the plotters, to the doubters, to those who conspired against Him.

Again, the point couldn't be clearer. The Sabbath was for the good of men, not for their destruction. The Pharisees had twisted God's law to their own purposes. They claimed faithfulness and obedience, but imposed their own purposes upon God's people. They used the Lord and His Scriptures to further their own interests and to justify themselves. Theirs was the error of Balaam.[6]

Balaam thought he was serving God. He was so blinded by his own self-righteousness that he couldn't see that God opposed what he was doing. When his donkey tried to tell him that God's angel was about to smite him dead, he beat the poor ass. He was so blinded by his own self-righteousness that a miracle of the first degree failed to alert Balaam to his own error. Balaam said all the right things, but was blind to God's leading, as were the Pharisees.

The Pharisees remained silent at the invitation to confess their intentions to the Lord of lords. Scripture says that Jesus "looked around at them with anger," and that He was "grieved by the hardness of their hearts" (v. 5). All we know is that the Pharisees "watched him closely" (v. 2), when Jesus responded with anger and grief for their souls. Did Je-

---

6   Numbers 22, See also Ross, Phillip A. *The Work at Zion—A Reckoning*, Fairway Press, Lima, Ohio, 1999, Vol. 2, p. 28.

sus jump to a conclusion here? Was He wrong to be so angry at them and to judge them so severely?

There are a couple of things here that are worth noting. First, there is a righteous anger that is not tainted with sin. Jesus cautioned His disciples to be careful with their anger.

> "Whoever is angry with his brother without a cause shall be in danger of the judgment" (Matthew 5:22).

But He didn't disavow all anger. There is a righteous anger that has a righteous usefulness. Jesus put the money changers out of the Temple in an expression of righteous anger. The point is that there is a right and a wrong use of anger. However, a double caution is advised because most of us are too quick to believe our own anger to be always righteous. However, righteous anger is only used in the service of the Lord, not in service to ourselves.

Jesus also judged the Pharisees as having hardened hearts. Basically He was saying that they were not saved because of the hardness of their hearts. Hardened hearts cannot receive salvation. Did this observation carry the weight of damnation?

Jesus said, "Judge not, that you be not judged" (Matthew 7:1). Yet, He never forbids the exercise of biblical judgment. He also said,

> "Do not judge according to appearance, but judge with righteous judgment" (John 7:24).

It is not judgment per se that is forbidden, but unrighteous judgment. That is, judgment that is not firmly grounded in Scripture, the only reliable guide for righteousness. Christians are not to use their own judgment against others, but always to apply God's judgment found in Scripture to themselves first and foremost, but also to others.

But, again, Jesus did not bring condemnation upon the Pharisees. They brought it upon themselves. In the midst of Jesus' anger and grief, He was not the cause of their condemnation. Rather, He showed mercy by healing the man with the withered hand. Similarly, Jesus doesn't condemn wayward churches, they condemn themselves. Nor does He simply condemn withered churches, sometimes He heals them. Ultimately, the Lord pours out His grace and mercy, and the abundance of His healing power to bring His church to her rightful glory. In every age Jesus protects and heals His withered church—sometimes by trial and chastisement, but always for a glory yet to come.

How was the man healed? "Stretch out your hand" (v. 5), Jesus commanded. He never asked the man if he wanted to be healed. He didn't quiz him about his faith. He didn't ask him to say the sinner's prayer. He commanded the man to stretch out his hand, the very thing that the poor man could not do on his own. His withered hand was not able to stretch out.

The verb *stretch* is used often in Scripture. God stretched out His hand and smote the Egyptians. Moses stretched out his hand and Aaron stretched out his rod and brought plagues to Egypt. The Hebrew *natah* means the simple action involved in reaching. It always signifies an action either by God or by men. To receive God's healing Jesus commanded the man to step forward and stretch out his weakness in public.

As the man obeyed he was healed. He stepped forward. He drew near to Jesus, and away from the crowd. He turned his attention to the Lord. Then he stretched out his withered hand. He revealed his weakness to Jesus and to the watching crowd. He acknowledged his weakness publicly. He offered his weakness to the purposes of the Lord. He came out of obscurity and embarrassment, and allowed God to make a public example of his weakness. And upon doing this, upon his obedience, upon doing the very thing that in his own strength he could not do, his hand was restored.

The Greek word for *restored* (*apokathistemi*) is used only eight times, six times referring to this story, once in Acts 1:6 regarding the restoration of Israel, and once in Hebrews 13:19 regarding the restoration of a man who had been disciplined by the elders. The Greek word that is usually used for healing is *therapeuo*, which is used forty-three times. The man was not healed therapeutically, he was restored, or reset to his proper condition.

Immediately upon the man's healing, the two factions of the Jewish church united and "plotted...how they might destroy (Jesus)" (v. 6). The demonstration of Jesus' power united the feuding factions in the church against Him. Those who had long fought against one another now joined forces to fight against Jesus. Putting this fact in modern parlance, we might say that both conservatives and liberals were threatened by the obvious power and authority of the Lord. Jesus was equally disdained by both the right and the left.

At this point Jesus "withdrew with His disciples" (v. 7). But the multitude heard of the healing of the man's withered hand, and they followed Him seeking yet more miracles and healings. Jesus, in His great compassion, "healed many" (v. 10). We don't know how many He healed, but Scripture tells us that

> "as many as had afflictions pressed about Him to touch Him" (v. 10).

Jesus' purpose in coming to earth was to put an end to the temporary system of Old Testament sacrifices, and to reestablish the biblical teaching of salvation by grace alone through faith alone in Christ alone, "and that not of yourselves" (Ephesians 2:8), as Paul said. But the crowds wanted miracles and healings.

They were looking for flash and instant gratification, not the long and patient methods of God's ordinary means—not the ministry of Word and Sacrament, not study, prayer, and fellowship—but miracles and healing. They sought to "touch Him" (v. 10), because their hopes were driven by the superstitions they had grown up with. It's not that touching Jesus couldn't provide healing miracles. It could indeed—and did, as in the healing of the woman with the twelve-year flow of blood (Mark 5:27).

All things are certainly possible with God, but such miraculous healings are not God's usual practice today. We will be much better off to employ God's ordinary means than to constantly expect Him to treat us extraordinarily. Miracles and healings are not beyond the power of God, but neither are they His normal practice. To insist on them is to pridefully insist that we are extraordinary people. Thus, the seeking of miracles originates in self-concern—pride.

Note also that Jesus encountered the "unclean spirits" (v. 11) again.

> "Whenever they saw Him, (they) fell down before Him and cried out, saying, 'You are the Son of God'" (v. 11).

They swooned in the realization of His divinity. Sound familiar? These unclean spirits occupied sinners who had been broken and overwhelmed by their own sinfulness.

On the one hand we are tempted to think that it is a good thing for such people to identify Jesus as the Son of God. While the Pharisees tripped over Jesus' divinity, these unclean spirits shouted it from the rooftops. Jesus kept trying to point His divinity out to the Pharisees, almost rubbing their noses in it. But here when the unclean spirits shouted it out for all to hear, Jesus

> "sternly warned them that they should *not* make Him known" (v. 12, italics added).

Why not? Why did Jesus not want to be associated with the unclean spirits? Didn't He come to save sinners? He did. However, there were several occasions that Jesus told various people not to tell anyone about Him or about what He had done regarding some particular healing or miracle.

Jesus was still a long way from the cross, which was His goal. His ultimate purpose was the atonement, which required the cross. He didn't want the crowds to interfere with His main purpose by distracting people with an inordinate concern about miracles and healing. Sure there were miracles and healings, but His primary purpose was atonement. At any point, Jesus could have turned to the crowds and asked them to choose between His atonement on the cross or miracles and healings. They would have chosen miracles every time!

But that was not what He came to do. So He continued to redirect people to His primary purpose because it is much more important than miracles and healings.

Has Christ called you? Have you engaged His ordinary means of grace? Or are you still looking for miracles and healing? His death on the cross is the means of your atonement, isn't that enough? It's what He came to do.

11. CALLED AND SENT

And He went up on the mountain and called to Him those He Himself wanted. And they came to Him. Then He appointed twelve, that they might be with Him and that He might send them out to preach, and to have power to heal sicknesses and to cast out demons: Simon, to whom He gave the name Peter; James the son of Zebedee and John the brother of James, to whom He gave the name Boanerges, that is, "Sons of Thunder"; Andrew, Philip, Bartholomew, Matthew, Thomas, James the son of Alphaeus, Thaddaeus, Simon the Cananite; and Judas Iscariot, who also betrayed Him. And they went into a house.
—Mark 3:13-19

A multitude followed Jesus as he went out of the synagogue where He had healed the man with the withered hand. Many people followed Him seeking healing, others wanted to witness miracles. The unclean spirits were extolling Him as the Son of God and falling down in a feint of enthusiasm. He healed some, and some witnessed miracles, but He "sternly warned" those with unclean spirits "not to make Him known" (v. 12). Their witness and their antics would not help the Lord accomplish His mission of atonement.

Escaping the press of the crowds again, Jesus "went up on the mountain" (v. 13). If we follow Mark's account closely we will see that when Jesus left the crowd they were in a bit of a tizzy. He had accused the Pharisees of having hardened hearts. He had dodged the crowds whose desires threatened to pull Him off course. He "sternly warned" the unclean spirits not to mention His name. And now He again abandoned the crowds for a select group of friends.

Mark said that He "called to Him those He Himself wanted" (v. 13). Jesus chose a few people for His own reasons. He didn't ask everyone to accompany Him up the mountain. Who did He take? Mark said that He went up the mountain to appoint the twelve apostles. Two things need to be noticed here: 1) the manner in which the apostles were chosen, and 2) the fact that they were not volunteers but appointees.

Were the apostles chosen because they were holier than everybody else? Not at all. In fact, we will see their lack of holiness and fickle commitment as we get further into Mark's story. But suffice it to say that it was not their abilities that caused the Lord to call them. In fact, Mark told us exactly why Jesus called these men and not the others. Jesus called "those He Himself wanted" (v. 13). He called them because He wanted them for His own reasons, not because of their spiritual sensitivities or any superiority in themselves.

The most obvious example of this fact is Jesus' choice of Judas. As an apostle Judas ultimately failed to love Jesus. Judas' apostleship served as a negative example. Judas failed the Lord by betraying Him. He also failed in his responsibility as the keeper of the money. Through his betrayal He left the job half done. He attained no personal success nor happiness, but was finally driven to suicide and damnation (Acts 1:18, John 17:12). Not a pretty picture. Why was he not ultimately chosen to be an apostle? Because he did not serve the Lord's purpose in that role. Judas had another role to play.

Peter was almost as bad. He, too, failed repeatedly to understand Jesus. His faith failed him on the water and he nearly drowned (Matthew 14:30). He, too, betrayed Jesus, not once, but three times (Mark 15:72). Yet Jesus persevered with Peter. Peter's failures served the Lord's purpose, as did those of Thomas. Thomas doubted the Lord during His entire earthly ministry (John 20:27). No, the apostles were not chosen because of their spiritual or worldly excellence, but because of God's purposes.

Neither did Jesus broadcast the invitation far and wide. He didn't invite anyone who wanted to come up the mountain. He called a few friends by name to leave the crowd and come with Him. Then He appointed them

> "that they might be with Him and that He might send them out
> to preach" (v. 14).

This calling and sending of the apostles doesn't apply to all Christians, but applies specifically to preachers. Not all Christians are called to preach, and even fewer were called to be apostles.

All Christians are called into faithfulness by the Lord, but not all are sent to preach. Actually, only a few Christians are called to preach, others are called to teach, others to serve as elders, others to serve in the collection and distribution of resources to the poor, and others for evangelism, etc. There are many gifts and many jobs that Christ calls His people to do. All Christians are called and commissioned for some kind of service.

All Christians, and especially preachers, are called to "be with" (v. 14) the Lord, to spend time with Him in prayer, study, and fellowship. This calling is not something extra, but is essential for discipleship. All Christians are commanded to worship, to pray, to fellowship together, to search out the Scriptures, etc. Not every Scripture has the same application.

The call to preach is given in many places (Matthew 10:7, 28:19; Romans 10:15, etc.). Mark said that the apostles were given "power to heal sickness and to cast out demons" (v. 15), but we know from experience that preachers don't generally have that kind of power today. Why not? It was given to the apostles—but even then only occasionally. Paul could not heal himself of his own affliction (2 Corinthians 12:7).

Because the discipline of discipleship requires reliance upon the ordinary means of grace, preachers must employ and encourage God's ordinary means of grace for spiritual growth. Preachers are neither endowed with miraculous powers nor commissioned to perform miracles —the apostles were, but preachers are not. With the completion of the New Testament, Christians are to depend upon the Word, not miracles. The gospel of Jesus Christ isn't about the ongoing performance of miracles, except the miracle of salvation. The miracles in Scripture were for the purpose of establishing the fact of God's salvation. And Jesus' death and resurrection established it.

Dependence upon the ordinary means of grace is not a sign of weakness, but a sign of faithfulness. Where miracles demonstrate a great power that is recognized by the world, the ordinary means of grace are seen by the world as weak and ineffective. But Christ said to Paul,

> "My grace is sufficient for you, for My strength is made perfect
> in weakness" (2 Corinthians 12:9).

The real power of God's ordinary means of grace is often viewed by the world and by the spurious as weakness. The faithful are often charged with being weak because they do not work miracles. But the faithful don't claim to heal or perform miracles or cast out demons, only to worship, pray, study, and fellowship together for the cause of Christ.

The reason that we are to depend only upon God's ordinary means of grace revealed in Scripture is because the Lord established them for our use. They may be nothing to the world, but they are precious to the saints because they reveal to us our own weaknesses and limitations.

They point out our own inability to save ourselves, even through the use of such means. Were we workers of miracles, able to bestow healing and prosperity, we would soon come to believe our own press reports, to believe in our own spiritual powers and abilities. Believing in our ability to work miracles we would soon turn from God's purpose.

Often, those who claim such powers claim that they come from the Lord, but they also claim themselves to be vehicles of such powers and miracles. Human pride soon moves the credit from the source (God) to the vehicle (man). Though they may mention God in the credits, workers of miracles soon enough pride themselves on their own abilities. We are as human beings so depraved that we can even be proud of our humility, and boast in our faithfulness.

Whenever people think that some healing has occurred, or some great miracle is underway, they flock to be near the person or place they identify with the miracle. Rather, than flocking to their own church to praise God as the true source of all miracles, they will travel across the country or round the world to pay homage to some place or person, as if the miracle had some worldly cause or local connection.

The so-called miracles of the virgin Mary fall into this category. The attributes of God are misapplied to weeping statues and local shrines, revealing rampant idolatry and the misunderstanding and misapplication of Scripture. In a similar fashion we see people flocking to Brownsville or Toronto (sites of purported revival) to be near reported outpourings of the Holy Spirit, as if God were bound by geography. Worldly limitations are attributed to God's Spirit, as if physical proximity to the Spirit (whatever that means) will cause the Spirit to spread, as if He were a fire or a disease that can be spread through contact and proximity.

But God only works miracles and healing out of necessity—His necessity, not ours. God works according to His own plans and timetables, not ours. How and why miracles and healings occur is not available to the understanding of man. All we know is that all miracles and all miraculous healings are the work of God alone—for His purposes, not ours. He alone is able, we are not. Such things occur by the necessity of the Holy Spirit, not by the whims of men.

Similarly, the presence of the Holy Spirit is necessary for all Godward movement in the lives of believers. Notice in Scripture that many unsaved people witnessed the miracles of Jesus. The healing of the ten lepers, for instance, shows that, while Jesus healed ten, only one returned to give thanks to the Lord (Luke 17:15). The implication is that only one of the healed lepers was truly saved by faith. The others were cured only to perish in the flesh. The significance being that their miraculous healing from leprosy did nothing to save their souls.

So what was the difference between the nine who were healed but lost, and the one who was saved? Scripture reveals nothing in them that made any difference. We don't know how or why one turned, or why the others didn't. All we know is that the one turned to the Lord and found salvation. He was not more holy than the others, nor did his healing make any critical difference. The only difference we can find is in God's grace.

The purpose of the story is to demonstrate that salvation is by grace alone, and is not dependent upon works of any kind, be they the ordinary works of ordinary men or the extraordinary works of God. People are not saved because they witness a miracle, or because they take part in a miracle, or because they are on the receiving end of a genuine miracle. Salvation is by grace alone. We can only believe and be saved by the grace of God. Salvation is dependent upon God. As God said to Moses,

> "I will be gracious to whom I will be gracious, and I will have compassion on whom I will have compassion" (Exodus 33:19).

Salvation belongs entirely to the Lord.

The lesson that we must learn is that the church is not called to be successful, because success is of the Lord. One plants, another waters, but God gives the increase (1 Corinthians 3:6). Our responsibility is planting and watering, not increase. The Lord will not hold us responsible for what He alone can do.

Rather we will be held accountable for our faithfulness to the gospel. Not growth and worldly success, but faithfulness is the true measure of the church. And of Christians.

So, how are you measuring up?

12. Divided Loyalties

*Then the multitude came together again, so that they could not
so much as eat bread. But when His own people heard about
this, they went out to lay hold of Him, for they said, 'He is out
of His mind.' And the scribes who came down from Jerusalem
said, 'He has Beelzebub,' and, 'By the ruler of the demons He
casts out demons.' So He called them to Himself and said to
them in parables: 'How can Satan cast out Satan? If a kingdom
is divided against itself, that kingdom cannot stand. And if a
house is divided against itself, that house cannot stand. And if
Satan has risen up against himself, and is divided, he cannot
stand, but has an end. No one can enter a strong man's house
and plunder his goods, unless he first binds the strong man.
And then he will plunder his house.'* —Mark 3:20-27

We left Jesus and His disciples as they entered a house (v. 19).
He had called the apostles to come apart from the crowd.
Mark may be collapsing the time involved here, but he appears to indicate that the next significant thing that happened was that
the crowds followed Jesus once again. This time they pressed themselves
upon Him and the disciples so that it was impossible to move about
enough to prepare or eat a meal. The point is that the house was extremely crowded.

Mark said, "But when His own people heard about this…" (v. 21).
Before we finish the sentence we need to determine who heard what.
The NKJV reads, "His own people," the NIV, "his family," the KJV, "his
friends." The Greek construction suggests those who were near Jesus in
either proximity or in relationship, i.e., family or followers, depending
on the context. The context could just as easily indicate His family, His
friends, or His disciples. The bottom line would indicate that those who
were concerned about Jesus heard something about Him.

But what did they hear? The Greek simply says that they "heard."
The translators have added either "about this" or "of it" for the purpose
of context and clarity—although the addition doesn't seem to me to clarify much. We must identify the nature of what they heard because their

reaction to what they heard was significant. A variety of suggestions have been made by scholars. Some have suggested that his family heard that He was drawing great crowds. Others that He suffered from hunger because "they could not so much as eat bread" (v. 20).

But more likely, they heard about His location, where He was. He had gone home to his Galilean base, His house or the house of a friend. And because of what they heard about His activities—His preaching against the Pharisees, the miracles and healings, etc.—His family came to get Him. Much as your family and friends would do, if you began publicly acting as if you were the Christ.

> "They went out to lay hold of Him, for they said, 'He is out of His mind'" (v. 21).

As if to bolster the case against Him, the scribes—lawyers from Jerusalem—had come down to establish a case against Jesus' sanity.

> "He has Beelzebub," *they said.* "By the ruler of the demons He casts out demons" (v. 22).

The scribes, equivalent to agents from the prosecutor's office in downtown Jerusalem, also came once word of Jesus' whereabouts reached them. Their presence, no doubt, reinforced the case His family thought they had against Him. From Jesus' family's perspective, this thing was already getting out of hand, and they wanted to minimize the damage that He had done to Himself and to the family name. The fact that scribes from Jerusalem had gotten involved surely made things worse. Nobody wants to tangle with city hall.

They charged Him with satanic complicity, "He has *Beelzebub*" (v. 22—italics added). The word is of uncertain origin. No one knows exactly what it means, but it is used in reference to Satan (*Ba'al*) or his minions or his powers. Both Matthew and Luke relate this story to Jesus healing a demon-possessed mute.

The thing to notice is that the scribes do not doubt that exorcisms are real. Notice also that the scribes were familiar enough with exorcisms to attribute them to the power of a god that they knew well enough to call by name, Beelzebub. They were probably also trying to associate Jesus with this pagan god of the underworld in order to discredit Him in the eyes of faithful Jews. The implications were clear. Jesus was either crazy or possessed by Satan. They completely disallowed the possibility that He might actually be who He said He was.

His family had not yet arrived (v. 31), so we can conclude that Jesus "called (the scribes) to Himself and (talked) to them in parables" (v. 23). However, it was not a private conference He had with them,. Rather, He talked to them in the midst of the pressing crowd in order to make a public point.

Though Jesus often talked in parables, it was not His intent to confuse or deceive people. Rather, the parables were often stories that illustrated His point. His intent was to clarify His point by leading the listeners to think for themselves about the subject at hand. By speaking in parables Jesus forced His listeners to make inferences and connections, and to draw conclusions that connect the parable with the point He is trying to illustrate.

The point of the parable was that divided kingdoms like divided houses cannot endure. It has long been known that the most effective strategy in war and politics is to divide your opponent. Whether that division consists of a physical division of forces or the breaking apart of their mental or psychological unity, division undermines organization. Divisions and the lack of unity will quickly tear any organization apart.

Unity is the primary ingredient for any organizational endeavor. Without unity at a deep and fundamental level, no organization can accomplish much or last long. But what is unity? What are the requisites for unity? What are the limits of organizational unity? What kind of unity is required for effective organizations?

Obviously, I want to talk about church unity, about the requisites and limits of church unity. And in order to do that we need to distinguish between surface unity and deep unity. We need to see that these different facets of unity are not just different, but are often antithetical. They are at times theologically opposed to one another, if only because one tends to a false unity and the other to a true unity.

In surface unity it often appears that everyone agrees about most everything. A concerted effort is made to gloss over all fissures and cracks (disagreements) that appear so that everything appears to be unified. The emphasis is upon appearance. Surface unity can be compared to plaster cracks that appear in the walls of homes as they age. It begins with a hairline crack, hardly noticeable. But over time it grows to the point that it must be fixed. So, out comes the Spackle and paint, and in no time at all the crack is covered up and the wall looks whole again. But after a few more years the same crack often appears again. It can be fixed again, but will continue to reappear over time.

The common plaster crack does not endanger the structure of a house. It is the result of the normal settling and shifting of soil that occurs everywhere. Plaster cracks don't look good, so they are repaired as a matter of appearance. But the fixing of a plaster crack is a surface repair. It does nothing to stem the tide of the shifting soil or to reinforce the foundational structure of the house in order to prevent the crack from reappearing.

As long as the foundation of the house is sound, plaster cracks will not seriously endanger the safety and well-being of the house. They are simply a recurring minor nuisance. Unless they are caused by a deteriorating foundation. Here we shift from a superficial problem of minor significance to a deep-rooted problem with serious consequences.

Where the uniform integrity of a foundation begins to disintegrate, cracks and deterioration of the foundation result. The first signs of such a problem will often be plaster cracks, just as we discussed before. However, the cause and the solution to a foundation problem is much more difficult, much more involved. The analogy begins to lose its application the more we press it for detailed meaning. But the point remains about surface unity and deep unity. So, what are the theological or church-related elements involved in surface unity and deep unity?

The elements of surface (or superficial or external) church unity are secondary things like time of worship, place of worship—and similar concerns with the building and grounds. There needs to be some basic agreements about when to worship and where to worship, what kinds of programs are permissible, and what are not permissible. Surface unity involves basic agreements about dress and behavior codes, be they spoken or tacit.

There are also some organizational considerations that fall into the surface category. They are composed of the kinds of things that Christians agree to disagree about, but are unwilling to break fellowship over. Here we find a variety of church traditions and practices that involve various ways to do things, i.e., different beliefs about communion, different beliefs about baptism, different ways to organize church government, different styles of preaching and worship music, even different eschatological interpretations of the end times.

I'm aware churches have split over some of these things, but I don't believe they usually merit the significance to justify church division, nor do they warrant someone leaving a church. Though I don't belong to the same church, I can be in genuine fellowship and unity with people of relatively diverse beliefs. So, the above list of what I call minor infrac-

tions in the church could be cause for the admonishment of many denominations which have come about over such petty concerns. These
kinds of cracks or tears in the Christian fabric can and should be repaired.

But there are other deeper theological differences of opinion that
cannot and should not be overcome. Paul said that

> "there must also be factions among you, that those who are
> approved may be recognized among you" (1 Corinthians 11:19).

In other words, there will always be significant doctrinal differences
among people in the church. They are necessary because the various
opinions and interpretations about the really important things will force
the church to identify God's essential truth in the midst of diversity—and
even falsity. This exercise will keep the faithful alert and attuned to the
Lord.

Organizational peace has never been a mark of the faithful church,
and it never will be. Christ's peace is not like worldly peace. God has not
called us to lounge in self-complacency. Rather, the church is filled with
the tensions of Scripture. Biblical tension in the church results from our
wrestling with deep and important spiritual issues. God wants us to
wrestle, not struggling against one another, but with His Word.

We must realize that such struggles will always come through one
another, but are not about one another. We are to wrestle with the deep
theological issues of Scripture—justification, sanctification, and salvation
itself. By wrestling with these issues we engage the Holy Spirit who
wrests us from the snares of Satan and sets us on the path of Christ's
righteousness.

A church that is not struggling with the tensions of these essential
biblical issues is most likely spiritually dead. Whereas a church that evidences such struggle is a church that is actively engaging the tensions of
Scripture, and is available to the leading of Christ. The church needs to
be a place of learning and free discussion of biblical issues. Yet, we must
also stand under the unity of Christ and of Scripture, and not allow our
differences to drive us apart.

The only way to do that is to make our primary unity a unity with
Christ and with His Word as it has come down to us through history.
We must first find unity by coming into agreement with Scripture regarding the deepest or most fundamental doctrines of Scripture—justification, sanctification, and salvation itself. Here we must seek continuity
with Scripture and evangelical history. Doctrinal unity at these deeper,

foundational levels will insure that superficial disagreements will pre-serve the unity of the church by not dividing the saints. By claiming and clinging to biblical truth the church can and will survive the stresses and struggles of being faithful in a fallen world.

Of course, we will differ in our assessments about these things, and that is as it should be. Our differences in conjunction with vigorous, free discussion will allow the Holy Spirit to lead the discussions. The purpose of such discussions is not to determine a conclusion, but to allow us to follow the Holy Spirit as He leads His people to genuine maturity in the faith.

13. Unforgivable

"Assuredly, I say to you, all sins will be forgiven the sons of men, and whatever blasphemies they may utter, but he who blasphemes against the Holy Spirit never has forgiveness, but is subject to eternal condemnation"—because they said, "He has an unclean spirit."   —Mark 3:28-30

We come now to one of the most difficult passages in Scripture. It is not all that difficult to understand, but it is difficult to accept, to receive as a truth of God. We have all been influenced by the secular liberalism so prevalent in our day. That influence obscures the plain reading of such passages as this one. The liberal mindset has such an ideological commitment to the belief that God is love—and nothing but love—that it refuses to recognize God's justice. Liberals readily accept that God's love issues in mercy. And, of course, that is true, but it is not the only truth about God.

There is another equally valid and necessary quality of God's character that exists in tension with God's love. The verse before us reminds us that God is also just. That He is moral, fair, righteous, and lawful. Justice demands that people receive what they are due, what they have earned. It reminds us that God's justice demands the punishment of the wicked, as it demands the reward of the righteous.

But Scripture also tells us that there are no righteous people,

> "for all have sinned and fall short of the glory of God" (Romans 3:23).

In other words, there is no one who deserves any reward in God's eyes because we are all contaminated with the sin of Adam. This world and its inhabitants are on a global Titanic, on a collision course with death and destruction as a direct result of the Fall of Adam.

Contrary to popular belief, people are not born into a morally neutral condition that is then made positive or negative by their decisions and actions. Scripture tells us that we are all condemned to hell because of Adam's rebellion against God. Adam declared war on God and on the things of God.

It is as if America (the world) were at war with God, as if a President had declared war many generations ago, and that war has continued. The war is not the fault of the children born after that declaration, yet it is a reality for them. As war shapes and conditions all the various social and economic factors of a society, so Adam's war against God shapes and conditions our lives.

It is into this situation, into the realities of Adam's war and God's curse, that Jesus has come with a message of mercy and reconciliation from God. As we study the gospel of Mark we will see both the nature of that message and its reception in the world.

There are two aspects of the Scripture before us that must be clearly understood. First of all, Jesus said that "all sins will be forgiven" (v. 28). Before we look at the single exception to this statement of God's grace, we need to gain an appreciation of the incredible grandeur of God's mercy. All sins will be forgiven! The Lord didn't say that all sins might be forgiven if people meet some basic requirements. But He said that all sins will be forgiven. The King James Version says it more forcefully,

> "Verily I say unto you, All sins shall be forgiven unto the sons of men."

Jesus Christ brings a message of peace and reconciliation to the sons of Adam, to those who have been caught up in Adam's rebellion against God. Christ doesn't bring a tentative message of peace, but a definitive message of grace. Jesus doesn't so much as offer peace to a sin-torn world, as He proclaims that God's grace through Him shall prevail. He brings the message that God's peace will eventually prevail because of the propitiation He made on the cross.

Propitiation is one of those words that has fallen on hard times. It occurs four times in Scripture (in the King James Version). For instance,

> "In this is love, not that we loved God, but that He loved us and sent His Son to be the propitiation for our sins" (1 John 4:10).

The NIV translates the Greek *hilasterion* as atonement.

> "He loved us and sent His Son as an atoning sacrifice for our sins."

To propitiate is to win over someone who has been offended, to make amends, and turn away wrath.

However, God didn't send Jesus to appease *our* hearts because we have been offended by the righteous character of God. Jesus didn't come with a message that God is sorry that His demands for justice and right-eousness have offended our sensitivities. Rather, Jesus came to satisfy *God's* requirement for justice. Jesus came to pay the price, to receive the just punishment for sin. The punishment has not been waived because of Jesus. It has been paid by the obedience of Christ, an obedience that led to the cross.

God's mercy is not that the punishment for sin has been reneged. God cannot alter His decrees without sacrificing the character and in-tegrity of His justice. No, the justice of God is intact. He demands and requires absolute justice in regard to His law. All infractions of that law must receive their due penalty. The laws of God are not abrogated in Christ, but fulfilled—satisfied in Christ.

God's mercy is not that He has canceled the just punishment for sin. God's mercy is that Christ received the just punishment for sin. God's judgment against sinners stands! It is irrevocable because God's decrees are irrevocable. God's character is unchanging. What He demanded yes-teryear through the Old Testament, He demands today through the New. God's laws and God's decrees are absolute. There is no abrogation of God's justice ever!

The two pillars of God's character are perfect justice and perfect love. These two pillars always stand together, never apart. They cannot be understood apart from one another. They make no sense by them-selves. Without reference to love and the grace provided by Christ, jus-tice is cold and unforgiving. Without reference to justice, God's love in-dulges our selfishness and mocks His law. If somehow grace could be given apart from the law being established, God would appear to be hard and cold. But when God's grace is shown after the establishment of the law, as is the case, then God is understood to be kind, loving, and merciful—even while the law is in force.

The grace that God has given through the propitiation of Christ is not the suspension of punishment for sin. All sin must be punished! Rather the grace that God has given through the propitiation of Christ satisfies the need to punish sin. The punishment for sin transpires be-cause Christ has received that punishment. God's mercy is not a stay of execution, but the provision of a substitute for the execution that you and I deserve.

Christ came into a world torn by sin and rebellion to be the propiti-ation for sin. Jesus said,

> "Assuredly, I say to you, all sins will be forgiven the sons of
> men...." (v. 28).

But God's love goes even further! We know that Jesus was charged with blasphemy by the High Priest. It was *the* charge that put Him on the cross. Blasphemy was punishable by death.

> "And whoever blasphemes the name of the Lord shall surely be put to death" (Leviticus 24:16).

Jesus said,

> "all sins will be forgiven the sons of men, and whatever blasphemies they may utter" (v. 28).

Not only has Jesus atoned for our sins, but He has atoned for our blasphemies as well. Whatever actions we take that oppose God and whatever words we utter in opposition or frustration against Him are all atoned for in the cross. Calvary covers it all!

> *Far dearer than all that the world can impart*
> *Was the message that came to my heart;*
> *How that Jesus alone for my sin did atone,*
> *And Calvary covers it all.*
> *The stripes that He bore and the thorns that He wore*
> *Told His mercy and love evermore;*
> *And my heart bowed in shame as I called on His name,*
> *And Calvary covers it all.*
> *How matchless the grace, when I looked in the face*
> *Of this Jesus, my crucified Lord;*
> *My redemption complete I then found at His feet,*
> *And Calvary covers it all.*
> *How blessed the thought, that my soul by Him bought,*
> *Shall be His in the glory on high;*
> *Where with gladness and song I'll be one of the throng,*
> *And Calvary covers it all.*
> —Mrs. Walter G. Taylor

We are talking about the effect of the atonement. All kinds of sin and all blasphemy will be forgiven, *shall* be forgiven—all except for one sin. Calvary almost covers it all. Calvary covers most of it. Calvary covers it all, except for this one unpardonable sin. There is one sin, said Jesus, that will not—shall not and cannot—be forgiven. What great grace and mercy God has extended! What a blessing that Christ has provided! But there is this *one* sin.

I would be less than faithful to the Scripture if I passed over it because it is important.

> "He who blasphemes against the Holy Spirit never has
> forgiveness, but is subject to eternal condemnation" (v. 29).

Matthew reported it this way,

> "every sin and blasphemy will be forgiven men, but the
> blasphemy against the Spirit will not be forgiven men" (Matthew
> 12:31).

Luke said that

> "anyone who speaks a word against the Son of Man, it will be
> forgiven him; but to him who blasphemes against the Holy
> Spirit, it will not be forgiven" (Luke 12:10).

There it is. It cannot be denied. To deny it is to deny Scripture itself. To try to deny it by redefining the plain meaning of the words is to
deny that language has meaning. Our secular world believes that God is
love and only love. But this false understanding stumbles on this stone,
this Rock of offense. People think that if God is going to be fair, if He is
truly just, then He must forgive all sin and not exclude anything.
Doesn't fairness require equal treatment under the law?

It does. But God's grace and mercy are not bound by the requirements of the law. It is justice that is bound by the law, not mercy. And
so God's justice demands that every sinner receive his just reward, that
every sinner receive the penalty for his sin. That's justice! If we want to
talk about fairness we should insist that we get what's coming to us!

No, grace and mercy are not bound by the demands of law. God's
grace is free from the demands of the law. God's grace and mercy are
free of the law. He can forgive whatever sins He wants to. And in the
face of justice, in the face of our own sinfulness, we can have no just
complaint against the grace and mercy of God. Grace is not about fairness!

The only thing left is to define this unforgivable sin. There has been
much speculation about it. Generally, it is understood to mean saying
nasty things about the Holy Spirit. Luke says that there is a difference
between blasphemy against the Son of Man (Jesus) and against the Holy
Spirit. Yet, the Holy Spirit is fully manifest in Jesus.

The Old Testament defined sin in terms of the Law. Sin was generally understood to be certain violations of the law—killing, adultery,
stealing, etc. In the New Testament Jesus reemphasized some of the for-

gotten factors of sin when He preached the Sermon on the Mount. For instance, He showed that actions issue from the heart. Therefore, sin originates in the heart. He pointed out that sin is a heart issue, an attitude issue, more than a behavioral issue. It was as if Jesus said, Straighten out your beliefs, and your attitudes and behavior will follow suit.

Therefore, the unforgivable sin also originates as a heart issue prior to its manifestation as verbal sacrilege. It is a certain belief or attitude that defies the whole idea of God's forgiveness. All sin that results in eternal condemnation stems from this central heart issue, from the denial of the reality of God, the denial of the things of God. There are a variety of ways that this sin can be played out.

There are many ways to deny God. Certainly, simple disbelief is a basic form of denial. Those who refuse to believe in God, or what is the same thing, to refuse to believe the truth of God's Word, simply turn their backs on God. They do not receive God's forgiveness because they turn and walk away from Him. That's an easy one to understand.

But there is another kind of denial that suffers the same end. It also denies the veracity or trustworthiness of God and His Word. But rather than simply turning and walking away from God, away from the propitiation He has provided, Scripture is redefined and reinterpreted to mean something other than its plain meaning. Here we find people redefining the meaning of propitiation, redefining the meaning of atonement, or of Christ's sacrifice, or God's grace and mercy. They are redefined in such a way that it appears that God forgives everybody for everything, that hell and damnation are not real. In short, that God condemns no one. But the Scripture is clear that many suffer the condemnation of God's law.

I don't want to dwell on it, but that is the plain meaning of many passages of Scripture. So, we must attend to it, though it creates a serious difficulty. It creates a real tension in our lives, a tension that we cannot resolve. That unresolvable tension will either drive us into the loving arms of Jesus, or it will drive us insane, where insanity is defined as separation from God and from God's love and protection.

The unforgivable sin is to turn your back on Jesus, to refuse to accept the propitiation that He has so freely given. Related to the unforgivable sin is the denial of the plain reading of His precious Word. God means what He says, and says what He means.

Open our eyes, Lord, that we may not walk away from the salvation that you have provided. Help us also to believe with integrity the wholeness of your Word.

14. Doing God's Will

*Then His brothers and His mother came, and standing outside
they sent to Him, calling Him. And a multitude was sitting
around Him; and they said to Him, 'Look, Your mother and
Your brothers are outside seeking You.' But He answered
them, saying, 'Who is My mother, or My brothers?' And He
looked around in a circle at those who sat about Him, and said,
'Here are My mother and My brothers! For whoever does the
will of God is My brother and My sister and mother.'*

—Mark 3:31-35

We know that Jesus' family had been concerned about Him.
They undoubtedly heard the reports of the miracles, and of
His preaching against the Jewish establishment. They were
aware that the authorities in Jerusalem were disturbed about Him.

Jesus had gone to His Galilean headquarters, the house where the
multitude had followed him seeking miraculous healings. He was in the
midst of that multitude when He received a message that His mother
and brothers were outside waiting to see Him.

Family has always played a significant role in Jewish life. Nothing is
more important than family relations. The same is true in the West, at
least it seems to have been true in the past. We pine for that past where
family was valued above all else. The politicians and many churches call
for a return to the family values of the past. Often we think that there
are no human ties that are more important than family ties. There can
be no doubt that family relationships play a key role in God's church
and in human society.

But we would make a terrible mistake if in the light of Christ's
gospel we thought that family values and relationships were the most
important relationships we have. I don't want to downplay the importance of families or family values in the hierarchy of biblical values.
However, we must acknowledge the meaning and importance of this
scene in Mark involving Jesus, His family, and His followers.

Jesus, in His characteristic way, corrected a misunderstanding current in Jewish society then and in most societies today. That misunder-

standing is that there is nothing more important than family relationships. Again, please understand that I am not saying that family relationships are unimportant. They are extremely important. But family concerns are not a Christian's highest concerns. At the apex of Christian
values stands God in Christ. He is the most important and our personal
relationship with Christ is the most important relationship that a person
can have—bar none!

When Jesus asked, "Who is My mother, or My brothers?" (v. 34),
He called attention to the proper biblical values which place not only
God but relationships among Christians above family relationships. Doing so does not devalue families, unless families have been mistakenly
overvalued. Rather, Jesus was restoring the importance and rightful
place of God's family, the church family. In other words, Jesus was not
suggesting that family relationships are of little concern because they are
less important than church relationships, but He is saying that as important as family values are, church relationships—proper relationships between brothers and sisters in Christ—are even more important.

It is easy to misunderstand this today because many of us, like the
Jews of old, have inverted biblical values in this regard. If a poll were
taken today among Christians generally, I'm sure that we would find
that most Christians mistakenly value their family relationships above
their church fellowships. Consequently, it is important for us to see that
Jesus intended to correct this mistaken belief.

> "For whoever does the will of God is My brother and My sister
> and mother" (v. 35).

Having established this biblical priority of values, we then must ask
what it means to do the will of God. The first thing that it means is that
in doing God's will we do not do our own will. A Christian's concern
for doing God's will must take precedence over doing what he or she
personally wants to do. It even takes precedence over doing what we in
ourselves think is the right thing to do. The admonition of Scripture is
not to treasure what *we* think, but what *God* thinks.

When someone offers an interpretation of a Bible passage that dif-
fers from yours, do you say, *Well, that's just your opinion. People have
different opinions about what it means, and all are equally valid.* If you
believe that understanding the Bible is primarily a matter of personal
opinion, then you will be unable to do God's will because you are unable to know God's will. Isaiah said,

"For My thoughts are not your thoughts, Nor are your ways My
ways...For as the heavens are higher than the earth, So are My
ways higher than your ways, And My thoughts than your
thoughts" (Isaiah 55:8-9).

Understanding Scripture is not a matter of my interpretation or your interpretation, Luther's interpretation or Calvin's interpretation, etc. It is a
matter of understanding God's intended meaning and purpose. God intended to convey a message in His Word. It is not the multitude of human interpretations that are significant, but it is God's intended meaning
that we must seek to understand.

The primary realization that Christians must have regarding Scripture is that God's Word is completely foreign to human thinking, to
their own thinking. God's Word is so utterly opposed to the human ego
and the desires of the flesh that it cannot be derived from human thinking. Even reason alone cannot establish it. God is an alien (supernatural)
being, who thinks alien thoughts, and commands His followers to take
up alien ways of life and living, ways that are completely opposed to
what we want for ourselves. The difficulty of understanding Scripture is
not its intellectual complexity, but its complete otherness.

This otherness is a predominant theme of Scripture. God's law opposes selfishness and self-centeredness at every turn. God's law is so foreign to the interests and concerns of human beings that we are not able
to conform to it on our own. For instance, God's demand for blood sacrifice as the only acceptable atonement for sin is beyond human understanding, though we try.

Christ's act of substitutionary atonement on the cross makes no human sense at all. How can Jesus pay the penalty for my sin? How can
my disobedience be accounted to Him? And how can His righteousness
and obedience be accounted to me? Aside from biblical categories and
biblical thought patterns, it truly makes no sense. It does not lend itself
to the natural understanding of humanity.

However, within biblical categories, within biblical thinking—particularly the Old Testament stories and ideas of sacrifice, blood atonement, etc.—Christ's atoning sacrifice produces a great wealth of meaning and wisdom to repentant sinners. And that is the importance of
learning and teaching biblical stories and concepts! The stories provide
the background and foundation for Christ's ministry on earth. If you are
not familiar with biblical thought, Christ will mean nothing to you.

Apart from its Old Testament grounding the gospel of Christ is
foolishness and insanity, or at best, it communicates the human values of

love, compassion, and sacrificial service. Love, compassion, and sacrificial service are good and valuable in themselves, but they do not explain or communicate the heart of the New Testament. They do not explain or communicate the purpose of the cross. They do not explain or communicate the necessity of the resurrection. They do not explain or communicate Christ's atonement for repentant sinners. They do not explain or communicate the gospel.

The gospel of Jesus Christ is not love, compassion, and sacrificial service—as good and valuable as these things are. The gospel of Jesus Christ is... what? Can you define the gospel in a sentence? You should be able to. What if someone asks you about it? What will you tell the Lord at the last judgment, when He demands an account of your faith?

The good news of the gospel is that Christ died for the salvation of repentant sinners. The great news of the gospel is that Christ died for *me*. Did He die for *you*? As Paul said,

> "Christ Jesus came into the world to save sinners, of whom I am chief" (1 Timothy 1:15).

We need to understand that Christ not only came to save sinners, but that He came for particular individuals—for me! Each and every saved sinner will testify to this fact.

Jesus said it this way in the gospel of John (6:38-40),

> "I have come down from heaven, not to do My own will, but the will of Him who sent Me. This is the will of the Father who sent Me, that of all He has given Me I should lose nothing, but should raise it up at the last day. And this is the will of Him who sent Me, that everyone who sees the Son and believes in Him may have everlasting life; and I will raise him up at the last day."

Even Jesus in the flesh did not satisfy His own fleshly will, but God's will. As disciples, then, we also need to satisfy the Lord's will and not our own. "Not My will, but Yours, be done," said Jesus. Not my will, but yours, be done, Lord Jesus, we must concede. Jesus did not work to please His human desires, but to please God in everything. "I always do those things that please Him" (John 8:29).

The bottom line is that you and I cannot accomplish God's will. We can't even understand it on our own! Rather, the Holy Spirit can do God's will through us. May we yield to Him through obedience to Scripture.

15. Parables

*And again He began to teach by the sea. And a great multitude
was gathered to Him, so that He got into a boat and sat in it on
the sea; and the whole multitude was on the land facing the sea.
Then He taught them many things by parables, and said to
them in His teaching: 'Listen! Behold, a sower went out to sow.
And it happened, as he sowed, that some seed fell by the wayside; and the birds of the air came and devoured it. Some fell on
stony ground, where it did not have much earth; and immediately it sprang up because it had no depth of earth. But when
the sun was up it was scorched, and because it had no root it
withered away. And some seed fell among thorns; and the
thorns grew up and choked it, and it yielded no crop. But other
seed fell on good ground and yielded a crop that sprang up, increased and produced: some thirtyfold, some sixty, and some a
hundred.' And He said to them, 'He who has ears to hear, let
him hear!' But when He was alone, those around Him with the
twelve asked Him about the parable. And He said to them, 'To
you it has been given to know the mystery of the kingdom of
God; but to those who are outside, all things come in parables,
so that "Seeing they may see and not perceive, And hearing
they may hear and not understand; Lest they should turn, And
their sins be forgiven them."' And He said to them, 'Do you not
understand this parable? How then will you understand all the
parables? The sower sows the word. And these are the ones by
the wayside where the word is sown. When they hear, Satan
comes immediately and takes away the word that was sown in
their hearts. These likewise are the ones sown on stony ground
who, when they hear the word, immediately receive it with
gladness; and they have no root in themselves, and so endure
only for a time. Afterward, when tribulation or persecution
arises for the word's sake, immediately they stumble. Now these
are the ones sown among thorns; they are the ones who hear
the word, and the cares of this world, the deceitfulness of riches,
and the desires for other things entering in choke the word,
and it becomes unfruitful. But these are the ones sown on good*

ground, those who hear the word, accept it, and bear fruit:
some thirtyfold, some sixty, and some a hundred.'

—Mark 4:1-20

As we come to the fourth chapter of Mark we find that Jesus has moved again. He is now teaching by the seashore. The crowds continued to follow Him. He got into a boat and preached to a crowd on the shore. The water would provide great acoustics in that the sound waves would reflect rather well off the water, assuming that the water was calm.

The parable of the sower should be a familiar story to most of us. The point is that we, the hearers of the gospel, are not all at the same place spiritually. Our hearts are as varied as the terrain of the earth. And our spiritual condition makes a great deal of difference to our reception and ability to make use of God's Word.

The parable speaks of four environments, or spiritual conditions—attitudes of the heart in which the Word is received. People are different, and the gospel is not equally revealed or useful to all. It is not equally given to all, nor are all equally able to understand it. As people schooled in democracy, we don't like the fact that God's Word and God's grace are not equally given to everyone. We think that if anyone should treat people fairly, it is God. So sometimes we want God to be fair and to treat everyone alike, to give everyone an equal chance at salvation. But such thinking is not biblical.

God's justice is fair, and God's fairness is evidenced in His law. All people are equally subject to God's law. The law is held up as the measure to meet if we want to revive God's favor. And the law is such a true blessing from God! We are so blessed to have it, and to be able to strive toward it. But no one measures up to it, "for all have sinned and fall short of the glory of God" (Romans 3:23).

The result of God's fairness, His sense of justice, brings damnation and punishment for sin. Here is God's fairness! Here God treats everyone equally, and the result is damnation. Yes, God is fair and just, and provides equal justice for all. But God's justice leads to damnation. God's fairness, God's justice is not an attribute that brings comfort or joy. Those who seek God's fairness know not what they seek! Lord, have mercy!

Mercy and grace should be the attributes of God that people seek. We have sinned and fallen short of Your measure, Lord, have mercy.

But alas, grace and mercy are not equally given, but are given according the secret purpose of God. I say *secret purpose* not because only a few people know about it, but because God's ultimate thoughts and purposes are not and cannot be fully known to the puny minds of men. The Psalmist proclaimed,

> "Such knowledge is too wonderful for me; It is high, I cannot attain it" (Psalm 139:6).

It is out of our reach.

The four kinds of people, or four attitudes, or heart soils that Jesus mentions are 1) the distracted, 2) the spurious, 3) the overwhelmed, and 4) the fruitful. Of these four groups only one will finally come to salvation.

The grace given to the distracted falls on the "wayside, and the birds of the air came and devoured it" (v. 4). The wayside is the side of the road. God's seed falls off the path, out of the way, into the gutter. The distractions that occupy such people are described by the Lord as birds that come and devour the seed He scatters. The grace of the gospel is devoured by the worldly distractions that occupy most people. Distractions are those things that busy our time and keep us from the godly concerns of Bible study, prayer, worship, fellowship, etc.

There are many distractions—sports, movies, entertainments of various kinds, work, property maintenance, politics, the arts, even school, etc. None of these are bad in themselves, but when we value them more than we value spiritual growth we have a problem. And that problem leads to damnation. Thus, Satan uses these kinds of activities to distract us from God and to move our primary commitment away from God. In fact, Jesus said that it is Satan himself who

> "comes immediately and takes away the word that was sown in their hearts" (v. 15).

Some of these people may even go to church, but they don't hear the Word preached. They hear the words but they don't *hear* the message. It doesn't mean anything to them because it isn't important to them. As such, it doesn't matter what message is preached—law or gospel, liberal or conservative, biblical exposition or personal anecdotes, religious or secular. It makes no difference because it isn't important. They just come to pass their time. They attend church in order to feel that they are justified in the eyes of God.

Most distracted people don't come to church at all, but those that do, come for their own reasons. Perhaps they are maintaining a social image or perhaps it pleases them to think of themselves as being noble Christians. It makes them proud to think that God blesses them. They come to assure themselves of God's blessing. One lady in my church in Evansville found Sunday mornings to be most productive. She regularly balanced her checkbook during the service.

Can the problem of worldly distractions be overcome? Not once the seed is devoured it is gone. The only solution is to prevent the seed from being devoured in the first place. Diligence and discipline must be engaged to overcome distractions, before distractions are engaged.

The second group Jesus mentions are the spurious, who are in equal spiritual danger. The spurious are those with stony-ground faith. God's grace falls on their unprepared and/or hardened hearts, where it doesn't have much "earth" (v. 5) or good soil in which to grow. Jesus said that the seed

> "sprang up because it had no depth of earth. But when the sun was up it was scorched, and because it had no root it withered away" (vs. 5-6).

Stony ground Christians are quick to see the light. They are quick to engage the depths of God's Word, and readily tell you so. They jump to conclusions and seem to make the most of the few spiritual resources they have. Their initial rapid spiritual growth leads them to be admired by many. Everything about their faith and understanding seems so right, so fast, and so natural that they can easily find their way into leadership positions.

Paul had such Christians in mind when he counseled Timothy "not (to) lay hands on anyone hastily" (1 Timothy 5:22). The difficulty with stony ground Christians is that their faith does not last. It does not hold up under stress or over time. Like those distracted with worldly concerns, their faith is only a brief distraction from their worldliness. Like the distracted, their minds flit from interest to interest—and the church is just another flitting interest. They are here today, and gone tomorrow.

Stony ground Christians have shallow spiritual roots. Their interest and attention are fixed on the superficial, temporary benefits that they can receive by being a Christian. Jesus said, "because (they) had no root (they) withered away" (v. 6). They do not have a deep understanding or consistent interest in spiritual things. Thus, they are not what they seem to be. They "endure only for a time" (v. 17). They "stumble" when God's Word brings "tribulation or persecution" (v. 17).

The third group that Jesus addressed I have called the *overwhelmed*.

> "And some seed fell among thorns; and the thorns grew up and choked it, and it yielded no crop" (v. 7).

The thorns Jesus speaks of are what we call weeds, fast growing, rapidly reproducing, good-for-nothing plants that infect every garden, and which thrive amidst neglect.

The point is that neglect of the means of grace—the disciplines of the faith—allows the growth and development of habits and desires that will overwhelm godly values. Just as the weeds will take over your garden if you let them, so bad habits and wrong thinking overtake your mind if you let them.

The damnable thing about weeds is that our doing nothing ensures their health and productivity. Weeding is a constant demand, and the best way to keep weeds to a minimum is to weed daily and catch them when they are small. Once they become large and abundant, they have crowded out the good seed. To fail to weed is to kill your garden with neglect. Even more, the "cares of the world" (v. 18) or bad habits are not mere neglect, but are practices that actively undermine God's values. Taking on the cares of the world is like fertilizing the weeds.

The last group that Jesus spoke about in this parable were faithful Christians. Such Christians regularly tend the gardens of their minds and souls. They weed and water. They work the soil (their hearts) in preparation, and continue to work it as their garden grows. Such Christians grow, not like weeds, but in the deliberate pace and patterns of faithfulness. They bear fruit and produce seed "some thirtyfold, some sixty, and some a hundred" (v. 8).

Obviously, the good-ground Christian is the ideal. He sets the standard for faithfulness. He is not distracted by the world, but is disciplined in the faith. He is disciplined in the hope and joy of salvation. He exercises the means of grace because he likes to please God, and because he is satisfied with the spiritual nourishment that God provides. He avoids worldly activities. He understands God's Word to the degree he needs to and is encouraged by it. Not everyone understands the Word. I wish it were otherwise, but it isn't. God has blessed some more than others. Nor are all of God's blessings alike.

> And He Himself gave some to be apostles, some prophets, some evangelists, and some pastors and teachers, for the equipping of

> the saints for the work of ministry, for the edifying of the body
> of Christ, till we all come to the unity of the faith and of the
> knowledge of the Son of God, to a perfect man, to the measure
> of the stature of the fullness of Christ; that we should no longer
> be children, tossed to and fro and carried about with every wind
> of doctrine, by the trickery of men, in the cunning craftiness of
> deceitful plotting, but, speaking the truth in love, may grow up
> in all things into Him who is the head—Christ—from whom the
> whole body, joined and knit together by what every joint
> supplies, according to the effective working by which every part
> does its share, causes growth of the body for the edifying of itself
> in love (Ephesians 4:11-16)

God has hidden His Word from some. He has withheld the blessings of understanding and faithfulness from others. That is what Scripture says. I don't like it myself. I wish it were otherwise, but that is what it says. And He said to them,

> "To you it has been given to know the mystery of the kingdom
> of God; but to those who are outside, all things come in parables,
> so that 'Seeing they may see and not perceive, And hearing they
> may hear and not understand; Lest they should turn, And their
> sins be forgiven them'" (vs. 11-12).

It's from Isaiah 6:8-13,

> "I heard the voice of the Lord, saying: 'Whom shall I send, And
> who will go for Us?' Then I said, 'Here am I! Send me.'"

It's a beautiful verse. Some of you know music written for this verse. But do you know the rest of the verse?

> And He said, 'Go, and tell this people: "Keep on hearing, but do
> not understand; Keep on seeing, but do not perceive. Make the
> heart of this people dull, And their ears heavy, And shut their
> eyes; Lest they see with their eyes, And hear with their ears, And
> understand with their heart, And return and be healed."' Then I
> said, 'Lord, how long?' And He answered: 'Until the cities are
> laid waste and without inhabitant, The houses are without a man,
> The land is utterly desolate, The Lord has removed men far
> away, And the forsaken places are many in the midst of the land.
> But yet a tenth will be in it, And will return and be for
> consuming, As a terebinth tree or as an oak, Whose stump
> remains when it is cut down. So the holy seed shall be its stump' (
> Isaiah 6:9-13)

Isaiah prophesied the coming of Christ. But he also prophesied hardened hearts and the destruction of Jerusalem. God's own people had grown hard-hearted. God didn't make them hard-hearted, but He punished them for their hard-heartedness. Just as Christians today can read Isaiah and see the prophecies of Christ, so could have the Jews of old. But they didn't. It's not that God hid those prophecies from them, but that the same Word that reveals Christ to the faithful, conceals Him from the faithless.

Yet, God is not the author of sin or evil. God is the bearer of light in a world darkened by sin. The teachings of Scripture are not pleasant to those who are proud of themselves and their accomplishments. The understanding of God's sovereignty, like the reception of His grace, cannot stand on a foundation of pride and self-concern.

None of us are without some lingering element of pride. Pride is the root of all sin. Consequently, we all struggle with the bold and clear proclamation of God's truth, which offends our pride. Often the trouble and problems that occur in churches are associated with this struggle against biblical truth. It is our own sin and pride that hides God's Word of truth. The parables of Jesus, like much of God's Word generally, both reveal and conceal. The faithful are comforted and fed by God's Word. The same Word brings discomfort to the faithless, who will not feed on the teachings of grace. Such teachings are scorned and rejected by the faithless for a variety of reasons.

But don't think that I'm saying that if you don't understand *me* it's because you are faithless. Not at all! It's not *me* that you must understand, it's *God.* I'm not the Son of God. My words are not Scripture. I do my best to reveal and proclaim God's Word, but I'm not perfect.

We must realize that the Bible teaches some things that will make us uncomfortable. None of us will like everything that the Bible teaches. But we are not free to pick and choose. We must accept what is clearly taught in the Bible. We don't need to understand it all. In fact, we can't understand it all. But we must accept what we find, and receive what the Lord has given.

It is instructive to note that those who are faithful to the Lord are faithful to varying degrees,

> "other seed fell on good ground and yielded a crop that sprang
> up, increased and produced: some thirtyfold, some sixty, and
> some a hundred" (v. 8).

We can lament that there is not equal fruitfulness in the kingdom or we can simply accept is as God's reality. One of the purposes of this inequality may be that it brings Christians into fellowship as those who are more fruitful share with those who are less. But we must remember that such sharing is not a matter of social status (increased by giving or decreased by receiving), but is a function of love, responsibility, and obedience. Leadership in the kingdom is service, not privilege.

16. Able To Hear

Also He said to them, 'Is a lamp brought to be put under a bas-
ket or under a bed? Is it not to be set on a lampstand? For there
is nothing hidden which will not be revealed, nor has anything
been kept secret but that it should come to light. If anyone has
ears to hear, let him hear.' Then He said to them, 'Take heed
what you hear. With the same measure you use, it will be mea-
sured to you; and to you who hear, more will be given. For
whoever has, to him more will be given; but whoever does not
have, even what he has will be taken away from him.' And He
said, 'The kingdom of God is as if a man should scatter seed on
the ground, and should sleep by night and rise by day, and the
seed should sprout and grow, he himself does not know how.
For the earth yields crops by itself: first the blade, then the head,
after that the full grain in the head. But when the grain ripens,
immediately he puts in the sickle, because the harvest has
come.' Then He said, 'To what shall we liken the kingdom of
God? Or with what parable shall we picture it? It is like a mus-
tard seed which, when it is sown on the ground, is smaller than
all the seeds on earth; but when it is sown, it grows up and be-
comes greater than all herbs, and shoots out large branches, so
that the birds of the air may nest under its shade.' And with
many such parables He spoke the word to them as they were
able to hear it. But without a parable He did not speak to them.
And when they were alone, He explained all things to His dis-
ciples.   —Mark 4:21-34

After explaining the parable of the sower, Jesus presented three
more parables, the explanations of which are not recorded.
Rather, the Lord has left the explanation of them to the Holy
Spirit.

First, He said that the light of Christ is not to be hidden, but set on a
lampstand for all to see. The primary instruction of this parable is that
the light that Christians receive is not for themselves, but for others.
Christians are called into service—to teach, to share, to help. So, if you

are not actively involved in Christian service, either your light isn't lit or you're hiding it.

By Christian service I don't mean that all Christians need to be employed by a church. Nor do I mean that everyone has to be a Sunday School teacher, or whatever. What I mean is that every Christian must

> "always be ready to give a defense to everyone who asks you a reason for the hope that is in you" (1 Peter 3:15).

Every Christian must be ready and willing to share the gospel with seekers, willing and ready to explain to anyone who asks what you believe about Christ and why you believe as you do. That is the sharing of Christ's light.

Over and again Jesus uses the phrase, "If anyone has ears to hear, let him hear" (v. 23). Clearly, He means that not everyone will understand Him. "Then He said to them, 'Take heed what you hear'" (v. 24). That is, pay attention to what He says because there is more in it than meets the eye. Christ calls us to think about what He says, to meditate on it, to dwell on it, and to obey it. To heed what someone says means to take it seriously, to respond with the understanding that what has been said is indeed true, and warrants a recognition not only in thought but in action as well.

"With the same measure you use, it will be measured to you" (v. 24) is another way of teaching the Golden Rule, "whatever you want men to do to you, do also to them" (Matthew 7:12). This is further commentary on the parable of the light under a bushel. Whatever God has given you—grace, mercy, understanding, wisdom, wealth, whatever—has not been given for you but through you. The gift is not yours to keep, but is yours to share.

Therefore, Jesus said, "to you who hear, more will be given" (v. 24). Those who understand God's Word are burdened with greater responsibilities. To meet those responsibilities is to grow in grace because the Lord will provide increased depth of understanding and increased joy for those who pursue it. But to neglect your responsibility is to admit your failure to understand, and to confirm your own faithlessness. Such a failure will ultimately harden your heart rather than enlarge it.

Secondly, Jesus said that the kingdom is like planting a crop, i.e., corn. There are several useful analogies here. First of all, corn doesn't just grow. You've got to plant it. If you do nothing, your garden will grow weeds. Yet, the planting of the seed does not guarantee the growth of the crop. In fact, planting does not cause crops to grow.

While planting is necessary, it is not sufficient. We can plant a crop, but we cannot make it grow. We can water it, but we cannot make it grow. We can fertilize and weed it, but we cannot make it grow. The growth of your garden depends more on what only God can do than on what we can do.

We can help, but we can't make it happen. This is the lesson of grace. The seed must be planted. Left to ourselves, none of us would ever seek God. Oh, we might get spiritual and seek for all sorts of things that we mistakenly believe to be God. But we are unable of ourselves to even want to seek the God of Scripture. He is too foreign to our experience. Paul asked,

> "How then shall they call on Him in whom they have not
> believed? And how shall they believe in Him of whom they have
> not heard? And how shall they hear without a preacher? And
> how shall they preach unless they are sent?" (Romans 10:14-15).

The preaching of the Word is God's principle means of planting gospel seed. Most Christians come to faith by hearing the Word preached and expounded, either by listening or reading.

Preaching is a means of grace. It is the ordinary way that the seed of the gospel is planted in the hearts of believers. To ignore the instrumentality of preaching is to expect corn where none has been planted. Like the preacher, the farmer is not the originator of the corn, nor can he guarantee that every seed planted will grow, nor is he responsible for the growth—only the planting. He sows his seed and goes about his business. Paul said,

> "neither he who plants is anything, nor he who waters, but God
> who gives the increase" (1 Corinthians 3:7).

We don't know why God's Word grows in one person and not in another. We can't explain it. But it does. We can see that this indeed is the reality.

When the Word does take root, it grows like corn,

> "first the blade, then the head, after that the full grain in the head"
> (v. 28).

It follows a definite pattern, growing in various stages and at its own rate. The stages and the rates are fixed—out of our control. We can only tend it, we cannot hurry it.

Yet, it is important to understand that at every stage it is alive. At every stage it is corn and not something else. From this we learn that

Christians, too, are alive in Christ at every stage of their spiritual growth. Like the blade of corn is corn, the tiniest and weakest baby Christian is fully Christian, as a fetus is a person. We shouldn't curse the blade because it is not a stalk, nor the stalk because it has no ears, nor the ears because they are not yet ripe. Rather, we wait and we tend what God has given, trusting God to complete what He has begun.

If God is anything, He is patient. And so must we be patient, too. We must not despise immature Christians because they are not fully grown. It is a thousand times better to have grace in the blade than to have no grace at all. Rather, we need to help them grow, water and weed them—not despise them.

Finally, we should note that there can be no harvest until the ear is ripe. To rush the process is to ruin the harvest. Such things are on God's timetable, not ours. Yet, when the crop is ripe, any delay in the harvest will be equally ruinous. When the crop is ripe it is foolish to wait for more yield. It won't come. Each crop is what it is, and must be harvested without delay when it is ripe. To illustrate the point Jesus added the parable of the mustard seed, which provides a lesson about patience with small beginnings. The little tiny mustard seed grows into a great thriving plant that provides both food and shelter for a variety of creatures.

Jesus spoke many parables for the edification and consternation of many people. God's Word is always suited to the understanding of the hearer. Those with ears, who pay attention and who love the Lord, hear much. There is much wisdom in God's Word. If you come eager to learn and willing to trust that God is who He says He is, you will be fed. Regardless of intelligence or preparation, God's people always draw sustenance from His Word, be it a little or a lot.

But if you come full of self and pride, full of your own ideas about how to improve God's way, boasting of anything, or with a chip on your shoulder and full of doubt and indignation, God's Word will only serve to harden your heart. If you come with simple faith and trust, your faith and trust will be multiplied. And if you come with doubt or indifference, these too will be multiplied. Jesus "spoke the Word to them as they were able to hear it" (v. 33). He always spoke plainly and clearly, "but without a parable He did not speak to them" (v. 34).

He spoke to them in such a way that interpretation, discernment, and understanding were always required. He always spoke so that the Holy Spirit was needed.

> "These things I have spoken to you while being present with
> you. But the Helper, the Holy Spirit, whom the Father will send

in My name, He will teach you all things, and bring to your
remembrance all things that I said to you" (John 14:25-26).

Understanding God's Word requires the presence of the Holy Spirit
in the believer's heart. Without Him there can be no understanding.
The Holy Spirit is our teacher and interpreter. So, if you have any biblical understanding at all, you can thank God. But you had better not get
smug and think that you are better than others because of it. The understanding is not yours, but God's. We have nothing to be proud of. Such
pride will always trip you up.

Spiritual growth or growth in biblical understanding, like corn, is
either growing or dying. There is no standing still. When you stop
growing, you start dying.

Are you growing? Are you helping others grow spiritually? Have
you really heard God's Word?

17. Who Can This Be?

> On the same day, when evening had come, He said to them,
> 'Let us cross over to the other side.' Now when they had left
> the multitude, they took Him along in the boat as He was. And
> other little boats were also with Him. And a great windstorm
> arose, and the waves beat into the boat, so that it was already
> filling. But He was in the stern, asleep on a pillow. And they
> awoke Him and said to Him, 'Teacher, do You not care that
> we are perishing?' Then He arose and rebuked the wind, and
> said to the sea, 'Peace, be still!' And the wind ceased and there
> was a great calm. But He said to them, 'Why are you so fearful?
> How is it that you have no faith?' And they feared exceedingly,
> and said to one another, 'Who can this be, that even the wind
> and the sea obey Him!'   —Mark 4:35-41

Jesus had been teaching several parables to the crowd of people who
had been following him. Prior to this He had dealt with His family,
who had attempted to rescue Him from Himself and the difficulties
that His ministry had brought Him. They were worried about the increasing difficulties and embarrassment that would ensue if He continued on this course. When we left Him last, He had taken the disciples
aside to "explain all things" (v. 34) to them privately.

At this point we have a picture of a man who had been giving His
all to His ministry—non-stop preaching, special services of healing that
included the emotional stresses and strains of dealing with demons, and
going against the advice of His family to back off. Now, in pursuit of
additional ministry opportunities Jesus asked for a boat to cross the sea of
Galilee, where the Gadarene Demoniac waited for Him. We must assume that Jesus knew that the Demoniac was there.

Understandably, Jesus took advantage of the trip to catch up on
some much needed rest. How often have we wondered how Jesus could
have possibly slept in that little boat in the midst of a storm? What faith
He must have had, we think. And rightly so, for He is God in the flesh.
No one could have more faith than God Himself.

But as true as that is we must not let it obscure the equally true lesson of Jesus' humanity. Here was a man who had been preaching, teaching, and healing practically every minute of the day for weeks. Wherever He went He was in the public spotlight. Most people don't know the stress and strain of being in the public spotlight. Most people avoid it for just those reasons. But that was not Jesus' lot. He was in the spotlight as often as He was awake.

Consequently, we need to see Jesus sleeping in the boat, not simply as a sign of His heavenly faith, but equally of His bodily weakness. He was tired, so tired that He remained asleep in the midst of a tempest. That's tired! Jesus was not just God, He was the Spirit of God in the body of a man. Here we find a statement of the humanity of Jesus, asleep in the boat in the midst of a storm so powerful that it threatened these seasoned sailors.

In fact, the Scripture indicates that this is the perspective Mark intended. He said that "they took Him along in the boat *as He was*" (v. 36, italics added). If everything had been normal, there would have been no reason to specify that they took Jesus as He was, for He would have been able to take Himself. He had given the order to cross the sea and then, I suspect, had fallen asleep as they acquired a boat and supplies for the journey. Unable to arouse Him, they simply took Him as he was— exhausted and asleep.

Even as they crossed the sea, the crowd did not stop following Him. They accompanied Him in "other little boats" (v. 36). Why did they hound Him so? There had been no prophet in Israel for four hundred years, so as they began to realize that Jesus may have been God's prophet, they were eager to follow and to test Him that they might be sure.

The disciples were not as tired as Jesus was. They hadn't been working as hard as He had. They were only listening, while He had been teaching. And, no doubt, they found themselves able to catch a few winks now and then during His sermons. That's what we find today, why should it have been any different for Jesus?

At any rate, a storm arose that was terrible enough to scare these seasoned fisherman. Squalls often developed quickly on the Sea of Galilee because of its geographical setting. Such storms were not uncommon, yet these seasoned sailors were frightened by this one.

They couldn't believe that Jesus continued to sleep as the storm raged. They didn't understand how tired He really was. He lay in the stern sleeping as the boat tossed to and fro in the wind and waves. Finally, they succeeded in waking Him up. "Teacher, do you not care that we are perishing?" (v. 38) they asked.

Because they were professional sailors, we can imagine that they had done everything they could before waking Him with the confession of their inability to deal with the situation. The boat had been taking on water faster than they could remove it, and if that situation continued, the boat would soon be overwhelmed and sink in the storm. Going to Jesus was their last resort. They were at their wit's end.

What can we learn from this incident with Jesus? First, we can note that most people will not turn to the Lord until they have exhausted their alternatives. The more options people have, the longer it will take them to play them out before turning to Christ. Though this situation seems terribly unfortunate, it is observably true in the lives of many Christians.

Secondly, we cannot expect to go through life without encountering storms and difficulties. We cannot expect God to provide clear sailing all the time. Storms, difficulties, and troubles are a natural part of life, and Christians are not exempt from them. Far from it! In fact, Jesus said, "If they persecuted Me, they will also persecute you" (John 15:20). Jesus promised the grace and mercy of free pardon for sin, not a life without affliction. In fact, we find that Scripture teaches that God uses afflictions to chastise, train, and strengthen His people. So, not only will God not keep us from afflictions, but at times He will bring them upon us Himself for His own reasons. And by receiving them from the hand of God, knowing that they are part of His sanctifying grace and mercy, we are enabled to grow in faithfulness because of them.

Here is the Christian joy that worldly people can never know. Here is the satisfaction of finding meaning and purpose in the midst of affliction. It is not a joy that the world even wants. Worldly people think that God ought to spare them the suffering of affliction. But Christians know that God is sovereign, and as such He redeems our suffering by using it to bring us to a greater spiritual maturity. That spiritual growth, then, provides a personal assurance of faith, and the assurance of faith is, in turn, a source of joy.

J.C. Ryle said it this way,

> "By affliction He shows us our emptiness and weakness, draws us to the throne of grace, purifies our affection, weans us from the world, makes us long for heaven. In the resurrection morning we

shall all say, 'it is good for me that I was afflicted.' We shall thank God for every storm".[7]

I suspect that no one knows this kind of joy like a mother. The pain of childbirth soon gives way to the joys of young motherhood. And as the child grows and finds his share of worldly troubles, his mother's love continues to grow deeper because of them.

When Jesus awoke, He stood up and "rebuked the wind, and said to the sea, 'Peace, be still!'" (v. 39). The word *rebuked* reveals His emotional tone. The word *peace* provides the content of His communication. In other words, He yelled at the sea and told it to be quiet. And it did!

Here we can learn about Jesus' power. As God He has power over nature. He spoke and nature obeyed. Today in the midst of the greatest technological power the world has ever known—bar none, we are helpless before nature's fury. We have tamed nature only to the extent that we can redirect a few of its forces. We reroute rivers, build bridges and dams, and live in relative safety because of it. Yet, natural disasters are among our worst enemies. We watch idly while storms, floods, and earthquakes take their toll in defiance of our pride in our technology. The lesson here is that Jesus, clothed in a first century robe and sandals, was more powerful than all of the technology of twenty centuries of scientific and technological progress.

Nothing is impossible with God (Mark 10:27). If only we will forsake our pride and come to Christ with the honest acknowledgment of our sinfulness and helplessness, God will not forsake that which He has promised. He will complete what He has begun. But He will do it His way, in His time, by His means.

We love to think that God is on our side, helping us to accomplish great things. People flock to those who teach that God wants to bless our best hopes and dreams for ourselves. And there is just enough truth in such a teaching for it to be dangerous. It is true that God blesses His people. But He does not bless the hopes of the world, nor the worldly dreams of His people. Rather, He blesses His own hopes and dreams, which run counter to the world, as He impresses them into the lives of His people.

Faithfulness is often sacrificed for worldly success. It doesn't have to be that way, but most often it is. It is rare indeed that true Christianity accompanies worldly success. Again, it is possible, but rare. God is not

---

7   *Mark*, Ryle, J.C., Banner of Truth, Carlyle, Penn., p. 83.

out to help us accomplish our hopes and dreams, but to use us to accomplish His hopes and dreams.

Jesus saw the fear of the disciples as an indication of their faithlessness. The storm caused them to reveal their worldliness, their concern about their boat and their lives. In the midst of the storm their self-preoccupation was revealed, and Jesus called it what it was—faithlessness. "Why are you so fearful? How is it that you have no faith?" (v. 40), He asked. They feared for their lives because they had no faith. He said that the disciples had no faith at that moment!

Jesus taught on another occasion that we should not worry about our lives,

> "what you will eat; nor about the body, what you will put on.
> Life is more than food, and the body is more than clothing.
> Consider the ravens, for they neither sow nor reap, which have
> neither storehouse nor barn; and God feeds them. Of how much
> more value are you than the birds? And which of you by
> worrying can add one cubit to his stature? If you then are not
> able to do the least, why are you anxious for the rest? Consider
> the lilies, how they grow: they neither toil nor spin; and yet I say
> to you, even Solomon in all his glory was not arrayed like one of
> these. If then God so clothes the grass, which today is in the field
> and tomorrow is thrown into the oven, how much more will He
> clothe you, O you of little faith? And do not seek what you
> should eat or what you should drink, nor have an anxious mind.
> For all these things the nations of the world seek after, and your
> Father knows that you need these things. But seek the kingdom
> of God, and all these things shall be added to you" (Luke 12:22-
> 31).

Such a teaching does not cause Christians to act stupidly and to neglect their own responsibility to earn a living and to take care of their families, but to trust that God has provided the means for doing just those things. As always, we must live according to God's precepts and by His means. He always provides the way when we submit to His judgment—even though we sometimes don't like His way.

Mark reveals an amazing thing at the end of chapter four. Jesus associated their fear of the storm with their faithlessness. Then Mark noted that

> "they feared exceedingly, and said to one another, 'Who can this
> be, that even the wind and the sea obey Him!'" (v. 41).

They feared for their lives in the midst of the storm. Then, when Jesus calmed it, they feared *Him* even more. Did this mean that they increased in faithlessness because of their increased fear? In a way, it does. Jesus presence among the disciples was the fullest revelation of God ever recorded. But the Gospels reveal the human reaction to God's revelation as well. That reaction shows us that God's revelation in Jesus Christ consistently demonstrated man's lack of faith.

When confronted by Jesus (God in Christ), people see themselves in a new light, and that light shows them the truth of their own hearts. In the light of Christ people see the bleakness of their lives without Christ, and the impossibility of them doing anything about that bleakness. The preaching of the truth of Christ crucified shines this same self-revealing light onto the hearts of all people and they personally experience the depth of their own desperation as they come face-to-face with the reality of their own sinfulness.

Thus, we are instructed by the response of the disciples, who were even more afraid of Jesus than of the storm! But note that they did not abandon Him. People generally flee from whatever they fear. But the disciples, in the boat with Jesus, had nowhere to go. They found themselves more terrified than ever and wondered,

> "Who can this be, that even the wind and the sea obey Him!" (v. 41).

Not long after this

> "Jesus and His disciples went out to the towns of Caesarea Philippi; and on the road He asked His disciples, saying to them, 'Who do men say that I am?' So they answered, 'John the Baptist; but some say, Elijah; and others, one of the prophets.' He said to them, 'But who do you say that I am?' Peter answered and said to Him, 'You are the Christ.' Then He strictly warned them that they should tell no one about Him. And He began to teach them that the Son of Man must suffer many things, and be rejected by the elders and chief priests and scribes, and be killed, and after three days rise again" (Mark 8:27-31).

They did not know who He was, He had to teach them. Consequently at this point they could not tell anyone else who He was because they did not know themselves. Jesus forbade the disciples to simply tell other people what they thought about Him or what they had personally experienced. He insisted that they first learn what He thought of

Himself. What He sought to teach them more than anything else was the purpose and meaning of His crucifixion.

Do you know who Jesus is? You can't really know Jesus until you know Scripture, and what it teaches about Him. Do you know Jesus Christ as revealed in Scripture? Or are you content with you own understanding?

18. Healing The Unclean

Then they came to the other side of the sea, to the country of the Gadarenes. And when He had come out of the boat, immediately there met Him out of the tombs a man with an unclean spirit, who had his dwelling among the tombs; and no one could bind him, not even with chains, because he had often been bound with shackles and chains. And the chains had been pulled apart by him, and the shackles broken in pieces; neither could anyone tame him. And always, night and day, he was in the mountains and in the tombs, crying out and cutting himself with stones. When he saw Jesus from afar, he ran and worshiped Him. And he cried out with a loud voice and said, 'What have I to do with You, Jesus, Son of the Most High God? I implore You by God that You do not torment me.' For He said to him, 'Come out of the man, unclean spirit!' Then He asked him, 'What is your name?' And he answered, saying, 'My name is Legion; for we are many.' Also he begged Him earnestly that He would not send them out of the country. Now a large herd of swine was feeding there near the mountains. So all the demons begged Him, saying, 'Send us to the swine, that we may enter them.' And at once Jesus gave them permission. Then the unclean spirits went out and entered the swine (there were about two thousand); and the herd ran violently down the steep place into the sea, and drowned in the sea. So those who fed the swine fled, and they told it in the city and in the country. And they went out to see what it was that had happened. Then they came to Jesus, and saw the one who had been demon-possessed and had the legion, sitting and clothed and in his right mind. And they were afraid. And those who saw it told them how it happened to him who had been demon-possessed, and about the swine. Then they began to plead with Him to depart from their region. And when He got into the boat, he who had been demon-possessed begged Him that he might be with Him. However, Jesus did not permit him, but said to him, 'Go home to your friends, and tell them what great things the Lord has done for you, and how He has

had compassion on you.' And he departed and began to pro-
claim in Decapolis all that Jesus had done for him; and all mar-
veled.   —Mark 5:1-20

W hen Jesus landed on the other side of the Sea of Galilee there was a welcoming party waiting for Him. This was not the first time that Jesus had encountered an unclean spirit. There was the man who had railed against Him the first time He taught in the synagogue (Mark 1:23), and the leper (Mark 1:40). And don't forget that the Pharisees claimed that Jesus Himself had an unclean spirit (Mark 3:30).

Each time Jesus healed a person with an unclean spirit, the spirit literally came out of him,

> "immediately there met Him out of the tombs a man with an
> unclean spirit" (v. 2).

The unclean spirit is clearly an evil foreign entity inhabiting a human body and/or mind. Scripture tells us that such people are demon possessed. I don't know about you, but most modern people dismiss demon possession as unreal on at least two counts.

First, most people do not believe in the reality of demons. And if they do, they believe that the freewill spirit of Western individualism and its stepchild, modern science (i.e., psychology, sociology, etc.) are able to resist any and all forces that threaten personal freedom. It would be great if we could just rebuke Satan and be done with him. But he's more cunning than that. Our self-confidence causes us to underestimate the enemy.

The Greek word that is translated as *unclean* (*akathartos*) pertains, first, to ceremonial uncleanliness, and secondly, to moral corruption in both thought and behavior. From a Christian perspective it means unsaved. Ephesians 2:8 tells us that

> "by grace you have been saved through faith, and that not of
> yourselves."

The justification—righteousness that comes with salvation—is not ours, but Christ's. His death supplies our justification. We are saved, not by our own righteousness, but by Christ's righteousness. Consequently, a person with an unclean spirit is a person who is in some sense spiritual, but unwashed in the blood of Christ.

Further evidence of the unsaved character of an unclean spirit is seen in the fact that this Gadarene Demoniac had been "dwelling among the tombs" (v. 2). So important is this fact that it is repeated,

> "immediately there met Him out of the tombs a man with an
> unclean spirit, who had his dwelling among the tombs" (vs. 2-3).

He was insane, crazy as a loon. The reference to tombs implies that this man, possessed by an unclean spirit, had been living in death. But since he was obviously alive in some sense, he must have been dwelling in spiritual death. The unsaved are often described as those who live in death, who are without the new life of the new birth. "All those who hate me love death" (Proverbs 8:36).

However, it was not the unsaved nature of this man that made him unique. Unsaved people were everywhere. This man's association with death was particularly strong. He lived in a graveyard. We must assume that he wanted to live in the graveyard because no one was able to stop him. Neither chains nor shackles could hold him. "Neither could anyone tame him" (v. 4). That is, he would not submit to even the basic rudiments of common society. At a practical level that might mean that he couldn't hold a job. He didn't want to work, and without work he was unable to fit into society.

> "Always, night and day, he was in the mountains and in the
> tombs, crying out and cutting himself with stones" (Mark 5:5).

He was a freak, and he hated himself for it.

The phenomenon of self-mutilation is not uncommon among troubled people. It seems to me that at some deep level such an act points to the biblical necessity of the shedding of blood for atonement. By shedding their own blood they inflict punishment upon their own flesh. Self-mutilation may involve some twisted understanding of sin and punishment.

> "When he saw Jesus from afar, he ran and worshiped Him" (v. 6).

Note that this man with the unclean spirit worshiped Jesus! In our modern quest for spiritual quick fixes, we often believe that simply knowing Jesus, or knowing and worshiping Jesus personally, is the essence of Christianity. But Mark said that this man with the unclean spirit knew Jesus and even worshiped Him. But neither his knowledge of Jesus nor his worship of Him provided salvation. As long as the man was inhabited by the unclean spirit his knowledge and worship were flawed. It was not real knowledge or worship.

If there was ever a lesson for the modern church it is here. The contemporary church has come to believe its own press (rather than Scripture), in that we too often think that people are saved by knowledge and action, for instance, knowing the four spiritual laws, praying the sinner's prayer, and worshiping Jesus in the church of our own choosing. We know Scripture. We have a personal relationship with the Lord. We come to church. What else could there be?

The problem is that when we tell people how to be saved, we provide a kind of cookbook recipe that is supposed to result in their salvation. The point is that this approach teaches salvation by works! There is no grace in it. If we are saved by grace, by the blood of Christ, then *we* don't make it happen by deciding, choosing, or worshiping. We cannot cause God to save us or anyone else.

As I say that, I can hear people thinking, If that's true, then there is no point in even trying, no point in prayer, Bible study, or worship! Be careful not to excuse yourself from the clear demands of Scripture. When people excuse themselves from obedience to God's Word, they reveal their own unrepentant hearts.

When God's people hear the clear preaching of His sovereign grace, they are not confounded about how to receive salvation. Rather, they are thankful that God has had mercy on them. More often than not, the thoughts of a saved person are more like, *Why me? Why have you saved me, Lord? I am not worthy. I am not any better than anyone else. In fact, I'm worse than many others. So, why me and not someone else? It doesn't seem fair, Lord, though I am eternally grateful. What must I do with this gift of salvation that you have so mercifully given to me? How can I make it up to you, Lord?*

The difference lies in the personal acknowledgment of their own personal worthlessness and God's gracious salvation. Coming face-to-face with one's own worthlessness is very humbling. The knowledge of one's own salvation comes, not from having performed particular tasks—not from knowing Scripture, praying, or going to church—but directly from the Holy Spirit Himself. It is not a salvation that will be true when certain conditions are met. Rather, it is a salvation that is already true, a salvation that required nothing but God's merciful grace and Christ's efficacious atonement.

God does not offer a *potential* salvation that can be activated by meeting certain conditions or doing certain things. Rather, God has already provided a *certain* salvation that cannot fail. God's salvation cannot be thwarted. God assures His salvation, and He is all-powerful and all-knowing,

> "declaring the end from the beginning, And from ancient times
> things that are not yet done" (Isaiah 46:10).

The man with the unclean spirit said to Jesus, "I implore You by God that You do not torment me" (v. 7). The sentence is in the Greek aorist tense, which means that the verb has no sense of past, present, or future time. There is no English equivalent for this tense, though it is generally rendered in the simple past tense. And here it should be rendered in the past tense as if to say, *Do not torment me any more or any longer.*

How could this poor soul have been tormented more than he had been already? The point is that he came to Jesus seeking an end to his torment, and Jesus set him free. "Come out of the man, unclean spirit!" (v. 8), Jesus commanded. The man had been possessed or driven by an unclean, unsaved, unrepentant spirit.

The Book of Revelation tells us that the saved are sealed on their forehead and right hand, and that the unsaved are marked in a similar way. Both the seal of God and the mark of the beast are signs of ownership or possession. This is the sense in which people are spirit possessed. They either belong to God or to Satan. The unclean, unsaved, unrepentant are in the grip of Satan.

The name of the unclean spirit was Legion, a word of Latin origin that indicates extremely powerful spiritual forces, like a division of combat ready spiritual soldiers. Curiously, the Lord didn't simply destroy Satan's legion that inhabited the man, but gave them permission to enter into a large herd of pigs, two thousand to be exact. When this legion of demonic forces possessed the pigs, they ran off a cliff and drowned in the sea. Not only did this actually happen, but it happened in order to convey a particular message in Scripture.

This was a large herd of pigs by any measure, and would have played a significant role in the local economy. But remember, the Jews considered pigs to be unclean, unfit for consumption or sacrifice. Consequently, those who handled pigs or made their living by them would have also been considered unclean. They were Gentiles.

The death of the pigs in the sea meant that the healing of the Gadarene Demoniac resulted in a significant economic disruption in his community. There is a lesson in this because genuine salvation will often have a serious effect on one's work. Christians often find that there are certain employment situations that offend their newly acquired Christian sensitivities. We could say that from an Old Testament perspective the Gadarene economy was polluted with the uncleanliness associated with pigs. It wasn't just the pigs, but unseemly habits and behaviors often come in complexes. Ungodliness tends to attract other ungodliness.

The healing that Christ brought had a peculiar effect on the local people. When they heard about it, they

> "came to Jesus, and saw the one who had been demon-possessed … sitting and clothed and in his right mind. And they were afraid. And those who saw it told them how it happened to him who had been demon-possessed, and about the swine. Then they began to plead with Him to depart from their region" (vs. 15-17).

It is curious that they witnessed the man's salvation and the miracle that Jesus had wrought—they even acknowledged that he was now in his right mind, yet they wanted the Lord of grace and mercy to leave them alone. They didn't want Him or any part of His salvation.

Why not? Perhaps they didn't want their economy disrupted. The salvation of one man had already cost them two thousand pigs, which would have had a tremendous effect upon the local economy. Jesus was a Jew, the disciples were Jews, the crowd that had followed Him were probably Jewish. Perhaps they thought that these Jews were out to eliminate their pig business. If they all had to become Jewish in order to be saved, they would lose the farm. They had maintained their pig farm in the midst of Jews. They knew about Jews and pigs, and they didn't want to lose their livelihood. They didn't understand that Jesus had been sent to the Gentiles. They didn't understand Christ's Gentile mission. In their fear they didn't want to hear about it.

Here Scripture shows us that many people reject salvation because they are afraid of the changes that it will bring. Often people aren't interested enough to want to know the truth, not even to correct their own misunderstandings. People are comfortable and habituated in their ways. These locals had adapted themselves to the aroma of pig farming, and the sweet savor of the gospel repulsed them.

The final vignette brings us back to the man who had been healed. He wanted to accompany Jesus, to serve Him, to be a benefit to the Lord and His mighty work. He "begged" (v. 18) Jesus to let him go with Him. This new convert had a newly acquired heart for the Lord and the lost, he was mission minded. He was ready to go anywhere with the Lord. So where did Jesus send him?

Home.

While we might be tempted to think that Jesus rained on this man's missionary parade, the truth is that the home is often the most difficult and neglected mission front. Young missionaries are often ready and willing to travel the world over to do what they have not done at home.

Home is a hard mission field. It requires absolute commitment, integrity, and perseverance. It is easier to convince a bunch of strangers that you are living a new life and walking with the Lord than it is to convince your own family. They know you too well and see you too often. In a most real and practical way family provides a genuine test of faithfulness and consistency for exactly these reasons.

I suspect that Paul counseled churches "not (to) lay hands on anyone hastily" (1 Timothy 5:22) by granting leadership to new converts for these same reasons. A church leader—and all missionaries should be considered to be church leaders—was to be

> "one who rules his own house well, having his children in
> submission with all reverence" (1 Timothy 3:4).

The proving ground for church leadership is the home, one's own family. So, Jesus sent the man who had been demon possessed home. There he could testify to the change in his life among those who really knew him. There he could live a new life among those who knew his old life. There he could share the gospel with and minister to Gentiles without all the baggage of Jewish misunderstanding.

Thus, Jesus had not merely sent him home, but had sent him home on a mission to the Gentiles.

> "And he departed and began to proclaim in Decapolis all that
> Jesus had done for him; and all marveled" (v. 20).

The first place that all disciples of Christ are called to minister is in their own homes. That's the place to begin. Yet today, faithful ministry in the home, family life according to the dictates of Scripture, has fallen by the wayside.

Lord, cleanse our polluted hearts with the blood of Christ. Keep us from the confusion of our own self-reliance. Cleanse our hearts anew, convert our minds afresh. Do what only you can do, in Jesus name. Amen.

19. Faith That Acts

Now when Jesus had crossed over again by boat to the other side, a great multitude gathered to Him; and He was by the sea. And behold, one of the rulers of the synagogue came, Jairus by name. And when he saw Him, he fell at His feet and begged Him earnestly, saying, 'My little daughter lies at the point of death. Come and lay Your hands on her, that she may be healed, and she will live.' So Jesus went with him, and a great multitude followed Him and thronged Him. Now a certain woman had a flow of blood for twelve years, and had suffered many things from many physicians. She had spent all that she had and was no better, but rather grew worse. When she heard about Jesus, she came behind Him in the crowd and touched His garment. For she said, 'If only I may touch His clothes, I shall be made well.' Immediately the fountain of her blood was dried up, and she felt in her body that she was healed of the affliction. And Jesus, immediately knowing in Himself that power had gone out of Him, turned around in the crowd and said, 'Who touched My clothes?' But His disciples said to Him, 'You see the multitude thronging You, and You say, "Who touched Me?"' And He looked around to see her who had done this thing. But the woman, fearing and trembling, knowing what had happened to her, came and fell down before Him and told Him the whole truth. And He said to her, 'Daughter, your faith has made you well. Go in peace, and be healed of your affliction.' —Mark 5:21-34*

Two thousand pigs died during the healing of the Gadarene De-moniac. The community of the man who had been healed feared the power of the Lord, and asked Jesus to leave. Jesus sent the healed man home to preach the gospel of grace to the Gentiles, and He returned to the other side of the lake of Galilee.

Note two things about healing generally. First, Jesus was rejected by the people, even after they witnessed a healing miracle. And second, the healing was never given for the sake of the person who received it, but for the sake of the gospel. The healed man served as an example of the power of the Lord to his own community, and as a messenger of the gospel to the Gentiles. The point was not that the man was made well, but that the gospel of Christ was revealed to the Gentiles.

Many people followed Jesus out of curiosity, but few followed as disciples. The ministry of Jesus cut across the normal divisions and categories of society. We saw earlier that the Jewish establishment rejected Jesus, as did the Gentile community of the Gadarene Demoniac. Yet, the healed Demoniac himself became a disciple. Now through the story of Jairus, we see that some within the Jewish establishment also had faith in the Lord.

Jairus was a ruling elder in the synagogue. Little is known of him. No doubt he was aware of Jesus from the discussions that must have occurred among the elders at the time. But while most of the elders rejected Jesus, we must conclude that Jairus had a measure of faith because he

> "came…and…fell at (Jesus') feet and begged Him earnestly" (vs. 22-23) to heal his daughter.

We might ask how Jairus had come by such faith, but we don't really know. Surely he had heard the claims of some that Jesus was the Messiah. Surely he had a good knowledge of the Bible, and had opportunities to hear the preaching of the gospel of Christ. But the truth is that the faithful are faithful because they are drawn into faithfulness by the Holy Spirit.

Jairus didn't come to Jesus and ask if Jesus was able to heal his daughter. He seems to have had no doubt in that regard. He reported that his daughter was at the "point of death" (v. 23), and he knew that Jesus only needed to "lay (His) hand on her, that she may be healed" (v. 24). How did Jairus know that? He was an elder in the synagogue. The laying on of hands had been practiced by the Old Testament priests and prophets as a way of communicating God's blessing. The practice of laying hands upon people was not new. But the amazing thing was that Jairus knew that Jesus was able to heal his daughter, which means that Jairus knew that Jesus wielded a measure of God's power.

We know that Jesus didn't need to actually go and lay His physical hands upon the girl because of His encounter with the Centurion, whose servant was ill (Matthew 8:5). The Centurion knew that Jesus needed only to give the word and his servant would be healed. But this elder believed in the laying on of hands. So, Jesus accommodated Himself to Jairus' belief. From this we learn that God often accommodates Himself to our feeble faith and understanding. He stoops down to our weakness in order to draw us up in His strength.

> "So Jesus went with (Jairus), and a great multitude followed Him and thronged Him" (v. 24).

Great was the crowd that had come to see, but few were those who approached Jesus with genuine faith.

Another story unfolded on the way to the home of Jairus. "A certain woman had a flow of blood for twelve years" (v. 25). She had spent everything trying to get some relief. But no one had been able to heal her. She was at her wit's end. Having heard about Jesus, she thought to herself, "If only I may touch His clothes, I shall be made well" (v. 28). She too believed that God's blessing was communicated by touch. So, in the press of the crowd she stole a touch of the Master's garment. And, sure enough, "she was healed of the affliction" (v. 29).

What did Jairus and this woman have in common? Faith. They believed what they had heard about Jesus and came to Him with simple faith, trusting that what they had heard was actually true. Their faith was not strong in the sense that it was well-supported on a solid foundation of right doctrine or by the intelligence that can distinguish the fine points of the great truths. Rather, their faith was weak. They were frustrated with their own efforts to bring about the healing they needed. Jairus, had, no doubt, employed all the means of healing at his disposal as an elder. He must have done what any elder would have done. He was a man of good standing in the community, a man of reputation and means. But, apparently, he was at his wit's end when He fell at Jesus' feet and begged Him to heal his daughter.

The woman with the blood flow was in the same situation. She had given all she had to the doctors of her day. She had tried everything, to no avail. The point is that they came to Jesus as a last resort. They had exhausted the ways and means of the world. Having exhausted all other means, they finally placed all their trust and faith in Christ alone. They had come to the point that their trust and faith were weak and nearly worn out. They were not puffed up with the pride of their own faithfulness, but were exhausted, having come to the end of their own efforts. But whatever faith they could muster at that point, they gave it all to Jesus.

Saving faith is not a work that people must achieve. It is not faith in *faith*, as if any faith will do. It is an open hand, an empty hand that reaches out to receive Christ. Blessed are those who come to Christ with this simple faith. But the truth is that such people are few in number. Similarly, most people will not turn to Christ until they have exhausted all other possibilities. But most people don't really believe in miracles, so they don't seek them. People don't really trust in Christ. People today trust in modern medicine, and give a speculative nod to Jesus just in case all else fails. They use Jesus like an insurance policy.

Yet, as soon as the woman touched Jesus' robe

> "the fountain of her blood was dried up, and she felt in her body
> that she was healed of the affliction" (v. 29).

Not only was she made well, but Jesus was aware that "power had gone out of Him" (v. 30), so He asked His disciples who had touched Him. The disciples were incredulous because the crowd pressed upon Him everywhere. He was in a sea of people, and He wanted to know who had touched Him! Well, the truth was that many people had touched Him in the midst of the crowd. That was their point. But *His* point was that while many had touched Him faithlessly, someone had touched Him faithfully. Not all touches are equal.

Again, the point Scripture makes is that some of the Gentiles had received Him, while most had rejected Him. And some of the Jews had received Him, while most had rejected Him. In the same way most of the crowd followed Him out of a faithless curiosity, but some among them (this woman) came to Him with genuine faith. The purpose of these stories was to point out that while most Jews and Gentiles rejected Jesus, His ministry cut across all social and cultural distinctions. He had not come for Jews or for Gentiles, but for the lost, Jew and Gentile.

The woman was still close enough to hear Jesus ask who touched Him. As Jesus looked around the crowd He probably looked right at this woman, who,

> "fearing and trembling, knowing what had happened to her,
> came and fell down before Him and told Him the whole truth.
> And He said to her, 'Daughter, your faith has made you well. Go
> in peace, and be healed of your affliction'" (vs. 33-34).

This whole scene must have happened in just a few minutes as Jesus was on His way to Jairus' house.

Jesus told her that her faith had made her well. The statement is completely true, but requires some explanation because of the potential for misunderstanding that surrounds it. We need to keep from turning New Testament faith into a kind of works-righteousness. That is always a temptation because people understand and desire works–righteousness. It is the folly of the flesh to think that we can make ourselves righteous and worthy in God's eyes.

The works-righteousness trap goes like this: If I can just learn enough about Jesus, or believe hard enough, or develop a strong enough faith, then I can be healed or saved. But Jesus did not mean that this woman or anyone could be healed or saved because of the strength or veracity of their own faith, as if faith itself is the means or cause of healing. Rather, He meant that this woman was able to receive the gift of healing because she was not full of self-confidence. She was at her wit's end, she leaned wholly upon Christ for what only Christ could give. It is not the quality or strength of one's faith, but the undeserved grace of God that causes healing or blessing or salvation. As the hymnist put it, "Nothing in my hand I bring, Simply to the cross I cling." In a logical sense, we can say that faith is necessary, and yet our own paltry efforts to be faithful are not sufficient. We must depend upon Christ and His faithfulness, not out own.

This woman of faith sought Jesus out. She didn't just sit back and wait for Jesus to come to her. She went to Him. She did everything in her power to avail herself of God's mercy.

As soon as He had healed her, He received word that Jairus' daughter had died. The message came with the implication that there was no longer any hope, nothing anyone could do. Tying it to the previous story, we could say that they thought that since the girl was dead, she could not possibly have the faith required for healing. If the woman with the blood flow was healed because of her faith, then this poor girl could not possibly be healed because of her faith—she was dead. Her own faith could not heal her.

The two stories are together because the one extends the lesson of the other. Jairus' daughter could have no role at all in her healing. She could not be healed by her own faith because she was dead. And dead people don't have faith! If she was going to be healed it would have to be by God's grace alone. Yet, Jesus wanted to show that faith still had a role to play. So, he turned to Jairus and said, "Do not be afraid; only believe" (v. 36). He asked Jairus to engage his faith in Christ on her behalf.

As He arrived people were weeping and wailing in sorrow at the girl's death. When Jesus told them that the girl was only sleeping, they laughed at Him. There was no doubt in their minds that she was dead!

He dismissed all but the girl's parents and the disciples. Then He took the girl's hand and told her to get up. And she did! He spoke a

Word to her and she responded. She was dead, and came to life. That is the proper order of events regarding healing. Healing, as well as grace and salvation, flow from God to man. God is the giver, we only receive the gift.

This girl's faith did not heal her. She was dead. But her father believed, and his faith played a part in her healing because she was under his household authority. The faith of her parents was the instrument of her healing. Her father's faith was not transferred to her, nor did her father's faith cause her to be healed. Rather, it was the means of her healing. In faith her father sought Jesus to heal her.

Think of it as fixing a leaky faucet. A wrench is the means or instrument of the fixing. But the wrench does not cause the repair of the faucet. The wrench cannot fix the faucet by itself, but is instrumental to the fixing. Similarly, faith was not the cause of the girl's healing, but the instrument of it. God used her father's wrench (faith) to fix her faucet (healing).

There is an interesting application of this teaching to infant baptism. The faith of the parent(s) can be instrumental to the salvation of their children. The parent's faith is not transferred to their children, nor does it cause the salvation of their children, nor does it guarantee the salvation of their children. But it can be instrumental to the salvation of their children in the sense that the faith of the parents brings the child into contact with the gospel of Jesus Christ.

The story closes like this:

> "But He commanded them strictly that no one should know it,
> and said that something should be given her to eat" (v. 43).

Again, Jesus performed a genuine miracle that brought life and salvation to the lost. Yet, He instructed His people to keep it to themselves. He did not tell them to go out and share their experience of the Lord or of their healing with others. Jesus was not interested in their experience or their understanding of His miracle. That was not the point. Rather, he told them to do something helpful. Get her something to eat.

So often we think that evangelism means telling others what Jesus has done for *us*, or what He means to *us*. Here was a perfect opportunity for Jesus' disciples to do exactly that. And Jesus told them not to! Scripture anticipates our every error. We've run across this before, and we'll run across it again. It is a most curious thing. It appears often enough and is clear enough that we should wonder if Jesus would approve our modern evangelism methods. This commandment of Jesus ought to be enough to cause us to doubt what we think we understand about evangelism.

Jesus wanted us to focus on the atonement, on His death on the cross, and not on what He could do for us in this world. He died on the cross to bring salvation to all believers. But He didn't die on the cross in order to guarantee us a better life here on earth. Name one apostle who lived the good life because of his commitment to Jesus. Name one martyr who experienced anything but trial and tribulation in this world. Of course they had joyous moments in their lives, don't get me wrong. But the point is that their faith brought them suffering.

Jesus died for the forgiveness of sins, for the salvation of sinners, for the healing of the breach between man and God, not so that we could each have two cars and a boat, not so that we might live long and prosper. Have you come to Jesus seeking what He alone gives, or have you come seeking what you want for yourself?

20. OFFENDED

Then He went out from there and came to His own country,
and His disciples followed Him. And when the Sabbath had
come, He began to teach in the synagogue. And many hearing
Him were astonished, saying, 'Where did this Man get these
things? And what wisdom is this which is given to Him, that
such mighty works are performed by His hands! Is this not the
carpenter, the Son of Mary, and brother of James, Joses, Judas,
and Simon? And are not His sisters here with us?' And they
were offended at Him. But Jesus said to them, 'A prophet is not
without honor except in his own country, among his own rela-
tives, and in his own house.' Now He could do no mighty
work there, except that He laid His hands on a few sick people
and healed them. And He marveled because of their unbelief.
Then He went about the villages in a circuit, teaching.

—Mark 6:1-6

As Jesus crisscrossed the Sea of Galilee preaching, healing, and
ministering, we have seen how His teaching and perspective
were at odds with people everywhere. Clearly the Jewish establishment opposed His teaching and His ministry everywhere they met it.
We have seen again and again that the vast majority of people were interested in Jesus for the wrong reasons. When Jesus sought to clarify His
teaching, to bring people into conformity with His will, they abandoned Him.

When Jesus cast out an unclean spirit, He was accused of teaching
new doctrine (Mark 1:27). When Jesus healed a paralytic, the scribes accused Him of blasphemy (Mark 2:7). When Jesus dined with Levi
(Matthew), the Pharisees accused Him of gluttony (Mark 2:16), charg-
ing that His disciples did not keep religious fasts. When He healed on
the Sabbath, the Pharisees and Herodians plotted to destroy Him (Mark
3:6). His own family thought that He was out of His mind (Mark 3:20).
When He cast out demons, He was accused of having a demon (Mark
3:22). When He taught the people, they did not understand His parables
(Mark 4:13). When He healed the Gadarene Demoniac, He was asked to

leave (Mark 5:17). And here in chapter six we find that He is rejected in His own home town.

Since His baptism Jesus had been ministering a lot around the Sea of Galilee. Chapter six finds Him returning home to the hills of Nazareth—Him and His disciples. Jesus hadn't come home simply to visit His old friends, He had come to minister. He had come home with twelve friends—but more than friends, the disciples were His followers. Imagine someone you used to know as a kid coming to visit with twelve guys who treat him like a king. Remember that Jesus' own family had already tried to divert Him from His Messianic role. They already thought He was nuts, and that word had undoubtedly circulated through the local Nazarene grapevine. And suddenly He shows up with a dozen converts!

He went to church that week and spoke up during the lesson. Jesus spoke and taught with authority, so we can imagine that He got some attention. A Jewish synagogue could be established wherever ten Jewish men could meet on a regular basis. Jesus came with twelve. In essence, the men He brought were equivalent to another church. It was as if a whole church had descended upon His hometown of Nazareth.

Jesus' teaching in the synagogue disturbed the regulars.

> "And when the Sabbath had come, He began to teach in the synagogue. And many hearing Him were astonished, saying, 'Where did this Man get these things? And what wisdom is this which is given to Him, that such mighty works are performed by His hands!'" (v. 2).

They were astonished. The Greek word is *ekplesso*, the root of which means to strike with panic, shock, or amazement. What it really means is that they were dumbfounded and offended.

Mark doesn't tell us exactly what Jesus taught, but it matters little. Everything He had been teaching had the same effect. Generally, people didn't understand it, and when they did, they didn't like it. But it was not unpopular because it was new and different. There were many new and different religious teachings being proclaimed during Jesus' lifetime that were quite popular. Rather, the gospel of Christ was unpopular because it struck a mortal blow to the heart of human pride.

Jesus had come with the simple message of salvation that He had preached since His baptism.

> "Jesus came to Galilee, preaching the gospel of the kingdom of God, and saying, 'The time is fulfilled, and the kingdom of God is at hand. Repent, and believe in the gospel.'" (Mark 1:15).

Repent and believe!

You might wonder what was so threatening about that? What could be more comforting than the knowledge of salvation? Well, nothing is more comforting than the knowledge of salvation. But in order to receive such knowledge, one must admit to one's present lack of salvation, and one's own sin.

To illustrate this we can point to the same issue which has occurred in the Mainline churches as charismatics have come into their midst proclaiming that they (the Mainliners) must be baptized in the Holy Spirit, by immersion, and by speaking in tongues. To some degree or other this Pentecostal message has been brought to nearly every denomination. The implication is that the Mainliners have missed it. I'm not arguing for immersion or speaking in tongues, but I am trying to suggest the emotional response that people had in the face of Jesus' invitation to salvation.

The issue is that in order to accept Jesus' teaching and salvation, people must admit that everything they have done previously has not brought them enlightenment or salvation. Jesus' offer of salvation was a slap in the face to the leaders of the Jewish synagogues, and more so to the Jerusalem Temple establishment. In essence, Jesus proclaimed that the whole Jewish tradition, as it operated in His day, was futile and ineffective. It wasn't working. It left the people unenlightened and unsaved.

It is the same accusation that charismatics bring against all non-charismatics. However, the fact that Christians and their churches are immersed in dead orthodoxy, doesn't prove that the charismatics are right. It only indicates that orthodox belief can be held without conviction, devoid of the Holy Spirit. But it doesn't mean that historic Christian orthodoxy is wrong.

This same concern was alive in Jesus' day. Jesus was not preaching against Jewish orthodoxy. Far from it! Rather, He begged the Jewish leaders to turn back to their own history and to the orthodoxy of their historic doctrines. Jesus wanted people to understand and believe the traditional doctrines of the Scriptures. He wasn't teaching a new doctrine, He was teaching the fulfillment of the old!

So, as Jesus taught in his home synagogue people were offended on two counts. First, they had so neglected their own Scriptures that they had difficulty understanding what He was talking about. They felt stupid and got mad. However, they were stumbled, not by the difficulty of Jesus' teaching, but by their own failure to know Scripture. Secondly, they were proud of what they thought they had accomplished through their religious practices. Again, the cause of the offense was not in what Jesus taught, but in what the people of Nazareth thought they already knew and thought they had already accomplished.

Who does He think He is! Coming in here and talking that Messiah stuff. He's no Messiah, He's Joseph's son, the carpenter. Why, He don't even got no schoolin'! "Where did this Man get these things?" wrote Mark.

> "And what wisdom is this which is given to Him, that such mighty works are performed by His hands!" (v. 2).

In their astonishment, they revealed that they correctly understood several things about Jesus. The truth is that we cannot attribute their unbelief to a lack of knowledge. They recognized that Jesus was full of wisdom. Real wisdom usually threatens people because its truth is convicting. Unable to deny the truth, people often respond with anger and frustration because they don't want to conform to the implications of God's truth. People who are comfortable with their lives don't want to change and resent being told that their comfort deceives them.

They also acknowledged that Jesus didn't teach His own ideas, but that the wisdom He taught had been given to Him. This insight was commonly missed by people as they variously accused Him. But those in His home synagogue knew that He wasn't teaching things that Joseph had taught Him.

In the Gospel of John (7:15-20) we find these words:

> "And the Jews marveled, saying, 'How does this Man know letters, having never studied?' Jesus answered them and said, 'My doctrine is not Mine, but His who sent Me. If anyone wants to do His will, he shall know concerning the doctrine, whether it is from God or whether I speak on My own authority. He who speaks from himself seeks his own glory; but He who seeks the glory of the One who sent Him is true, and no unrighteousness is in Him. Did not Moses give you the law, yet none of you keeps the law? Why do you seek to kill Me?' The people answered and said, 'You have a demon. Who is seeking to kill You?'"

So, if Jesus' hometown people correctly understood Him, why were they not converted? That is an important question that we would do well to answer. Why are some people converted, and some not? We'd like to be able to say that the difference is found in their upbringing and education, that a Christian family and Christian education makes the critical difference. And while we are tempted to believe it, our own experience knows that it's wrong. We need only look at our own families to know the gospel truth. Some are saved and some aren't. Yet, generally speaking, our various family members have had the same upbringing and Christian education.

Now, I'm not saying that upbringing and education make no difference at all. They do! They are important! But they don't make the *necessary* difference. Certainly, children who are raised in Christian families by born again parents who provide a Christian education have a tremendous advantage. Such children have a leg up on the salvation horse. But having a leg up on the horse is not the same as being in the saddle.

We know enough to know that family training, Christian education, and church attendance do not save anyone. We are not saved by such things. We are saved by grace alone through faith alone in Christ alone through Scripture alone to the glory of God alone. While family training, Christian education, and church attendance are means of salvation, they themselves do not save. Just as a wrench cannot fix a leaky faucet by itself, but can be used for that purpose. Similarly, God sometimes uses family training, Bible study, and church attendance to accomplish His salvation. But sometimes He doesn't.

Who can explain it? I can't, and Scripture doesn't. Scripture simply teaches that Jesus saves. God said to Moses,

> "I will be gracious to whom I will be gracious, and I will have compassion on whom I will have compassion" (Exodus 33:19).

Another time Jesus had been preaching the same message and knowing that His disciples complained about it,

> "He said to them, 'Does this offend you? What then if you should see the Son of Man ascend where He was before? It is the Spirit who gives life; the flesh profits nothing. The words that I speak to you are spirit, and they are life. But there are some of you who do not believe.' For Jesus knew from the beginning who they were who did not believe, and who would betray Him. And He said, 'Therefore I have said to you that no one can come to Me unless it has been granted to him by My Father'" (John 6:61-65).

These are the very words of Jesus, yet they make many people uncomfortable with their implications. They point to doctrines that have stumbled many. People don't dislike them because they don't understand them; people dislike them because they strip us of the very thing that we pride ourselves on—the ability to control our own lives, and our own destinies.

People want to believe themselves to be good people because they choose to be good. People want to believe that anyone who chooses to be good can do so. This is the moral argument for righteousness. But God says that

> "none (are) righteous, no, not one" (Romans 3:10),

> "for all have sinned and fall short of the glory of God" (Romans 3:23).

> "For by grace you have been saved through faith, and that not of yourselves; it is the gift of God" (Ephesians 2:8).

Finally, those Jews in the Nazarene synagogue where Jesus taught that day knew that mighty works had been performed by Jesus (v. 2). His miracles were not in question, yet they did not believe, but "were offended at Him" (v. 3).

Though they knew of His mighty miracles, and believed them to be authentic, and Him to be a genuine worker of miracles, they did not savingly believe. Their knowledge of Jesus as the kid down the street kept them from seeing Him as the Savior of the world. Their familiarity with Him bred contempt for His ministry. Consequently, Jesus did no great miracles or works in their midst. But because all things are possible with God, Jesus certainly could have done miracles there. Nor was their unbelief greater than His ability to work miracles, as if their unbelief retarded His miracle working ability.

Rather, because God has ordained salvation to come by faith, Jesus chose not to attempt any miracles among the Nazarenes. Jesus never tried to cram faith down the throats of the faithless. He let them be. He allowed them to suffer the consequences of their own choices. What Jesus did was to encourage those with little faith to grow in faith.

But Jesus did not ignore His Nazarene friends. He didn't condemn them to hell because they didn't believe. Rather, "He went about the villages in a circuit, teaching" (v. 6). He taught them even though they didn't believe. Why did He teach them when He knew that they didn't believe? Perhaps He knew that though they didn't believe themselves, He knew that some of them would have believing children.

What a God we have! What a great compassionate, faithful, and patient God! He cares for us in ways that we do not know and cannot understand. Praise God!

21. REPENTANCE REITERATED

And He called the twelve to Himself, and began to send them out two by two, and gave them power over unclean spirits. He commanded them to take nothing for the journey except a staff —no bag, no bread, no copper in their money belts— but to wear sandals, and not to put on two tunics. Also He said to them, 'In whatever place you enter a house, stay there till you depart from that place. And whoever will not receive you nor hear you, when you depart from there, shake off the dust under your feet as a testimony against them. Assuredly, I say to you, it will be more tolerable for Sodom and Gomorrah in the day of judgment than for that city!' So they went out and preached that people should repent. And they cast out many demons, and anointed with oil many who were sick, and healed them.

—Mark 6:7-13

As Jesus went "about the villages in a circuit, teaching" (v. 5) He fully realized the extent of the need for solid, biblical instruction. Thus.

"He called the twelve to Himself, and began to send them out two by two" (v. 7).

When you think of people going out two by two, what do you think of? Do you think of genuine Christian missionaries? Probably not. Most of us think of Jehovah's Witnesses or Mormons. It is amazing how much this simple evangelism technique has been abandoned by otherwise faithful churches. To even suggest that going out two by two is an essential ingredient in Christian missions is practically unheard of. It seems too cultish, too radical, too unchristian. Yet, that is exactly what Jesus commanded His disciples to do.

And He "gave them power over unclean spirits" (v. 7). Essentially, unclean spirits were opposed to what Jesus taught. If we understand that Christian righteousness (or cleanness) is not our own but Christ's, then uncleanness means a lack of Christ's righteousness. And because Christ's righteousness is extended to all who are willing to receive it, those who don't have it have rejected it. Normally, the first step in the rejection of Christ's righteousness—which is salvation itself—is the refusal to admit one's own sin and repent of it. Consequently, the power over unclean spirits consisted of the power to bring people to repentance.

Secondly, Jesus told the disciples to "take nothing for the journey" (v. 8) except a few bare necessities. What are we to make of the fact that Mark records that Jesus told them to take a staff, but Matthew and Luke record that Jesus forbade them to take a staff? Is this a Bible contradiction? It would be easy to see it as a contradiction. But if we apply what we know to be true—that the Bible does not contradict itself, we are compelled to seek another explanation. The Bible often forces us to learn how to think for ourselves by teaching things that can be considered to be contradictory. By dealing with them correctly we learn important subtleties in biblical logic.

The Greek word for *staff* is *rhabdos*, and it can refer to both a walking stick and a royal scepter, a traditional symbol of power and authority. Consequently, we can suppose that Jesus meant that the disciples should take a walking stick to help them in their journey, but that they should not take any worldly vestiges of power and authority. Such an explanation fits well with what we know of Jesus and His ministry.

What can we make of Jesus' injunction to take nothing with them? There are several possibilities. One is that they were not going very far, that their primary mission was to reach their immediate neighbors. There is much to be gained by such a reading. Another is that they were to go to backslidden Jews who at least maintained the biblical injunctions of hospitality to travelers. Jews were scattered throughout the land and would provide hospitality, many of them even becoming bases for ministry as they were converted. But whatever Jesus meant we can surmise that He intended the gospel to travel along lines of friendship and hospitality.

And in an effort to maintain the friendships they made, they were to remain with those particular friends as long as they ministered in that particular village.

> "In whatever place you enter a house, stay there till you depart
> from that place" (v. 10).

In this way the disciples would maintain their friendships. Jesus' plan seemed to be twofold: 1) to spread the gospel, and 2) to grow disciples into greater spiritual maturity over time by maintaining significant relationships between them, much like a husband and wife grow deeper as they live together. Jesus seemed to value long term relationships over short term relationships as the means for successful church development.

Notice also that Jesus directed His disciples to avoid disputes.

> "Whoever will not receive you nor hear you, when you depart from there, shake off the dust under your feet as a testimony against them" (v. 11).

Where the disciples were received they were to stay, and where they were not received, they were to pronounce a curse and leave—but not to argue with people.

The curse was to be given only if the whole town rejected them. Otherwise, they were to continue to seek a place of hospitality as a base of operations. They were to preach the gospel, argue for the gospel, but not argue against objections grounded in faithlessness. Where they met such objections, they were to leave. But note that the curse was not for individuals, but for any city or town that rejected them. If there was no one in a city who would receive the gospel, that city was indeed cursed because God's curse essentially means being separated or apart from God.

And so the disciples went out in obedience to Jesus' command and preached the gospel. The first thing they did was to preach the gospel. They didn't do Vacation Bible School or Sunday School in order to attract the kids so they could reach the parents. They preached. They didn't set up small groups or Bible studies. They preached. The first thing they did was to preach the gospel. Even before they stayed at someone's house, they went into a town and began preaching. Where did they preach? Wherever they could, just as Jesus did. Often they preached in local synagogues, sometimes in homes.

Why begin with preaching? What is the purpose of preaching? Preaching is not teaching, though they are related. Preaching is the setting forth of the gospel by lifting up Christ crucified. Teaching comes later. Teaching is the explanation of the gospel. But preaching, we might say, is running Christ up the flag pole. Do you know the rest of that saying? Run it up the flag pole and see who salutes.

The purpose of preaching is not merely to draw a crowd, but to draw the elect, to sound forth the voice of the Shepherd that His sheep may hear Him and come. The purpose of preaching is to gather the sheep, to draw Christians together. Once they are together all sorts of other things can happen, and a church begins to grow. Sharing your faith is fine. Giving your testimony is great. Bible study is wonderful.

But all such things will fall flat where they are not appreciated. And they are not appreciated where Christ is not appreciated.

Jesus had already been drawing large crowds, but they disappointed Him. Most of the people who had been attracted to the large crowd scene followed Him for the wrong reasons, seeking the wrong things. As Jesus turned up the spiritual heat, drawing people into a deeper relationship with Him, most abandoned Him. Most people were not looking for the glory of the cross. Most people just wanted a quick fix and a handout.

If the truth be known, at this point, not even the disciples themselves wanted the glory of the cross. As we continue to study Mark we will see again and again that even the disciples were oblivious to it, until after it happened, and until the Holy Spirit came upon them. The point is that Jesus was on His way to Jerusalem, to a gruesome yet glorious death. Without the proper groundwork the cross doesn't connect with the felt needs of the average person.

When we speak of the gospel we usually mean the atoning death and resurrection of Christ as the propitiation for sin, resulting in forgiveness. But at this point Jesus had neither died nor resurrected. So what gospel did they preach? John's gospel of repentance. "They went out and preached that people should repent" (v. 12). Preaching repentance is not much more popular than preaching the glory of the cross. People really don't want to hear it. Why? Because before you get to the benefits of repentance and salvation, you need to hit on the heart of sin in a way that connects with people personally. And as much as people don't like to be told about their sin, they like it even less when it is clearly and irrefutably demonstrated in public.

It's embarrassing. And embarrassment is usually what we mean when we say we are offended by it. If whatever is said that offends you is blatantly false, you can disprove it or slough it off. But when it is true, people get angry because they are embarrassed. Yet, the purpose of preaching is not to offend people. Not at all! That approach is not only foolish, but dangerous. Rather, the purpose of preaching is to set forth the gospel, to make God's grace and mercy plain without belittling His justice and law. The object in preaching is not to offend people, but to keep from offending God by leaving out crucial elements of His gospel. The preacher's job is to clearly and correctly set forth the gospel, not to try to slant the message one way or another in an effort to appeal to a particular group of people.

When it is clearly and boldly set forth, the Holy Spirit uses the proclamation of the gospel to draw or repel whosoever He will. The gospel, rightly set forth, always demands a response. That response should not be a response to the preacher, although it is often misconstrued to be such. But it should be a response to Christ's call to salvation. The call is Christ's, not the preacher's. The issue of the gospel is not whether or not you like the preacher, but whether you will repent and respond to the gospel of Christ.

Finally, we learn that

> "they cast out many demons, and anointed with oil many who were sick, and healed them" (v. 13).

Some demons and unclean spirits were cast out from individual personalities. We saw that in the healing of the Gadarene Demoniac and others. We also learn that the disciples anointed and healed many who were sick. It is instructive to know what these people were healed of. What was their sickness? The Greek word is *arrhostos*, which literally means *without strength*. The term indicates spiritual weakness or moral slackness. Thus, we can surmise that they were healed of, among other things, a lack of spiritual commitment.

Jesus didn't heal people just to make them feel better. He always healed for the sake of His church, not simply for the sake of the individuals involved. In a sense, Jesus sent the disciples out to preach and teach for the sake of an ailing church. Jesus' purpose was not to establish a new church, but to reform the old. The Evangelical church did not begin with the birth or death of Christ, but as Paul says, with the calling of Abraham (Genesis 12:1-3).

By anointing those who were sick, those who were spiritually and morally weak, the disciples used the means of grace—the established pattern, the organizational structures and relationships within the church—for the purpose of healing the church itself. The process of anointing has been from ancient times the prescribed process of conferring power and authority within the church. As Old Testament priests and kings were anointed into office with oil, so were New Testament elders and deacons anointed into office by the laying on of hands.

The process of anointing the sick alluded to the established lines of power and authority within the church. What we are looking at, in addition to the physical healing of those who were ill, is the healing of the ancient governmental structure of the church. The apostles established the pattern of the New Testament church as a corrective for the Old.

Adhering to that pattern, then, would provide for the healing of *arrhos-tos*—the spiritual and moral weakness—into which the church had fallen.

Have you fallen into spiritual and moral weakness? Jesus bids that all who are weary and weak should come to Him. Christ is our healing. Christ is our rest, and our strength. But, alas, we cannot come unless and until we repent, until we acknowledge our own personal weakness, our inability, our error, our sin, and our selfishness. So, we must begin there, and not be afraid to admit our errors, and seek God's guidance.

Wouldn't it be great if repenting were just a one time thing! We could do it once and be done with it. But because sin is a lingering real-ity, we must linger in repentance as well.

22. Too Personal

Now King Herod heard of Him, for His name had become well known. And he said, 'John the Baptist is risen from the dead, and therefore these powers are at work in him.' Others said, 'It is Elijah.' And others said, 'It is the Prophet, or like one of the prophets.' But when Herod heard, he said, 'This is John, whom I beheaded; he has been raised from the dead!' For Herod himself had sent and laid hold of John, and bound him in prison for the sake of Herodias, his brother Philip's wife; for he had married her. For John had said to Herod, 'It is not lawful for you to have your brother's wife.' Therefore Herodias held it against him and wanted to kill him, but she could not; for Herod feared John, knowing that he was a just and holy man, and he protected him. And when he heard him, he did many things, and heard him gladly. Then an opportune day came when Herod on his birthday gave a feast for his nobles, the high officers, and the chief men of Galilee. And when Herodias' daughter herself came in and danced, and pleased Herod and those who sat with him, the king said to the girl, 'Ask me whatever you want, and I will give it to you.' He also swore to her, 'Whatever you ask me, I will give you, up to half of my kingdom.' So she went out and said to her mother, 'What shall I ask?' And she said, 'The head of John the Baptist!' Immediately she came in with haste to the king and asked, saying, 'I want you to give me at once the head of John the Baptist on a platter.' And the king was exceedingly sorry; yet, because of the oaths and because of those who sat with him, he did not want to refuse her. Immediately the king sent an executioner and commanded his head to be brought. And he went and beheaded him in prison, brought his head on a platter, and gave it to the girl; and the girl gave it to her mother. When his disciples heard of it, they came and took away his corpse and laid it in a tomb. —Mark 6:14–29

The story of the beheading of John the Baptist is a classic story that demonstrates the effects of truth upon the human conscience. As conscience guides human behavior, so truth guides conscience. Conversely, as a lack of conscience is an encouragement to sin, so ignorance of truth is a discouragement to the development of conscience. Conscience feeds upon truth, and ignorance of truth starves conscience.

We should note that verse 14 provides a testimony to the accepted belief in resurrection. Even King Herod understood resurrection to provide a testimony to spiritual reality. So established was this common understanding that it was repeated in verse 16,

> "But when Herod heard, he said, 'This is John, whom I
> beheaded; he has been raised from the dead!'"

John's beheading is stated simply and straightforwardly.

King Herod had been incestuously cohabitating with his brother's wife, Herodias, and John publicly chastised the royal couple for their disregard of the marriage covenant. John was simply preaching the truth of God's law, when the truth he preached pricked the conscience of Herodias. She took offense at John's preaching, and at John himself.

Interestingly, King Herod did not,

> "for Herod feared John, knowing that he was a just and holy
> man, and he protected him. And when he heard him, he...heard
> him gladly" (v. 20).

Herod's appreciation of John, no doubt, was an additional burr under Herodias' saddle.

Sin often results when one person takes up the cudgels for another, when one person defends the honor, reputation, or values of another. Rather, we should fight our own battles, and not become someone else's lackey, because when we do we often become Satan's lackey. In essence, we should guard ourselves against manipulation by others or on behalf of others. Vigilance must be maintained because it is the nature of manipulation that it occurs even when people don't realize that they are being manipulated. In fact, that is when manipulation is most successful.

King Herod was drunk when he promised to give Herodias' daughter anything she wanted. He spoke those fateful words at a public gathering. The daughter, likely to have been manipulated by her mother into dancing before the drunken party in the first place, then sought her mother's counsel regarding the promised gift.

Herodias had long been seeking an opportunity to put John away for the public embarrassment he had caused her. So, she told her daughter to ask for John's head. Upon hearing the request, Herod was "exceedingly sorry" (v. 26), but because of his pride and his concern for what people thought about him—peer pressure, he gave the order. John's head was brought to him forthwith. And he "gave it to the girl, and the girl gave it to her mother" (v. 28).

It's a story about how the conviction of sin works in people's lives. It's a story about the power of preaching as an effective means of penetrating people's defenses and touching their consciences. But it's also a story about the dangers of preaching God's truth, and of the necessity for the faithfulness of those who preach.

By and large, Christians don't mind preaching that is directed against the generic sins of the world. Christians know that the world is in bad shape and in need of reform, and as long as the preacher talks about generic sin, or the specific sins of someone else, the message is tolerable—even morally rousing at times. But when the preaching is directed against one's own personal but error-ridden worldview or one's own personal sins—especially one's favorite or treasured sins, it is received as meddling. Even Christians don't like it!

The first sign of conviction often occurs when people feel as if the preacher is talking about them personally, as if he is sharing some of their personal matters in a public forum. Though no names are mentioned, people sometimes think that they are being singled out and publicly reprimanded by gospel preaching, when in truth it is not the preacher who singles people out, but one's own guilty conscience that feels the sharp edge of gospel truth.

God's truth convicts by means of the Holy Spirit. The more truthful the more convicting; and the more convicting, the more relief is sought by sinners. The purpose of preaching is to goad sinners into seeking the grace of God for the relief of forgiveness. But unrepentant sinners balk at God's forgiveness and seek relief elsewhere, often by reducing the weight of God's truth upon them by attacking either the truth of the message itself, or the one who conveys it.

We see both of these unrepentant strategies in our own day. There is a seemingly coordinated effort among the unrepentant to prove the folly of God's truth. Biblical truth is systematically undermined and attacked everywhere by those at the helm of contemporary culture. Media, education, government, advertising, and even the church itself have become weapons of retaliation against God's biblical truth.

In addition, those who faithfully hold and proclaim God's truth are subjected to personal criticism and harassment—harassment being a mild form of persecution. God help you if the conscience of your employer is pricked by your witness—in the church or out. The excessive concern about offending or being offended that is so prevalent today and known as "political correctness" is the result of the denial of the conviction of sin by contemporary society. So-called hate crimes involve the lashing out of unrepentant sinners at whoever they believe to be the source of their feelings of conviction.

Whites attack Blacks because they believe that Blacks are the source of their guilt. Blacks attack Whites because they believe that Whites are the source of their shame. Liberals attack Conservatives because conserving God's Word leads to feelings of guilt. Conservatives attack Liberals in order to shift the blame for their own failures to those who are perceived to be worse than they. Don't we often point out the sins of others in order to justify ourselves. People think, *I'm not as bad as that guy. So before you go blaming me, you need to deal with him.* Blame shifting is as old as Eden itself.

But the biggest problem in contemporary society regarding this whole issue continues to be peer pressure. Herod was not able to do what was right because he was concerned that others would accuse him of going back on a public promise. Forget that the promise was made in a drunken stupor! Herod's interests were politically motivated. He was willing to sacrifice what he knew to be right for the sake of appearances —to appease Herodias and honor his public commitment to her daughter. That by definition is peer pressure, regardless of the ages or social status of those involved. John wrote that

> "even among the rulers many believed in Him, but because of
> the Pharisees they did not confess Him…for they loved the praise
> of men more than the praise of God" (John 12:42-43).

Mike O'Brien got on a ferry boat in Macao. The year was 1943. He forgot his passport. He couldn't get off in Hong Kong, nor could he get off on the return trip to Macao. For weeks he went back and forth between the two cities while the various embassies discussed his case. Some called him a Hungarian, others an Irishman or an American.

There are many people in this world who shuttle between two opinions, who can't commit themselves to God, nor to anything else. Such people, like Mike O'Brien, are spiritually homeless. They cannot abandon their earthly citizenship, nor can they claim a home in heaven.

Such people are always learning and never arriving at a definitive knowledge of the truth. Such people "falter between two opinions" (1 Kings 18:21).

Salvation is based upon a personal relationship with Jesus Christ, a relationship which we do not ourselves create, but receive. Similarly, true conviction of sin is also a personal conviction, not of our own making. The point is that without the pain of conviction, there can be no joy of salvation. It is as if the pain creates a capacity for the joy. In order to receive the joy of forgiveness and salvation, we must go through the door of conviction—the personal admission of our own guilt and complicity in our sin.

> "A satisfied soul loathes the honeycomb, But to a hungry soul
> every bitter thing is sweet" (Proverbs 27:7),

says the writer of Proverbs. In other words, there is no salvation for those who are self-satisfied. But to those who have experienced the personal destructiveness and sorrow of sin, to those who can acknowledge their personal sin and their personal need for salvation, the admission of personal sin and guilt yields the sweet savor of forgiveness.

> "If we confess our sins, He is faithful and just to forgive us our
> sins and to cleanse us from all unrighteousness" (1 John 1:9).

If we confess, if we repent, if we ask, if we seek, God is faithful to all His promises. Praise be to God!

23. God Provides

Then the apostles gathered to Jesus and told Him all things,
both what they had done and what they had taught. And He
said to them, 'Come aside by yourselves to a deserted place and
rest a while.' For there were many coming and going, and they
did not even have time to eat. So they departed to a deserted
place in the boat by themselves. But the multitudes saw them
departing, and many knew Him and ran there on foot from all
the cities. They arrived before them and came together to Him.
And Jesus, when He came out, saw a great multitude and was
moved with compassion for them, because they were like sheep
not having a shepherd. So He began to teach them many
things. When the day was now far spent, His disciples came to
Him and said, 'This is a deserted place, and already the hour is
late. Send them away, that they may go into the surrounding
country and villages and buy themselves bread; for they have
nothing to eat.' But He answered and said to them, 'You give
them something to eat.' And they said to Him, 'Shall we go and
buy two hundred denarii worth of bread and give them some-
thing to eat?' But He said to them, 'How many loaves do you
have? Go and see.' And when they found out they said, 'Five,
and two fish.' Then He commanded them to make them all sit
down in groups on the green grass. So they sat down in ranks,
in hundreds and in fifties. And when He had taken the five
loaves and the two fish, He looked up to heaven, blessed and
broke the loaves, and gave them to His disciples to set before
them; and the two fish He divided among them all. So they all
ate and were filled. And they took up twelve baskets full of
fragments and of the fish. Now those who had eaten the loaves
were about five thousand men.   —Mark 6:30-44

Jesus had sent out the twelve with orders to preach the gospel wherever they were received by people. Upon returning from their preaching mission, they reported all that happened to Jesus. The process of
reporting is evidence of the accountability that existed between Jesus

and His disciples. They did not go off and do their own thing, but they went out under the Lord's orders. Their preaching, no doubt, helped to gather the crowd of five thousand.

Having faithfully completed the task Christ set before them, He called them aside to rest a while. The work of ministry is never finished, so it naturally attracts workaholics, and tends to burn them out unless ample opportunity for rest is taken. Mark said that there was much "coming and going," so much that "they did not even have time to eat" (v. 31). Sounds a lot like modern life. It's not that ministers are busier than other people, but their busyness is of a different order and intensity than others. We could all stand to get away from our busy-ness more often. But the problem is that when we go on vacation, we don't get away from it at all. Rather, we try to take it all with us! For most people vacations are not restful. It is hard to get away at all today. Our modern conveniences like phones and computers make it increasingly difficult.

But neither could Jesus' twelve disciples get away. They tried,

> "but the multitudes saw them departing, and many (followed
> them) on foot from all the cities" (v. 33).

Jesus and His twelve preachers were tired and worn out. They sought rest, but found none. Many in the crowd beat Jesus and the disciples to the isolated place they were going. Apparently, it was a retreat spot that people knew about.

Mark twice mentioned it was an isolated or "deserted place." Apparently, the fact of its isolation was an important element of the story. Generally speaking, isolated spots have no cultural provisions, which sets up the miracle. They were in the wilderness. The accouterments of life were not available.

When Jesus saw the people He was moved with compassion for them. He felt bad or sorry for them because they were like sheep without a shepherd. When we hear Jesus describe people as sheep, we usually imagine scenes of pastoral beauty and romantic quietude. But the fact of the matter is that sheep are dumb. They don't have any sense. You may have come across a dumb dog at some time in you life. Well, dumb dogs are way ahead of smart sheep. Most sheep simply wouldn't survive without the shepherd's care. And that is the heart of Jesus' analogy. Neither would we.

So, Jesus began to teach them. He spent the rest of the day engaged in teaching. As the day drew to a close, the disciples came to Him and suggested that He send them away so that they could find food and provisions for the night. They reminded Jesus that they were a long way from anything.

> "This is a deserted place, and already the hour is late. Send them
> away, that they may go into the surrounding country and
> villages and buy themselves bread; for they have nothing to eat"
> (vs. 35-36).

It is not insignificant that the disciples suggested that the people be dismissed so that they could buy food. The point is that the disciples were culturally dependent. They could not imagine any source of food other than what was supplied by the local economy. Where would so many people get food in such an isolated place? They forgot or ignored or just didn't know about God's providence. God always provides for His people. The feeding of the five thousand was reminiscent of Israel in the wilderness. Israel depended upon God's provision. The point was clear: God still provides for His people. Nothing has changed in that regard.

Who knows exactly what happened on that particular day? The value of Scripture is never realized by trying to figure out how God works. *How* is the engineer's question. Engineers always want to know how so that they can do it themselves. But Scripture doesn't tell us how God works miracles, only that He sometimes does. The how question simply isn't answered. But the why question is. Scripture encourages people to ask why? Why did God multiply the loaves and fishes? Why does God provide for His people? To ask why is to ask about God's purpose. But the how question seeks to be like God, to try to appropriate His power.

Indeed, that is the very issue that resulted in the Fall of Man in the first place! Does that mean that all engineers are sinners? Well, all engineers are sinners, but not because they are engineers, but because they are fallen men. Nor is engineering a particularly sinful occupation. As long as it serves God, all is well. But that's true about any occupation. It is only as work begins to serve the selfishness of the individual or the human-centeredness of social causes does it begin to reveal the tenacity of man's fallen nature.

Jesus told His disciples to give the crowd something to eat. The disciples responded with astonishment, thinking that Jesus wanted them to spend their entire purse on one meal. The sense of the dialog here suggests that the disciples didn't have a clue about what Jesus wanted them to do.

Jesus always directs people to faithfully depend on God. But the disciples either didn't get the point, or didn't know what to do about it. So when it came to providing for the crowd, all they could think of was buying food for them. But that wasn't at all what Jesus meant.

He told them to see what supplies they had with them. Five loaves and two fish. It wasn't much, but it was enough. While the disciples added little to the miracle that day, they gave all they had. Like the poor widow who put her only pennies in the Temple coffers (Mark 12:42), or the time God multiplied the widow's flour to keep Elijah alive (1 Kings 17:16). God knows how to multiply.

John mentioned that a boy contributed "five barley loaves and two small fish" (John 6:9) to the cause. But there is no mention that anyone else contributed anything to their meal that day. Scripture simply says that the boy's five loaves and two fish were distributed and everyone was satisfied. And that's right! We simply contribute what we have to the Lord. We must be willing to offer God whatever we have, and be content when we have nothing to contribute, and receive whatever God provides. Miracles are miracles precisely because they are beyond our means and our understanding. Explanation has a way of crowding out the miraculous.

But another thing happened that day. Jesus organized the people. Earlier He commented that they were like sheep without a shepherd, lost and without order. But here in verse 39 we see that Jesus imposed order upon them. He divided them into groups or ranks of fifty and a hundred. In Exodus 18:21 we find Moses imposing a similar organizational pattern upon Israel. Moses said,

> "you shall select from all the people able men, such as fear God,
> men of truth, hating covetousness; and place such over them to
> be rulers of thousands, rulers of hundreds, rulers of fifties, and
> rulers of tens."

Consequently, we can surmise that Jesus was in some way reinstating an ancient social organization that had fallen into disrepute, reemphasizing that ancient social order.

When we remember that Jesus' primary purpose was the establishment of His church and not the mere satisfaction of bodily desires, we will begin to look for the deeper significance of the miracle of the mass event that day. That the real miracle was institutional and related to the church is demonstrated by the similarity of the feeding of the five thousand to the service (institution) of holy communion.

"And when He had taken the five loaves and the two fish, He
looked up to heaven, *blessed and broke* the loaves, and gave them
to His disciples to set before them…" (v. 41, italics added).

Communion requires the institution of Christ's church. Communion is an institution of the church. It requires a kind of liturgical order
—not just an order of worship like a church bulletin, but an authoritative
order within the church that allows for the proper administration of
communion. Serving communion requires the division of labor and the
establishment of church authority—pastors, elders, deacons, etc. The two
things are bound up together into a functional unity. The point is that
the liturgical activity of the church requires the proper organization of
the church. Consequently, seeing this miracle as the mere provision of
bread and fish for five thousand people misses the deeper institutional
significance of the miracle. Jesus had taken a bunch of lost sheep and
moved them toward becoming a communion receiving body.

Yet, Christ's church was not yet born that day. John said that many
of the five thousand left the Lord as He continued to teach some of the
harder truths (John 6:66). Mark tells us in verse 52 that even the disciples

"had not understood about the loaves, because their hearts were
hardened."

Jesus had not yet completed His mission. He was headed for Jerusalem,
to the cross. The cross was the central element in His ministry and He
must accomplish God's purpose on the cross in order to establish the
gospel offer of forgiveness of sin.

What was missing that evening of the feeding of the five thousand
was the reality of the Holy Spirit in the lives of believers. The Holy
Spirit had not yet been poured out. That would come later. And as it
came the disciples would then remember this feast with the Lord, and
how He began to organize lost sheep into a functional church and
miraculously fed them with the bread of heaven, the bread of life.

The miracle was far from over. Not only was there the application
of it to the organization of the church, but the miracle that happened
that day provided a great abundance of God's blessing—more bread and
fish than they could eat. They were not only satisfied by the miracle of
Christ, but the miracle had provided an abundance of blessing to share
with a hungry world. The disciples gathered up baskets of leftovers.
Scripture doesn't tell us what they did with the leftovers, but it's easy to
imagine that they used God's blessing to feed the saints, and to reach the
lost with gospel of salvation.

24. Eyes of Faith

Immediately He made His disciples get into the boat and go before Him to the other side, to Bethsaida, while He sent the multitude away. And when He had sent them away, He departed to the mountain to pray. Now when evening came, the boat was in the middle of the sea; and He was alone on the land. Then He saw them straining at rowing, for the wind was against them. Now about the fourth watch of the night He came to them, walking on the sea, and would have passed them by. And when they saw Him walking on the sea, they supposed it was a ghost, and cried out; for they all saw Him and were troubled. But immediately He talked with them and said to them, 'Be of good cheer! It is I; do not be afraid.' Then He went up into the boat to them, and the wind ceased. And they were greatly amazed in themselves beyond measure, and marveled. For they had not understood about the loaves, because their heart was hardened. —Mark 6:45-52*

Jesus was exhausted before the feeding of the five thousand. He and the disciples had been on their way to a well-deserved vacation in the country, away from the press of the crowds, when word leaked out about their destination and the crowds followed them into the wilderness. There had been no opportunity for rest. As soon as Jesus saw the people and their pitiful condition—leaderless and purposeless—He began to teach them. He taught them all day.

He knew there would be no rest as long as the crowds were present. So, immediately following the miraculous meal, He gathered the disciples together and sent them across the sea. Jesus did not go with them, but remained behind to dismiss the people and to pray. Scripture doesn't tell us what was on Jesus' mind, just that He dismissed the crowd and "departed to the mountain to pray" (v. 46).

The setting of this scene is significant, so it will benefit us to make sure we see it. Evening had come and darkness had settled on the land. Jesus had sent the disciples away. He Himself remained behind to pray. Jesus had put a distance between Him and the disciples.

135

He was praying, while they were rowing. He was being refreshed in prayer, they were working up a sweat rowing against the wind. They were rowing against the natural flow of their environment. Their boat no doubt had sails, but they were heading directly into the wind. So, they had to row rather than tack. The fact that they were rowing against the wind meant that they were moving toward their destination under their own power. They were going where Jesus told them to go, but they were doing it under their own effort.

> "Then He saw them straining at rowing, for the wind was against them" (v. 48).

Interesting. Darkness had fallen, the disciples were out in a boat, Jesus was on the mountain praying, when He saw them. We don't need to spiritualize it by saying that Jesus saw them with the eyes of prayer. He could have, but He could just as well have seen them out on the water from His position high in the hills under a clear, moonlight sky.

It doesn't matter how He saw them, just that He saw them straining, toiling in the dark and apart from Him, against their natural environment, to get where He had sent them. Against the wind. They were straining against the wind. The wind was blowing against them, and they were working hard to travel against its current.

In many ways the disciples on that little boat that night on their way to Bethsaida in obedience to the Lord were a lot like the church. The scene serves as an analogy for the church, in a way. The church is like a boat with a sail. In and of itself it is useless, it requires wind to make it useful. The church is too often working up a lather trying to get where the Lord has sent it, straining against its natural environment, which blows and howls against it in the darkness. The church is too often in the dark without the Lord, working under its own power.

It was the fourth watch, late into the night, at the darkest hours of the night. Storm clouds were about to overtake the disciples, as they breathlessly pressed for the goal set before them. It's an interesting image that can provide a lot of food for thought.

Then Jesus "came to them" (v. 48) at the darkest point of the night. They were staining against their environment in the dark when He came to them. They hadn't called on Him. Rather, He had come to them unbidden. And how did He come to them? Quite unexpectedly. He came to them in a way that they could not have imagined was even possible. He came to them "walking on the sea" (v. 49).

There is no doubt why the disciples thought they saw a ghost. No man could walk on water. So, what looked like a man, they concluded, was a ghost, "and they cried out" (v. 49). They were frightened, scared out of their wits. Mark tells us that "they all saw Him and were troubled" (v. 50).

Troubled puts it mildly! Miracles are always troubling because they disturb our most fundamental categories of thought. They challenge our basic understanding of reality. They make us doubt what we thought we had understood. Genuine miracles are deeply disturbing. They shake the foundations of our knowledge and of our society, indeed, of our very sanity. Jesus came to them walking on the sea!

It would have been bad enough to have just seen Jesus walking on the water that night. But it got worse, more intimidating, more disturbing. If we could just rack it up to fatigue or some sort of hallucination, we could dismiss it. But Jesus spoke to them. Seeing a ghost is scary enough, but having one talk to you is even worse. Worse because it becomes more difficult to dismiss, more difficult to explain, more difficult to admit that you don't know as much as you thought you did. Or that you can't trust what you thought you knew as much as you want to.

"Be of good cheer!" Jesus said, "It is I; do not be afraid." (v. 50). Right! They just had the rug pulled out from under their very comprehension of reality itself, and Jesus wants them to be glad about it! Be happy. It's a lot like working hard all your life for retirement, and then one day something happens and you lose everything—a death, a flood, a bankruptcy, an accident. The nest that you had feathered for so many years, the rock upon which all your hopes have rested, is suddenly down the river, and some guy comes along and says, *Cheer up.*

Notice that Jesus' greeting is the same as all of the angelic greetings of Scripture. Angels always tell people not to be afraid, which suggests that seeing something divine usually elicits a response of fear. In the case of the disciples in the boat that night, the very thing that they feared— Christ coming to them unexpectedly—was the Rock of their salvation. Imagine that! The very thing that they feared so much turned out to be the means of their salvation.

It was bad enough to see a ghost, even worse to have the ghost speak to them, but when He "went up into the boat to them" (v. 51) they were scared to death, ready to abandon ship. Now we're talking heart failure! Notice that Mark said that Jesus spoke to them, but he didn't say anything about them speaking to Jesus. Matthew recorded that Peter answered Jesus,

"Lord, if it is You, command me to come to You on the water"
(Matthew 14:28).

You gotta love Peter! In his impetuosity he was ready to meet the
Lord in the water. You can imagine him thinking, *If He can do, then I
can do it!* And sure enough, The Lord commanded it, "Come."
So Peter got

"out of the boat (and) walked on the water to go to Jesus"
(Matthew 14:29).

But as soon as Peter realized the awe inspiring situation he was in he began to be afraid. When he realized that he was actually walking on water in the middle of the lake in the midst of a brewing storm he was
overcome with fear. He knew that he couldn't walk on water by his
own power, and that the situation was proving to be more than he
could handle. So he called upon the Lord to save him—which He did. As
Jesus grabbed Peter's hand to keep him from going under He pointed
out Peter's problem, "O you of little faith, why did you doubt?"
(Matthew 14:31). Peter had enough faith to get out of the boat and try
it, but not enough to sustain himself. That was often Peter's problem.

Whatever else happened that night, when Jesus finally got into the
boat the disciples were awe struck. Matthew said that they "worshiped
Him saying, 'Truly, You are the Son of God'" (Matthew 14:33). Mark
said that

"they were greatly amazed in themselves beyond measure, and
marveled" (v. 51).

And John said that they "willingly received Him into the boat" (John
6:21). John's point is well taken. Though they were afraid, astonished,
and awed they received Him willingly, not without fear, astonishment
and awe, but willingly nonetheless.

As soon as the Lord got into the boat with them, "the wind ceased"
(v. 51). The storm passed. The sea calmed. Mark didn't say that they quit
rowing, but with Christ in the boat they quit working so hard to get to
their destination. Perhaps they raised the sail, Scripture doesn't say. But
whatever else happened, it was easier with Christ in the boat.

At that point they were, no doubt, relieved, at least a little. So, with
Jesus at the helm they could just kick back and enjoy the trip, right?
That's not what Mark said. Mark said that "they were greatly amazed in
themselves beyond measure" (v. 51). They were having a kind of salvation experience. First they were scared to death, then they were saved

from the storm that threatened them. And finally they were amazed beyond measure. That's a lot of amazement!

Everybody wants to be saved. People don't even mind a little amazement now and then. But nobody wants to be scared to death. The disciples were scared when Jesus came to them. Had they called on Him, they might have been prepared. But He came to them of His own choosing. He came to them before they realized who He was. He came to them before they knew that He could save them. He came to them unexpectedly.

The miracle of Jesus walking on the water is a perfect demonstration of a loving God saving a perishing people. But verse 52 comes like a cold shower first thing in the morning. They didn't get it! The *disciples* didn't get it. They didn't understand. They saw the miracle all right, but they didn't understand it. They saw the suspension of the laws of nature that allowed Jesus to walk on water—and Peter as well, but they failed to see its deeper purpose or meaning.

Inside the story of the physical miracle of Jesus walking on the water there is a greater, spiritual miracle, a more important miracle. It's wonderful that Jesus could walk on water, but what is walking on water compared to salvation itself. The Lord had come unbidden to save them from perishing, and they were worried about how He could walk on water! God brought them salvation, and they were worried about their sanity. Never mind that they were saved from a certain death in the midst of a violent storm! They were worried about what they would tell their friends.

Mark said that

> "They had not understood about the loaves, because their heart
> was hardened" (v. 52).

These are the *disciples*, mind you! Why is it that they had just been saved by the Lord walking out on the sea to rescue them, and Mark tells us that they never understood about the feeding of the five thousand? What's the feeding of the five thousand got to do with the walking on water?

The common theme is that they didn't understand either miracle. Jesus had just performed two back-to-back miracles right in front of the disciples. And they didn't get it! When Mark said that "their heart was hardened" (v. 52) he meant that their heads were like bricks. Mark's point was that they had just witnessed two genuine miracles. They were mightily impressed with what Jesus could do—multiply food, walk on water. And those were certainly miraculous things. The disciples had actually witnessed them and marveled about them. They had been there. They raved about the multiplication of food and walking on the sea.

They witnessed miracles, and marveled at their wonder. They proclaimed that Jesus was a miracle worker. But in spite of it all, Mark said, they didn't understand the miracles. They thought of them like they thought of magic, and that wasn't it. The disciples had missed the most important thing about Jesus' miracles.

It is as if Mark was trying to rub the reader's nose in the deeper significance of the miracles. By calling our attention to the fact that the disciples didn't understand the miracles, Mark called his readers to look more closely for the deeper purpose and significance of Jesus' miracles. Mark was trying to tell us that the miracles were not what they seemed to be, that there was more to them than appearances, more than what meets the eye, more than the mere supernatural manipulation of nature.

If all we understand is that Jesus multiplied loaves and fish to feed hungry people, we will miss it too. If we believe that Jesus can walk on water and leave it at that, our hearts and heads are as hard as the disciples. Mark is calling us to see the deeper spiritual reality that underlies the miracles. He wants us to see the purpose of the miracles.

Can you see it? Or are you frightened by what you don't understand? Are you afraid of the future? Of the unknown? Afraid of what it holds for you? Or are you trusting in Jesus? Are you willing and able to follow Jesus into deeper truth?

25. THE MASTER'S TOUCH

When they had crossed over, they came to the land of Gen-
nesaret and anchored there. And when they came out of the
boat, immediately the people recognized Him, ran through that
whole surrounding region, and began to carry about on beds
those who were sick to wherever they heard He was. Wherever
He entered into villages, cities, or in the country, they laid the
sick in the marketplaces, and begged Him that they might just
touch the hem of His garment. And as many as touched Him
were made well.　　　　　　　　　　　　　—Mark 6:53-56

When Jesus and disciples disembarked the boat the people recognized Him. In order to understand the importance of this recognition and the reaction of the people we must understand where this took place. Jesus crisscrossed the Sea of Galilee several times during His ministry, so we need to know where He has now landed according to Mark, and who these people are who recognized Him.

Jesus began His ministry in Galilee, which is located West of the Sea of Galilee. On the Northwestern coast lay Capernaum, the seaport of Tiberias was on the Southwestern coast. In the Western hills were Cana and Nazareth. Thus, Jesus' ministry began on the Western side of the Sea of Galilee. There He preached the "kingdom of God" (Mark 1:15), and began gathering His disciples (Mark 1:17). At Capernaum He cast out an unclean spirit (Mark 1: 25), and healed Simon Peter's mother-in-law (Mark 1:31). In Galilee He preached repentance (Mark 1:38) and cleansed a leper (Mark 1:41). At Capernaum He healed a paralytic (Mark 2:5).

It was at Capernaum that Jesus began to encounter outright resistance to the gospel. When the Pharisees questioned Him about why His disciples did not fast, He proclaimed Himself Lord of the Sabbath (Mark 2:27). To establish His Lordship over the Sabbath, Jesus healed a man with a withered hand during worship at a Capernaum synagogue (Mark 3:5).

The public healing and ensuing conflict caused a great multitude to follow Him. "He healed many" in that multitude (Mark 3:10), and cast out many "unclean spirits" (Mark 3:11) from them. Then He withdrew from the crowds to commission the twelve disciples (Mark 3:14), but the multitudes continued to follow Him wherever He went (Mark 3:20).

At this point those sent from Jerusalem accused Jesus of being a divisive radical (Mark 3:22), to which Jesus responded by telling them that if they didn't recognize the presence and power of the Holy Spirit, they would put their eternal salvation at risk (Mark 3:29). His family then tried to dissuade Him from the prophetic path He had taken (Mark 3:31), to no avail. And again, the crowds pressed Him as He told the parable of the sower and explained the purpose of the parables to the twelve disciples (Mark 4:12).

When He finished telling several parables to the multitude, He and the disciples crossed over to the other side of the Sea of Galilee to the Eastern shore. There He healed the Gadarene Demoniac, and disturbed the Gentile pig farmers, who asked Him to leave. He went back to the Western side (Mark 5:21), and healed the woman with the twelve year blood flow (Mark 5:25), and resurrected the twelve-year-old daughter of an elder of a nearby synagogue (Mark 5:38).

Rejected in his home town of Nazareth (Mark 6:3), Jesus sent out the twelve disciples into the countryside to preach repentance, to heal the sick, and to cast out unclean spirits (Mark 6:7). When the disciples returned from that preaching tour, they went with Jesus to a secluded place to rest (Mark 6:31). But the crowds again followed them (Mark 6:33). There Jesus fed the five thousand (Mark 6:44). That evening Jesus sent the disciples back across the Sea of Galilee (Mark 6:45), and during that trip they encountered Him walking on the water (Mark 6:48).

When they returned,

> "when they had crossed over, they came to the land of
> Gennesaret and anchored there" (Mark 6:53).

Gennesaret was near Capernaum on the Western side of the Sea of Galilee. That is significant because the Western side was where most of Jesus' ministry had taken place, and that is why the people there recognized Him. But what did they recognize about Him?

They took Him to be a healer and a worker of miracles. The point is that the people did not yet recognize that He was the Promised Messiah, but thought of Him as another Prophet in the Old Testament tradition. That is to say, that they sought from Him healings, miracles, and guidance, but not salvation. We can surmise this because of how the people responded to Him when they recognized Him.

We should not underestimate the value or importance of the biblical prophets. They were highly valued and historically significant individuals, who in many cases were miracle workers and healers themselves. The Promised Messiah, however, was in an altogether different category. So, we should not be surprised that they didn't recognize Jesus as Messiah at this point. But we should simply note the fact that they didn't. They

> "ran through that whole surrounding region, and began to carry about on beds those who were sick to wherever they heard He was" (Mark 6:55).

The people (not the disciples, but the people) went about proclaiming Jesus to be a healer, but said nothing about Him being the Messiah. The people flocked to Jesus, not for eternal salvation, but for the healing of their temporal aches, pains, and diseases.

As we have been discussing for some time now, this understanding of Jesus, while true—He could heal and perform miracles—missed the more important significance of His ministry. Jesus came to put an end to the Old Testament system of religious sacrifices, to offer Himself as the only acceptable sacrifice for the atonement of sin, and to open the eternal gospel of grace to the whole world. None of which required healing or miracles of the kind that the crowds continued to clamor for.

Yet, in spite of the fact that the crowds failed to understand the real purpose or nature of His ministry, Jesus accommodated Himself to their ignorance. He reached down to their level of ignorance in order to pull them up into a greater understanding of God's truth. He healed them because He knew that their pain and sickness would only distract them from God's deeper truths. If they were to come to any understanding of His real ministry and mission, they needed to be relieved of those things that distracted them, that stole from them the ability to concentrate and contemplate higher things, deeper things, greater things.

What a great God we have! In spite of God's perfect wisdom and power and might, He humbly stooped to accommodate Himself to our poor and faulty understanding, so that we might not only be saved, but become His friends. Through Christ, God reaches out to heal—yes, but more importantly, to save. And once He does, He so loves and cares for His people that He wants them to grow and mature in grace through

His mercy and tender care, so that they may be in a meaningful and personal relationship with Him through His Beloved Son, Jesus Christ.

In order to

> "come to the unity of the faith and of the knowledge of the Son
> of God, to a perfect man, to the measure of the stature of the
> fullness of Christ" (Ephesians 4:13),

we all must enjoy a measure of health and healing. But to think that our health and healing is the end or purpose of Christ's coming is to seriously misunderstand and misinterpret the gospel.

Yet, because of our depravity and sin, we find that the better our health, the more tempted we are to forget God. Few are the people who enjoy good health and at the same time truly love the Lord as He commands. Why that is I don't know! But it certainly seems to be true. Those for whom life is pleasant and easy are most often farthest from the Lord. So, while it is true that too much illness can distract us from God, so can too much health.

Consequently, it seems that in order to keep us appropriately focused and occupied with Godly concerns, He provides healing for some of the sick and chastisement for all those whom He loves.

> "For whom the Lord loves He chastens, And scourges every son
> whom He receives" (Hebrews 12:6).

God's purpose is not simply to make people feel better. His purpose is to shape His people into the likeness of Christ. And more often than not, God's chosen means for doing this is suffering.

But those whom Christ healed in the land of Gennesaret that day didn't know that, nor could they have known the fullness of Scripture at that point because the fullness of Scripture wasn't available to them. All they had was Christ (and the Old Testament), and though they misunderstood the deeper significance of His ministry, they understood His power and His grace and His mercy. So they

> "begged Him that they might just touch the hem of His
> garment" (Mark 6:56).

Oh, that God's people would have that kind of passion and commitment for Christ today, when we know that the real significance and meaning of Christ's ministry is not found in His garment, nor in the healing of our maladies, but in the eternal significance of His Word! Yes, Christ is the light of the world, but we don't have Christ in the flesh today. Rather, He has given us and the whole world something far greater than miraculous signs and wonders. He has given us, who live so far from the Jesus of history, a greater revelation of the fullness of His grace and mercy by leaving to us His Word, His Holy Spirit and His Church. His Word to instruct us, His Holy Spirit to guide us, and His Church in which to dwell.

These gifts are so much greater than the passing satisfactions of bodily healing. What is the healing of my body compared to the salvation of the world in Christ Jesus? Similarly, what is the death or destruction of my body compared to the insurmountable wisdom of God's Word and the indomitable strength of His Holy Spirit?

It is not my suffering that is significant, but Christ's death on the cross. It is not my aches and pains that keep me from Christ, but the distractions and desires of my own lusts. It is not the healing of my arthritis that will make the critical difference in my life, but the salvation of my soul by Christ's atonement of my sin.

God sent His only Begotten Son to die on the cross for the salvation of your soul. Isn't that enough? What more do you want? God has accommodated His glorious wisdom to our foolish ignorance. He has provided us with the fullness of His Word, the presence of His Holy Spirit, and the blessing of His Church. Isn't that enough? Of course it is.

26. Far From God

Then the Pharisees and some of the scribes came together to Him, having come from Jerusalem. Now when they saw some of His disciples eat bread with defiled, that is, with unwashed hands, they found fault. For the Pharisees and all the Jews do not eat unless they wash their hands in a special way, holding the tradition of the elders. When they come from the market-place, they do not eat unless they wash. And there are many other things which they have received and hold, like the washing of cups, pitchers, copper vessels, and couches. Then the Pharisees and scribes asked Him, 'Why do Your disciples not walk according to the tradition of the elders, but eat bread with unwashed hands?' He answered and said to them, 'Well did Isaiah prophesy of you hypocrites, as it is written: "This people honors Me with their lips, But their heart is far from Me. And in vain they worship Me, Teaching as doctrines the commandments of men." For laying aside the commandment of God, you hold the tradition of men—the washing of pitchers and cups, and many other such things you do.' He said to them, 'All too well you reject the commandment of God, that you may keep your tradition. For Moses said, "Honor your father and your mother"; and, "He who curses father or mother, let him be put to death." But you say, "If a man says to his father or mother, Whatever profit you might have received from me is Corban"— (that is, a gift to God),then you no longer let him do anything for his father or his mother, making the word of God of no effect through your tradition which you have handed down. And many such things you do.' —Mark 7:1-13

The scribes and Pharisees from Jerusalem caught up with Jesus again. The last time Jesus encountered them in Mark they had gone

> "out and immediately plotted with the Herodians against Him,
> how they might destroy Him" (Mark 3:6).

They now caught up with Jesus in the midst of His ministry in this crowd. They were out to get Him and they immediately set to work. They came looking for a reason to find fault.

> "Now when they saw some of His disciples eat bread with
> defiled, that is, with unwashed hands, they found fault" (v. 2).

Spiritual purity was the perfect issue to confront Jesus with, or so thought the Pharisees. They thought themselves to excel in spiritual purity. That's what being a Pharisee was all about. They figured that they had the upper hand regarding spiritual purity, so when they saw these lowly fishermen eating without even washing their hands, they drew their line in the sand. Everybody knew that

> "the Pharisees and all the Jews do not eat unless they wash their
> hands in a special way, holding the tradition of the elders. When
> they come from the marketplace, they do not eat unless they
> wash" (vs. 3-4).

They figured that they had Him right where they wanted Him, on the defensive. He would have to defend His obvious spiritual impurity, His violation of God's Law. They thought they had Him. He was obviously guilty, and they nailed Him! They spat their words at Jesus with a sense of moral superiority that would come to be known the world over as Pharisaic hypocrisy,

> "Why do Your disciples not walk according to the tradition of
> the elders, but eat bread with unwashed hands?" (v. 5).

Jesus' reply is quite startling to our contemporary sensitivities, understanding Jesus as a kind and compassionate hero who loved everybody and who bent over backwards to make sure that no one was offended. We've turned Jesus into a kind of nanny, or a cruise director, whose job it is to see that everyone is happy and has their needs met. Gentle Jesus, meek and mild.

"You hypocrites!" *Jesus said.* "Well did Isaiah prophesy of (you)..." (v. 6)! Hypocrisy appeared to be a major sin in Jesus' day. At least He railed against it an awful lot. And the Pharisees provided a ready target. Worse than thieves and prostitutes, worse than sodomites and murderers were the hypocrites, in Jesus' opinion. Hypocrisy is the act of presenting one's self—one's character, feelings, or beliefs—as being other than they really are. It's putting on a false face. It's hiding your feelings. It's saying you do when you don't, or saying you don't when you do. It's pretending to be someone you aren't. Its root is deceit. The word comes from the Latin which literally means pretender.

There's a great commercial on TV about hypocrisy. Maybe you've seen it. A dedicated sports fan tells us that he is definitely not superstitious. Then you see him at a game, going through several superstitious gyrations that are supposed to provide good luck for his team. I'm not even sure what it advertises. But the point is that this guy engages in behavior that he just denied ever doing. It's so ridiculous that it's funny. But as we laugh at such bizarre behavior, we grow more accustomed to accepting hypocrisy as normal. However, something is not right just because a bunch of people do it.

Then there's the TV show called *The Pretender.* It's about a guy who is an expert at pretending to be someone he's not. He pretends to be a doctor or a lawyer or whatever, and has many exciting exploits doing so. He is the envy of all who watch because he seems to be able to go anywhere and do anything. He is the epitome of personal freedom. But he is a hypocrite by definition.

Jesus quotes Isaiah's definition of hypocrisy.

> "This people honors Me with their lips, But their heart is far from
> Me. And in vain they worship Me, teaching as doctrines the
> commandments of men" (vs. 7-8).

Lord, let the scales fall from our eyes and the cotton from our ears so that we may acknowledge the truth of your Word, the truth of our own sanctimoniousness. These words of Scripture are for anyone who claims to be religious, and everyone who claims to be spiritual. This is the very heart of Jesus' message to the world. The fact that Jesus offers salvation to all implies that all are hopelessly lost without Him.

The Jews took particular offense at this implication because they considered themselves to be God's elect, the chosen people of God. They had the Law and the Prophets. They thought that their salvation was guaranteed by the promises of Scripture. They were the ones who maintained the ancient traditions and sacrifices instituted by Moses. Who was Jesus to tell them that they were lost? That was the issue. That was the rub. They thought that they were already saved. They thought that they didn't need what Jesus offered. Had Jesus been a good Rabbi Himself, He would have joined them in condemning the world. Sure, everybody else was damned, but not them. Not the Jews, especially not the Pharisees!

The funny thing is that we Christians can (and do) argue the same position today. Christians are God's elect. Claiming to be a Christian means being saved by the blood of Christ. So when people come into our churches saying that we aren't Christian or arguing the necessity of a so-called second blessing or of some additional charismatic experience of some kind, we balk. What are you talking about? We're already saved!

Are you?! If Christian salvation is genuine, then why does the world not believe it? Why do those who don't claim to be righteous, or spiritual, or Christian accuse the church and/or Christians of hypocrisy? If Christian salvation—commitment to Christ—is so genuine, why is the world so able to see through it? People claim to be Christian, yet various polls indicate that there is no significant difference between Christians and non-Christians in any area of social behavior or morality.

We know we are not saved because of our morality. We know that obedience is an expression of thankfulness for salvation, not the cause of salvation. But it seems that fewer and fewer Christians practice any biblical morality at all. Why? Are the second blessing people right? No, they are not. The problem is not that Christians need another spiritual experience to cement their salvation. The problem is that the church as a whole has allowed itself to become diluted with the desires and imaginations of men (humanity). Churches are more concerned about making everyone happy than defending the integrity of the Word of God. The problem is not the need of a second blessing. The problem is the hypocrisy of believing you are a Christian when there is no evidence to support your claim. What evidence? Walking in the faith, of course.

The purpose of the church is not to make people feel good about belonging to such a great and noble institution. The purpose of the church is not to esteem people into thinking that God is pleased to receive whatever little devotion or worship or stewardship that people begrudgingly give. The church is God's anvil upon which the hearts of repentant sinners are broken. It is the operating table upon which the Lord performs heart transplants. It is the hospital in which repentant, broken-hearted sinners recover. And when we try to make it anything other than that, when we try to make it conform to our own thoughts and desires, we move it away from God's purpose.

If there is a verse that the Jews could point to that justifies their accusation of Jesus, it is surely verse 9. Jesus said to the Pharisees,

"you reject the commandment of God, that you may keep your
tradition" (v. 9).

He told them that the religion they practiced was not of God. He accused the Pharisees—the keepers of God's Law—of having substituted
their own desires for God's. He accused the leaders of Judaism of being
man-centered rather than God-centered. In essence, He accused them of
idolatry, of substituting something other than God for God Himself.

This was not a new sin. Jesus quoted Isaiah, who had encountered
the same problem in his day. But the problem is older than Isaiah. It
goes back to the Golden Calf, even further to the Garden of Eden. Idolatry is very near the root of original sin itself. The problem of sin in our
lives is not something that gets taken care of in a flash. Rather, it is a fre-
quently recurring problem. The issue of sin is closely related to confusing our own personal thoughts and desires with God's thoughts and desires for us. It is about the correct discernment of God's will, about understanding God's Word, and about obedience.

How could those who were charged with keeping and defending
God's Word be guilty of misunderstanding, misinterpreting, and dis-
obeying it? I wish that this were an uncommon problem, an unusual oc-
currence in history, but it isn't. It is among the most common of sins, so
Jesus dealt with it directly. In order to stop the loss of blood from a
bleeding church, Jesus pressed hard upon the wound itself, like a medic
on a battlefield trying to save the life of a wounded soldier.

The practice known as *corban* was just such a sore spot. Jesus used
corban as an example to support His accusation that the Pharisees vio-
lated the Commandments of God. It pertains to the Fifth Commandment, "Honor your father and your mother" (Exodus 20:12). The Pharisees did not openly deny this commandment. They probably placed
much verbal importance on it, yet they contrived to make it void, of no
effect. How did they do this?

> "They taught that a man might dedicate to God's service, as
> sacred, any part of his property which might be applied to the
> relief of his parents, and so discharge himself from any further
> expense about them. He had only to say that all his money was
> '*corban*,'—that is, given over to holy purposes,—and no further
> claim could be made upon him for his father's or mother's
> support. Under pretense of giving God a prior claim, he set
> himself free from the burden of maintaining them forever. He
> did not flatly deny his duty to minister of his worldly substance

to his parents' necessities. But he evaded it by setting up a human tradition, and asserting a higher call of duty, even duty to God."[8]

In other words, financial contributions to the church obtained such a status as to take total precedence over other obligations. In this case the obligations of family responsibilities, obligations of obedience to the Ten Commandments, were overridden by either the individual's desire to support his church or the church's desire to solicit his money. A similar situation developed regarding indulgences during the Middle Ages. And it still happens today as contemporary cults and ministries solicit monies that God has a prior claim upon.

The bottom line of this practice was "making the word of God of no effect through your tradition" (v. 13). That is, anything that distracts from the effectiveness of God's Word is a kind of *corban*. And it is particularly detrimental when people claim to be godly, when people say that they are faithful, but are not. (This was the sin of Ananias and Sapphira, Acts 5:1–ff). Consequently, Jesus taught that the false profession of religion was worse than the sins of extortioners and harlots.

The difficulty with a false profession of religion is that people don't usually make such a profession with the intention of deceit. Rather, people justify their own beliefs and behaviors so that they seem good, or at least they don't appear to be bad. Rather, it is done out of genuine misunderstanding. People believe falsities about God or about Scripture or about themselves that cause them to believe something to be true which is not true.

For instance, people may claim that there is life on Mars. They may sincerely believe it, and tell others about it. They may be well read on the issue, may be able to explain many theories about life on Mars. They may live their lives with the hope and expectation that man will someday live on Mars. But when all is said and done there is no evidence of any life on Mars. They could have the best of intentions, and still be wrong.

I could have the best of intentions and still be wrong, as could you. So, how can we know that we are saved?

Jesus told Nicodemus, a Pharisee,

"unless one is born again, he cannot see the kingdom of God" (John 3:3).

So important was it that He repeated it,

---

8   Ibid., p. 139.

> "Most assuredly, I say to you, unless one is born of water and the Spirit, he cannot enter the kingdom of God" (John 3:5).

To be born again is to receive the gospel, to be saved. Salvation is not the fruit of what we have accomplished, nor of what we believe. Nor does salvation require any second blessing or charismatic experience. We are saved when God has slain the Old Man, and given birth to the New.

27. THE GOD WITHIN

When He had called all the multitude to Himself, He said to them, 'Hear Me, everyone, and understand: There is nothing that enters a man from outside which can defile him; but the things which come out of him, those are the things that defile a man. If anyone has ears to hear, let him hear!' When He had entered a house away from the crowd, His disciples asked Him concerning the parable. So He said to them, 'Are you thus without understanding also? Do you not perceive that whatever enters a man from outside cannot defile him, because it does not enter his heart but his stomach, and is eliminated, thus purifying all foods?' And He said, 'What comes out of a man, that defiles a man. For from within, out of the heart of men, proceed evil thoughts, adulteries, fornications, murders, thefts, covetousness, wickedness, deceit, lewdness, an evil eye, blasphemy, pride, foolishness. All these evil things come from within and defile a man.' —Mark 7:14-23

Having accused the Pharisees of hypocrisy, Jesus turned His attention to the crowd of people who had been following Him. Praying fervently that His preaching would not suffer the fate of Isaiah's, He commanded them to both listen and understand. While we might think that listening and understanding are the same thing, we find in Isaiah evidence that they are not the same.

The Seraphim that anointed Isaiah's lips for ministry instructed him to

> "Go, and tell this people: 'Keep on hearing, but do not understand; Keep on seeing, but do not perceive'" (Isaiah 6:9).

Jesus had earlier quoted these very words from Isaiah (Mark 4:12). God had prepared Isaiah for the fact that the people of his own generation would not understand or heed him. Understanding Isaiah's ministry would require the fulfillment of his prophecy. We, of course, know that Isaiah prefigured the coming of Christ, that Isaiah's prophecy would be fulfilled some seven hundred years after it was written.

Jesus gave His listeners a one sentence parable.

> "There is nothing that enters a man from outside which can
> defile him; but the things which come out of him, those are the
> things that defile a man" (v. 15).

The source of human sin is nothing other than the unrepentant heart,
the unconverted mind, the unsaved habits that infect and affect everybody. No one is exempt from the plague of original sin, the tendencies
of the flesh to seek their own satisfaction.

Medical doctors tell us that we all have residing within our bodies
every disease known to man. Every virus or germ that can steal our
health is already alive within us. However, we are protected by an immune system that keeps the numbers of these aberrant viruses to a man-
ageable level. The immune system acts like a police force that keeps the
parasitic organisms in check. There is an analogy between the physical
state of our bodies and the condition of our souls.

We are often prone to think that the children we know and love—
be they neighbors, grandchildren, or our own children—are "good"
children, and that they are negatively affected by the bad examples of
other "not-so-good" children, or by the negative effects of television,
etc. We naturally want to think that our good children are corrupted by
the negative elements in society. And such a belief is partially true! Paul
cautioned,

> "Do not be deceived: 'Evil company corrupts good habits'" (1
> Corinthians 15:33).

That is true enough.

But there is another truth that is prior to that. I'm talking about the
truth of original sin, sometimes called total depravity or reprobation.
Man is totally depraved by nature. But depravity does not necessarily
mean someone who is so whacked out as to be a candidate for institu-
tionalization. It simply means someone who is morally corrupt, morally
impure according to God's standards. Similarly, a reprobate is someone
who is unprincipled or irreverent. And again, we are talking about
God's standards as given in Scripture.

Those who don't live up to God's moral standards are depraved
reprobates. That makes for a long list of people, for there is no one who
is not on it; "for all have sinned and fall short of the glory of God" (Romans 3:23). If we don't get this point clear, all our other thinking tends
to be obscured as well. We can read Romans 3:23 and understand that

all people are sinners, but unless the impact of the implications of this doctrine brings us to our knees in tears and to Godly sorrow that causes, not just feelings of repentance, but a life of repentance as well, we, like Isaiah's audience, have heard, but not understood what Jesus is trying to say.

Jesus said, "If anyone has ears to hear, let him hear!" (v. 16). What a curious thing to say! What does it mean? Why did He say that? He could have said, *Those who have ears to hear….* But He didn't. He said, "If anyone has ears to hear…," as if He meant, *Can anyone at all hear what I'm saying?!* We must remember the frustration Jesus had experienced because so many people had failed to understand Him so often. We tend to think that everyone can understand the Christian gospel, but not everyone chooses it. However, that is not what Jesus said.

Jesus distinguished between those who have physical ears and those who have ears to hear, suggesting that He knew that not everyone would understand Him. We know that Jesus did not mean that every-one was blessed with ears to hear the gospel. Otherwise this comment—which is heard so often from Jesus—would be a pointless redundancy. Why would He point out those with ears to hear unless He was address-ing a select group within His larger audience. Imagine Jesus' frustration as He pulled His disciples aside only to find that they, too, were among those who did not understand Him. "Are you thus without understand-ing also?" (v. 18).

He had just read the Pharisees the riot act, accusing them of reli-gious hypocrisy, and now He discovers that His own disciples don't have a clue as to what He is talking about. Neither the academically trained religious experts nor the self-taught, self-proclaimed religious experts knew what Jesus was getting at. This encounter in chapter seven demonstrates that genuine spiritual understanding comes neither from academic discipline nor from personal devotion or enthusiasm. Just as salvation does not come from the works of men, neither does spiritual understanding come from human effort.

That's not to say that human effort is not useful, it is! While prayer, study, and service are not the causes of salvation or of spiritual under-standing, they are the products of God's grace. While it is true that the fruits of the Spirit indicate the presence of God's grace, it is also true that God's grace is not evident in every human heart. Many unsaved people accomplish noble things in their lives, through their own efforts, and we should not discourage such noble productivity. But in the long run, works-righteousness cannot save. We should encourage hard work for good causes from the unsaved as well as the saved. But we should never be so confused as to think that God will save anyone because of their good works.

For instance, eating a healthy diet is a good thing to do whether or not you are a Christian. Washing your hands before you eat should be practiced by everyone. Honesty and integrity will be a blessing to all, both Christians and pagans. All people should strive for excellence of character and genuine spiritual understanding. However, astute Bible students will realize that such efforts can only be accomplished by the power of the Holy Spirit, and that those who genuinely engage Godly discipline also confess Jesus Christ as Lord and Savior.

Now, that does not mean that living a Godly life will cause a person to be saved. Rather, it means that the presence of the Holy Spirit in someone's life normally produces an increase of sincere Godly living. It's a subtle difference, but an important one. The logic flows in one direction only, just as genuine grace flows in only one direction, inexorably drawing the faithful into greater Christian maturity.

We should not be surprised by human sinfulness. It is our natural condition. God has promised to cure us of it, but not all at once. Rather, in Christ we live day by day, always in the midst of sin, but always with the hope of salvation from it. And always with the confidence that in Christ we shall overcome it. Even when we succumb to our temptations we must not lose hope. We must persevere in the difficult struggle to actually live our lives according to God's Word.

Husbands and wives must engage one another biblically. Parents and children must relate to one another biblically. Members of the church must gather and organize themselves according to the dictates of God's Word. To do anything less—even if we are assured of our salvation—is to forsake the fullness and the richness of the blessings that God has for His people. To live other than as God dictates—even if we are saved by grace—is to limp along, suffering the slings and arrows of outrageous fortune.

We must understand that the purpose of the church is not completed with a confession of salvation, rather Christian living *begins* with such a confession. While individual evangelization is fulfilled with the confession of Christian faith, sanctification is not. We are called to salvation—yes! But we are also called into Godly living and Godly relationships that bring spiritual maturity to our growth in grace. That maturity will increasingly produce genuine biblical worship and faithful biblical patterns of relationship and church government.

Too many churches stagnate spiritually because their whole focus is on bringing people to Christ. That's only half the job. The other half is helping the faithful grow in Christ, bringing others into a responsible and mature community of people who live the gospel personally and as a church to the best of their ability through the power of the Holy Spirit according to the Word of God.

Have you confessed Christ? Shared your personal commitment to Him with your brothers and sisters in Christ? If you have, are you growing in faithfulness? Are you learning? Are you relating to others biblically? Or are you content to just sit back and be a religious consumer? To be fed yourself—to receive, but not to help feed others—to receive but not give?

28. Dogged Persistence

*From there He arose and went to the region of Tyre and Sidon.
And He entered a house and wanted no one to know it, but He
could not be hidden. For a woman whose young daughter had
an unclean spirit heard about Him, and she came and fell at His
feet. The woman was a Greek, a Syro-Phoenician by birth, and
she kept asking Him to cast the demon out of her daughter.
But Jesus said to her, 'Let the children be filled first, for it is not
good to take the children's bread and throw it to the little dogs.'
And she answered and said to Him, 'Yes, Lord, yet even the little dogs under the table eat from the children's crumbs.' Then
He said to her, 'For this saying go your way; the demon has
gone out of your daughter.' And when she had come to her
house, she found the demon gone out, and her daughter lying
on the bed.*   —Mark 7:24-30

Jesus went to the "region of Tyre" (v. 24), but didn't want anyone to
know about it. The area had a long history of wicked ungodliness. It
was a port of sin, a haven for the heathen.

Mark isn't clear whether Jesus didn't want people to know that He
had gone to Tyre, or that He didn't want them to know that He had
gone into that particular house. Nor does Mark tell us why Jesus wanted
to keep it a secret, only that He did. Perhaps He was concerned about
the rumors that could develop if people had known that He visited such
a place. Was He hiding some secret sin? We know that He was not, but
the people of every age are prone to gossip. He had already been falsely
accused of many things.

Perhaps it wasn't so much that Jesus was concerned that people
knew of His journey to Tyre, but that on His journey "He entered a
(particular) house" (v. 24) in that vile land. Jewish custom forbade the
entering of a Gentile home. It could have been that that particular house
was known for its sinfulness, as if it were a house of ill repute. Or perhaps it was enough that Jesus entered the house of a woman in Tyre.
The issue of Jesus being with a woman behind closed doors reminds us
of our own political rumors, and of the damage they can wreak.

Mark said that Jesus didn't want anyone to know that He entered that house, but that Jesus' presence could not be hidden no matter where He went. There is no indication that Jesus made any attempt to cover the story up, only that He preferred that people not know about it.

Does this mean that Jesus cannot be the incarnation of God because if He was He would have known everything? And Mark would not have spoken as he did? That a divine Jesus would have known that people would find out? Not at all. The story is not given in its fullness—many things happened that are not reported. Rather, God has adapted Mark's story for our sake, that we might better understand the full revelation of God in Christ. The story, like all Bible stories, is adapted to the limitations of humanity and the necessities of God.

Jesus went to Tyre to perform a miracle, and, as often was the case, He didn't want the whole truth of the miracle to leak out prematurely. Several times He performed miracles and asked the recipients not to tell anyone. Jesus was in that kind of situation in Tyre.

The woman may have been a single mother, as there is no indication that a man lived with them—husband or otherwise. The woman was also a pagan, a Gentile, a "Syro-Phoenician by birth" (v. 26). Mark made a special effort to point out this fact because it relates to Jesus' ministry to the Gentiles. She was not Jewish, not familiar with the Jewish Law or Prophets. She had none of the advantages that the Jews had for recognizing and dealing with the ministry of Jesus. The Jews, of all people, should have recognized Jesus as the Messiah. But over and over we see that they didn't. Rather, we find that Gentiles were somehow better able to receive Jesus and the salvation he brought.

The woman's concern was not for herself, but for her daughter. Her concern was that Jesus "cast the demon out of her daughter" (v. 26). What demon? Mark said that the daughter had an "unclean spirit" (v. 25). Jesus had run into unclean spirits before. *Akathartos* means unclean in a ceremonial sense that relates to the Levitical law, and in a moral sense it means unclean in thought and life. We might best understand the word and Mark's use of it to mean unsaved, in the sense that salvation cleanses the heart of sin and guilt. In essence, then, the woman was unsaved, as all Gentiles are unsaved by definition. She was unsaved in the sense that she should have not understood the things of God. Yet, in spite of the fact that she was a Gentile, she hounded Jesus to cast the demon out of her daughter. She was engaged in intercessory prayer, lifting up her daughter before Jesus continually.

We find in this story the value and power of intercessory or incessant prayer, the value of a mother's prayer for her children. One of the most helpful things that we can do for someone else is to pray for them. Parent's prayers for their children are so precious in the sight of God, so valuable, so effective. We must never lose sight of the value of such prayer. This woman simply refused to give up hope. She hounded Jesus about it, asking and begging Him to do what she knew He alone could do.

We don't know how she knew about Jesus. Tyre was quite a way from the hills of Galilee. We can surmise that stories about Jesus abounded. But why did this particular woman believe the stories when so many others didn't? We don't know. And that is certainly part of the lesson that this story conveys. We don't know how the mercy and grace of God works. We don't know who will receive it and who won't. In fact, Scripture is replete with the frustration of human expectations in this regard. The Jews should have received and understood Jesus, but didn't. The Gentiles had no basis for understanding, but often did!

Furthermore, Jesus confounds our modern understanding of how ministry is supposed to work. Jesus wasn't nice to this woman. He wasn't kind to her. He wasn't patient with her. Rather, it seems that He tried to discourage her from spiritual pursuits.

> "Let the children be filled first, for it is not good to take the
> children's bread and throw it to the little dogs" (v. 27).

In essence Jesus called her a dog. How would you feel if you came in for counseling and I referred to you as a dog? Not very well, I think. You would probably get angry with me. But what if Jesus called you a dog? Would you get mad at Him?

The Jews commonly referred to all Gentiles as dogs. So, there was a social context for Jesus' words. That doesn't make it okay. Nonetheless, we simply note that such words could be expected from the lips of a Jew. So, let us understand these words to give credence to the human reality of this story because they point to the humanity of Jesus, because they carried a bit of a sting.

The point to notice is that Jesus didn't gush all over this woman by encouraging her to become a Christian or to receive God's grace or to receive the gospel. None of that! Rather, Jesus told the woman that the gospel was not for people (dogs) like her, that it was sent first to the Jews, that she should not expect anything because He had not yet reached the Jews. Let the children—that is the children of Israel—be first, He said. Matthew records Jesus as saying,

> "Do not give what is holy to the dogs; nor cast your pearls before swine, lest they trample them under their feet, and turn and tear you in pieces" (Matthew 7:6).

This woman replied almost as if she was familiar with this saying of Jesus. Jesus' concern here was the loss of respect for the wisdom of God, but this woman responded by saying that in her case there would be no loss of respect, but that, in fact, she would feed on whatever God would give her. She would not trample God's grace under foot. Rather, she would make use of it. That's a big difference. She acknowledged her "doghood"—her sin and unworthiness, and promised to feed on whatever crumbs of grace that came her way.

This is the essence of faith! Here was a woman who had nothing but faith in Christ. We don't know how she acquired that faith, but there is no evidence that she had any theological or biblical training. All she had was her faith and a prayer for her daughter.

Too many people today are quick to give up their faith unless they are coddled and spoon-fed at every point. People today want to be esteemed by their religion. People think that their faith or their church or their religion should make them feel good about themselves. So, when resistance or difficulties or "bumps" are encountered, they are quick to abandon the rough waters and go in search of smoother sailing. A statement like the one Jesus made in today's world would be poorly received. People would be offended and incensed. How many people, having received such a comment today, would persevere in faith like this woman did? Not many. And that's the point!

Faithfulness is not simply receiving God's grace, but it is persisting in that grace come what may. This woman believed that Jesus was the Messiah without any evidence or witnessing of miracles, and nothing would dissuade her. She wanted for her daughter something that she herself could not provide. Being a woman of Tyre she probably had not lived a clean life herself. She had not lived on the basis of God's wisdom, and she knew it. She didn't want her daughter to follow in her ways. But she could not prevent it herself.

So, she hounded Jesus to rid her daughter of the unclean spirit that inhabited her. Unclean spirits inhabited so many! She asked and prayed for Jesus to save her daughter from the corruption of a sinful world. To be clean, ceremonially and morally clean according to Scripture, is to be saved. The woman prayed for the salvation of her unsaved daughter. That's what the story is about.

Jesus was perfectly aware that He had come across a faithful woman, a woman who had sinned greatly, for sure! But a faithful woman nonetheless, not because she was herself pure or perfect, but because she depended on Jesus' purity, Jesus' perfection, and Christ's righteousness.

Because of this woman's confession, because of the words from her mouth and the prayers of her heart, Jesus said, "go your way" (v. 29), continue doing as you have done, continue believing and praying as you have, for "the demon has gone out of your daughter" (v. 29). She and her daughter were saved by her faith, by her persistent faithfulness.

Jesus had gone to Tyre to extend the gospel to the Gentiles. He had been utterly frustrated in Jerusalem and Samaria. His own people and His own family—even His own disciples—had failed to understand, failed to receive the grace He ministered. The prophets had warned that His own people would reject Him, and they did.

But this poor, uneducated, Gentile woman found salvation. She had the tenacity, the dogged persistence to hang in there with the Lord, even when it seemed as if He did not treat her well. She persisted in believing. She persisted in praying. Her situation in Tyre was pretty much hopeless. She had lived an unclean life, and her daughter was following in her footsteps, when Jesus unexpectedly went to Tyre and saved them both.

Could it happen to you? Can you be saved in spite of your sin and confusion? Does your situation seem hopeless, personally, or for your children? Don't believe it. Rather, believe the Lord for whom anything is possible, and pray.

29. Ears to Hear

Again, departing from the region of Tyre and Sidon, He came
through the midst of the region of Decapolis to the Sea of
Galilee. Then they brought to Him one who was deaf and had
an impediment in his speech, and they begged Him to put His
hand on him. And He took him aside from the multitude, and
put His fingers in his ears, and He spat and touched his tongue.
Then, looking up to heaven, He sighed, and said to him, 'Eph-
phatha,' that is, 'Be opened.' Immediately his ears were opened,
and the impediment of his tongue was loosed, and he spoke
plainly. Then He commanded them that they should tell no
one; but the more He commanded them, the more widely they
proclaimed it. And they were astonished beyond measure, say-
ing, 'He has done all things well. He makes both the deaf to
hear and the mute to speak.' —Mark 7:31-37

L eaving Tyre Jesus went to Decapolis, Southeast of the Sea of
Galilee. Mark mentioned Decapolis earlier. When the Gadarene
Demoniac was healed of his unclean spirit, Jesus sent him to Decapolis to preach the gospel (Mark 5:1-20). Perhaps Jesus had gone to
visit the man He had healed, and to see how his preaching had fared.

The Gadarene Demoniac must have had some success in his preaching for there were many who had heard that Jesus was able to heal.

> "Then they brought to Him one who was deaf and had an
> impediment in his speech, and they begged Him to put His Hand
> on him" (v. 32).

We need to look at this man's affliction and what his friends proposed
Jesus do about it.

The Gadarene Demoniac was sent to preach the Word in Decapolis.
No doubt, many were saved by his preaching. We know that preaching
or hearing God's Word is the ordinary means of salvation. People are
normally saved by hearing the Word. But this man could not hear the
Word preached because he was deaf. If salvation depended on physically
hearing the Word, this man could not be saved. He was different from

the Pharisees and the crowds who had refused to hear the Word from Jesus' lips. They were physically able to hear, but unwilling to receive God's Word. This man had another problem, he couldn't physically hear.

Neither could he speak. Those who work with the deaf know that learning to speak requires hearing because we learn to speak by mimicking others. The deaf can sometimes learn to speak a little, but it is stilted and difficult speech to understand because they don't know how words are supposed to sound. The man's speech impediment served to establish the authenticity of his deafness. He was not a stranger who proclaimed to be deaf, but a resident of Decapolis, a man people knew. They knew him to have been deaf from childhood, and brought him to Jesus.

But what did they want Jesus to do to him? Interestingly, they proposed the means of this man's cure—the laying on of hands. They knew, or thought they knew, that healing was effected by the laying on of hands. I'm reminded of the ads for prescription drugs that are occurring more regularly on television. People are encouraged to go to their doctor and tell him what cure they require. The methodology is backwards. The thinking reverses the standards of medical science. Patients don't tell doctors what they need to heal them, doctors tell patients.

They were frustrated because this man couldn't receive God's grace because he couldn't hear the gospel. Perhaps others had tried laying hands on him without success. So, they figured, if Jesus laid hands on him, he'd be healed for sure. They thought they knew how God's grace worked. And, knowing how it worked, they were ready to exploit it. We are all like that. As soon as we figure out the right method, we exploit it to serve our own desires. Those who think they know a surefire way to play the stock market, or to win at gambling, are quick to engage the process in the hope of striking it rich.

Surely Jesus could have healed this deaf man by merely speaking the Word, or even willing it to be so, as He had done to the Centurion's son (Matthew 8:13). But He didn't. No doubt, Jesus wanted to solve two problems here. First, He wanted to heal this deaf mute, and second, He wanted to mature the understanding of those who thought they knew how to control the grace of God. If healing, and by implication salvation, can be controlled by the laying on of hands, then it is no longer a function of God's grace. If we give it or cause it to be given, then it is no longer a gift. It's not grace when we control or effect it. Grace is grace only when it issues from the unconditional will of God.

Jesus "took him aside from the multitude" (v. 34) so that casual observers wouldn't think that they could heal someone by sticking their fingers in his ears and spitting on him. Someone would be sure to try it! So He pulled the man aside. Those who brought him were undoubtedly with him, watching. But the healing was not open to the whole crowd that had gathered.

What Jesus didn't do was to lay hands upon the man, as people expected Him to do. Rather, He

> "put His fingers in his ears, and He spat and touched his tongue"
> (v. 33).

Weird! What can we make of this? If we conclude that deaf people can only be healed with spit, we will have missed something important. Some people might be tempted to think that the healing was the result of saying a special or magical word because Jesus

> "look(ed) up to heaven, ...sighed, and said to him, '*Ephphatha*,'"
> (v. 34).

People are not beyond thinking such things. But again, such thinking is wrong.

Now, I can't tell you how this man was healed. I don't know—and that's the point Jesus was making. The Lord is not limited to prescribed methods of healing. He isn't limited by anything. His healing, His miracles, His grace and mercy cannot be controlled by us, nor can they be predicted by us. The Lord is simply not bound to heal or work miracles or extend His grace by prescribed methods, nor according to our thoughts and desires. That's the point Jesus made here. He confounded the expectations of those who thought they knew how God was supposed to work.

He also demonstrated that nothing can keep people from hearing the Word of God, except their own unwillingness. Not even physical deafness was an obstacle to hearing God's Word. Therefore, those who heard but didn't hear were without excuse. The gospel is to be preached to all. As God's love is unconditional, that is, not dependent upon any human circumstances, so the gospel is to be preached to everyone indiscriminately.

God intends that everyone hears the gospel for two reasons. First, to show His great mercy and compassion in that salvation is not reserved for any particular class of human beings—not Jews alone, not Gentiles alone, not males alone, not the rich and powerful alone, not adults alone.

None of that! Rather, the gospel is set before the whole world. And by this we see the greatness of God's mercy. And because no particular class of people is denied the gospel, we see that salvation is rejected only by the stubborn refusal of particular individuals, who of their own accord refuse to receive it.

In the midst of this healing miracle, Jesus "sighed" (v. 34). The Greek word is *stenazo*, which is used in the Septuagint for groaning in childbirth (Jeremiah 4:31), for mortal conflict (Ezekiel 26:15) and grief for the dead, for suffering, for judgment or eschatological events (Isaiah 24:7), and as a sign of penitence. Here it conveys the sense of grief. Jesus rolled His eyes skyward and sighed a sigh of grief. But why? What was the nature of Jesus' grief? He was about to heal this poor man. He should have been happy for him. But He was overwhelmed by grief. Why?

His grief was an expression of His disappointment because so many people were so spiritually blind. We recall His interaction with the Pharisees and the crowds that continued to follow Him—even His own disciples didn't understand. And now these Decapolites came to Him with a deaf mute, sure that they knew exactly how He ought to be healed—by the laying on of hands.

In conjunction with Jesus' sigh was the word *ephphatha*. Because Mark provided both the Aramaic and the Greek, we can surmise that the word was difficult to understand, or that it didn't translate easily or clearly. The best English rendering is "be opened," or "be no longer blocked or plugged." Jesus commanded that this man be open and receptive to His Word, that he not only be open to hearing in general, but that he be able to hear Jesus in particular. The implication is that the man be opened to hear God's Word, to have ears to hear the gospel.

No sooner had Jesus spoken the word, and the man's ears were opened and his tongue untied. He heard clearly and spoke plainly. Who can explain such a miracle? I certainly can't. Nor does it need explanation. It simply indicates that in Christ, nothing can keep a person from hearing the gospel. And that without Christ there can be no hearing of it.

Jesus commanded the man and his friends not to tell anyone about the miracle. Curious. Jesus restored the man's hearing. We have been talking about how the man was probably saved as well because it seems that he was healed, not only of his physical inability but of his spiritual inability as well. Finally, he heard the gospel and was saved.

His friends were standing around watching, and as soon as he was healed, they began shouting and praising God. They could hardly contain themselves. Caught up in the excitement of the moment, they weren't thinking about the lesson Jesus provided about the means of God's grace and mercy. They just began to praise God, to proclaim what God had done for their friend. It was a momentous occasion.

But they failed to hear what Jesus said. Thus, they failed to do what Jesus asked. "Tell no one," He commanded (v. 36). But they themselves failed to hear Him. It seems as if the more Jesus insisted, the less attention they paid to Him. It was great that this man had been healed, but the people of Decapolis did not listen to Jesus. One man was healed of deafness, yet many still failed to hear the Master. In direct disobedience to His words, the

> "more He commanded them, the more widely they proclaimed it" (v. 36).

Jesus was not trying to work reverse psychology here. He really didn't want the word to get out yet. So why did these otherwise faithful people not listen? Good question. Why are some people saved and others not? Good question. Why aren't the saved perfectly obedient to God's will? Good question. These are all great questions for which we don't have satisfactory answers. But why not?

The answers to these kinds of questions come with spiritual maturity. There is a difference between being saved and being spiritually mature. For many decades contemporary Christians have focused on issues of salvation and neglected issues of spiritual maturity—doctrine and history. The problem is that most everybody wants to be saved, but few are willing to engage the disciplines that produce maturity.

Consequently, we may have a lot of saved Christians these days, but certainly have few mature Christians. What do I mean? I mean that too few people have really applied themselves to Bible study. Too few people are familiar with Christian history and doctrine. Most people are content to get just enough "Spirit" to make them feel good, but not enough to make any real difference. While God wants all His people to go to heaven, knowing that you are heaven bound is not the end of the matter.

Rather, the assurance of one's own salvation is simply a prerequisite for the more difficult work of doing God's will "on earth, as it is in heaven." Salvation is not the end of the process, but the beginning. Being saved doesn't mean lying back and coasting into glory. Being saved is the first step in giving your life to Christ in grateful service.

Christ died that we may live. The confession of salvation is the confession that we have died to ourselves, so that Christ may live through us. His death serves our life, and our death, our spiritual death to ourselves, then, serves His life. Once we acknowledge our own death and rebirth, we are faced with living our lives in service to Him—not just now and then when it's convenient, but all the time. And that's where many people have missed the boat.

What about you? How are you serving Christ?

30. No Sign

In those days, the multitude being very great and having noth-
ing to eat, Jesus called His disciples to Him and said to them, 'I
have compassion on the multitude, because they have now
continued with Me three days and have nothing to eat. And if I
send them away hungry to their own houses, they will faint on
the way; for some of them have come from afar.' Then His dis-
ciples answered Him, 'How can one satisfy these people with
bread here in the wilderness?' He asked them, 'How many
loaves do you have?' And they said, 'Seven.' So He commanded
the multitude to sit down on the ground. And He took the
seven loaves and gave thanks, broke them and gave them to His
disciples to set before them; and they set them before the multi-
tude. They also had a few small fish; and having blessed them,
He said to set them also before them. So they ate and were
filled, and they took up seven large baskets of leftover frag-
ments. Now those who had eaten were about four thousand.
And He sent them away, immediately got into the boat with
His disciples, and came to the region of Dalmanutha. Then the
Pharisees came out and began to dispute with Him, seeking
from Him a sign from heaven, testing Him. But He sighed
deeply in His spirit, and said, 'Why does this generation seek a
sign? Assuredly, I say to you, no sign shall be given to this gen-
eration.'   —Mark 8:1-12

hapter eight brings another mass feeding miracle. There are
many similarities between this feeding of the four thousand and
the feeding of the five thousand. However, it is commonly understood that these are not differing reports of the same miracle, but actually different miracles of the same kind. I suspect that Jesus repeated
them for the sake of emphasis.

At this point in Jesus ministry the multitude that followed Him was
very large and had "nothing to eat" (v. 1). The fact that they had nothing to eat suggests that they were unprepared. It is not difficult to speculate that in those days people took food and provisions with them when

they traveled. That being the case, we surmise that the crowd that followed Jesus had probably taken some food and with them when they began. But they failed to accurately assess the distance that they would need to go in order to follow Jesus. Because they ran out of food they were ill-prepared for the journey that following Jesus would involve.

We also know, based upon Jesus previous experience, that the multitude followed Jesus for reasons of shallow curiosity—because of Jesus' reputation as a miracle worker and healer. They weren't concerned about what He taught, but about seeing something special and feeling good. They wanted a magician to entertain them and a healer to make them feel better.

It would be a stretch of the imagination to think of this crowd as having salvation. The Gospels don't record every person whom Jesus saved, but the pattern we have seen is that a few were saved out of the multitudes who followed. Yet, Jesus had compassion even upon these unsaved people. He said,

> "I have compassion on the multitude, because they have now
> continued with Me three days and have nothing to eat" (v. 2).

Jesus was concerned for all those who followed Him, even those whose understanding was shallow, even those who followed for the wrong reasons, even those who would not be eternally saved. Jesus was concerned about them, much as Jeremiah had counseled Israel to work for the good of those who had taken them captive because the prosperity of Israel in captivity would be effected by the prosperity of those who had taken her into captivity (Jeremiah 29:28). Thus God's blessings flow beyond the merely saved and touch upon the general population.

Note also that this event took place in Decapolis, which meant that in all probability many of these people were Gentiles. Jesus had compassion on Gentiles because He was extending the gospel to them. It was all part of His outreach mission to the Gentiles.

The story unfolds much as the feeding of the five thousand had. Jesus raised the issue about feeding the crowd, and the disciples responded that there were too many people and not enough food. Jesus got specific. "He asked them, 'How many loaves do you have?'" And they said, "Seven'" (v. 5). The point is that there were a lot of people and not enough food.

As in the feeding of the five thousand, Jesus brought order to the crowd by asking them to sit. Mark didn't mention that the crowd sat in groups as did Luke, but we can imagine it because of the orderliness of the procedure. Then Jesus

> "took the seven loaves and gave thanks, broke them and gave
> them to His disciples to set before them; and they set them before
> the multitude" (v. 6).

Do you see the communion pattern here? Jesus gave them, not to the crowd, but to the disciples who then "set them before the multitude." The Greek word translated *set before* (*paratithemi*) carries the sense of serve, as a waitress might set your dinner before you.

Not only were the people fed, but the disciples were given an opportunity to exercise their primary function, that of service to the Lord. They served the Lord by obeying His command, demonstrating that leadership in the church means service to others, not being served by others.

They also had some fish, which Jesus blessed and gave to the disciples who also set them before the multitude. Everyone ate their fill and there were seven baskets of leftovers. The result of the miracle was the same as the feeding of the five thousand. Everyone was satisfied and there was much left over. God provided, and He provided abundantly.

When the miracle had been wrought and the numbers had been confirmed—four thousand people fed with seven loaves and a few fish, and seven baskets remaining—Jesus sent the multitude away. He gathered His disciples and went to Dalmanutha, near Magdala, back across the Sea of Galilee.

Not long ago (at the beginning of chapter 7) Jesus had tangled with the Pharisees over purification rites. His words had been direct and to the point. He accused them of ignoring the heart of God's Word by pretending outward obedience, thereby forsaking the commandments of God and conforming to the traditions of men. In essence, the Pharisees had attempted to run God's church by popularity polls, seeking to please men rather than God. He tangled with the Pharisees again at Dalmanutha.

> "Then the Pharisees came out and began to dispute with Him,
> seeking from Him a sign from heaven, testing Him" (v. 11).

The way Mark phrased this shows the intent of the Pharisees. They were not looking for a sign in order to strengthen their faith, as many who followed after Jesus did. Rather, they came disputing Jesus, with the intent to disprove Him by demanding a miracle. They believed Him to be a charlatan and hoped to trip Him up and expose His folly.

Mark said that in response Jesus "sighed deeply in His spirit" (v. 12). Remember the sigh that He had earlier (Mark 7:34), this one was just like it, only deeper. Paul used the same word in Romans 8:22-23, where it is translated as *groan*.

> "For we know that the whole creation groans and labors with birth pangs together until now. Not only that, but we also who have the firstfruits of the Spirit, even we ourselves groan within ourselves, eagerly waiting for the adoption, the redemption of our body."

That's the kind of sigh Jesus sighed.

Then Jesus answered the Pharisees,

> "Why does this generation seek a sign? Assuredly, I say to you, no sign shall be given to this generation" (v. 12).

All of the synoptic gospels record this saying of Jesus, but the others put it more boldly. According to Matthew 16:4 Jesus said,

> "A wicked and adulterous generation seeks after a sign, and no sign shall be given to it except the sign of the prophet Jonah."

Luke's version is more like Matthew's than Mark's.

Mark's context clearly belongs to the first century. When Mark said "this generation" he meant those alive at that time. But Matthew and Luke have a different thrust. They applied it more widely by saying that Jesus not only intended that particular generation, but any wicked, evil and adulterous generation. Jesus meant that the seeking of a sign as the Pharisees did was always itself evil and wicked.

Criticizing the people of his time, Paul later said,

> "For the message of the cross is foolishness to those who are perishing, but to us who are being saved it is the power of God. For it is written: 'I will destroy the wisdom of the wise, And bring to nothing the understanding of the prudent.' Where is the wise? Where is the scribe? Where is the disputer of this age? Has not God made foolish the wisdom of this world? For since, in the wisdom of God, the world through wisdom did not know God, it pleased God through the foolishness of the message preached to save those who believe. For Jews request a sign, and Greeks seek after wisdom; but we preach Christ crucified, to the Jews a stumbling block and to the Greeks foolishness, but to those who

are called, both Jews and Greeks, Christ the power of God and
the wisdom of God" (1 Corinthians 1:18-24).

We are to seek, not signs, nor wisdom, but Christ crucified. Christian preaching, Christian worship is not about signs or wisdom, it's about Christ crucified, about the cross of Christ, about the death and resurrection of Christ, who died that we may live.

No sign, but Jonah! Jonah, of course, was three days in the belly of a whale. The allusion is to Christ's death and resurrection, three days in the tomb. This is the only sign we need, the only sign that will ever prove efficacious. The gospel is not about signs or wonders or the wisdom of this perishing world. It's about the death and resurrection of Jesus Christ.

What are you looking for? What are you waiting for? A miracle? A healing? A special revelation of the Spirit? Christ died for your salvation! What more do you want?

31. Leaven of Heaven

And He left them, and getting into the boat again, departed to the other side. Now the disciples had forgotten to take bread, and they did not have more than one loaf with them in the boat. Then He charged them, saying, 'Take heed, beware of the leaven of the Pharisees and the leaven of Herod.' And they reasoned among themselves, saying, 'It is because we have no bread.' But Jesus, being aware of it, said to them, 'Why do you reason because you have no bread? Do you not yet perceive nor understand? Is your heart still hardened? Having eyes, do you not see? And having ears, do you not hear? And do you not remember? When I broke the five loaves for the five thousand, how many baskets full of fragments did you take up?' They said to Him, 'Twelve.' 'Also, when I broke the seven for the four thousand, how many large baskets full of fragments did you take up?' And they said, 'Seven.' So He said to them, 'How is it you do not understand?' —Mark 8:13-21

The Pharisees sought to disprove Jesus by asking Him to perform a miracle, not realizing that He just completed the miracle of the feeding of the four thousand. Matthew records a clarification of this verse.

> "How is it you do not understand that I did not speak to you concerning bread?— but to beware of the leaven of the Pharisees and Sadducees. Then they understood that He did not tell them to beware of the leaven of bread, but of the doctrine of the Pharisees and Sadducees" (Matthew 16:11-12).

What is at issue here, what Jesus is warning us about, are two classic errors that have always opposed God's truth. From time immemorial Satan has tried to pull the faithful off track with either one of two errors— formalism or skepticism. Formalism generally belongs to religion and manifests itself in moral legalism or ritualistic formality. Skepticism, on the other hand, is a product of doubt and manifests as liberalism and permissiveness. One makes too much of the Law, the other makes to little of it.

We'll come back to these two concepts. But first we need to look at the context in which they arise. Jesus was on the boat, crossing again to the "other side" (v. 13) of the Sea of Galilee. They

> "had forgotten to take bread, and they did not have more than one loaf with them in the boat" (v. 14).

The disciples are shown to be as ill-prepared for their journey as were the multitudes who followed Jesus into the wilderness. Everything that we said about the multitude being unprepared for the journey with Jesus applies to the disciples as well. They were just like everyone else, which suggests that they were not selected to be disciples because of their moral or intellectual superiority, but were selected by God's grace and for God's purpose alone.

Jesus sat down with them in the boat and began to teach them. Jesus was a good teacher who always used the appropriate teaching techniques. He didn't coddle them or try to protect them from the sharp edge of the truth, but simply and plainly confronted them with the demand for repentance. Repentance, the first fruit of the gospel, involves the conscious recognition of one's own sin and the intentional turning away from it. It involves a rethinking of one's values, priorities, and understanding (or world view).

Jesus had mentioned the "leaven of the Pharisees and the leaven of Herod" (v. 15). As the disciples discussed among themselves what He meant, Jesus interrupted them. They had come to the conclusion that He was referring to the bread and provisions that they had forgotten to bring aboard.

Jesus did not want to be misunderstood on this point, so He corrected them, *Why are you talking about bread?* Jesus asked.

> "Do you not yet perceive nor understand? Is your heart still hardened?" (v. 17).

Notice the reason that Jesus suggested as the cause of their misunderstanding. In this case we can assume that a hardened heart means callused and insensitive perception. A hardened heart cannot understand God's truth because it is closed to that truth. God's truth is not perceived by a hardened heart. A hardened heart is impervious to truth because it does not recognize or honor God's truth.

Remember that Jesus was talking to the *disciples* here. He had called these men to be disciples. They were in personal relationship with the Lord. They were walking with Jesus. But they had missed something very fundamental. And if they missed it, so could we. If the disciples were guilty of this hardheartedness, none of us can be exempt from it. In fact, overcoming this deficiency is a normal part of Christian maturity.

For many people this realization of self-fallibility brings great discomfort. It is, at heart, to admit that you are wrong. Normally people can more readily admit that they used to be wrong. Such people will tell you how wrong they were, how wrong they *used to be*. And in doing so they are quick to add that they have since corrected that error, which means that they still believe themselves to be right. The point is that it is incredibly difficult for people to admit that they are presently wrong about something, and that they do not know the truth. Modern people are especially like that. We like to think that we know everything. Jesus pointed out the error of the disciples in the boat that day.

> "'Having eyes, do you not see? And having ears, do you not
> hear? And do you not remember? When I broke the five loaves
> for the five thousand, how many baskets full of fragments did
> you take up?' They said to Him, 'Twelve.' 'Also, when I broke
> the seven for the four thousand, how many large baskets full of
> fragments did you take up?' And they said, 'Seven.' So He said to
> them, 'How is it you do not understand?'" (vs. 18-21).

He pointed out that He had twice performed miracles that were witnessed by thousands of people, yet each time the miracles were denied by those who didn't believe. He was showing them that the miracles that everyone wanted were immaterial to the gospel. The gospel is about truth, not miracles. The gospel is about God's salvation of humanity, not about curing the infirmities of the body. He had performed miracles and still people refused to believe. Even those He healed refused to obey. And obedience is the first fruit of faithfulness. The miracles witnessed to the authority of the gospel, but added nothing to it.

So, why did people not believe? Jesus suggests here that they had been deceived by the leaven of the Pharisees and of Herod. The Greek word for *leaven* is *zume*. The fact that Israel celebrated the Feast of the Unleavened Bread suggests that there was a negative connotation regarding leaven. The process of leavening is related to the process of fermentation. Both provide a subtle change over time to the character of a thing. Leavening bread makes it light and less substantial. Fermented grapes become intoxicating.

The issues are not clear-cut because some leavening is good and some isn't. Fermentation, rightly done, produces a fine wine, wrongly done, the whole batch is ruined. Leavening, as Jesus used the term, then, refers to issues of purity—that is, legalism, and of impurity—or liberalism. Biblical truth involves holding to core values without sliding to the right or to the left. Formalism (legalism) pulls us one direction, skepticism (liberalism) pulls the other.

J.C. Ryle, writing in 1857, notes that formalism and skepticism

> "have been chronic diseases in the professing Church of Christ.
> In every age multitudes of Christians have been infected by
> them. In every age men need to watch against them, and be on
> their guard."[9]

And we are no different than those who have gone before us. Ryle's caution—Jesus' caution really—is for us if we believe ourselves to be faithful.

Formalism effects two religious areas—rituals and morals. Ritualistic formalism amounts to thinking that everything in the church needs to be done in a certain way. Mostly it effects worship practices (liturgy), but is not limited to worship. Ritualistic formalism is no more than getting stuck in a liturgical rut. Repeating the past for the sake of repetition. There is a right honoring of the past and there is a rote honoring of the past.

The Pharisees were terribly afraid of the changes that Jesus represented. They had their ways of doing things. They had their four hundred laws that "interpreted" Scripture. They had their sacrifices and their social prestige. And they were unwilling to give any of that up for gospel truth. So, they branded Jesus a heretic.

Skeptics, on the other hand, doubt everything. They doubt Jesus like the Pharisees doubted Jesus. But they also doubt the Law. Science is skeptical. The scientific method employs skepticism until proven otherwise. The scientific method is antithetical to faithfulness. It works well for science, but makes a mess of faith. Science doubts until proven otherwise, whereas faith trusts until proven otherwise. Skeptics apply the scientific method to the study of Scripture, and assume that none of it is true until it is proven to be true. That was the attitude of the Pharisees regarding Jesus' miracles.

This is the attitude of liberalism. Liberals are not all atheists. Many are agnostic, some even purport themselves to be Christian (Matthew

---

9   Ibid., p. 158.

7:21-ff). And because they don't believe Scripture, they feel themselves free to disregard God's Law and to do whatever seems to them to be good in regard to morals and worship. In morals they are permissive, and in worship they are self-expressive, doing whatever they like.

Legalism applied to morality produces works righteousness, believing that people are saved because they live moral lives, because they do good things. The opposite danger—liberalism—believes that God is not concerned about morality, that because people are saved by grace they are free to behave however they like. It is true that people are not saved because of their morality. Rather, they are saved in order to live by Christ's morality. It is very easy to err one way or the other. Holding fast to biblical truth is simple, but it is not easy.

The disciples were not saved by or because of Jesus' miracles. They witnessed them. They were part of them. But the miracles didn't make any difference to their salvation. Nor did they grow in spiritual understanding by witnessing miracles. But neither were the disciples saved because of their superior morality. They were ordinary men in every sense of the word, sinners like everyone else.

Rather, they were saved because Jesus called them. He called them and they followed. Grace is the leaven of heaven. It's a good leaven, it makes the saints grow.

Perhaps Christ has called you. How can you tell?

By your following.

32. SEE, DON'T SAY

Then He came to Bethsaida; and they brought a blind man to Him, and begged Him to touch him. So He took the blind man by the hand and led him out of the town. And when He had spit on his eyes and put His hands on him, He asked him if he saw anything. And he looked up and said, 'I see men like trees, walking.' Then He put His hands on his eyes again and made him look up. And he was restored and saw everyone clearly. Then He sent him away to his house, saying, 'Neither go into the town, nor tell anyone in the town.'   —Mark 8:22-26

The lesson of the healing of the blind man at Bethsaida is a lesson in humility. At least it should be. We should come away from it with a deeper understanding of our own spiritual blindness. The miracle is much like the healing of the deaf mute (Mark 7:31-37). As they did with the deaf mute, the crowd asked Jesus to touch this blind man. These people also thought that they knew the means of healing and implored Jesus to use it. As before, that means was the laying on of hands. So often people come to the Lord to tell Him just what they need and how He ought to give it to them. A story titled Providence illustrates the point.

The only survivor of a shipwreck was washed up on a small uninhabited island. He cried out to God to save him, and every day he scanned the horizon for help, but none seemed forthcoming. Exhausted, he eventually managed to build a rough hut and put his few possessions in it. But then one day, after hunting for food, he arrived home to find his little hut in flames, the smoke rolling up to the sky. The worst had happened; he was stung with grief. Early the next day, though, a ship drew near the island and rescued him. "How did you know I was here?" he asked the crew. "We saw your smoke signal," they replied.

The writer of Proverbs said that God's wisdom is more precious than rubies and beyond comparison (Proverbs 3:15). God is not bound by methods or formulas or precedents. God is free to do whatever He chooses. Yet, God normally chooses to operate according to His ordinary means of grace. God rarely contravenes the laws of nature. Oh, it may seem like He does, but the discrepancy is more in our understanding than in God's methods.

The point is that the crowd thought that they knew how Jesus ought to heal this poor blind man.

> "So He took the blind man by the hand and led him out of the town" (v. 23).

Just as with the healing of the deaf mute, Jesus took the man away from the crowd. And as He had employed spit to heal the deaf mute, He spit on this blind man's eyes and "put His hands upon him" (v. 23). This same procedure healed the deaf mute, but this time it seemed to work only partially. Jesus asked the man if he could see. The man "looked up" and said, "I see men like trees, walking" (v. 24). He could see, but only partially. His vision was confused and unclear.

There is medical evidence that the restoration of sight requires more than mere vision. The process of seeing is actually a complex phenomena that involves mental recognition and understanding as much as visual perception. Any fool can see the pieces on a chess board, but not everyone can see the dangers or the right moves. Similarly, the blind man could not distinguish between men and trees. Perhaps he just saw fuzzy blobs, and noticed that some of them moved. Not having seen before, he didn't know what distinguished men from trees. He had to learn to discern. Though his vision may have been okay, he had to learn how to make sense of what he saw. And that is the significance of this story.

This healing miracle is unique in that it documents the fact that healing is not always instantaneous. I suspect that the truth of the matter is that genuine healing is seldom instantaneous because of God's preference to employ His ordinary means of grace.

The traditional Protestant understanding in this regard is that God's first concern in history was the completion of Scripture. God established His Word as the means of salvation, and his Word established the Sacraments. When that was accomplished through the death and resurrection of Christ and the closing of the Canon, God turned His people to seek Him through His Word, the Bible, and through the proper administration of the Sacraments.

When I was young my father assembled my Christmas presents for me. When I got older, he gave me the instructions. It's a maturity thing.

First, Jesus "spit on his eyes and put His hands on him" (v. 23). That brought partial healing.

> "Then He put His hands on his eyes again and made him look
> up. And he was restored and saw everyone clearly" (v. 25).

When Jesus healed the deaf mute He had looked up. We thought about that in conjunction with Jesus' sigh of disappointment. This time the looking up seems to be of a different sort. There was no sigh related to it. And this time it was not Jesus, but the blind man who looked up, but could only see "men like trees, walking" (v. 24). Then Jesus put His hands on the man's eyes again and "made him *look up*" (v. 25, emphasis mine). It almost seems as if when the man had looked up, at first the light was so bright that he looked away. He was only able to see "men like trees, walking." Then Jesus made him look up longer or harder or whatever. And he was healed as he looked up, or because he looked up. The looking up became part of the healing process.

The analogy is that of looking up to Jesus. Jesus is our healing and in as much as we look to Him, we are healed or saved. We are reminded of the story of Moses putting a fiery serpent on a pole to cure those who had been bitten by snakes. They only had to look up at it and they were healed (Numbers 21:4-9). It foreshadowed looking to Christ on the cross for salvation.

Mark said that the man "was restored and saw everyone clearly" (v. 25). The Greek word for *restore* is *apokathistemi*, which means to restore to its former state. The curious thing is the emphasis upon a return to a former condition. Had the man previously been able to see? Was his blindness the result of an accident or some condition that came later in life? We don't know. There is no indication of any such thing. More likely the word *restore* indicates not only that this man had been healed of his blindness but that he had been saved as well, that he was restored in his relationship to God. Salvation restores that broken relationship with God.

Upon saving the man, Jesus told him not to speak to anyone about it. We've seen this a number of times before. But what can we make of it? We know that Jesus' purpose was Calvary and that He didn't want anything to interfere with that. It is no doubt true that He wanted to keep a lid on things until the appointed time.

But there is another way that we can understand Jesus asking various people to keep quiet about their healing or their salvation. Just because someone is saved doesn't mean that they know anything about salvation. People can be saved and not understand it at all. People can be saved and have a wrong understanding of salvation. Salvation and the understanding of salvation are quite different things.

The sense I get from this story is that Jesus was trying to point out the progressive nature of salvation. It can all happen in an instant, but it doesn't usually happen that way. We must remember that salvation is made up of two components—justification and sanctification.

Justification happens in an instant because it is God's doing. God justifies His people on the basis of Christ's sacrifice. Justification is like an accounting entry made in God's heavenly books. But sanctification takes a lifetime to complete. Sanctification is the progressive reshaping of our character in the likeness of Christ. Sanctification is a matter of learning, a matter of edification and admonishment. It's a kind of training in Godliness.

The point is that someone's justification does not imply the end of their sanctification, but the beginning. New Christians often have a shallow and faulty understanding of the faith. Don't get me wrong, Christian maturity is not a matter of time in grade. Just because you've been a Christian for twenty or thirty years doesn't necessarily mean that you are a mature Christian. Maturity—sanctification is a work. It is first and foremost God's work. He works it in us. But it is also our work. You must, as Paul said, "work out your own salvation with fear and trembling" (Philippians 2:12). Those who do not work at it do not mature in the faith.

Paul meant that we must engage God's ordinary means of grace—Word and Sacrament. We must study God's Word, and pray fervently. We must serve the Lord with gladness, love His people, and avoid everything ungodly, unloving, and unholy.

This man who had been healed of his blindness had been genuinely healed and saved—restored. But his understanding of it all was probably immature and faulty. We can imagine that whatever he would say at this point in his walk would not contribute to the truth of the gospel. So Jesus told him to go home and not talk to anyone about it.

We don't know what this man did. Jesus said the same thing at the healing of the deaf mute. But those people didn't listen to Jesus.

> "The more He commanded them, the more widely they proclaimed it" (Mark 7:36).

They spread the errors of their immaturity.

There are two possible responses to Jesus' request not to tell anyone. Like the friends of the deaf mute, people often get puffed up, proud that they are associated with such a miraculous event. Such people usually take things into their own hands and do what they think best. They tell people what they think, whether it's right or not. Their concern is not correct understanding. Their concern is to let people know they are associated with powerful people and events. That response issues out of pride.

The other response is a response of humility. In essence Jesus told these people that they didn't know what they were talking about. And because they didn't know what they were talking about, it would be best if they didn't do any talking at all. Jesus said that spreading no information was better than spreading wrong information. In humility we must honestly acknowledge our own limitations and not pretend to know what we don't know. Having surgery does not make a person a surgeon. Nor does regeneration qualify one to teach the gospel. All teachers need to be born again, of course, but not every born again Christian can formally teach. Sometimes saying nothing is better than saying anything.

Salvation was accomplished by Christ on the cross. His blood justified His people. All healing and salvation issue from Christ, who is God's Word. Neither Christ's touch nor His spittle were necessary for the man's healing. We know that Jesus could heal simply by willing it. Yet, the Lord chose to use these elements in conjunction with the man's faith to bring about this man's healing. But the point is that by faith the blind man looked up to Christ and was healed. Praise be to God!

33. ROCK OF CONFESSION

Now Jesus and His disciples went out to the towns of Caesarea
Philippi; and on the road He asked His disciples, saying to
them, 'Who do men say that I am?' So they answered, 'John the
Baptist; but some say, Elijah; and others, one of the prophets.'
He said to them, 'But who do you say that I am?' Peter an-
swered and said to Him, 'You are the Christ.' Then He strictly
warned them that they should tell no one about Him. And He
began to teach them that the Son of Man must suffer many
things, and be rejected by the elders and chief priests and
scribes, and be killed, and after three days rise again. He spoke
this word openly. And Peter took Him aside and began to re-
buke Him. But when He had turned around and looked at His
disciples, He rebuked Peter, saying, 'Get behind Me, Satan! For
you are not mindful of the things of God, but the things of
men.'   —Mark 8:27-33

Jesus and His disciples journeyed forty miles north of the Sea of
Galilee to Caesarea Philippi. This was the only recorded visit Jesus
made to this town. It may be significant that He had not ministered
in this town before. The question Jesus asked His disciples there is a key
gospel question. The gospel hinges on the answer. "Who do men say
that I am?" (v. 27). Or as Matthew 16:13 records it, "Who do men say
that I, the Son of Man, am?" Let's consider who the question is addressed
to and what it specifically asks.

The Greek word for *men* is *anthropos*, which means humanity as a
species. Jesus directed His question at both specific individuals and man
in general. He wanted to know what reputation He had outside the specific areas in which He had been ministering. What were the rumors
about Him? But Jesus didn't ask as a way of polling public opinion. He
didn't ask for His sake, but for ours. It's not that Jesus was concerned
about public opinion, that He wanted to know what people thought of
Him. Rather, He intended to demonstrate to His disciples the contrast
regarding public opinion about Him and the truth of who He actually
was/is.

Understanding the true identity of Jesus is essential to Christian living. A faulty understanding of who Jesus is will result in a faulty walk and a lousy witness. The question is addressed to every disciple in every age because true discipleship begins with the right answer to this question. Who is Jesus Christ? Answer the question for your five-year-old son or granddaughter. Answer it for your teenage daughter or grandson. Answer it for your neighbor in the house next to you. Answer it for yourself. To answer this question correctly is to proclaim the gospel.

It is important to see who specifically Jesus was talking to. He was traveling with His disciples when "He asked His disciples" (v. 27). He didn't single Peter out, but asked the disciples as a group.

> "So they answered, 'John the Baptist; but some say, Elijah; and others, one of the prophets.'" (v. 28).

There was a variety of opinion about exactly who Jesus was. Clearly belief in reincarnation was in vogue. Though Elijah had ministered in Israel nine hundred years earlier, Malachi had prophesied that God would send Elijah "before the coming of the great and dreadful day of the LORD" (Malachi 4:5). We also see that the people believed John the Baptist to be a bona fide prophet, equivalent to Elijah. And they classified Jesus in the same category as a prophet of God.

For them to have had such an understanding of Jesus was no minor thing. To give Jesus the authority of a prophet was an exceedingly great honor. There had been no prophetic voice in Israel, other than the recent emergence of John the Baptist, for hundreds of years. So, to accord that honor to Jesus was to grant Him tremendous authority. In essence, they said that His words were equivalent to Scripture, for the Prophets wrote Scripture.

Yet, the testimony of the people was confused. The opinions were not only conflicting, but inadequate. The opinions of men, like the traditions of men, cannot do justice to God's truth. The question and its answer demonstrate that people simply did not know who Jesus was. They didn't know and they couldn't know. Our best thoughts, our wildest speculations, our most popular rumors always fall short of the truth. That is the point demonstrated by Jesus' question. Men, in and of themselves, cannot discover the truth. We can't figure it out ourselves. Contrary to popular opinion truth is not acquired by piecing together the various opinions and beliefs of mankind into a kind of quilt of truth. Like the Tower of Babel our cooperative efforts cannot ever reach God's truth.

So, how then is the truth revealed? It is revealed by the One who is the Way, the Truth, and the Life. Christ is the revealer and He does the revealing. He draws back the curtain, we cannot. That is the point!

Finally Jesus asked the disciples, "Who do you say that I am?" (v. 29). Peter answered. For himself—yes; for the others—perhaps. His answer provided the foundation upon which Christ would build His Church. Peter confessed, "You are the Christ," (v. 29), the Anointed One, the Messiah of God. More than a prophet, Peter confessed Jesus to be God in the flesh, the One for whom all history had been written, the One who was, is, and always will be God Himself.

At this point Matthew expands the story by reporting that

> "Jesus answered and said to him (Peter), 'Blessed are you, Simon Bar-Jonah, for flesh and blood has not revealed this to you, but My Father who is in heaven. And I also say to you that you are Peter, and on this rock I will build My church, and the gates of Hades shall not prevail against it. And I will give you the keys of the kingdom of heaven, and whatever you bind on earth will be bound in heaven, and whatever you loose on earth will be loosed in heaven'" (Matthew 16:16-19).

Whatever this means, however you interpret it, it cannot be denied that something foundational happened here. Jesus conferred power and authority for the building of His Church. But upon what does this power and authority rest? Upon Peter's realization, or upon Christ's revelation?

Surely, they are like the different sides of a single coin. Yet, they are neither the same nor equal. One exemplifies the true Head of the Church and one does not. One will prevail against the gates of Hell, and one will not. One provides the keys of the kingdom, and one does not. A misunderstanding at this point could wreak great havoc in a world that much prefers the thoughts of men to the truth of God.

Jesus already indicated which side of the coin was heads. He said that flesh and blood had not revealed this to Peter, but that God in heaven had revealed it. The realization did not originate with Peter, but with God. The Rock of Christ's Church was neither Peter's manhood nor his office. Rather, Christ Himself who is the embodied revelation of God was (is) Himself the Foundation Stone upon which the Church was built.

Jesus was perfectly aware that His disciples did not understand this. No one did. At this point in Jesus' ministry, as we have clearly seen from our study of the gospel of Mark, no one understood who He was or what He was doing. At best people thought He was a Prophet. Most thought of Him as a healer or a worker of miracles, and sought after Him for what they could get for themselves—healing, status, prestige. Even those who had been miraculously healed and saved were unable to appreciate the magnitude of the reality of Christ.

So Jesus asked His own disciples to "tell no one about Him" (v. 30) for the same reasons that he told others not to say anything. Because they didn't understand they would only spread their own faulty opinions and speculations. Because the revelation of Christ was not yet complete, they could not yet understand it. So, Jesus told them to keep quiet.

In the silence, then, Jesus began to tell them the truth about His mission, that He

> "must suffer many things, and be rejected by the elders and chief
> priests and scribes, and be killed, and after three days rise again"
> (v. 31).

The word *must* is emphatic. Jesus *must* suffer these things. These things were not optional, not probable, but certain. Without them there could be no propitiation, no satisfaction of God for the sins of men, no reconciliation with God, no grace, nor forgiveness. These things were essential to the ministry of Jesus. He must pay the price. He must atone for the sins of His people. He must.

The contrast between popular opinion—which the disciples held at this point—regarding who Jesus was and what He was about was so great that Peter and the disciples were nauseated. The truth of Christ from the very lips of Christ was utterly rejected by His own disciples!

Not only could the gates of Hell prevail against Peter as a man, but almost immediately upon Peter's confession that Jesus was the Christ he was overpowered by Satan himself. Peter spoke for the disciples,

> "Far be it from You, Lord; this shall not happen to You!"
> (Matthew 16:22).

How could Peter contradict the teaching of Jesus when He had just made the confession of salvation? As soon as Peter understood himself as having made the confession, received the power and authority of Christ, he contradicted the Lord Himself!

Jesus put Peter in his place.

> "He ... turned around and looked at His disciples, (and) rebuked
> Peter, saying, 'Get behind Me, Satan! For you are not mindful of
> the things of God, but the things of men'" (v. 33).

Peter, who had just confessed that Jesus was the Christ, had a different understanding about what the Christ should be doing than Jesus did. In spite of Peter's confession, he did not understand the gospel. And Jesus told him so! Peter's thinking was guided by the flesh, not by the Spirit.

If Peter could be guilty of failing to understand the gospel, even after having confessed Jesus to be the Christ, isn't it possible that your understanding might be flawed. I'm not talking to anyone in particular. Rather, I believe that the Scripture addresses this issue to all disciples in every place and in every time.

People choose to become Christians because they believe that they understand the gospel, or Jesus, or the Bible, etc. They believe that they understand to whatever degree what God is doing and they want to be a part of it. So they say *yes* to Christ, or they receive Christ, or join the church, etc. That's exactly what Peter had done. Peter thought he knew, and spoke his mind.

What's the practical application of all this? Don't trust your own understanding.

> "Trust in the Lord with all your heart, And lean not on your own understanding; In all your ways acknowledge Him, And He shall direct your paths" (Proverbs 3:5-6).

> "He who trusts in his own heart is a fool, But whoever walks wisely will be delivered" (Proverbs 28:26).

> "And if anyone thinks that he knows anything, he knows nothing yet as he ought to know. But if anyone loves God, this one is known by Him" (1 Corinthians 8:2-3).

But if you don't trust in your own understanding, whose understanding can you trust? Trust that which has stood the test of time. Be a student of history. Trust the Lord, trust the Bible, and trust those to whom God has given leadership. If you can't trust your leaders, then get rid of them or go to a church that has godly leaders. It's your right, and your duty.

We live in horrendous times. Leadership itself is in doubt from the President on down. A spirit of doubt and distrust pervades every relationship. The cancer of doubt and distrust clouds the relationships even among God's people. Trust must be restored, and I suggest that it can only be restored by trusting *first* in Christ. Christ is our Rock in the whelming flood.

Whatever you do *you* had better be on the side of the Lord yourself, and have godly, biblical reasons for doing whatever you do. Irrespective of current leadership, that is what Christians are called to do anyway.

Is that what you are doing?

34. Take Up Your Cross

When He had called the people to Himself, with His disciples also, He said to them, 'Whoever desires to come after Me, let him deny himself, and take up his cross, and follow Me. For whoever desires to save his life will lose it, but whoever loses his life for My sake and the gospel's will save it. For what will it profit a man if he gains the whole world, and loses his own soul? Or what will a man give in exchange for his soul? For whoever is ashamed of Me and My words in this adulterous and sinful generation, of him the Son of Man also will be ashamed when He comes in the glory of His Father with the holy angels.' —Mark 8:34-38

We finally come to the crux of the gospel, the nut, the rub, the central tenet of Christianity—the cross. Jesus laid out the scenario for Peter and the disciples regarding His suffering and death on the cross. It is not difficult to understand what Jesus meant, but it is quite difficult to accept. Jesus suffering and dying on the cross was not what Peter thought should happen, and he told Him so.

Jesus was fulfilling the role of the Suffering Servant (Isaiah 53). Isaiah had prophesied that the Messiah would suffer, and the disciples should have been familiar with the prophecies of Isaiah. Yet, they had a great deal of difficulty connecting these things. It seems that they could accept Isaiah's prophecy, or they could accept that Jesus was the Messiah. But they struggled to accept them both.

Prior to this time Jesus and His disciples had preached faith and repentance as the means of salvation. That message seemed to produce much misunderstanding among the people as Jesus was thronged for miracles and healings. There appeared to be no let up as rumors and stories circulated about His miraculous powers. No one had come to Jesus full of repentance or desiring repentance. A few had been healed by faith. Most came to see a miracle show or to receive a miraculous healing. People came for what they could get for themselves.

Finally Peter confessed that Jesus was the Christ, but still misunderstood what that meant. When Jesus told the disciples about the cross, they rejected it. In the face of all this misunderstanding, then, Jesus set out the truth of His ministry and the crux of salvation.

> "Whoever desires to come after Me, let him deny himself, and take up his cross, and follow Me. For whoever desires to save his life will lose it, but whoever loses his life for My sake and the gospel's will save it" (vs. 34-35).

As Jesus then taught the truth of the gospel He spoke to everybody, and avoided teaching one thing to one group and another thing to another group. That preference can be seen in who Jesus addressed. Mark said that

> "He had called *the people* to Himself, with His disciples also" (v. 34, italic added).

He was not content to simply tell the disciples and allow them to tell the people. Rather, He called everyone together and told them all. He didn't tell some select inner group, but He told all "the people." He didn't preach one thing to His inner circle and another to the masses, but He preached the hard edge of the gospel truth to everyone alike.

The truth is the power of the gospel, and He gave this truth, this power to the people, "with His disciples also" (v. 34). The central pillar of the gospel is self-denial, not the kind of denial that exists where people cannot face some uncomfortable truth so they pretend that it isn't true, but the kind of self-denial that sacrifices its own concerns for the sake of others.

The kind of self-denial or self-sacrifice that Jesus taught is a necessary fruit of the gospel. Of course, we know that self-denial does not produce salvation. You can't earn salvation by being a selfless person. Rather, salvation produces self-denial in the character of the saved. It works one way, but not the other.

While it is true that self-denial is interested in meeting needs, it doesn't seek to meet its own needs, but the needs of others. On the other hand, Christians who expect to have their own needs met have failed to understand and to practice the gospel at a very fundamental level. In the old days the practice of self-denial was called *mortification*. The word literally means to put to death the desires of the flesh, or the desires of the self. People made a practice of abandoning their own desires through prayer, fasting, study, and service.

From this central teaching of Jesus we see that Christianity manifests primarily as a religion of self-sacrificing service to others. Again, we must understand that we are not talking about works-righteousness.

Service does not make you a Christian. Yet, being a Christian results in serving others, even if all you can do is pray.

Jesus also taught the importance of the soul. The same Greek word, *psuche*, is translated both *life* and *soul*.

> "For whoever desires to save his life will lose it, but whoever loses his life (*psuche*, soul) for My sake and the gospel's will save it. For what will it profit a man if he gains the whole world, and loses his own soul (*psuche*, life)?" (vs. 35-36).

The soul is a moral entity that is designed for everlasting life. The soul is what survives the body at death. It is eternal, and in its resurrected body is destined for heaven or hell.

Morality involves a positive comparison and likeness to a standard. Immorality fails to meet the standard. Because the idea of the soul is tied to a moral standard, God's moral standard (the Ten Commandments and Jesus' two Great Commandments), the idea of the soul cannot be separated from morality. But again, we must guard ourselves from thinking in terms of works-righteousness. We cannot attain a saved soul by being moral. Why not? Because we can't be moral without Christ. Christ is our morality. He is the strength of moral decisions. He is the guiding factor whenever anyone does what is right. So, Christians are moral because they are saved, but they are not saved because they are moral. If you have to be righteous before you can be saved, no one would ever be saved because of our fallen nature.

Jesus said that a person who loses his life because of his morality, because he chooses to do the right thing, to take a moral stand, assures his salvation. Because salvation is assured—not granted or given, but assured by moral behavior—Christians can always afford to do the right thing, the moral thing.

Conversely, preferring physical life over salvation or moral righteousness is a sure sign of damnation. Those who desire to save their own skins, or their own necks, will lose their souls, their lives, and their morality because of their self-centeredness. Those who insist on having their own needs met, those who are unwilling to sacrifice their own needs for the sake of others, will find themselves outside the kingdom of God when the doors are shut.

The preservation of the morality of one's soul is more valuable than all the treasures in the world. Your soul, the protection of your moral character, is more important than anything else. That's what Jesus said.

That's why lying and cheating puts your soul at risk. Bodily injury does not effect the soul, but moral failure can mean certain and eternal death.

That doesn't mean that there isn't forgiveness. Of course, God forgives our sins, even those sins that persist into our Christian walk! But over time, we should find ourselves growing more moral, not less, more godly, not less. People who use forgiveness to justify sin are not walking with the Lord. That is not what Jesus meant. God's forgiveness does not eliminate God's demand for righteousness.

In the Old West it was said that "a man was as good as his word." That saying originated from this teaching of Jesus. A man's word, his promise, his faithfulness, his honesty and integrity were grounded on the intent of his heart. If he said he would, he would. If he said he wouldn't, he wouldn't. Come hell or high water, he would do what he said he would do because he valued his honor, his soul, his morality above all else. And when that is lost in a man or a society, it is a great loss indeed. It is a perilous loss. That's why Jesus said it was so important to protect it.

Jesus concludes by teaching about shame.

> "For whoever is ashamed of Me and My words in this adulterous
> and sinful generation, of him the Son of Man also will be
> ashamed when He comes in the glory of His Father with the
> holy angels" (v. 38).

This verse not only teaches that we should not be ashamed of the gospel, but it teaches that we will be tempted to be ashamed of the gospel. That is a most curious thought. What part of the gospel embarrasses us? If we were to ask ourselves if we are ashamed of the gospel we would, no doubt, overwhelmingly say that we are not. But are there some aspects of the gospel that you hesitate to talk to people about? If you are honest, you know that there are.

Hell, while we believe it is a reality, is not a topic of conversation that we are likely to raise with people. The stronger our belief in Hell, the less likely we are to bring it up, especially with our family. All of those hard sayings of Jesus are not difficult to understand, they are difficult to accept. They don't set well with human understanding. They cause us to come to unpleasant conclusions about God, or about ourselves.

Those unpleasant conclusions about God are not true. But until we come to terms with our shame and our embarrassment about the gospel, they can cause us a great deal of consternation. And that is as it should be. If we don't struggle with our understanding of God, we have too shallow an understanding.

God wants us to struggle, as Israel struggled with the angel, as Abraham struggled with the thought of sacrificing his own son, as Moses struggled with the commandments of God, as the Prophets struggled with God's judgment, etc. The reason the Bible continues to be a best selling book is because it continues to challenge people. It does not admit to any easy solutions to human problems, but engages us at a very deep level.

Don't we all struggle with the biblical teachings on election and predestination? On God's sovereignty and the issues of free will? Christian literature is filled with such struggles. Such doctrines are troubling. The more I understand them, the more I understand why people are troubled by them. Yet, they are in the Bible. To deny that you are chosen by God for salvation is to deny and reject the Bible and your own salvation. To claim your own absolute free will is to deny God's sovereignty. God calls us from eternity, yet we must confess Christ as Lord and Savior. How can God call us to a salvation that we are not able to accomplish?

We can't ignore these classic issues. Nor are we free to believe whatever we want about them. If people can believe whatever they want, then truth has no value. Rather, Scripture teaches that right belief is critical. We must resolve these issues. And the resolution will cause us to embrace or deny our own salvation, to embrace or deny God's sovereignty, to embrace or deny Christ as Lord and Savior. That is the conundrum that God has given us. We must either embrace Him or refuse Him. He allows no middle ground.

All of these classical doctrines lead us to the acceptance or refusal of salvation. That's the purpose of Scripture. We are not free to redefine biblical terms to suit ourselves. We are not free to believe whatever we want. We are not free to ignore the hard parts and just pick and choose what makes us feel good. We are not free to leave these matters unresolved. We must come to terms with the biblical issues of salvation and damnation.

The way to do that, said Jesus, is to deny ourselves, take up our cross, and follow Him. When God comes in glory with his holy angels He will be ashamed of those who are ashamed of the gospel. The glory of God means that all the credit, all the honor, all the power belongs to God, not to us. We cannot give God the glory and hold on to some of it for ourselves. Our God is a jealous God, jealous about His glory.

We cannot take up our cross with the hope of finding personal satisfaction. The cross is not a means of happiness. To take up our cross means to give ourselves to death. The cross is an instrument of death. It serves no other purpose. The cross is the universal Christian symbol. It is the essence of Christianity.

This teaching about self-denial, about taking up our cross, about giving ourselves to death was given to the people and the disciples to correct the misunderstandings that had arisen about Jesus and His ministry. Christianity has been sorely misunderstood, not because it is a difficult thing to understand, but because it is a hard thing to accept.

Salvation involves the mortification of the flesh, but not for its own sake. In turning to Christ we must turn away from ourselves. But if we just turn away from ourselves without turning to Christ, we are still lost. Jesus preached John's gospel of repentance. "Repent, and believe in the gospel!" (Mark 1:15). Repent! Turn around! Go the other way! To repent is to notice that you are going the wrong way, thinking the wrong things.

But the only way that we can turn away from our sin is to turn to Jesus. Jesus *is* the Gospel of God! Christian repentance is not just turning away from sin, it is also turning to Christ.

35. TRANSFIGURATION

And He said to them, "Assuredly, I say to you that there are
some standing here who will not taste death till they see the
kingdom of God present with power." Now after six days Jesus
took Peter, James, and John, and led them up on a high moun-
tain apart by themselves; and He was transfigured before them.
His clothes became shining, exceedingly white, like snow, such
as no launderer on earth can whiten them. And Elijah appeared
to them with Moses, and they were talking with Jesus. Then
Peter answered and said to Jesus, "Rabbi, it is good for us to be
here; and let us make three tabernacles: one for You, one for
Moses, and one for Elijah"—because he did not know what to
say, for they were greatly afraid. And a cloud came and over-
shadowed them; and a voice came out of the cloud, saying,
"This is My beloved Son. Hear Him!" Suddenly, when they had
looked around, they saw no one anymore, but only Jesus with
themselves. Now as they came down from the mountain, He
commanded them that they should tell no one the things they
had seen, till the Son of Man had risen from the dead. So they
kept this word to themselves, questioning what the rising from
the dead meant. And they asked Him, saying, "Why do the
scribes say that Elijah must come first?" Then He answered and
told them, "indeed, Elijah is coming first and restores all things.
And how is it written concerning the Son of Man, that He
must suffer many things and be treated with contempt? But I
say to you that Elijah has also come, and they did to him what-
ever they wished, as it is written of him."   —Mark 9:1-13

For some time people had been following Jesus around seeking
miracles, healing, and other manifestations of God's power. Some
wanted the benefits of association with such power, like healings
and mass feedings. Others, no doubt, sought signs of proof for Jesus' divinity. As we have seen earlier, Jesus rebuked many for their selfish and
petty concerns. Yet, He nonetheless healed many, fed many, and produced other signs of His divinity.

However, the Scripture just preceding this provided a high point in the Gospel of Mark when Jesus predicted His death on the cross, and demanded that true disciples must take up their own crosses and follow in the way that Jesus led. The fact of Jesus' prediction of His death on the cross is intimately related to this vision of His transfiguration. Where His death on the cross is dark and depressing, the vision of His transfiguration is brilliant and uplifting. The two visions must be held in tension because together they provide both the depth and height of Christ's ministry.

The first part of the transfiguration vision provided a tangible hope for the people living when Jesus addressed them. He said that those who heard Him speak would live to "see the kingdom of God present with power" (v. 1). They would live to see the greatest manifestation of God's power because God would move decisively to establish His kingdom among them. And what might that expression of God's power be? The resurrection of Jesus Christ from the dead. Paul said that

> "if Christ is not risen, then our preaching is empty and (our) faith
> is also empty" (1 Corinthians 15:14).

In other words, Christ's resurrection is the primary proof of His divinity. If the resurrection is not true, the entire New Testament is faulty. Christ's resurrection is the definitive foundation of the coming kingdom of God.

Mark said that the journey to the mountain of transfiguration took place "after six days" (v. 2). That is to say that it took place on the seventh day, the Sabbath. On that day high on a mountain Jesus "was transfigured before them" (v. 2). The Greek word is *metamorphoo*, which means a metamorphosis, a change into another form. It is a very significant and thorough change of the type that transforms, for instance, a caterpillar into a butterfly. What is changed becomes remarkably different, yet remains the same. People have speculated about the meaning of Jesus' transfiguration for eons. And speculate is all we can do. Something changed and yet remained the same.

Matthew said that

> "His face shone like the sun, and His clothes became as white as
> the light" (Matthew 17:2).

Luke said that

> "the appearance of His face was altered, and His robe became
> white and glistening" (Luke 9:29).

There is no doubt that something visible happened, but more importantly something spiritual also happened. The gospel writers were not simply using a literary technique, but were attempting to communicate something of the deeper reality of what happened. The effort to communicate a deeper understanding required them to use metaphorical language.

By using the terms *clothes, robe,* and *raiment* the writers point to other biblical usage of similar terms. For instance, Psalm 132:9 reads, "Let Your priests be clothed with righteousness." Speaking of Christ, Isaiah (11:5) said that

> "Righteousness shall be the belt of His loins, And faithfulness the belt of His waist."

Isaiah made clothes equivalent to righteousness, as if righteousness were something that could be put on. Paul spoke of the "armor of righteousness" (2 Corinthians 6:7) and the "whole armor of God" (Ephesians 6:13), suggesting that righteousness could be worn as a kind of protection. Mark said that

> "His clothes became shining, exceedingly white, like snow, such as no launderer on earth can whiten them" (Mark 9:3).

Mark's description pushes us into a metaphorical consideration. The allusion to super-laundered clothes points to the brilliance of Christ's righteousness. Somehow the righteousness of Christ was revealed on that mountain, as if Christ Himself had put on some emblem of righteousness.

The fact that Moses and Elijah talked with Christ establishes their agreement in doctrine and Christ's alignment with the Old Testament patriarchs. Luke tells us that they

> "spoke of His decease which He was about to accomplish at Jerusalem" (Mark 9:31).

They discussed the necessity and effectiveness of Christ's death on the cross. Remember that the sacrifice of Christ required that He be a lamb without spot or blemish (1 Peter 1:9), that is, perfect in righteousness.

Peter's desire to build three tabernacles simply demonstrated that Peter did not correctly understand what was going on. The disciples simply did not understand the ministry of Jesus until after His ascension when the Holy Spirit was poured out upon them in the Upper Room. They repeatedly failed to understand His death. For the time being they were dominated by fear, which overshadowed them and clouded their vision and understanding. Yet, even in their confusion they heard a voice which provided important guidance for them and for all disciples in every age. "This is My beloved Son. Hear Him!" (v. 7).

The voice said two things: 1) Jesus is the Son of God, therefore, 2) heed Him. What ministers say is not of primary importance, nor what the church as an institution says, nor what the great councils or best scholars said, but what Christ said. Scripture is preeminent. Our lives, our families, our schools, our societies cannot endure unless they are founded and grounded in the Word of God. There is no area of life that is exempt from the guidance and judgment of God.

Immediately after this mysterious voice sounded on the mountain, Peter, James, and John looked around and saw only Jesus. This part of their vision points to the supremacy of Jesus Christ over the Old Testament. Though Moses and Elijah conferred with Jesus, only He remained. The final scene of the vision revealed only Christ alone, as if to reinforce the importance of faith alone in Christ alone.

As they returned down the mountain after this incredible vision, Jesus told them not to tell anyone. People love to talk about extraordinary things, and of their associations with the powerful. Doing so makes people feel important. But Jesus told the disciples to keep it under wraps "till the Son of Man had risen from the dead" (v. 9). So, they kept it to themselves, but they wondered what Jesus meant by "risen from the dead."

They were familiar with the prophecy of the coming of Elijah written in Malachi 4:5, the last book of the Old Testament. Jesus' answer to their question about Elijah was cryptic. He acknowledged the truth that Elijah's return would precede the coming of the Son of Man, and pointed them to the accompanying prophecies about the suffering of the Son of Man. They couldn't understand the allusions Jesus made about the cross, so He pointed them to the Old Testament prophecies concerning it.

When He said that Elijah had already come, He made the point that the time for the suffering of the Son of Man was upon them. Jesus made no effort to identify the return of Elijah with anyone in particular. To have done so would have taken away from His point about the impending cross. He was trying to point them to the cross, not to the identity of Elijah. Consequently, we will be better served to look to the cross ourselves. Some said that John The Baptist fulfilled the role of Elijah, and maybe he did. But the point was not to identify John the Baptist, but to identify Jesus the Messiah.

This will be a recurring theme in the gospels. Jesus continued to point the disciples to the cross. But they didn't want to see it. They kept turning away from it, until the time they could not deny it. Their reception of the Holy Spirit and their realization of the centrality of the cross were equivalent. The Spirit would reveal the necessity of the cross, and their realization of the centrality of the cross would create an opportunity for the Spirit.

The primary purpose of Jesus' life, death, and ministry is the cross. The gospel is the news that Jesus died on the cross as a substitutionary sacrifice for the atonement of sin. Believe that, hold on to that, and you will have life everlasting.

36. Help My Unbelief

And when He came to the disciples, He saw a great multitude around them, and scribes disputing with them. Immediately, when they saw Him, all the people were greatly amazed, and running to Him, greeted Him. And He asked the scribes, "What are you discussing with them?""Then one of the crowd answered and said, "Teacher, I brought You my son, who has a mute spirit. And wherever it seizes him, it throws him down; he foams at the mouth, gnashes his teeth, and becomes rigid. So I spoke to Your disciples, that they should cast it out, but they could not." He answered him and said, "O faithless generation, how long shall I be with you? How long shall I bear with you? Bring him to Me." Then they brought him to Him. And when he saw Him, immediately the spirit convulsed him, and he fell on the ground and wallowed, foaming at the mouth. So He asked his father, "How long has this been happening to him?" And he said, "From childhood. And often he has thrown him both into the fire and into the water to destroy him. But if You can do anything, have compassion on us and help us." Jesus said to him, "If you can believe, all things are possible to him who believes." Immediately the father of the child cried out and said with tears, "Lord, I believe; help my unbelief!" When Jesus saw that the people came running together, He rebuked the unclean spirit, saying to it, "Deaf and dumb spirit, I command you, come out of him and enter him no more!" Then the spirit cried out, convulsed him greatly, and came out of him. And he became as one dead, so that many said, "He is dead." But Jesus took him by the hand and lifted him up, and he arose. And when He had come into the house, His disciples asked Him privately, "Why could we not cast it out?" So He said to them, "This kind can come out by nothing but prayer and fasting."
—Mark 9:14-29

Like Moses returning from Mt. Sinai, Jesus came down from the Mount of Transfiguration to a scene of some confusion. His disciples were caught up in a heated discussion in the midst of a growing crowd. The people were "amazed" at the sight of Jesus. The Greek word is *ekthambeo* and means to throw into terror or amazement. No doubt Jesus still had some transfiguration residue about His person, which suggested something of His divinity.

He didn't ask His disciples what was going on, but He asked the scribes (lawyers)—as if a father were asking about his children. *What are you doing with my children?*

The scribes must have hesitated for a moment because someone in the crowd answered Him. In fact, it was the father of a mute boy. He had brought his son to the disciples to be healed. It will be helpful to know the nature of the child's affliction because one of the points of the story is that the disciples were unable to heal him.

At this point the boy's father said that he was afflicted with "a dumb spirit" (v. 17, KJV). The Greek word is *alalos*, which simply means speechless. The word for *spirit* can also be translated as *soul*. But in verse 25 Jesus identified it as an unclean spirit—*akathartos*, "foul" in the King James. The boy had an unclean spirit or soul. We have come across unclean spirits before. They seemed to follow Jesus' wherever He went.

There was the man in the synagogue with an unclean spirit. When Jesus rebuked and cast it out the people

> "were all amazed, so that they questioned among themselves, saying, 'What is this? What new doctrine is this? For with authority He commands even the unclean spirits, and they obey Him'" (Mark 1:27).

Then there was the time that Jesus was pressed by the crowds.

> "For He healed many, so that as many as had afflictions pressed about Him to touch Him. And the unclean spirits, whenever they saw Him, fell down before Him and cried out, saying, 'You are the Son of God.' But He sternly warned them that they should not make Him known" (Mark 3:10-12). We can't forget that Jesus Himself was accused of having an unclean spirit (Mark 3:30).

The Garadene Demoniac was also possessed by an unclean spirit (Mark 5:1-20). Jesus had also given the disciples power over unclean spirits (Mark 6:7). Finally, a Gentile woman who had a daughter with an unclean spirit had been healed by Jesus (Mark 7:24-30).

This young boy, whatever else he was afflicted with, whatever the reason for his speechlessness, also had an unclean spirit. The fact that there are so many repetitions of the same affliction suggests that the spiritual nature of the boy's ailment is important. Biblical healings affect both physical and spiritual aspects of being.

The father told Jesus that he had brought the boy to the disciples for healing, but they could not heal him. But why not? Jesus had given them power over unclean spirits. The story suggests that the disciples had been working in the flesh, without Jesus. Jesus had not been with them.

The application is that disciples can do nothing without Jesus. We must learn to strive to receive the grace and presence of the Lord in all that we do. Without Him we can do nothing of significance, but with Him "all things are possible" (v. 23). Not some things, not a few things, but *all* things. In Christ, all breaches can be healed, all arguments mended, all divisions overcome.

This poor father, having just described the situation to Jesus—no doubt looking for Jesus to remedy the situation, received a very surprising answer.

> "O faithless generation, how long shall I be with you? How long shall I bear with you? Bring him to Me" (v. 19).

Does this strike you as curious, or is it just me? Jesus identified the source of the problem to be faithlessness on the part of everyone involved. The literal translation here is *unbelieving* (*apistos*) and is contrasted with the word *believe* (*pisteuo*) in verse 23. "If you can believe, all things are possible to him who believes." The lack of healing stemmed from a lack of belief, said Jesus.

The father of the child was immediately brought to tears. We don't know if they were tears of joy because he understood that Jesus would indeed heal his son, or if they were tears of frustration because he knew that his belief was weak and mingled with unbelief. He used the same words for belief and unbelief that Jesus used.

Here we see a pretty clear example that the faith that is required for healing is not faith in the faith of the believer, but faith in the faith of Christ. It is Christ's faith that heals, not ours. Even when Christ's faith is given to us, it is never perfect but always impure because it is mixed with our human nature. Our faith is always weak, our motives always mixed. Jesus said, in essence, that all things are possible for those who believe in Christ because it is the power of Christ that makes all things possible. The power to make all things possible does not reside in me, but in Christ. The power is not transferred or lent to me, but always belongs completely to Christ alone.

The next thing that happened was that Jesus "rebuked the unclean spirit" (v. 25). To rebuke means to tax with fault, to chide, rebuke, reprove, to censure severely, to admonish. The unclean spirit at this point was still in the boy. So, while we know that Jesus did not rebuke the boy himself, it sure looked like He did. If you weren't paying close attention it might have seemed as if Jesus called the boy names.

> "Deaf and dumb spirit, I command you, come out of him and
> enter him no more!" (Mark 9:25).

This was standard operating procedure for Jesus, He always rebuked unclean spirits like that.

If that wasn't enough, after Jesus' rebuke the boy went into another seizure, which "convulsed him greatly" (v. 26). The unclean spirit then visibly or audibly or somehow came out of the boy. At the conclusion of the boy's last convulsion, he then appeared to be dead. People in the crowd began saying that he was dead.

The application of this part of the story is to see that, spiritually, the boy was indeed dead, and had been dead all his life. His soul, his spirit could not hear or speak. That is the classical definition of what it means to be spiritually dead. The carnal soul is deaf and dumb to the Holy Spirit. We are all dead to the Spirit until we are born again. Now, there is no way that we can cause someone to be born again. Only Christ's Holy Spirit can do that. We cannot argue someone into being born again. We can't teach anyone how to be born again—its not a matter of having the proper education or training. It's not a technique that anyone can learn. Christ alone is the author and dispenser of the grace of regeneration.

Jesus then took the boy's hand and "lifted him up" (v. 27) The Greek word here is *egeiro*, used by Mark to describe many healings and resurrections or resuscitations. With this the boy's healing was complete.

The disciples then asked Jesus why they were unable to cast out that particular unclean spirit. Jesus answered them, "This kind can come out by nothing but prayer and fasting" (v. 29). Here it seems that Jesus gave credence to the fact that spiritual maturity is progressive. It is unlikely that He meant to say that anyone who prayed and fasted enough could attain the power to do such healing. Rather, he suggested the spiritual immaturity of the disciples at the time. Spiritual maturity is a matter of trusting Christ more often, not a matter of learning how to employ the power of God for our own purposes.

If you think that you can become holy by prayer and fasting, you have another think coming! That kind of religion is works-righteousness and is everywhere condemned in Scripture. We cannot manipulate God by prayer and fasting, or any other technique. All we can do is trust and obey more often. If you genuinely trust the Lord, prayer and fasting can provide more opportunities to practice obedience. In this way saints can grow and mature. But neither prayer nor fasting is a magic bullet that always produces desired results.

There were three important lessons in this story. First, our faithlessness is the source of sin. Since our faith is always a mixture of belief and unbelief, we are prone to sin as long as we live.

Second, even saved Christians can do things in the flesh, apart from the Lord. One temptation is to get ahead of the Lord and try to do God's work for Him, the other is to get behind the Lord and try to let Him do it without you. We must always wait when God waits, and move when God moves.

Third, spiritual maturity is a progressive work in the lives of believers. That means that spiritual maturity comes in stages and in fits and starts. No one becomes suddenly mature. We can be suddenly born again, but not suddenly mature. Growth is a process. So, be patient with yourself, and with others.

The flip side here is that spiritual growth requires spiritual birth. Our salvation is accomplished by the mediatorial work of Christ alone. Salvation is credited to Christ's death and resurrection. It's not a complicated matter, but it is a matter of faith and belief.

37. Great Misunderstanding

Then they departed from there and passed through Galilee, and He did not want anyone to know it. For He taught His disciples and said to them, "The Son of Man is being betrayed into the hands of men, and they will kill Him. And after He is killed, He will rise the third day." But they did not understand this saying, and were afraid to ask Him. Then He came to Capernaum. And when He was in the house He asked them, "What was it you disputed among yourselves on the road?" But they kept silent, for on the road they had disputed among themselves who would be the greatest. And He sat down, called the twelve, and said to them, "If anyone desires to be first, he shall be last of all and servant of all." Then He took a little child and set him in the midst of them. And when He had taken him in His arms, He said to them, "Whoever receives one of these little children in My name receives Me; and whoever receives Me, receives not Me but Him who sent Me." —Mark 9:30-37*

After healing a boy of an unclean spirit, Jesus left and went through Galilee. Scripture says that He didn't want anyone to know. Know what? The NIV says that He didn't want anyone to know "where they were." The NKJV adds an "it" at the end of the verse, "He did not want anyone to know it." It could have been that He didn't want anyone to know about the healing He had just performed. He often told people to say nothing to anyone about their healing. Or it could be that the verse refers to the concern that follows regarding His betrayal. Actually, the two things are related.

Jesus had become a marked man. The authorities wanted to stop Him from preaching and teaching because they believed that He was dangerous. Everywhere He went He gathered crowds and was at the center of riots and near riots. It was not that Jesus incited riots, but rather, those who disagreed with Him made every effort to stir people up against Him. That was the source of the riots, not Jesus.

Jesus again taught the disciples about His impending death on the cross, that He would be betrayed and killed, but would be resurrected.

The people had been clamoring for miracles. But where they were interested in healing their aches and pains, Jesus would give them the ultimate miracle of miracles—His resurrection. And just as all His miracles were intended to teach about the kingdom of God, so His resurrection would be the greatest miracle. It would confirm His divinity and establish for all time the truth of His gospel.

The disciples, of course, didn't understand Him. We can hardly blame them. We would not have understood either had we been in their shoes. We have the advantage of two thousand years of theology and Christian history, which provides a great benefit to the saints.

God always knows in advance how the future will play out, but we don't. Furthermore, it is to our benefit that we don't have God's foreknowledge. It is much better that we simply trust the Lord on the things we don't understand. However, that doesn't mean that we should not endeavor to know God's truth in its full measure, as it has been given. The trick is to study to know God's Word, but to keep from probing where God's Word does not go. God has some secrets that are best left alone. We need to be content with His self-revelation. God has revealed as much about Himself as He wants us to know—and, believe me, it's plenty!

It is instructive that the disciples did not understand what Jesus was talking about, and that they were afraid to ask Him about it. Here we see an important truth about all genuine disciples. That truth reveals that disciples may not fully understand Jesus or Scripture, and that they have a healthy fear of the Lord that keeps their curiosity from wandering where it shouldn't.

One of the main themes of Scripture is the difference between those who are led by God and His Word, and those who are led by their own imaginations. The key discernment in the Christian life is the difference between God's leading and one's own leading, between the truth as revealed by Scripture and the truth as revealed by human imagination. False images are forbidden by the Second Commandment. The intent of that commandment is to keep us from wandering in the rich fields of our own imaginations and believing that we are led by God.

Here is the importance of maintaining God's truth as it has been handed down to us. If we are to understand the Bible correctly, we must maintain the biblical perspective that has been handed down through the ages. Why? Because God's truth doesn't change. We certainly need to make it our own. We will undoubtedly describe it in different words. But the heart of the gospel as we understand it must maintain fidelity with the gospel as the saints through the ages have understood it. To drop the ball in this regard is to lose the gospel itself. That's why we must understand the gospel from an historical perspective, and not just from the perspective of our own culture.

This is a very real danger that the church has struggled with in every generation. The issue is heresy and Christian history is full of it. The great issues of heresy are always with us. They are reinvented in every generation through the fertility and creativity of the human mind. To fail to study and understand history is to open ourselves up to the dangers of heresy. Heresy always begins with a few very simple ideas. The disciples that day wrestled with some heretical ideas.

Heresy is nothing other than believing what is contrary to church teaching. For Roman Catholics that means believing other than the teaching of the Roman Catholic Church. For evangelicals it means believing other than what is commonly held as evangelical theology among the historic evangelical churches. But that presents a difficulty for us Protestants because at this point in history there are churches that identify themselves as evangelical that believe every which way. For instance, Mormons and Jehovah's Witnesses, while not considered to be evangelical by most Christians, understand themselves to be true Protestant evangelical churches.

While the issues are deep and the histories complex, the root of heresy is always a simple misunderstanding that grows over time. Scripture provides an example of the roots of heresy in the story of the disciples arguing about who would be the greatest among them.

Jesus taught that He must die on the cross for the propitiation of sin. He would give Himself as a sacrifice for sin. In a similar way, those who would follow Jesus must also give themselves in sacrificial service to Him. Christians must be other-directed, not self-directed. Jesus had just taught this in Mark 8:34,

> "Whoever desires to come after Me, let him deny himself, and take up his cross, and follow Me."

Christians are to deny themselves, not satisfy themselves. We are to sacrifice our needs for the sake of the needs of others.

Yet, here were the disciples arguing about who would be the greatest disciple. They were defending their own greatness, rather than seeking to be humble. The direction of their lives, the direction of their concerns was all wrong. It was as if they hadn't heard a thing Jesus taught. They needed to have a complete revolution in personal values. They had yet to repent. Jesus had called them into discipleship, and they had followed Him. But they hadn't yet repented, and repentance is the beginning of a genuine Christian life. To repent is, of course, to turn around and go the other way.

In order to set them straight, Jesus called them together and said,

> "If anyone desires to be first, he shall be last of all and servant of all" (v. 35).

Jesus worked with their very human desire to be top dog, and told them that in the kingdom of God the top dog was on the bottom. Thus, he envisioned for them a complete reversal of their most fundamental thoughts and values. Such a reversal is called repentance.

To illustrate this teaching Jesus took a little child—an infant, "and set him in the midst of them" (v. 36). The disciples had been arguing, and Jesus put a baby in the middle of their argument. We can learn several things from that simple gesture. First, the disciples were not traveling alone, but with their families. Jesus and the disciples had separated themselves from the crowds, and were hiding from the law. Yet, there were children and infants among them. They apparently traveled in families, maybe not all the time, but some of it. Jesus always used whatever was readily available to illustrate his teaching, and a baby was readily available.

How does a baby illustrate self-sacrifice? Babies themselves are little bundles of pure selfishness. However, caring for babies causes the most selfish parents to sacrifice their own desires for the sake of their baby. Jesus was illustrating a point that related to Christian leadership. The disciples were arguing about their leadership positions in God's kingdom. While it's true that to receive the kingdom like a child points out the grace of Christ's gift because an infant can do nothing but receive. However, by putting a baby in their midst, Jesus made the point that Christian leaders are like parents who must sacrifice their own desires for the sake of their children.

Obviously, that doesn't mean that parents give their children everything the children want. Rather, it means that they do what is best for the growth and development of their children. Parents become the servants of their children, just as church leaders become servants of the church. But again, that doesn't mean that as servants parents give their children whatever *they* want. When that happens the children only become spoiled and self-centered.

Rather, the job of parenthood is to serve God's interests for the sake of your children. God knows and wants what is best for children. A good parent gives them, not what they want for themselves, but what God wants for them, what is best for them. So it is with Church leadership. Church leaders are called to be servants of the church, but that doesn't mean that they are to always do what's most popular. Rather, they are to do what *God* wants for the church. Leaders lead.

That's why in the earliest Congregational churches the leaders could veto a vote of the body, just as the body could veto a vote of the leaders. Where there is such disagreement, the best thing to do is more study and prayer.

Church leaders are to pledge themselves to serve the peace and purity of the church. And that's no easy task! It turns out that what serves the peace often corrupts the purity, and what serves the purity often disturbs the peace. Nonetheless, the church is called to both peace and purity among her members. Jesus said,

> "Whoever receives one of these little children in My name
> receives Me; and whoever receives Me, receives not Me but Him
> who sent Me" (v. 37).

To receive someone in Jesus' name is to treat him or her like a Christian. The analogy relates to the church. The church will be made up of infants in Christ, and the disciples as church leaders must receive them as they are. And what are they? They are little sinners chosen by God, given to the church for instruction in righteousness. The church is to parent these baby Christians, to "bring them up in the training and admonition of the Lord" (Ephesians 6:4)—not merely doing what *they* want, but doing what *Christ* wants for them.

Christ died for the reconciliation of sinners, for the likes of you and me. He died for us so that we may live for Him. If you have received God's gift of grace through the death and resurrection of Christ, don't neglect your responsibility to live for Christ, as if Christ is living in you.

38. What About Him?

Now John answered Him, saying, "Teacher, we saw someone who does not follow us casting out demons in Your name, and we forbade him because he does not follow us." But Jesus said, "Do not forbid him, for no one who works a miracle in My name can soon afterward speak evil of Me. For he who is not against us is on our side. For whoever gives you a cup of water to drink in My name, because you belong to Christ, assuredly, I say to you, he will by no means lose his reward."

—Mark 9:38-41

It is not coincidental that verse 38 follows verse 37. Though my Bible has inserted a section break between these verses, they belong together. The point of verse 37 is that whoever receives another in the name of Christ receives Christ Himself. That doesn't mean that the other person is to be regarded as Christ Himself, but that Christ is intimately involved in the process of recognizing someone as a Christian.

The point is made more emphatic by suggesting that the one to be recognized as a Christian may be a child. Remember that the word *children* in verse 37 literally means infant. Jesus said that to recognize another person as a Christian—particularly an infant—requires the presence of Christ Himself. But note that it doesn't simply require the presence of Christ in the one to be recognized, but it requires the presence of Christ in the one who does the recognizing as well. This is the more significant teaching of this verse.

In other words, it requires the presence of Christ in one's self to recognize the presence of Christ in another. John captured Christ's words another time that spoke to the same issue.

> "No one can come to Me unless the Father who sent Me draws him; and I will raise him up at the last day. It is written in the prophets, 'And they shall all be taught by God.' Therefore everyone who has heard and learned from the Father comes to Me" (John 6:43-45).

The difference between Mark 9:37 and verse 38 is the referent. John understood the issue clearly because he had learned it. At first John was concerned because they

> "saw someone who *does not follow us* casting out demons in
> Your name, and we forbade him because he does not follow us"
> (v. 38—italics added).

John's concern was that the man they saw did not follow them—the disciples. At that point in their spiritual walk anyone who followed the disciples would be utterly lost because the disciples themselves had yet to recognize the Lord's real mission. It was not other disciples they were to follow, but Christ.

Christ is Lord and Savior, not John or Mark or Augustine or Calvin or Luther or Wesley. To think of ourselves as Johanites or Markians, or Augustinians or Calvinists or Lutherans or Methodists is to miss the mark. It is to substitute shadow for light. It is to fail in a fundamental sense to understand the gospel. However, that does not mean that we should avoid the counsel of other disciples, particularly those whom history has shown to be helpful.

Too often contemporary Christians understand the Protestant doctrine of Sola Scriptura to mean that Christians should only read the Bible. The first article of the National Association of Evangelicals Statement of Faith reads,

> "We believe the Bible consisting of the Old and New Testament,
> to be the only inspired, inerrant, infallible, authoritative Word of
> God written."

It means that the Bible is the only sufficient and completely trustworthy document that deals with God's Word. But it doesn't mean that we should shy away from Calvin, Luther, Wesley, etc.

Jesus speaks against a faith that is so closed-minded that it fails to see Christ in other disciples, particularly those baby Christians who have yet to show a worthy measure of their faith. We must guard ourselves against thinking that *we* have it right, and that others are wrong unless they agree with us. That is the spirit that Jesus forbids here. But that doesn't mean that everyone has a right to his own opinion. Nor does it mean that we shouldn't try to convince others to believe as we do. Theological discussion is to be encouraged, not discouraged.

Rather, it applies to me or anyone else, should we think that we have the final word on what Scripture means. The Lord Himself would undoubtedly say that the crucial thing is not what Calvin or Luther or

Wesley said, but what Christ said. Yet, by the same token what Calvin and Luther and Wesley said is important. It is, in fact, very helpful. Thus it is important for the church to listen to these faithful disciples, but to remember that they are only disciples.

It is also important to note that Christ's teaching here does not undermine the function or authority of church leaders—theologians, pastors, elders. Too many Christians argue that because Christians are to follow Christ, they are not to follow their own church leaders. There is a sense in which that is true, but there is also a sense in which it is false. We have talked about how it is true. Christ is Lord, not me or Calvin or Wesley, etc. But in what way are Christians to honor and respect the leadership of their pastor, elders, and deacons? In what sense are Christians to follow their church leaders?

Leaders are to be called by God Himself to serve. Their leadership must then be recognized by the church through appointment or election. The point is that church leaders do not represent the church in the courts of God, as if they are a constituency bringing their thoughts and concerns to the Lord. Rather, they represent God to the church, bringing His thoughts and concerns to His people.

While there should be a healthy give and take in the flow of thoughts and ideas among church leaders and their people, instruction in biblical thinking usually flows from the leaders to the people. The pastor and teaching elders are to teach. This doesn't mean that the people have nothing to teach the leaders. Good leaders are always learning, and are willing to learn from any source. But generally speaking, teachers teach and students learn.

The disciples saw a man healing and casting out demons in Jesus' name, but they didn't know him. He claimed to be a disciple of Christ, but the disciples didn't know who he was, or whether he was a genuine disciple or not. The issue was the ability of the disciples to recognize other Christians. Jesus said (in part), "he who is not against us is on our side" (v. 40). Jesus told them that the man was not doing anything unchristian, and should be considered to be a disciple.

The ministry of this man was not opposed to the ministry of the disciples, so the disciples should not oppose him. The gospel may move forward while it is unopposed. If that is all that Jesus said on the matter, it would be a straightforward lesson. But it is not. Both Matthew and Luke present a different take on this important lesson. For Jesus also said,

"He who is not with Me is against Me, and he who does not
gather with Me scatters abroad" (Matthew 12:30, see also Luke
11:23).

Here Jesus seems to say the opposite of what He said before. However, Jesus is not contradicting Himself. Rather, He is dealing with two
different situations. We can think of the two different situations as two
levels of commitment to the gospel. The first one (vs. 40) suggests a low
level of commitment. There a man was healing and casting out demons.
The work he did was not opposed to Christ. But because it is phrased as
it is, it again suggests that the man wasn't doing much for Christ either.
The best that the Lord could say was that he wasn't opposed to the work
of the gospel. And that is good, to an extent.

Commitment to Christ cannot begin until we stop opposing the
Lord. Remember that people are sinners and at enmity with God. Unsaved people resist and oppose Christ at every turn. They do not like
Him, they do not understand Him, they want nothing to do with Him.
So, when people stop opposing the Lord and His gospel, they have begun to turn around. The lack of opposition is the beginning of commitment.

But people cannot remain in the neutral position of not opposing
Christ for long. It is a temporary position because everyone will either
be attracted to or repelled from Christ. No one can sit for long under
the preaching and teaching of the gospel without being effected one
way or the other. Linleigh Roberts said,

"If truth is not the means of conversion, it becomes the grounds
for condemnation."[10]

Commitment to Christ will either increase or decrease over time, but it
will not remain stagnant. It can't, the Lord won't let it.

The second situation was altogether different. There Jesus dealt with
the scribes and Pharisees who had accused Him of being possessed by an
unclean spirit. There Jesus was not dealing with someone sitting on the
fence of commitment, but with staunch representatives of the opposition. There Jesus was talking about Israel as a whole being a divided
kingdom. There He said that all genuine spiritual growth must be
growth toward God, and anyone who was not growing toward God
would be opposed to Christ.

---

10 Roberts, Linleigh. *Let us Make Man*, Banner of Truth, Carlyle, Penn., 1988, p.
    92.

Even genuine Christians are for a time uncommitted to Christ. And that's okay. It must be that way for a time, as people are in the process of conversion. But once people have moved off the fence, they are either with the Lord or they are not. And that leads to a discussion of one of the greatest errors that Christians make—judging others.

Generally speaking Christians are not to judge others. "Judge not, that you be not judged" (Matthew 7:1). We are in no position to be pointing a finger at someone else. Most of the time we should not stand in judgment of anyone else. Those passages of Scripture that accuse are not to be used against others, but are to be used in our own lives to help us flee from sin. God's law accuses us all, and rightly so. Who among us is living as he should?

But the purpose of God's law is to chase sinners into the ever-loving arms of Jesus Christ for salvation, or into the pit of hell for damnation. That is the good news of Jesus Christ to a world lost in sin and corruption. God sent Jesus to save it through the judgment of His Word. The gospel of Christ forces people off the commitment fence, but it doesn't force them into His arms. They must either embrace Him as Lord and Savior, or flee Him because He is the just Judge who either saves or condemns them.

However, that is the Holy Spirit's role, not ours. And we err when we try to act in that role. Thus it is not for Christians to point a con-demning finger. This is a good, sound general rule, but there are excep-tions to it. There are times when it is our duty to point out sin and fail-ures of faithfulness. Such responsibilities belong primarily to church offi-cers—pastors, elders, and deacons—as they engage the process of church discipline, and not to ordinary Christians generally.

Suffice it to say that we should not point God's judgment at anyone other than ourselves. The purpose of preaching is to help us do that, to bring God's Word to bear in a practical way upon *our own* lives, both positively to encourage, and negatively to admonish. Christians are duty bound to bring God's Word to bear upon themselves in order to grow in grace and in the

> "unity of the faith and of the knowledge of the Son of God, to a
> perfect man, to the measure of the stature of the fullness of
> Christ" (Ephesians 4:13).

Generally speaking, we should not worry about the other guy and what he's doing. Worry about yourself and what you are doing—and not doing. The first responsibility for Christians is to get their own houses in order. Christ died, not to bring wrath and judgment to a sinful world, but to bring His faithful people home.

39 WHEN SALT OFFENDS

"But whoever causes one of these little ones who believe in Me to stumble, it would be better for him if a millstone were hung around his neck, and he were thrown into the sea. If your hand causes you to sin, cut it off. It is better for you to enter into life maimed, rather than having two hands, to go to hell, into the fire that shall never be quenched—where 'Their worm does not die, And the fire is not quenched.' And if your foot causes you to sin, cut it off. It is better for you to enter life lame, rather than having two feet, to be cast into hell, into the fire that shall never be quenched—where 'Their worm does not die, And the fire is not quenched.' And if your eye causes you to sin, pluck it out. It is better for you to enter the kingdom of God with one eye, rather than having two eyes, to be cast into hell fire— where 'Their worm does not die, And the fire is not quenched.' For everyone will be seasoned with fire, and every sacrifice will be seasoned with salt. Salt is good, but if the salt loses its flavor, how will you season it? Have salt in yourselves, and have peace with one another." —Mark 9:42-50

The "little ones" that Jesus talks about in verse forty-two is a reference to the "little child" that He set before them while they were arguing about who would be the greatest disciple in the kingdom of God. It is important to make that connection because Jesus is still dealing with that issue as He speaks of being offended by the gospel. Where He had just said that it is imperative for the disciples to recognize and receive all true disciples—even elect children and infants, He now underscores the importance of this teaching by saying that those who cause other disciples to stumble—even children and infants in faith, who cause Christians to doubt their salvation or believe wrongly— would receive a punishment worse than death.

He is pointing to the critical importance of teaching and leading other disciples correctly. Those who would teach or lead other Christians have an awesome responsibility to get the gospel right. The emphasis here is clearly on the correct or orthodox teaching of the gospel, the Word of God. Those who are immature in the faith can stumble. They can misunderstand or fail to properly discern God's Word. While we know that a wrong understanding of the gospel cannot completely destroy the salvation of God's people, it can be the source of much diffi-culty and trouble.

Thoughts and ideas have consequences in the real world. What we think and believe do make an important difference in our lives, and in the lives of others. There is a right understanding of the gospel, as there are wrong ways to understand it. There must be, otherwise God's Word wallows in the cesspool of relativity. If we are free to believe different, contradicting interpretations of the Bible, then God Himself is not telling the truth. If we are free to choose what to believe ourselves we are not subject to Him, but He is subject to us. Of course, we all have a right to our own opinions. But as Christians we have an even greater responsibility to understand God's truth correctly. Your opinion or my opinion are of no real consequence, but God's Word is.

If only it were so easy as that! But it isn't—and you know it. God's Word is always mediated through human channels. The prophets who wrote it were human. Those who translated and preserved it through the ages have all been human. And those who receive it today are hu-man. And there is much human difference of opinion about the right way to understand God's Word. So, how are we to sort through the many differences of opinion in order to receive and believe God's ortho-dox opinion?

Jesus said here that God's orthodox truth itself would offend many people. Thus we face a difficulty. We are not to offend other believers, yet the gospel itself will offend many. It will be impossible to eliminate the offense of the gospel without eliminating the gospel itself—which is an option that many churches have taken. They decide what to teach and preach by shying away from certain Scriptures and issues that they find troublesome. That is an alluring solution to the problem because it plays to the positive warmth of love and unity in the gospel that appeals to saint and sinner alike.

However, it offends God because it does not treat His Word with integrity. It avoids what seems at first glance to be negative and judg-mental by focusing only on certain aspects of the Bible. Thus liberalism is not an inclusive truth because it does not include all of the Bible itself. Its primary focus and concern is man—the people in the church, and not God or Scripture.

Roman Catholics have another solution to the problem. They believe that the Roman Catholic Church has preserved the truth, and people should trust the Church leaders and believe what they say is true.
Our difficulty is that we know that much of what Roman Catholicism
teaches is not true according to Scripture itself.

But how do we know that? How do we know that both the liberals
and the Catholics are wrong? How do we know that we are right?
That's the issue that Jesus is dealing with here. The problem is not that
our beliefs sometimes offend others, it is that our beliefs sometimes offend *God*. The lesson that Jesus teaches here is that people will be offended by the gospel. Everyone must struggle with the narrow and bi-
ased aspects of the gospel.

> "Because narrow is the gate and difficult is the way which leads
> to life, and there are few who find it" (Matthew 7:14).

But what we must not do is offend God by failing to correctly understand and teach His Word. But again, how do we know what the correct understanding of God's Word is?

Before Jesus answered the question, He spelled out the consequences for failing to get the right answer. He wants us to know that
the stakes are high, and that He is playing for keeps.

> "If your hand causes you to sin, cut it off. It is better for you to
> enter into life maimed, rather than having two hands, to go to
> hell, into the fire that shall never be quenched" (v. 43).

How are we to understand this verse? To misunderstand it could
mean that a lot of Christians will be missing hands.

> "And if your foot causes you to sin, cut it off. It is better for you
> to enter life lame, rather than having two feet, to be cast into hell,
> into the fire that shall never be quenched" (v. 45).

Who among us can say that their hand or their foot have not caused
them to sin? And finally,

> "if your eye causes you to sin, pluck it out. It is better for you to
> enter the kingdom of God with one eye, rather than having two
> eyes, to be cast into hell fire" (v. 47).

A misunderstanding of God's Word here can be the source of much
pain and difficulty.

There is no way to twist Jesus' words and make it appear that He is
not talking about cutting of hands and feet, and plucking out eyes. That

is clearly what He said. But what does He mean? Are we to take this teaching literally? I assume that Christians that aren't missing any body parts don't take it literally.

The point that Jesus makes is that it is more important to avoid hell than to preserve our own bodies. So, can hell be avoided by cutting off hands and feet and plucking out eyes? No, it can't. We know that we cannot simply take the literal meaning of Jesus' words here because we know that doing so will not in itself keep anyone from hell. Thus, it is not the hand or foot or eye that we are to eliminate, but whatever causes them to sin. Jesus calls us to eliminate the causes of sin in our lives, be those causes actions that we do (signified by "hand"), places we go (feet), or things we see (eyes). We must eliminate whatever tempts us to sin.

Is that possible? Can we do that? Can we truly eliminate the causes of sin in our lives? If you say yes, you deceive yourself because

> "If we say that we have no sin, we deceive ourselves, and the truth is not in us" (1 John 1:8).

And if you say no, you deny the command of God's Word,

> "Do not be overcome by evil, but overcome evil with good" (Romans 12:21).

We now have two issues before us. First, how do we know what to believe about God's Word? And second, how can sin and its causes be eliminated from our lives? These two issues arise out of this section of Scripture, and both are answered in the same way. When Paul struggled with the weakness of his flesh the risen Lord said to him,

> "My grace is sufficient for you, for My strength is made perfect in weakness." Paul responded, "Therefore most gladly I will rather boast in my infirmities, that the power of Christ may rest upon me" (2 Corinthians 12:9).

God's strength is demonstrated through our weakness. So, when our own strength is showing, God's is not.

We are not able to eliminate sin from our lives, but God is. It is not something that we can do for ourselves. Rather, it is something that God does for us. We don't need to cut off our hands or our feet or pluck out our eyes. We need to rely on God. We need to turn our lives over to Him. We need to let Him sit in the driver's seat. We need to do what He wants us to do. We need to go where He wants us to go. We need to see what He wants us to see. The more we yield to God's guidance the more sin will be eliminated from our lives.

And how do we know that this is true? Two ways: by the inward conviction of the Holy Spirit, and by the testimony of the saints.

People can only understand God's Word by the power and presence of the Holy Spirit. It is the Spirit of God at work in the hearts and minds of His people that causes His Word to ring true. We believe by faith, not because we can demonstrate the truth of God's Word.

And who are the community of saints? It's not a particular denomination. Rather, it is those people throughout history who have been saved by grace alone through faith alone in Christ alone, according to Scripture alone, to the glory of God alone. It is the living and historical witness of all such people. To illustrate the character of the community of saints Jesus talked about salt. Salt, like the community of saints, has a particular character and purpose. It is both a preservative and a flavor enhancer. Like Christian faith, it makes everything taste better and last longer. The community of faith increases our enjoyment of God's Word, and it preserves the character and integrity of God's Word.

But when salt loses its flavor, it does nothing. Its flavor, its character is what makes it powerful. In a similar way, the character of the community of the saints is salty. It is and it must be strong and distinct. It must not be like everything else. It must both preserve the character that it has inherited, and it must season the world with the Word of God.

The church must be prepared to offend the whole world for the sake of the integrity of God's Word, yet it must be careful not to offend God Himself. What a high calling that is! Yet, the only way to do such a thing is to concentrate on not offending God—to treat His Word with absolute honor and integrity, and let the Holy Spirit be responsible for drawing together the community of saints. Our job is to keep our eye on the cross, to preach and to hear the gospel.

Jesus died for this purpose, for the saving of sinners by the power of the gospel. We must allow the gospel to do its work, first in our own lives, and then in others. We must allow it to draw whosoever it will. When a church shifts its primary purpose from maintaining the integrity of the gospel to maintaining the attendance roster it is in serious trouble. Christ didn't die so that friends can sit in church together. He died to bring all who believe to the crisis of faith that leads to salvation.

This lesson that Jesus taught here is summed up in His last words,

> "Salt is good, but if the salt loses its flavor, how will you season it? Have salt in yourselves, and have peace with one another" (v. 50).

To have salt is to be strong and distinct. It is to be a clear, articulate, and bold witness for Christ, and to permeate the society in which we live with the Word of God. But in order to do that we must first be at peace with one another. Christian peace cannot be the shallow go-along-to-get-along mentality that avoids doctrinal differences. Rather, it is the deep peace that has searched God's Word out, wrestled with its offenses, and stands under Christ in the unity of His faith.

40. NUPTIAL BONDS

Then He arose from there and came to the region of Judea by the other side of the Jordan. And multitudes gathered to Him again, and as He was accustomed, He taught them again. The Pharisees came and asked Him, "Is it lawful for a man to divorce his wife?" testing Him. And He answered and said to them, "What did Moses command you?" They said, "Moses permitted a man to write a certificate of divorce, and to dismiss her." And Jesus answered and said to them, "Because of the hardness of your heart he wrote you this precept. But from the beginning of the creation, God 'made them male and female.' 'For this reason a man shall leave his father and mother and be joined to his wife, 'and the two shall become one flesh'; so then they are no longer two, but one flesh.' Therefore what God has joined together, let not man separate." In the house His disciples also asked Him again about the same matter. So He said to them, "Whoever divorces his wife and marries another commits adultery against her. And if a woman divorces her husband and marries another, she commits adultery." —Mark 10:1-12

As we come to the Lord's discussion of marriage, we need to realize that the primary concern here is not merely marriage vows but integrity and fidelity themselves. We must understand that marriage was not instituted for our purposes, but for God's purpose of covenant fidelity. The covenant bond that was instituted in marriage is only a shadow of the primary covenant bond between God and His people. The issue of marriage fidelity impacts the greater concern of fidelity to God's covenant. Thus, what Jesus said about marriage has a wider application than mere marriage.

Jesus continued to travel and to teach. Here in part we see Jesus' amazing patience with people. We have seen in our study of Mark that people rarely understood much of what He said to them. People continued to come to Him seeking signs, wonders, healings, and miracles, and He continued to teach and interpret biblical doctrine. He explained the Old Testament and corrected common spiritual misunderstandings—

knowing all the while that few among them had any understanding at all of what He was talking about.

Yet, He persisted. And His persistence provides a great deal of hope, assurance, and guidance for us. Jesus knew that His words were falling on many deaf ears, yet He did not stop teaching, nor did He give up hope. Similarly, we who teach and preach—Sunday School teachers, Bible study leaders, etc.—are not to give up either. We are not to give up teaching simply because the progress we see doesn't match our expectations. Rather, we are to work steadfastly and boldly, ever maintaining the biblical principle that the duty is ours and the results are God's. It is not the good and successful servant that will enter into the joy of the Lord, but the "good and *faithful* servant" (Matthew 25:21, italics added). The Lord will reward people according to their labor, not their success (1 Corinthians 3:8). This is a great encouragement to persevere in the faith.

In the midst of Jesus' teaching, the Pharisees came again to test the Lord. Their question was designed to entrap Him so they could condemn Him. "Is it lawful for a man to divorce his wife?" (v. 2), they asked. If he answered *yes*, they would condemn Him as a libertine who was undermining their society by relaxing divorce laws. And if He answered *no*, they would condemn Him for denying the law of Moses. Jesus was a master at seeing through these tests and turning the tables on those who set out to trap Him by taking them back to the intent of Scripture.

What did Moses command? He asked them. They knew that Moses had permitted men to write certificates of divorce. Jesus then took them, not to the legal aspects of divorce laws, but to their purpose. First, we must realize that the law of Moses was not merely the law of Moses, but the Law of God written by Moses. It is God's Law that is under fire here, not man's.

Marriage is a creation ordinance. It was never intended to be a social convenience, but rather reflects the truth of the relationship that exists between men and women because of the nature of creation. Marriage is the fulfillment of humanity. That is, in marriage people become whole. Husband and wife are fused into one flesh, not merely in the sense of sexual union, but in the more important and foundational sense of spiritual union. While marriage is quite mysterious, it is not grounded on spiritual mysticism, but on God's covenant. Marriage is an expression of God's covenant relationship with humanity—not the only expression, but an important one.

Don't jump to the conclusion that being single makes a person somehow less human or less complete. It doesn't. Rather, marriage serves as a concrete example of our relationship with God. Spiritually, the church is described as the bride of Christ. Christians, then, are in a kind of marriage relationship with God, where Christ is the Husband and we are the wife. Thus, Christ as the Head of His church rules the wife, and she serves Him.

In Christ we are united in a covenantal bond that resembles marriage. Human marriage is not necessary for such a covenantal relationship with the Lord, but serves as a means to understand the greater spiritual reality. The deeper reality is that people become whole, not merely through the unity of the marriage covenant, but more fundamentally Christians are brought into spiritual unity through God's covenant in Christ.

The question about divorce, then, is not merely a question about human relationships, but more importantly about our relationship with God as well. While we must certainly address the practical concerns of marriage and divorce, Jesus pointed out that we must first deal with the spiritual reality of our relationship with God. Understanding the Old Testament laws regarding divorce requires a prior understanding and commitment to God's covenantal relationship with His people.

God's purpose in allowing for divorce was not to provide for the greater happiness of His people. He allowed it because of their hardheartedness, because of their sinfulness. Divorce stands as a testament to human sinfulness. It originated, not in God's mercy, but in human sinfulness. While God treated divorce with a measure of mercy, divorce is not an ordinance of creation, but a consequence of the fall. Thus, divorce always originates in human sin, not in God's mercy.

The other thing that we need to realize is that Moses' divorce laws were instituted for the protection of women. His intent was to disallow divorce for trivial reasons. The Old Testament knows of no such thing as marital incompatibility because marriage was grounded in God's covenant. And the power of God to establish His covenant was greater than the personal likes and dislikes of His people. Marriage as a covenant relationship between husband, wife, and God is not and cannot be easily broken.

Infidelity was the only basis for Old Testament divorce. Should a husband desire a divorce, he must write out his reasons and give them as a certificate to his wife. If those reasons were anything other than her sexual infidelity, the husband would be writing out a testament of his own infidelity to God's law. For him to divorce because he had found a better relationship with someone else required him to publicly denounce his own adherence to the law of God. Thus, divorce is never an expression of God's mercy provided for an intolerable relationship, but is always an expression of human sin, of the falling away from God's covenantal relationship by either one or the other or both of the parties involved.

This, of course, does not mean that God doesn't forgive those who have been divorced, whether or not it was their fault. There is no sin that God cannot forgive, except the sin that refuses to receive God's forgiveness. Forgiveness is always possible with God.

Jesus was trying to tell us that the divorce problem won't be solved by addressing the issues and concerns of divorce procedures, but by addressing the underlying issues and concerns of marriage. The problem is that people start off on the wrong foot, with the wrong understanding of what marriage is supposed to be. The epidemic of divorce in modern society could be greatly helped if people would consider three things prior to getting married.

First, Paul commends Christians to marry "only in the Lord" (1 Corinthians 7:39). That is to say that Christians should only marry Christians. That's not narrow-mindedness, it's obedience to Scripture. The biblical injunction to marry only within the family of faith demonstrates the importance of spirituality in marriage. Christian marriage can only work when both husband and wife are in a covenantal relationship with God before they marry. Spiritual agreement is a great benefit to marriage.

The marriage covenant is built upon God's covenant. A marriage that does not rest on God's covenant does not rest on a firm foundation. Again, that doesn't mean that God can't convert husbands and wives after the wedding. He can, but as a general rule it is better to postpone the wedding until after the conversion. If the relationship is of God's making, there is no hurry to tie the knot, nor is there any reason to disregard the biblical foundation of marriage.

Second, marriages will have much more happiness and satisfaction when husbands and wives keep their expectations to a minimum. When people look to marriage to solve their problems, they are setting themselves up for sure disappointment. The truth is that marriage is not the solution to life's problems, but is a major source of them. Marriage is not a problem solver. It's a problem generator. That's why we need to have our faith in proper order first. We must understand and realize that marriage is not a perfect union between angels, but a very imperfect union between sinners.

Third, each marriage partner should always strive for the sanctification of the other. Sanctification is, of course, spiritual growth—growth in holiness. Where justification is imputed righteousness, sanctification is infused righteousness. In justification God accounts sinners righteous, in sanctification God makes sinners righteous. It takes a lifetime, but our faith must make us more and more like God—holy, pure, and righteous. The more holy, pure, and God-like married people are, the more happiness they will experience in their marriage. But again, that's true whether people are married or not!

Christ died to bring such holiness and purity to His people. He died for your sin so that you may live for His righteousness. Christ died to bring the whole world to the fulfillment of God's covenant. Marriage can be a tremendous benefit to our spiritual growth, but only if it is done right—God's way. Otherwise, it becomes, not a benefit but a detriment.

41. As A Child

Then they brought little children to Him, that He might touch
them; but the disciples rebuked those who brought them. But
when Jesus saw it, He was greatly displeased and said to them,
"Let the little children come to Me, and do not forbid them; for
of such is the kingdom of God. Assuredly, I say to you, who-
ever does not receive the kingdom of God as a little child will
by no means enter it." And He took them up in His arms, put
His hands on them, and blessed them.　　　—Mark 10:13-16

Following Jesus' discussion of marriage and divorce, someone in
the crowd brought some children to Him, "that He might touch
them" (v. 13). The disciples resisted and rebuked those who
brought them. What would cause the disciples to be so concerned about
Jesus handling some babies? Perhaps they thought Jesus to be above such
mundane concerns, as if Jesus were too important to waste His time
dealing with a bunch of children. Or perhaps it was because the disciples
were aware that Jesus often healed by touching people, and so perhaps
the disciples revered His touch as a means of grace. Perhaps they didn't
want to misuse or denigrate the Lord's blessing. Scripture doesn't tell us
the reasons for the disciple's action, just the fact of it.

But whatever the disciples thought is immaterial because Jesus corrected them. They were wrong and He would have nothing to do with
such nonsense. He had both the time and the concern to "touch" the
children. By treating them as He did, He demonstrated the fact that
children are people too. His concern was for the salvation of humanity
and children are no less human that adults.

In Scripture every time that Jesus "touched" someone they received
grace and healing. "As many as touched Him were made well" (Mark
6:56). Both the Old Testament church and the New Testament church
practiced the laying on of hands as a means and/or symbol of a blessing.
Note that verse 16 confirms Jesus' intent to bless the children.

> "He took them up in His arms, laid His hands on them, and
> blessed them."

Scripture itself makes the connection between Jesus' touch and His laying hands upon them. By doing so, Scripture makes this little incident a
lesson in God's grace. To that lesson we now turn.

There are two sides or perspectives that are addressed in this story:
1) Jesus receives the children, and 2) the children receive the kingdom.

Sometimes the disciples saw themselves as the custodians of God's
grace. We saw this earlier when John wanted to forbid the casting out
of demons in Jesus' name by an unknown person (Mark 9). The disciples
forbade him to continue because he was not associated with their group.
Jesus reprimanded their decision to forbid him saying, "he who is not
against us is on our side" (Mark 9:40).

Now we find the disciples again attempting to control God's grace
by forbidding children—infants—from receiving the Lord's blessing.
However, this does not mean that people can do whatever they want regarding God's grace. Nor does it mean that God's grace operates in a
mechanical way, as if we can simply do the right thing or say the right
thing and cause God's grace and/or blessing to be imparted. Not at all!

God is not a vending machine in the sky where we put in our order
or our quarter, pull the right lever, and receive or impart God's grace.
The cause of the receiving or imparting of God's grace is not under human control. We must not err by thinking that Scripture teaches that
people are free to use Jesus or His blessing and grace however they
want, as if God's grace were under *our* direction.

The point is that the disciples are not to control God's grace, but to
acknowledge it. The disciples are to discern—to understand, to acknowledge—the genuine presence of God's grace. It's the difference between noticing and causing.

But while we are not able to dispense God's grace as we think fit,
God is. God is the one who provides grace and blessings for His people.
God is free to dispense His grace however He wants to whomever He
wants. God is not bound by any particular means, yet He normally uses
means to impart grace. The church has long acknowledged that the
principle means of grace are Word and Sacrament.

To say that grace is imparted by the Word of God, means that salvation is usually received as people interact with God's Word, the Bible.
God has chosen to reveal Himself through His Word. He usually works
through Scripture—prayer, preaching, and Bible study.

Additionally, the sacraments of baptism and communion normally
function as signs and seals of God's promises revealed through His
Word. This is to say that Christ's presence in baptism and communion is

a real presence, a genuine presence, though it is not always discerned to be so. Furthermore, the sacraments work, not magically or mystically, but by the power of God's Word. The sacraments are particular actions that accompany God's Word. But the actions themselves are effective only because they depend upon God's Word. Furthermore, they are only effective when accompanied by the power and presence of the Holy Spirit.

The point is that God blesses whomever He chooses to bless. In order for grace to be grace, it cannot in any way be dependent on those who receive it. To be grace it must be a pure gift. It cannot be dispensed according to the desires of men, not by priests or pastors, nor by evangelists or mystics. And it cannot be dispensed by any kind of ceremonies either, not by baptism or communion, nor by walking the aisle or praying a prayer. If we as human beings have any control of the reception or dispensing of God's grace, then by definition it cannot be grace. If I can cause you to give me a gift, then what I receive from you is not a genuine gift.

Thus, Jesus rebuked the disciples for getting in the way of little children who were coming to Him. *Let them come,* He said, *do not forbid them.* We might expect Him to say next, *Whoever does not receive little children will by no means enter the kingdom of God.* But He doesn't. Rather, He said,

> "…whoever does not receive the kingdom of God *as a little child* will by no means enter it" (v. 15—italics added).

The analogy is not about receiving children, but about receiving the kingdom. We don't enter the kingdom by receiving children. Rather, we enter the kingdom when we receive it as a child receives it.

The other thing that Jesus says here is that little children—infants—are received into God's kingdom. This is an astonishing statement to many people, but it's true. If people must receive the kingdom as a child, then there is nothing that precludes children from receiving the kingdom.

But, someone might ask, isn't faith the condition that must be met in order to receive the kingdom? Doesn't Paul say, "For by grace you have been saved through faith" (Ephesians 2:8)?

Of course he does, but he doesn't mean that we must have faith in order to receive God's grace. It's not that we receive grace only when we have sufficient faith, for that would be works-righteousness. Rather, Paul said that faith is the means or vehicle by which people are saved.

We are not saved because we have faith. Rather, we have faith because we are saved. Faith does not precede God's gift of grace, it follows it.

> "For by grace you have been saved through faith, and that not of yourselves; it is the gift of God" (Ephesians 2:8).

The "it" here refers to faith. Faith is a gift of God. The engine of God's grace pulls the train, the caboose of human faith doesn't push it.

Children are not able to receive God's kingdom because they have the right kind of faith, nor because their faith is strong enough. People are not saved by having the right kind, quality, degree, or amount of faith. All such thinking makes salvation into a kind of works-righteousness. Rather, people are saved by the blood of Jesus Christ, who died on the cross for the atonement of sin. We are saved by what Christ did, not by what we do in response. Salvation is a gift, not a reward.

Of course we must receive it, and faith is the means by which it is received. But faith does not cause salvation to happen. Rather, salvation causes faith to happen. And that is the good news of the gospel. It is great news because salvation is entirely the work of God, and is not dependent upon us. Glory, Hallelujah! It's in God's hands, not mine. I am not saved because I am faithful, I am faithful because I am saved. It's a gift! What a joy!

The joy of salvation is the fact that it has been freely given to unworthy people. God's people know the joy of salvation. In spite of my sins and imperfections, God has chosen to save me! Though I am not worthy—no more worthy than anyone else, God has saved me. To ask, *Why me?* is the wrong response. Thankfulness is the right response. Receiving salvation provides no grounds for pride or boasting. We have nothing to boast about. The knowledge of personal salvation humbles the saints. It's almost embarrassing that God would choose such a flawed vessel in which to manifest the glory of His salvation.

When someone has done us a favor we feel indebted to that person. Even more so when the favor bestowed is something that we cannot do for ourselves. Such a favor puts us into that person's debt. We feel like we need to do whatever we can to return the favor. So it is with Christ. We are in His debt because He has saved us from our sins. The favor that we need to return is to live under the obligations of His righteousness. Thus, in thankfulness for His salvation, we strive to become righteous and holy because that's what He wants us to be. And we do it without regret, remorse, or pretense—as a child. To genuinely receive the kingdom of God is to receive it genuinely.

42. What We Trust

Now as He was going out on the road, one came running, knelt before Him, and asked Him, "Good Teacher, what shall I do that I may inherit eternal life?" So Jesus said to him, "Why do you call Me good? No one is good but One, that is, God. "You know the commandments: 'Do not commit adultery,' 'Do not murder,' 'Do not steal,' 'Do not bear false witness,' 'Do not defraud,' 'Honor your father and your mother.'" And he answered and said to Him, "Teacher, all these things I have kept from my youth." Then Jesus, looking at him, loved him, and said to him, "One thing you lack: Go your way, sell whatever you have and give to the poor, and you will have treasure in heaven; and come, take up the cross, and follow Me." But he was sad at this word, and went away sorrowful, for he had great possessions. Then Jesus looked around and said to His disciples, "How hard it is for those who have riches to enter the kingdom of God!" And the disciples were astonished at His words. But Jesus answered again and said to them, "Children, how hard it is for those who trust in riches to enter the kingdom of God! It is easier for a camel to go through the eye of a needle than for a rich man to enter the kingdom of God." And they were greatly astonished, saying among themselves, "Who then can be saved?" But Jesus looked at them and said, "With men it is impossible, but not with God; for with God all things are possible." Then Peter began to say to Him, "See, we have left all and followed You." So Jesus answered and said, "Assuredly, I say to you, there is no one who has left house or brothers or sisters or father or mother or wife or children or lands, for My sake and the gospel's, who shall not receive a hundredfold now in this time—houses and brothers and sisters and mothers and children and lands, with persecutions—and in the age to come, eternal life. But many who are first will be last, and the last first."
—Mark 10:17-31

In the Rich Young Ruler we see a spiritual seeker, a man who had made a sincere effort to follow God according to the Old Testament law. He approached Jesus because he was actively pursuing righteousness and faithfulness. Like the Pharisees he had made no mean effort to be faithful. He was a student and a product of the teaching of the Pharisees in that he strove with great energy to obey the law.

There is no reason to think that his religious pursuits or his inquiry about wanting to grow spiritually were anything but genuine. There is no indication that the Pharisees had put him up to laying a trap to ensnare Jesus. When he referred to Jesus as "Good Teacher" (v. 17), he did not pretend to honor Jesus. It was not so much a false intention on his part as it was a wrong understanding of the nature of salvation.

The Rich Young Ruler had been a student of the Pharisees, and had learned their system of works-righteousness very well. His spiritual efforts were genuine in that he seemed to believe in what he was doing. Those who subscribe to a works-righteous faith are not insincere. Often their spiritual efforts put others to shame. They are often highly motivated in what they do. Works righteous theology produces many good, sincere, hardworking people. The man's sincerity and integrity were not in question here.

The doctrine of imputed righteousness, the heart of the Protestant Reformation, understands Scripture to teach that God saves sinners, not that God saves those who are morally good.

> "But God demonstrates His own love toward us, in that while we were still sinners, Christ died for us" (Romans 5:8).

God doesn't save the righteous—because there aren't any! God saves sinners in order that they may become righteous. We are not saved because we are righteous, rather, we are able to grow in righteousness only because we are saved. We do not do good works in order to be saved, rather we are saved in order that we may do good works.

What we see in this Rich Young Ruler is not a lack of sincerity or integrity, but a lack of the proper understanding of Scripture. Jesus told him to consider the Old Testament commandments,

> "Do not steal, Do not bear false witness, Do not defraud, Honor your father and your mother" (v. 19).

Jesus didn't list all ten of them, and perhaps that's why the young man said that he had kept all those that Jesus had listed.

But honestly, what child has never lied or disobeyed his parents? By saying that he had fulfilled even these commandments, he revealed a clear lack of understanding of the depth and breadth of the Commandments, and the all-encompassing contagion of sin. The man was not guilty of insincerity, but of failing to understand himself as God understood him. He had a good self-image in that he thought highly of himself, but his self-image was inaccurate according to God's Word. He saw himself as obedient to God's law, whereas Scripture teaches that the purpose of the law was to reveal to people their inability to fulfill God's law. Thus, the gift of the gospel is a gift of grace because there are no righteous people, "no, not one" (Romans 3:10).

The man's response revealed his ignorance of Scripture and of himself. Thus, Mark said that Jesus *looked* at him. The Greek word is *emblepo* and suggests that Jesus saw him for what he was. Jesus saw through his wrong understanding of God's Word. Something blinded this young man to God's truth, and Jesus saw what it was in a flash of insight.

This young man endeavored to love and serve both God and worldly riches. His love of mammon kept him from seeing the truth of Scripture. He wanted to serve God, but he didn't want to stop serving himself. He wanted to do what he wanted to do in such a way that it would serve God secondarily.

And aren't we all like that! We all want to be saved, but we don't want to give up doing what we want to do. We are like the monkey who reached into the cookie jar, grabbed a cookie, but found that the cookie jar opening was too small to allow his hand to escape as long as he held anything in his hand.

We all want what we want and we don't want to let it go. But Jesus said to him, *Give up what you want for yourself, get rid of your own plans and desires, then* "come, take up the cross, and follow Me" (v. 21). The cross! It always comes down to the cross. That's what the disciples themselves had failed to understand. People have a difficult time realizing that true discipleship is a function of the cross.

People want the joy and the glory. The disciples argued among themselves about who would receive the greatest glory. People don't want the cross. But salvation is not about what you and I want, it's about what God wants for us. And that's the rub. That's the stumbling stone. That's the sticking point. Christianity would be much more appealing without the cross.

Jesus had nailed him. He put His finger on the one thing that clearly revealed the man's misunderstanding. This man's liability was his money. Why was it a liability? Because it got in the way of his salvation. It got in the way of his commitment to Christ. It interfered with his re-lationship to the Lord.

We know that Jesus had no problem with wealth itself. Money was not the problem. Many of the faithful saints in the Bible were men of great wealth. So, what was the problem? Paul said,

> "For the love of money is a root of all kinds of evil, for which
> some have strayed from the faith in their greediness, and pierced
> themselves through with many sorrows" (1 Timothy 6:10).

Not money itself, but the love of money. The issue is not money per se, but what we love, what we trust. To have faith in Christ means to trust the Lord. It's not simply a matter of believing that God is real or that Christ is the way of salvation. Rather, it is a matter of actually living on the understanding that God will take care of us in such a way that we need depend upon nothing else.

The issue is what *we* love, what we are devoted to. To be devoted to something involves spending a great deal of time and thought about it. When people fall in love they spend a lot of time thinking about their loved one. They want to spend time together, not doing anything in particular, just being together. And when they are apart they think and pine about each other. That is the nature of real devotion. Thus, we are devoted to what we spend our time doing and thinking about.

Some people are devoted to sports—you have to be if you want to be good at it! Others are devoted to watching sports. Some people are devoted to their work. Some people are devoted to food, or travel. And some people are devoted to their money, playing the markets, nursing their retirement nest egg. What are you devoted to? What do you spend your time doing? What do you spend your money on?

If Christianity were to become illegal, would there be enough evi-dence to convict you of being a believer? Does simply going to church make you a believer? Does your devotion to Christ carry over into your home life or your work life? Are you actively devoted to the Lord, giv-ing to Him generously of your time, talent, and treasure? How much should you give? What did Jesus say to the Rich Young Ruler?

> "One thing you lack: Go your way, sell whatever you have and
> give to the poor, and you will have treasure in heaven; and come,
> take up the cross, and follow Me." (v. 21).

Again, Jesus has no problem with money per se. It's not how much you have that is important. Rather, it's what you do with it. It's what it means to you. Money is nothing in and of itself. It's just a piece of paper, or a piece of gold—a rock. Money is only important because it is a means of exchange. The dollar bill in your pocket is really a promise, a promissory note. It represents a promise that if you give it to someone, they will give you a dollar's worth of something.

Your checkbook is another example. A check is nothing more than a promise either. It's an I. O. U. When you give someone a check, you are giving them your promise. Such promises have value in the marketplace. They are bought and sold as commodities. Thus, our entire financial system is built upon promises. Wealth is a measure of the value of our promises.

The issue is not just the value of your promises, but the value of God's promises. Can you trust God to take care of all your needs by trusting the value of God's Word? Will you devote yourself to the Lord, serving Him and studying His Word? Or will you devote yourself to the values of this perishing world by trusting in the value of money? The issue is not money, but trust—truth.

If we trust our lives to the things of the world, like money and technology, we will wake up one day with nothing to hold on to. Thus, Jesus said to the Rich Young Ruler, *You must let go of your false values before you can take up God's eternal values. You cannot hold both at the same time.* What was his response?

> "He was sad at this word, and went away sorrowful, for he had
> great possessions" (v. 22).

He could not take up the cross because he couldn't let go of his own concerns. What about you?

Jesus looked around at His disciples as He asked the question because it applied to them as well. *How hard it is!* He said. We would all like to think differently, or at least think that we are different from those who are tainted by worldly temptations. We all know that, like power, money corrupts. And like power, the more you have, the more corrupt you grow—not always, but usually. But people tend to think that they are exceptions to the norm.

However we might understand the camel and the eye of the needle, the point is that wealth provides a formidable barricade to heaven.

> "It is easier for a camel to go through the eye of a needle than for
> a rich man to enter the kingdom of God" (v. 25).

As poor as the disciples were—and they were average working men, they understood Jesus clearly. "Who then can be saved?" (v. 26) they cried. They understood themselves to have enough money to interfere with their salvation. But if they thought they were rich enough to be at risk in this regard, what about you?

Again, Jesus' response points to the fact that people are not saved by what they have or don't have. People are not saved by what they do or don't do. People are saved by the grace of God, period!

> "With men it (salvation) is impossible, but not with God; for
> with God all things are possible" (v. 27).

In other words, we are not to look to anything but Christ for salvation. And looking to Christ, we must understand that nothing can keep us from salvation. Wealth creates a tremendous problem, but Christ provides an even greater solution.

Peter tried to tell Jesus that he and the disciples were different than the rest of the people because they had given up everything to follow Jesus. Peter began to make a case for his own (infused) righteousness. But Jesus cut him off by saying that it wasn't just the love of money that distracted people from salvation, but the love of family or property as well. He implied that the love of any worldly goods and/or relationships created the same difficulties as the love of money.

But, said Jesus, *Whoever gives it all up for Me and for the kingdom will be repaid a hundred-fold. Whatever sacrifices people make will be more than generously compensated for. The gift of eternal life is a hundred times more valuable than anything on earth.*

Jesus concludes this argument by saying that "many who are first will be last, and the last first" (v. 31). Here Jesus exhorted the disciples to persevere in faithfulness. Just because Jesus had called them early in His ministry did not necessarily mean that they would be the first to enter the kingdom, or that they would have the best places in the kingdom. Rather, Jesus said, our concern is not when the kingdom comes—only God knows that. Our concern is to persevere in faithfulness to the end.

43. What You Ask

Now they were on the road, going up to Jerusalem, and Jesus was going before them; and they were amazed. And as they followed they were afraid. Then He took the twelve aside again and began to tell them the things that would happen to Him: "Behold, we are going up to Jerusalem, and the Son of Man will be betrayed to the chief priests and to the scribes; and they will condemn Him to death and deliver Him to the Gentiles; and they will mock Him, and scourge Him, and spit on Him, and kill Him. And the third day He will rise again." Then James and John, the sons of Zebedee, came to Him, saying, "Teacher, we want You to do for us whatever we ask." And He said to them, "What do you want Me to do for you?" They said to Him, "Grant us that we may sit, one on Your right hand and the other on Your left, in Your glory." But Jesus said to them, "You do not know what you ask. Are you able to drink the cup that I drink, and be baptized with the baptism that I am baptized with?" They said to Him, "We are able." So Jesus said to them, "You will indeed drink the cup that I drink, and with the baptism I am baptized with you will be baptized; but to sit on My right hand and on My left is not Mine to give, but it is for those for whom it is prepared." And when the ten heard it, they began to be greatly displeased with James and John. But Jesus called them to Himself and said to them, "You know that those who are considered rulers over the Gentiles lord it over them, and their great ones exercise authority over them. Yet it shall not be so among you; but whoever desires to become great among you shall be your servant. And whoever of you desires to be first shall be slave of all. For even the Son of Man did not come to be served, but to serve, and to give His life a ransom for many."
—Mark 10:32-45

Jesus and the disciples were on the road again, going up to Jerusalem. Mark said that "Jesus was going before them" and "they were amazed" and "afraid" (v. 32). Jesus was no doubt leading them physically down the road, but He was also leading them spiritually into a deeper understanding of the gospel.

Notice that they were amazed and afraid before Jesus predicted His impending crucifixion, death, and resurrection, which means that their amazement and fear were not directly related to Jesus' prediction at that time. Surely, their amazement and fear related to Jesus' crucifixion because the gospel is related to His crucifixion. But because their amazement and fear preceded His prediction, the source of their concern at that time was other than Jesus' prediction. So, what were they amazed and afraid of?

If we take the immediate context and consider that they were still reeling from His teaching about money and salvation to the Rich Young Ruler we can surmise that they were amazed at God's incredible grace, so freely given to sinners. And they were afraid of the implication of actually depending on God's grace rather than depending upon money themselves. Jesus had applied His injunction—to

> "sell whatever (they) have and give to the poor... and come, take
> up the cross, and follow (Jesus)" (v. 21)

—to them as well as to the Rich Young Ruler.

A literal reading of this injunction is quite distressing. Forsaking family, friends, and property for the gospel is a tall order, and no one should take it casually. In addition, Jesus had mentioned something about impending persecutions (v. 30). What was that all about? All these thoughts tumbled in the disciples' heads as they walked. No wonder they were amazed and afraid.

Then Jesus told them why they were going to Jerusalem. It wasn't exactly clear, but several of Jesus' words continued to rattle them—*betray, condemn, mock, scourge, kill.* Is it any wonder they missed Jesus allusion to the resurrection? They were still choking on betray, condemn, mock, scourge, and kill.

This was the third time that Jesus had mentioned His death and resurrection But it was such a foreign concept that it is little wonder that they had trouble understanding what Jesus was talking about. Their own preconceived ideas about the Messiah of God continued to dominate their awareness. In fact, what we see in the gospel of Mark generally is the incredibly tenacious power of preconceived ideas to pervert the gospel of Christ. More often than not, what we as human beings see in a given situation is what we expect to see. Human perception tends to conform to human expectation. Thus, God's truth so often lies in obscurity in the minds of most people.

The proclamation of the gospel must always begin with the doctrine of sin as total depravity—the inability of man to save himself and to rightly understand God. The ways of God—crucifixion, resurrection, vicarious atonement, free grace to sinners, strength in weakness, etc.—are not the ways of man. So, until we realize that God's Word is utterly foreign to human understanding, our own expectations, our own hopes and dreams will continue to direct our perceptions. People are unable to perceive or understand the gospel rightly until they abandon their own preconceptions. That is, until they receive the guidance of the Holy Spirit.

The history of the church is the history of the struggle between orthodoxy and heresy, between God's truth and human misunderstanding. The recalcitrant thoughts and expectations of men continue to erode God's biblical foundations. In other words, the foundations of the gospel need to be renewed and refreshed in every generation because of the tenacity of fleshly hopes and dreams. The trick is to reform and renew the gospel without changing it.

We can see this tendency exhibited in the disciples as James and John come to Jesus with a slightly refined but essentially identical concern about their own positions of power and authority in the kingdom of God. Previously they had argued about who among them would be the greatest in the kingdom (Mark 9:33-ff). In spite of all that Jesus had taught and said, that discussion continued unabated among the disciples.

Here it erupts again as James and John told Jesus that they wanted Him to do for them whatever they asked (v. 35). Such audacity! They, like we, want God to work for us. Such thinking is entirely backwards. God does not work for us, we work for Him! In the same way that our human thinking gets reversed about the ways of salvation, so the disciples continued to think that God was in their service, rather than them being in God's service.

History shows that we easily get things reversed. For instance, we do not do good works in order to be saved, but we are saved in order that we may do good works. We are not saved because we grow in righteousness, but we grow in righteousness because we are saved. The Rich Young Ruler put his own concerns before God, just as James and John did here. This reversal is always a matter of putting ourselves before God, making salvation depend upon what we do rather than on what God has done.

Jesus asked them what they wanted Him to do for them. Who were they concerned about? Themselves. They wanted to sit on His right and left in the kingdom. They wanted the seats of honor and power for themselves. Oh, they would let Jesus be the King of kings all right, but they wanted to be in charge of everyone else!

Jesus told them that they didn't know what they were talking about. They hadn't yet understood the necessity or role His death and resurrection played in salvation. They were afraid of the word *persecution*. They didn't understand that values in the kingdom will be reversed—the first will be last, the last will be first, God's strength will be found in human weakness, etc. When Jesus asked them if they were able to drink from His cup or be baptized with His baptism, His meaning was that they were not able.

The word *cup* here indicated the crucifixion experience that awaited Jesus in Jerusalem. It was another allusion to His suffering, death, and resurrection. The allusion to Jesus' cup was a direct reference to words Jesus had used earlier—betray, condemn, mock, scourge, kill. This was the baptism that Jesus would undergo.

But the disciples, still under their own personal delusions and expectations, thought themselves able to follow Jesus into His baptism. They thought that they could indeed drink His cup and receive His baptism. Remember that the Holy Spirit had not yet been bestowed upon them, so they were talking in the flesh. Like the Rich Young Ruler, they thought they could do it themselves. Their theology was still works-righteous. And it shouldn't surprise us that they were as they were. They had lived under the teaching of the Pharisees all their lives.

Little did they know what was in store for them. But Jesus did. Anticipating the outpouring of the Holy Spirit and their martyrdom, Jesus assured them that they would indeed receive His baptism and drink His cup. However, their concern about their places or roles in the kingdom was at best premature. Once they received the Holy Spirit their minds would be changed. Then they would understand things differently.

The other disciples heard Jesus correcting them and jumped in, berating them as if *they* understood what Jesus was talking about. Jesus knew that they didn't. The Holy Spirit hadn't come upon them either. They were in no position to say anything.

Jesus called them to Him to explain to them all their position as disciples and leaders in the kingdom. The leaders in the world rule over those they lead. They look down on them, and boss them around. They think that they are "above" other people. But kingdom leadership is not like that, He said. kingdom leaders are servants of those they lead. Ours is a servant leadership. Christian leaders are the servants of those they lead. The highest position in the kingdom is the "slave of all" (v. 44).

The disciples had been seeking prestige and power, but Jesus offered personal insignificance and service. The disciples had been seeking glory and self-importance, but Jesus offered the cross and self-denial. The disciples wanted power and security, Jesus offered weakness and vulnerability.

It reminds me of a poem:

Confederate Soldier

I asked God for strength That I might achieve.
I was make weak That I might learn to obey.
I asked for health That I might do greater things.
I was given infirmity That I might do better things.
I asked for riches That I might be happy.
I was given poverty That I might be wise.
I asked for power That I might have the praise of men.
I was given weakness That I might feel the need of God.
I asked for things That I might enjoy life.
I was given life That I might enjoy all things.
I got nothing that I asked for, But everything I had hoped for.
Almost despite myself My unspoken prayers were answered.
—An Unknown Confederate Soldier

44. Blind, But Now I See

*Now they came to Jericho. As He went out of Jericho with His
disciples and a great multitude, blind Bartimaeus, the son of
Timaeus, sat by the road begging. And when he heard that it
was Jesus of Nazareth, he began to cry out and say, "Jesus, Son
of David, have mercy on me!" Then many warned him to be
quiet; but he cried out all the more, "Son of David, have mercy
on me!" So Jesus stood still and commanded him to be called.
Then they called the blind man, saying to him, "Be of good
cheer. Rise, He is calling you." And throwing aside his garment, he rose and came to Jesus. So Jesus answered and said to
him, "What do you want Me to do for you?" The blind man
said to Him, "Rabboni, that I may receive my sight." Then Jesus said to him, "Go your way; your faith has made you well."
And immediately he received his sight and followed Jesus on
the road.*   —Mark 10:46-52

We all know that when Joshua fought the battle of Jericho, the walls came tumbling down. Joshua's victory at Jericho was a decisive battle in the conquest of Caanan. Jericho was highly fortified. Her defensive walls were thick and high, practically im-pregnable. Yet, the ancient Israelites—or rather God—brought those walls down without firing a shot. You remember the story. Joshua in-structed his soldiers to circle Jericho seven times without saying or do-ing anything. At the end of the seventh circumnavigation they were to raise a triumphant shout of God's name. As they did so, the walls came tumbling down. In a significant way the ancient defeat of Jericho opened the way for the conquest of Caanan.

Whatever Jesus did in Jericho stirred up a great following because as He left that city "His disciples and a great multitude" (v. 46) followed Him. Where was He going? To Jerusalem for the final showdown. As He left Jericho, Bartimaeus, who was known for his blindness, called out to Him. We don't know much about Bartimaeus, except that he was blind and that his father's name was Timaeus. No doubt Mark men-tioned his father's name because Timaeus was well known for some reason—good or bad we don't know. This detail provides us with the fact that Bartimaeus was a real individual who was known to be blind.

Bartimaeus was begging by the side of the road when Jesus passed by. Bartimaeus knew that something was going on because of the crowd that gathered. When he heard that Jesus of Nazareth was the center of activity, he cried out, "Jesus, Son of David, have mercy on me!" (v. 47). This plea, issued by blind Bartimaeus, evidenced genuine faithfulness.

Three things are worthy of note in this cry. First, it is a fervent cry to the Lord. It comes out of a sense of utter and complete hopelessness that looks to the Lord as the only remedy. This position or attitude—utter hopelessness apart from Christ's intervention—provides fertile soil for the seed of faith to bloom and grow.

Every Christian must cross this field of helplessness and be stripped of those things upon which they falsely and vainly depend, those things that encourage us to trust in ourselves or in the things of the world, rather than in Christ. Bartimaeus' cry was a cry of desperation, not despondency or hopelessness but rather the desperate realization that only one hope remained for him—Christ. It was not a cry of defeat, but the valiant cry of a soldier with his back up against a wall and the enemy coming down upon him. It was a cry of determination, not a cry of desolation.

How do we know that? Because of the two things that Bartimaeus said in his cry. Bartimaeus recognized the fact that Jesus was the Son of David. The phrase "Son of David" is pregnant with messianic meaning. Grounded in the Old Testament, the title belonged to the long awaited Messiah of God, who would bring salvation to the lost and lame. Old blind Bart knew by faith that Jesus was indeed the Messiah of God. But not only did he know it personally, he proclaimed it in the midst of the crowd.

Above all the noise and commotion of the crowd, Jesus heard Bartimaeus cry out. Why? Because that's exactly what Jesus was looking for. He was looking for a sign that someone understood that He was not just a good preacher, not just a talented healer, but the very Messiah of God. And who recognized that fact? A blind beggar! While so many around Jesus, including His disciples, failed to see Jesus' identity, a blind beggar at the side of the road announced it publicly. Peter had recognized Jesus as the Christ earlier, but from all appearances the others disciples had not. And Peter had yet to understand his own confession.

In this way Bartimaeus had the correct object of faith. He did not have faith in himself. He did not have faith in the church. He did not have faith in miracles. He had faith in Christ, and in his desperation his faith was turned to Christ alone. But he not only had faith in Christ, he understood how faith worked.

"Have mercy on me" (v. 47), he cried. God's mercy is synonymous with God's grace. The gift of mercy is the gift of grace. Bartimaeus knew that the only way that he could enter into the kingdom of God was by an act of God's gracious mercy. He was a blind beggar at the side of the road. As the hymnist wrote, "Nothing in my hand I bring, simply to the cross I cling." He had nothing and could contribute nothing toward his salvation. Yet, he trusted or knew that Christ was God's Messiah, and that salvation came by grace alone.

It is curious that many people in the crowd warned Bartimaeus to be quiet. Why would the crowd not rejoice in Bartimaeus' insight into the identity of Jesus and the nature of salvation? Apparently, they didn't see what was so significant about what Bart said. They either didn't understand it or didn't like it. Yet, Bartimaeus went against the desires of the crowd and began shouting his confession. Jesus is the Messiah! Salvation is by God's gracious mercy alone!

When Jesus heard his cry, He stopped and commanded His disciples to bring the man to Him. Providence had provided another object lesson for His followers. Jesus commanded that the man be called over. Three times Mark used the word *call* in verse 49. Jesus commanded the man to be called, they called him, telling him that Jesus had called him.

It is not a coincidence that people are Christian because God calls them. Christians are people who are *called* by God. Some Scriptures tell us that Christians are called out or called apart by the Lord. The Greek word *ekklesia*—church—means a people who are called out or called apart or called together. The word itself sets up a tension between those who are called into the church and those who are not. The distinction reflects the ancient division between the saved and the lost.

We remember that the Rich Young Ruler was not saved. He had turned away from Jesus, hanging on to what he had—his material possessions. But here blind Bartimaeus, who had nothing, responded to Jesus call by "throwing aside his garment" (v. 50). The only thing of any value that this poor, blind beggar had was his garment, his coat or blanket. Yet, he relinquished his only possession and came to Jesus. Bartimaeus' response is contrasted with the response of the Rich Young

Ruler. The poor, blind beggar threw aside his only possession, while the Rich Young Ruler clung to all that he had.

The question that Jesus asked him was the same question that He had just asked His disciples, James and John, What do you want Me to do for you? Mark thus contrasted the response of the disciples with blind Bartimaeus. Bartimaeus responded by calling Jesus "*Rabboni,*" which means "My Great One." Again, Bartimaeus acknowledged the divinity of Jesus and his personal response or relationship to Him as Lord. Other than Peter, the disciples had made no such acknowledgment.

Bartimaeus wanted to receive his sight, to be restored to his original, intended condition of being a fully functioning human being created in the image of God. He did not ask for personal advantage, but only that his personal disadvantage would be removed. The disciples, on the other hand, had asked for positions of power and influence in the kingdom of God. The disciples sought their own advantage.

Bartimaeus had the insight to see that Jesus was the Messiah and that salvation was by grace alone. Whereas James and John couldn't see past their own desires. The story invites us to contrast the two kinds of vision and to assess which is more important—physical sight or spiritual insight.

Finally Jesus said, "Go your way..." (v. 52). He could tell Bartimaeus that because he was already standing firmly in God's Way. Thus, Bartimaeus did not go his own way, he followed Jesus. Jesus also said to him, "your faith has made you well," or "healed you." The King James Version reads, "thy faith hath made thee whole." The Greek word is *sozo*, which literally means to save. Bartimaeus' faith had saved him.

It is clear here that Bartimaeus' salvation preceded his sight. Jesus told him that his faith had already saved him. The verb is in the past tense. He was already saved because of his faith in Christ as the Messiah of God. After Jesus told him that, then "he received his sight" (v. 52). Yes, Bartimaeus received his sight, but more important he was saved. And even more important, his salvation became an object lesson that clearly gave all the glory, all the credit to God. Having received his sight, Bartimaeus then proceeded to "follow Jesus" (v. 52).

In Mark's gospel the salvation/healing of Bartimaeus was for Jesus what Jericho had been for Joshua—a significant and determinative event. The capture of Jericho represented an important foothold or breakthrough into Caanan from which the Israelites could mount increasingly successful forays. So, Bartimaeus' salvation/healing represented an important foothold or breakthrough for the gospel of Jesus Christ because

Bartimaeus understood the two pillars upon which it rested—the divinity of Jesus and the grace of God. From this foothold, Jesus set out for Jerusalem.

We are saved by grace alone through faith alone in Christ alone according to Scripture alone to the glory of God alone. What's so important about the word *alone*? It emphasizes that our salvation is not a matter of personal merit or works. It emphasizes that faith is the only instrument of salvation—not the church, not priests or pastors, not ceremonies. And it emphasizes that Jesus Christ is the only Savior. Do you call Christ your Lord and Savior? To call Him Lord is to be His willing servant twenty-four hours a day.

Lord, help us to see that if we are not your servants we are servants of your enemy. Help us to see, as Bartimaeus did, that you are the only hope we have. Help us to see you as the Christ you are, and to accept and receive your precious gift of grace. Amen.

45. Faith in God

Now the next day, when they had come out from Bethany, He was hungry. And seeing from afar a fig tree having leaves, He went to see if perhaps He would find something on it. When He came to it, He found nothing but leaves, for it was not the season for figs. In response Jesus said to it, "Let no one eat fruit from you ever again." And His disciples heard it. So they came to Jerusalem. Then Jesus went into the temple and began to drive out those who bought and sold in the temple, and over- turned the tables of the money changers and the seats of those who sold doves. And He would not allow anyone to carry wares through the temple. Then He taught, saying to them, "Is it not written, 'My house shall be called a house of prayer for all nations'? But you have made it a 'den of thieves.'" And the scribes and chief priests heard it and sought how they might destroy Him; for they feared Him, because all the people were astonished at His teaching. When evening had come, He went out of the city. Now in the morning, as they passed by, they saw the fig tree dried up from the roots. And Peter, remember- ing, said to Him, "Rabbi, look! The fig tree which You cursed has withered away." So Jesus answered and said to them, "Have faith in God. For assuredly, I say to you, whoever says to this mountain, 'Be removed and be cast into the sea,' and does not doubt in his heart, but believes that those things he says will be done, he will have whatever he says. Therefore I say to you, whatever things you ask when you pray, believe that you re- ceive them, and you will have them." —Mark 11:12-24

The story is simple to report, but difficult to explain. Jesus cursed a fig tree that was in leaf out of season but had no fruit. "It was not the season for figs" (v. 13) so what did Jesus expect? Most people probably don't know that fig trees produce fruit before they pro- duce leaves. The fruit is the first thing out, then they produce leaves and the fruit ripens. Therefore, if the tree had leaves it should have had fruit, even though this particular tree was blooming out of season. Jesus then cursed the tree for being what it was—fruitless.

Mark then moves from there directly to the cleansing of the Temple. We're familiar with the scene. Faithful Jews were required to make regular sacrifices of various sorts of animals on various occasions. The animals needed to be without spot or blemish. The trip to Jerusalem was often long and arduous, so for expediency sake a system was developed where pilgrims could purchase first class animals raised especially for sacrifice. It made things much easier on the pilgrims by making travel easier and utterly eliminated the risk of presenting an unfit sacrifice.

What had begun as an aid to struggling pilgrims had become the center of activity as merchants contracted with the Temple to provide a kind of "one-stop shopping for all your sacrificial needs." Business got to be pretty good, and as it is with business success, soon the interests of the business overrode the purpose of the whole sacrificial system. The atoning purposes of the sacrifice took a back seat to the commercial opportunities at hand. The business no longer served the purpose of the Temple, but the Temple served the purpose of the business.

The synoptic gospels report that Jesus called the Temple a "den of thieves." But we must also consider John's version, "a house of merchandise" (John 2:16). John's word was *emporion*, which is just as it sounds—an emporium, marketplace. By calling it a den of thieves we might be tempted to think that the merchants were cheating people somehow. But it seems to me that even if the merchants had been completely honest in their dealings, Jesus response would have been the same. The merchants had Temple permission to do what they were doing. The issue wasn't dishonest business practices, but the subverting of divine to worldly purposes.

Jesus suggested that there is a fundamental problem with subsuming ministry values under market values. We might ask, *Is nothing sacred?* Was the Temple not a sacred space that had been "set apart," sanctified for God's purposes? The merchandising of Temple sacrifices revealed a fundamental lack of understanding and concern regarding the atoning purpose of the sacrifices. The main problem was that neither the merchants nor the Priests had any problem with what they were doing. Thus, the cleansing of the Temple by Jesus was a straightforward story with a fairly simple lesson about spiritual purity.

On the way out of Jerusalem the next day when Peter noticed that the fig tree that Jesus had cursed the day before had "withered away" (v. 21). The fact that Mark sandwiched the cleansing of the Temple between the cursing and the withering of the fig tree suggests that they are related. We need to establish that relationship before we look at the lesson conveyed.

There is general agreement that the fig tree represents the Old Testament Jewish church/establishment of Jesus' day. The fig tree motif itself has long been used in Scripture. The leaves that Adam and Eve covered their nakedness with were fig leaves (Genesis 3:7). The fig tree had become a symbol of safety and salvation during the reign of Solomon (1 Kings 4:25). The examples are numerous.

The most common understanding was that Christ had come during a time of spiritual darkness. The nations of the earth did not have a true understanding of God, all except Israel, that is. Israel represented a nation out of season. It was green and lush with the teaching of God through the Temple sacrifices and Old Testament revelation. Thus, it alone among the nations seemed to be alive in a Godly sense, like the lone fig tree the day Jesus passed it by.

But as abounding as Israel was with the things of God, it was spiritually fruitless. It was all leaf and no fruit. Israel was spiritually bankrupt, as evidenced by the merchandisers in the Temple. We might say that there was plenty of "green" (money), but little of spiritual substance to show for it. Israel lacked appropriate fruits of the Spirit. God's purpose was to grow spiritual fruit, and the one place that should have manifested such fruit—Israel, the Temple—was barren. Like the fig tree.

So Jesus, acting in His divinity as God Himself, cursed it. He cursed the barren fig tree, just as God cursed the barren Temple. Jesus had said that

> "every tree that does not bear good fruit is cut down and thrown
> into the fire" (Matthew 7:19).

Over night the fig tree then withered away! And sure enough, within the lifetime of some of those who had known Jesus personally, the Temple and all of Jerusalem burned to the ground at the hands of the Romans (A.D. 70).

What does all this mean? Jesus told us what it means. His answer in the Greek was preceded by, *gar amen* (and means *amen!*). The KJV translates *gar,* "For *verily* I say unto you…" (italics added). The words indicate that what was said next provided a kind of conclusion about what was said previously. Peter had noticed the withered fig tree and said,

"Rabbi, look! The fig tree which You cursed has withered away"
(v. 21). And *gar amen*, "So Jesus answered and said to them,
'Have faith in God'" (v. 22).

The lesson about the withered fig tree and the merchandising of the
Temple was to have faith in God.

How so? Was Jesus being mystically cryptic here? No. In fact, He
put His finger on the very thing that ties the two stories together—faith,
or a lack of it really. Faith was the missing ingredient in the fig tree and
in the cleansing of the Temple. How so? The fig tree and Israel—the
Temple and its practices—were barren. Neither had produced the fruit
that the Lord wanted—figs in the case of the tree, and the fruits of the
Spirit in the case of Israel. The cause of spiritual fruitlessness is a lack of
faith. Faith produces spiritual fruit. Israel had failed to produce spiritual
fruit in her people, so the Lord cursed her.

"Have faith in God" Jesus said,

> "For assuredly, I say to you, whoever says to this mountain, 'Be
> removed and be cast into the sea,' and does not doubt in his
> heart, but believes that those things he says will be done, he will
> have whatever he says. Therefore I say to you, whatever things
> you ask when you pray, believe that you receive them, and you
> will have them" (vs. 22-24).

Does that mean that you can have whatever you want as long as
you want it hard enough? No, not at all. Who has no doubts in his
heart? Only God Himself, for all of us human beings are tainted with sin
and doubt (Romans 3:23). Who actually believes that whatever he says
will in fact be done? Only God Himself has that kind of power. Only
God can command mountains to move with the sure expectation that
they will comply.

Therefore, Jesus was saying by way of analogy that He was God,
and that we should have faith in Him by wanting what He wants for us.
When we want for ourselves what God wants for us, we will surely receive it because God will make it happen. Jesus was not teaching visual-
ization, like they do in sports and business seminars. People are taught to
visualize their success or a particular play or move and by visualizing
themselves going through the motions, they are more likely to make it
actually happen. Or so people are taught. But that is not what Jesus
taught here.

Here Jesus taught people to believe in the reality of a God who is
completely able to do whatever He wants. Jesus taught the reality of a

sovereign God who is in absolute control of all things. First, said Jesus, believe in this sovereign God, this omnipotent, all-powerful God. Believe that He is real! Then, believe that you as an individual have been granted His favor, that He has given you His grace and His mercy, that He has given all things for the salvation of His people, of which you are one. Whatever you ask, believe that God can provide it, and that God in fact wants you to have it. Believe that you are a special concern to the God who is omnipotent. That's what Jesus was teaching here—not that we can have anything we want in the flesh, but that we can and will have whatever God wants us to have.

46. ALREADY LATE

*Now when they drew near Jerusalem, to Bethphage and
Bethany, at the Mount of Olives, He sent two of His disciples;
and He said to them, "Go into the village opposite you; and as
soon as you have entered it you will find a colt tied, on which
no one has sat. Loose it and bring it. "And if anyone says to
you, 'Why are you doing this?' say, 'The Lord has need of it,'
and immediately he will send it here." So they went their way,
and found the colt tied by the door outside on the street, and
they loosed it. But some of those who stood there said to them,
"What are you doing, loosing the colt?" And they spoke to
them just as Jesus had commanded. So they let them go. Then
they brought the colt to Jesus and threw their clothes on it, and
He sat on it. And many spread their clothes on the road, and
others cut down leafy branches from the trees and spread them
on the road. Then those who went before and those who followed cried out, saying: "Hosanna! 'Blessed is He who comes in
the name of the Lord!' Blessed is the kingdom of our father
David That comes in the name of the Lord! Hosanna in the
highest!" And Jesus went into Jerusalem and into the temple. So
when He had looked around at all things, as the hour was already late, He went out to Bethany with the twelve.*
—Mark 11:1-11

O n the day that we know as Palm Sunday Jesus and His disciples
went to Jerusalem, but did not enter it until certain prepara-
tions had been made. They first went to the Mount of Olives,
a hill outside of Jerusalem near the villages of Bethpage and Bethany.
The word *Bethpage* literally means "the house of unripe fruit." It was
the lack of fruitfulness that caused Jesus to curse the fig tree (Mark
11:14), and which led to the cleansing the Temple (Mark 11:15). The
word *Bethany* literally means "the house of dates or of fruit." The two
villages are contrasted in both a literal and a spiritual sense.

Jesus had come to save the Jews, but found them spiritually fruitless.
It was the Jews who had rejected Him and the salvation He brought at

every turn. But the Gentiles had, by and large, received Him. He had sown and seen fruits of salvation among the Gentiles, but not among the Jews. This scene of preparation to enter into Jerusalem suggests the analogy of fruitlessness. Bethany, the fruitful village, was the home of Mary, Martha, and Lazarus. It was the place from which Jesus entered Jerusalem.

Jesus told two disciples to "go into the village opposite you" (v. 2— italics added). The Greek word that indicates the particular village Jesus referred to is *katenanti*, which means over against, before, or opposite. It suggests that Bethpage was across a valley or ravine. But the analogous point is that Jesus was in a fruitful village when He sent the disciples on an errand to the fruitless village. The fruitless imagery of fig (date) trees applies to Israel and the Old Testament religion of the Jews. That connection is established by the story of the cursing of the fig tree.

From a spiritual perspective Jesus said, *Go into the fruitless village in the opposite place from where I am. There you will find a colt tied and bound.* The Greek word is *deo*, which simply means tied, but it also means to bind, put under obligation. Jesus used the same word in Matthew 18:18,

> "Assuredly, I say to you, whatever you bind on earth will be
> bound in heaven, and whatever you loose on earth will be loosed
> in heaven."

Indeed, the colt represents a humble power that resided in the fruitless village that no one used. No one had sat upon it. No one engaged this humble power in the fruitless village. So Jesus told His disciples to untie it, to unloose it, to free it from its bondage and bring it to Him. Clearly, the story suggests, as does the cursing of the fig tree, a transfer of power and authority from what was fruitless to what is fruitful.

If anyone asks you what you are doing, said Jesus, *tell them that the Lord needs it.* Who? The Lord, *kurios.* Two things are suggested here. First, Jesus identified Himself as the Lord, and second, He identified His disciples as His servants. The disciples did not want the colt for themselves, they were simply on an errand for the Lord, who had need of it. And because the disciples did exactly as the Lord had told them, they were able to accomplish what He sent them to do. Their obedience to the Lord kept them from being charged as thieves. The will of God was (and is) greater than the laws of men.

The colt was tied up, just as God's grace was bound to the sacrificial system of the Temple. The colt represents the power of God, Jesus rides upon it humbly into Jerusalem with the doctrines of grace. It had the same power and authority in its bound condition, but because it was bound no one used it. God's grace, God's power cannot be bound, it is boundless. The analogies are significant and many-faceted.

When they brought the colt to Jesus they "threw their clothes on it" (v. 7) or "threw their cloaks over it" (NIV). Time and again Scripture alludes to the righteousness of God as a cloak or covering. We are saved, not by our own righteousness, but by Christ's righteousness. His righteousness is imputed to us, it is put upon us as a cloak that does not belong to us but which protects and covers us. Here the disciples threw their own righteousness upon the colt—upon the symbol of the power and effectiveness of God's grace. And Christ sat on it. That is, they discarded their own righteousness for the glory of Christ's righteousness.

Others "spread their clothes (or cloaks) on the road" (v. 8). They also surrendered their own righteousness to the righteousness of Christ. It was an act that honored Jesus. Just as the four and twenty elders cast their crowns before Jesus as an act of submitting their authority, their righteousness to the Lord (Revelation 4:10), so God's people that day threw before Jesus the symbols of what little authority and righteousness that they had. They threw the symbols of their own righteousness into the dirt. Their own righteousness was useless before the glory of Christ's righteousness.

In addition, because Jesus had not yet died on the cross for the atonement of sin, those who trusted in His righteousness that day did so on faith alone. Jesus had not yet endured His crucifixion. Perhaps He would chicken out. Perhaps things would not go as He predicted. The crowd that day claimed the completed and fulfilled righteousness of Christ by faith alone. It was not yet completed when they claimed it by faith.

Look at this other detail Mark provided,

> "others cut down leafy branches from the trees and spread them on the road" (v. 8).

If cloaks represent righteousness, what do leafy branches represent? What did they represent in the story of the cursing of the fig tree? There the fruitless fig tree represented Israel. Israel was a tree that should have produced spiritual fruit, but didn't. That is the essence of the story.

Here the people cut, not just leaves, but entire branches and cast them before the Lord. The symbolism is the same: Israel, the fruitless tree—green, but fruitless, was subservient to the Lord Jesus Christ. Israel, in a sense had paved the way for Christ as He rode into Jerusalem. The Old Testament law and sacrificial system of the Temple paved the way for Christ, the ultimate gift of God. Grace triumphed over law, grace trampled the burden of Pharisaical law under foot.

The people of Jerusalem suddenly understood who Jesus was—not all of them, but some of them. Jesus was not just another prophet, He was the promised Messiah Himself. People still didn't understand that He must suffer and die on the cross, but they understood that He was the Son of God, the One who had come to save them from their sins. They didn't yet know how He would save them, how He would suffer and die as a sacrifice for sin. How could they have known? Nobody knew that but God. Every time Jesus tried to tell them, they didn't believe Him. They couldn't believe Him. It was too foreign. It still is! Who can understand it? We don't understand it—oh, we try but fail. However, we are not saved because of our understanding, we are saved by faith alone in Christ alone through Scripture alone.

"Blessed is He who comes in the name of the Lord" they cried!

> "Blessed is the kingdom of our father David That comes in the
> name of the Lord! Hosanna in the highest" (vs. 9-10)!

In Christ the kingdom of God broke into human history. With this announcement "Jesus went into Jerusalem and into the Temple" (v. 11). In Jerusalem, in the Temple, Jesus looked around. He assessed the situation, seeing it for what it was. As a result of His assessment, He said that "the hour was already late" (v. 11). Evening would be upon them.

He had much that He wanted to do and say in Jerusalem but, the hour being late, people would not be attentive. He and the disciples then returned to Bethany, to the village of figs and dates.

Are you ready to hear what Christ has to say?

47. Neither Will Your Father

*"And whenever you stand praying, if you have anything
against anyone, forgive him, that your Father in heaven may
also forgive you your trespasses. But if you do not forgive, neither will your Father in heaven forgive your trespasses." Then
they came again to Jerusalem. And as He was walking in the
temple, the chief priests, the scribes, and the elders came to
Him. And they said to Him, "By what authority are You doing
these things? And who gave You this authority to do these
things?" But Jesus answered and said to them, "I also will ask
you one question; then answer Me, and I will tell you by what
authority I do these things: The baptism of John—was it from
heaven or from men? Answer Me." And they reasoned among
themselves, saying, "If we say, 'From heaven,' He will say,
'Why then did you not believe him?' But if we say, 'From
men'—they feared the people, for all counted John to have been
a prophet indeed." So they answered and said to Jesus, "We do
not know." And Jesus answered and said to them, "Neither will
I tell you by what authority I do these things."*

—Mark 11:25-33

S o here we are in the middle of Jesus' lesson about faith and prayer.
We have already seen that the faith that Jesus required was not a
matter of our human ability to work ourselves up to a sufficient
degree of faithfulness to qualify for salvation, but a matter of having received the gracious gift of faithfulness provided by God. The faith that
the Lord described was a gift of God, not a work of man.

Having then received that gift of faith, and having the right object
of faith—Jesus Christ, faithful saints will seek and want what God wants
for them. With that proviso, Jesus said, God would provide whatever
His faithful people ask. That is, God will provide what *He* wants for His
people.

Verse 25 then teaches how faithful saints can increase the effectiveness of their prayers. Because God's forgiveness of sins is at the very
heart of salvation, forgiveness is also at the very heart of effective prayer.

God has forgiven His people through the sacrifice and atonement of Christ on the cross. And because Christians are to be imitators of Christ and to grow in the likeness of Christ we must also share the gift of forgiveness we have received by forgiving others for their wrongs against us. Forgiveness is not a gift that we keep to ourselves, but is a gift that is not truly received unless it is passed on to others. This is the lesson in the Parable of the Unforgiving Servant (Matthew 18:35).

This teaching is so important that Jesus states it both positively and negatively to insure that there will be no misunderstanding. Stated positively, He said that God will forgive us like we forgive others. Stated negatively, He said that inasmuch as we fail to forgive others, so God will fail to forgive us. But notice Jesus' language, "if you have anything against anyone, forgive him" (v. 25). Jesus places the burden of initiating forgiveness on the person who has been offended.

Normally the process of offense and forgiveness happens like this: Person A offends person B. After person B apologizes, person A extends forgiveness. But that is not the procedure that Jesus recommends. Jesus said that when person A offends person B, person B must go directly to person A and extend forgiveness without waiting for the apology. In other words, the burden of forgiveness belongs to the person who has been offended. Yet, that is not the way that the world thinks about forgiveness. The world insists that an apology be offered before any forgiveness can be extended. But Jesus said, "If you have anything against anyone," if you are troubled or bent out of shape by something that someone has said or done to you, then you must not wait for them to apologize, but you must go directly to them and extend forgiveness by apologizing.

That's what God has done through His gift of grace. God did not wait for us to come to Him, hat in hand seeking His forgiveness.

> "God demonstrates His own love toward us, in that while we were still sinners, Christ died for us" (Romans 5:8).

That is our model for treating others. While others are actively engaged in sin against us, we are to seek them out and extend forgiveness.

Exactly what are we supposed to do? The Greek word translated *forgive* is *aphiemi*. It means to let go, give up a debt, to forgive, to remit, to keep no longer. The sense of Jesus' instruction here directs us to quit holding on to the offense that someone has committed against us. The burden is not on the person who has done the offending to apologize, but is on the person who has been offended to let go of their resentment.

Jesus was speaking to everyone who holds a grudge of any kind against anyone else. At one time or another everyone has held a grudge against someone else. Clearly His intent was to break the cycle of offense and retaliation that so perpetuates sin and evil and malice among people. And particularly, as Jesus was in Jerusalem at the time, He spoke to the Pharisees and Sadducees who were offended and irritated with Him. The self-righteous always take offense at Jesus. The self-righteous dislike Jesus' teaching and Person because He both reveals the folly of self-righteousness and establishes the righteousness of Christ as the only righteousness that is acceptable to God. In essence, Jesus taught that self-righteousness itself is a sin.

Jesus was in Jerusalem for what we call Holy Week. He was in and out of the Temple. He had previously thrown out the moneychangers and purveyors of merchandise, which no doubt caused quite an uproar, some people supported Him and others did not. Verse 27 tells us that on another occasion when Jesus was in Jerusalem—in the Temple

> "the chief priests, the scribes, and the elders came to Him. And they said to Him, 'By what authority are You doing these things? And who gave You this authority to do these things?'" (vs. 27-28).

What things did they refer to? Surely they meant His cleansing of the Temple, but they also meant His teaching generally. They perceived that Jesus was teaching and acting upon an understanding of Scripture, an understanding of God that differed significantly from what they taught. The priests and the scribes (lawyers), representing the ecclesiastical and legal authorities, had gained the support of the Temple elders. They not only brought the biblical and spiritual authority represented by the priests against Jesus, and the legal authority represented by the scribes, but now they had the authority of the Jewish community represented by the elders as well. All areas of accepted authority were represented by the coalition that objected to Jesus.

Interestingly, they came to Jesus with the right question. The question of Jesus' authority is a central issue regarding His ministry. Unless we understand Jesus' authority correctly, we will get wrong everything else that He taught, we will misunderstand everything that Jesus represents and everything that He has done for His people. By what authority did Jesus act? In other words, just who did He think He was!

Jesus' answer brings us face to face with another issue that has troubled the Christian church from its inception—baptism. Jesus told them that He would be happy to tell them about His authority if they would first tell Him about the authority of the baptism of repentance that John the Baptist had practiced. "Was it from heaven or from men?" (v. 30). Because Jesus had merged His own practice of baptism and ministry with John's (John 10:40-42), the question applies to the baptism of the Christian church as well.

For this reason I suggest that the question about the authority of John's baptism is an equally important question about the authority—that is, the source and nature—of Christian baptism. By what authority are people baptized? Is it a heavenly authority (spiritual) or a human (institutional) authority? Jesus identified His authority with the authority of baptism.

The Pharisees were shrewd politicians, so they stopped to think before they replied. The difficulty was that John the Baptist, like Jesus, stood outside of the Temple establishment. John was not employed by, supported by, or formally connected to any part of the Temple administration. We might say that John had not been duly ordained and installed by the Temple as a prophet of God.

Thus, the Pharisees reasoned among themselves that if they answered Jesus that John's baptism was grounded in the heavenly authority of God's kingdom, they could be charged with failing to accept John's prophetic office. If John had been truly appointed by God Himself to be a prophet, they were obliged to accept and receive John as a prophet, which they did not. But if they answered that John's baptism was "from men" (v. 32), that is, not grounded in God's spiritual authority, they would face a popular uprising because the mass of the people believed John to have been a genuine prophet. Either answer would land them in hot water.

So they declined to answer, and Jesus then declined to tell them of His authority as well. But before we talk about why Jesus didn't answer them, let's apply the situation to the current difficulties regarding baptism. All Christian churches agree that Christians must be baptized, but they disagree as to what constitutes baptism. We differ about the appropriate modes of baptism—sprinkling, pouring, or immersion. We differ about the candidates for baptism—infants, children, or only confessing adults. And we differ about the extent of baptism, whether it produces salvation (i.e., Roman Catholic), or is a mandatory part of salvation (i.e., Anabaptist), or is a matter of obedience to Scripture (i.e., Evangelical and Reformed), or is a nice but merely symbolic ceremony (i.e., Quaker). The point is that there is a lot of disagreement among contemporary churches about baptism.

But the central issue is this question Jesus asked the Pharisees. What is the source and nature (authority) of baptism? Every Christian must answer this question. Jesus, of course, taught that John's baptism carried the authority of heaven. Jesus believed that baptism generally is grounded in the authority of the kingdom of God. It is first and foremost a spiritual event. The ceremony, though not insignificant, is not as important as the reality. Jesus suggests that He is not as concerned about the procedures or institutional practices regarding baptism as He is about the spiritual reality of soul cleansing that baptism represents.

In other words, Jesus doesn't seem to be concerned about the modes of baptism—sprinkling, pouring, or immersion. He never personally baptized anyone with water. Nor does He seem to be concerned that the candidates for baptism be humanly qualified, because no one is qualified to received baptism or salvation—"all have sinned and fall short of the glory of God" (Romans 3:23). Because salvation is not dependent upon our confession, but upon God's grace, baptism—which symbolizes initiation into the church—is a gift of grace before it is a response of confession and commitment.

We would do well to understand that the church is not identical with the kingdom of God, nor is baptism equivalent to salvation. Baptism does not save a person, nor is baptism mandatory for salvation to be effective. Not every baptized person is saved, nor is every unbaptized person unsaved. Rather, salvation belongs to the Lord, and baptism is a function of obedience to Scripture. Thus, if a person is an adult Christian and refuses to be baptized, he does so in disobedience to Christ, and on that basis he must question his own salvation.

The same thing can be said about church membership. Church membership is no guarantee of salvation. And at the same time, some people who are not members of any church will be saved. However, if a person is an adult Christian and refuses to become a member of a local church, he does so in disobedience to Christ, and on that basis he must question his own salvation because God's people are obedient (Romans 12:4-5).

Inasmuch as we cooperate with God, He will cooperate with us. And inasmuch as we fail or refuse to cooperate with God, He will fail or refuse to cooperate with us. The same argument that Jesus used to describe God's manner of forgiveness can be used to describe His authority. As people believe in Christ's authority He exercises that authority over them, providing protection and blessing. But as much as people don't believe it, He doesn't exercise His authority over them, leaving them without His protection or blessing.

The Pharisees failed to answer Jesus' question about authority. They also failed to extend their forgiveness to Jesus. They held onto their grudge against Him. Thus, Jesus neither told them of His authority, nor did He extend to them God's forgiveness. May we not be like the Pharisees.

48. DESTINED FOR REJECTION

Then He began to speak to them in parables: "A man planted a vineyard and set a hedge around it, dug a place for the wine vat and built a tower. And he leased it to vinedressers and went into a far country. Now at vintage-time he sent a servant to the vinedressers, that he might receive some of the fruit of the vineyard from the vinedressers. And they took him and beat him and sent him away empty-handed. Again he sent them another servant, and at him they threw stones, wounded him in the head, and sent him away shamefully treated. And again he sent another, and him they killed; and many others, beating some and killing some. Therefore still having one son, his beloved, he also sent him to them last, saying, 'They will respect my son.' But those vinedressers said among themselves, 'This is the heir. Come, let us kill him, and the inheritance will be ours.' So they took him and killed him and cast him out of the vineyard. Therefore what will the owner of the vineyard do? He will come and destroy the vinedressers, and give the vineyard to others. Have you not even read this Scripture: 'The stone which the builders rejected Has become the chief cornerstone. This was the LORD's doing, And it is marvelous in our eyes'?" And they sought to lay hands on Him, but feared the multitude, for they knew He had spoken the parable against them. So they left Him and went away. —Mark 12:1-12

The challenge before us today is to understand the parable of the wicked vine dressers in a way that makes a positive impact upon our faithfulness. The positive point of the story is not in question, yet to arrive at the positive understanding we must cross a mine field of human depravity.

There are three primary characters in this story, the owner of the vineyard, the keepers of the vineyard, and the son. The story is a parable, an allegory, a metaphor, where the main parts of the story are not to be understood literally, but symbolically. The story as a whole sets forth a moral or principle that applies to salvation.

The man who planted the vineyard, of course, represents God, who created the heavens and the earth. The vine dressers or keepers represent Israel (or humanity), to whom God gave the law and the temple for their order and benefit. The servants who were sent to gather some of the fruit of the vineyard represent God's prophets and preachers. And the son of the owner represents, of course, Jesus Christ.

The story is about earth and Israel's role among the nations.

> "The Lord God took the man and put him in the garden of Eden
> to tend and keep it" (Genesis 2:15).

The blessing of this gift fell to Israel, through Abraham, Isaac, and Jacob. There are several important points of the story to note. Israel did not own or control the vineyard or its products. Israel was only a steward, who took care of the property for the owner. When you put your money in the bank, the bank becomes your steward. The bank doesn't own your money, it merely cares for it until you call for it.

Notice also that the owner of the vineyard had done all of the work to establish it. He

> "planted (it) and set a hedge around it, dug a place for the wine
> vat and built a tower" (v. 1).

He, no doubt, employed labor to accomplish the work for him. Nonetheless, the finished product did not belong to the laborers, but to the owner. Just as when you employ someone to build a house for you. The completed home does not belong to the laborers, but to the owner.

The owner then "leased it to vinedressers and went into a far country" (v. 1). He didn't give it to them, but leased or rented it to them. The ancient Israelites, as Christians of all ages, are only "sojourners and pilgrims" (1 Peter 2:11) in this world. The citizenship of Christians has its first and foremost allegiance to the kingdom of God. Christians are only secondarily citizens of an earthly country. Our first allegiance must always be to God, according to the First Commandment.

The parable goes on to say that at vintage or harvest time the owner sent a servant to collect "some of the fruit of the vineyard from the vinedressers" (v. 2). Those who went in the service of the owner were called "servants." They were his servants, not servants of the vine dressers. They owe their first allegiance to God. They did not come to contend with the vine dressers, but to work with them that the owner might enjoy some of his crop—not all of it but only some. Ideally the owner's servants and the vine dressers would work together to satisfy the owner's desires. But that's not how the story went.

For a reason that is not stated the vine dressers

> "took (the servant) and beat him and sent him away empty-
> handed" (v. 3).

The owner tried a couple more times, sending other servants, but each time the vine dressers treated them the same. Finally the owner sent his son, thinking that they would surely respect his son. But when the vine dressers found out that it was the owner's son, they divulged the reason for their actions—selfish greed. They

> "said among themselves, 'This is the heir. Come, let us kill him,
> and the inheritance will be ours'" (v. 7).

This parable teaches the sinfulness and depravity of man. Without reason or provocation the vine dressers (representing humanity) acted sinfully, selfishly, and savagely toward all who represented the owner. At this point we can ask an important question: Didn't God know that His servants and even His Son would be mistreated and killed? If God is God, surely He would know these things. We need to pay close attention to the words of the owner because he represents God.

> "Therefore still having one son, his beloved, he also sent him to
> them last, saying, 'They will respect my son'" (v. 6).

The owner did not say that they would respect his son right away. He didn't say that they would not mistreat him as well. In fact, if you look at his words as a decree, you can understand him to have decreed or commanded that they would eventually respect his son. "They will (someday) respect my son." There is no indication that the owner thought that his son would command instant respect. If not, why did the owner send his son?

The answer involves the gospel itself. Knowing that the owner represents God and the son, Jesus Christ, we apply to this story what we know about why God sent Jesus. The owner, having himself built and established the vineyard, leased it to the vine dressers. This was all done because of the generosity, grace, and mercy of the owner. Even when his servants were treated poorly, the owner responded in mercy by sending his own son to solve the problem.

Because we know Scripture we know that God knew that Jesus would be "wounded for our transgressions," He knew that Jesus would be "bruised for our iniquities" (Isaiah 53:5). The whole of the gospel of God's grace is found in this story. The mistreatment of God's representatives, His servants—prophets and preachers, is no surprise to God. But God's grace is always a surprise to man. We don't expect God to be gracious, we expect Him to be just—to give us what we deserve.

In verse 9 we find the proclamation of God's grace. Listen for it.

> "Therefore what will the owner of the vineyard do? He will come and destroy the vine dressers, and give the vineyard to others."

Do you hear God's grace or God's justice here? The Pharisees, the "priests, the scribes and the elders" (Mark 11:27) who had come to Jesus to question His authority, those who came to the Lord full of accusations, trying to trip Him up, saw only the cold justice of God. They heard that God would meet justice out to those who killed His son. They heard Jesus to say that God would condemn and destroy them. They heard Jesus bring a curse of God's wrath upon them, bringing upon them the deserved consequences of their own actions. This perspective is there! "He will come and destroy the vinedressers."

But that is not the end of the story. Jesus said,

> "He will come and destroy the vinedressers, and *give the vineyard to others*" (v. 9—italics added).

The story does not end with God's justice, but with His grace and mercy as He again gives to others what they do not deserve. This story, of course, prefigures Christ's mission to the Gentiles. The gospel and the kingdom are taken from Israel and given to the church of Jesus Christ. The gospel and the kingdom are taken from those who reject Christ, and given to those who receive Him. This is the gospel of Jesus Christ, and it still happens exactly this way.

Those who reject Christ find this parable hard and harsh and full of God's justice. It appears quite negative to them. But those who receive Christ find God's grace and mercy in it. To the one the story is the aroma of death leading to death, and to the other the aroma of life leading to life. And who can understand these things? (2 Corinthians 2:16).

> "The Lord gave, and the Lord has taken away; Blessed be the name of the Lord" (Job 1:21).

It is interesting to note that God sent His only Son, Jesus Christ, to die for the salvation of undeserving sinners. What an amazing fact! The life that Jesus lived and died was not of His own choosing, but was of God's choosing. When Jesus was in the garden he prayed,

> "Father, if it is Your will, take this cup away from Me;
> nevertheless not My will, but Yours, be done" (Luke 22:42).

The Greek word for *will*, *thelema*, means choice, inclination, desire, pleasure. My destiny is not my choice, not my inclination, not my desire, not my pleasure, but Thine, said Jesus.

The life Jesus lived followed and fulfilled a plan that God made before time itself. Every aspect of Jesus' life, every event recorded in Scripture unfolded according to God's plan. Jesus' life unfolded according to God's plan because Jesus was obedient to God's will. In everything Jesus obeyed the Lord, and thus, fulfilled His destiny.

> "He humbled Himself and became obedient to the point of death,
> even the death of the cross" (Philippians 2:8).

Does the Scripture clearly teach this? It does. Does the Scripture clearly call all of God's children to obedience? It does. Does the Scripture call all of God's children to obedience to God's will in the fulfillment of God's salvation plan? It does.

> "God from the beginning chose you for salvation through
> sanctification by the Spirit and belief in the truth" (2
> Thessalonians 2:13).

Children of God, take heart. God has called you to fulfill His eternal plan.

> "Moreover whom He predestined, these He also called; whom
> He called, these He also justified; and whom He justified, these
> He also glorified" (Romans 8:30).

God began it, and God will complete what He began. Herein lies our faith in the grace of God, through the obedience of Christ.

49. What About Government?

Then they sent to Him some of the Pharisees and the Herodi-
ans, to catch Him in His words. When they had come, they
said to Him, "Teacher, we know that You are true, and care
about no one; for You do not regard the person of men, but
teach the way of God in truth. Is it lawful to pay taxes to Cae-
sar, or not? Shall we pay, or shall we not pay?" But He, know-
ing their hypocrisy, said to them, "Why do you test Me? Bring
Me a denarius that I may see it." So they brought it. And He
said to them, "Whose image and inscription is this?" They said
to Him, "Caesar's." And Jesus answered and said to them, "Ren-
der to Caesar the things that are Caesar's, and to God the things
that are God's." And they marveled at Him.   —Mark 12:13-17

This story begins with the caution that the Pharisees and Herodi-ans had joined forces in order to trap Jesus and accuse Him either before the Sanhedrin or Pilate. If He answered that taxes should be paid, they would accuse Him before the Sanhedrin as a traitor to the Jewish cause of independence from Rome. And if He answered that taxes should not be paid, they would accuse Him before Pilate as an insurrectionist.

But even more interesting is the religious union that was formed between these two opposing parties. The Pharisees represented what we know today as Conservatives, and the Herodians represented what we know as Liberals. Neither of these factions had a genuinely biblical perspective. The conservative Pharisees were religious legalists, and the liberal Herodians were antinomians—they opposed religious law. The same tendencies exist today. Most religious conservatives interpret God's Law too narrowly, while most religious liberals believe that it no longer applies at all.

It is interesting how those who oppose the genuine biblical teaching of the gospel of God's grace can put their differences aside and join forces to oppose those who proclaim God's truth. Many who would otherwise have nothing in common unite to oppose genuine Christianity. Such was the merger of Pharisees and Herodians.

They then came to Jesus pretending a belief that He was a genuine teacher of the truth. "Teacher, we know that you are true" (v. 14). Part and parcel of Jesus' commitment to truth was His impartiality. They said that they were aware that Jesus "care(d) about no one" (v. 14). The allusion here is important. For them, the reference was found in Deuteronomy(10:17):

> "For the LORD your God is God of gods and Lord of lords, the great God, mighty and awesome, who shows no partiality nor takes a bribe."

> "You shall not pervert justice; you shall not show partiality, nor take a bribe, for a bribe blinds the eyes of the wise and twists the words of the righteous" (Deuteronomy 16:19).

We can also find this sense of biblical impartiality in Acts 10:34,

> "Then Peter opened his mouth and said: 'In truth I perceive that God shows no partiality.'"

They didn't mean that Jesus didn't like or respect individual people, only that His sense of justice and fairness would not be influenced by people of power, position, or sympathy. In this they were correct. Their disagreement with Jesus was not blatantly false, but contained a good measure of truth. Most false teachings are not completely wrong. Satan knows how to pack his kernels of falsehood in the midst of great truths. But like an arithmetic problem, whether it's wrong a lot or a little, it's still wrong. The smallest error generates a wrong answer.

The question of whether to pay taxes or not was a finely crafted argument intended to force Jesus into the hands of either the conservatives or the liberals. They asked Him a yes or no question hoping to catch Him in their nets however He answered. But Jesus saw through their plans. He knew their hypocrisy. How did He know it? He read their hearts. Their intentions were written all over their faces. Their words dripped with the thick syrup of evil intentions. Even children on the playground know when someone is trying to pick a fight with them. There isn't anything mystical about it. It just involves common sense.

The first thing that Jesus did was to call them on their intentions, "Why do you test me?" (v. 15), He asked. The Lord's treatment of the *denarius* proved to be a stroke of absolute spiritual genius. The useful, spiritual allusions are legion.

> "Render to Caesar the things that are Caesar's, and to God the things that are God's" (v. 17).

The coinage of the government is material, but the coinage of the kingdom is spiritual. The image on the coin was worldly, but the image in which God's people were created is spiritual. Give whatever money you owe to the government, but give your heart, your life, and your spirit to God.

Clearly Jesus distinguished between the different authorities of the two realms—government and church. Indeed there is a separation of power, authority, and jurisdiction between them. What is appropriate for governments and other worldly organizations is not appropriate for the church. For instance, the government wields the sword of justice—the power to enforce laws and inflict punishment for disobedience. The church, on the other hand, wields the hand of mercy—God's Word, the power of love and forgiveness.

The question the Sadducees asked deals with what people owe their government. We are obliged to obey the laws of the state in which we live, even if we don't like them. We are also free to work to change those laws, but we are not free to pick and choose which ones we will obey and which ones we won't. Among those laws are laws regarding taxes. We may not like the tax laws, we may disagree with the rates and procedures, but we are bound to conform to them.

Interestingly, taxes play an important role in Scripture. Before Israel was a nation the people clamored for a king so they could be like the other nations. They didn't want God to be their king, they wanted a man, like the other nations. The Prophet Samuel disagreed with the people, but when he took the concern to God, God agreed to give them a king like the other nations. But He told them that they wouldn't be happy with it.

> So Samuel told all the words of the LORD to the people who asked him for a king. And he said, 'This will be the behavior of the king who will reign over you: He will take your sons and appoint them for his own chariots and to be his horsemen, and some will run before his chariots. He will appoint captains over his thousands and captains over his fifties, will set some to plow his ground and reap his harvest, and some to make his weapons of war and equipment for his chariots. He will take your daughters to be perfumers, cooks, and bakers. And he will take the best of your fields, your vineyards, and your olive groves, and give them to his servants. He will take a tenth of your grain and your vintage, and give it to his officers and servants. And he will take your male servants, your female servants, your finest young men, and your donkeys, and put them to his work. He

> will take a tenth of your sheep. And you will be his servants.
> And you will cry out in that day because of your king whom
> you have chosen for yourselves, and the LORD will not hear you
> in that day. (1 Samuel 8:10-18).

God said from the very beginning that worldly government would not satisfy the desires of the people, but would only serve as an irritant. Government was given by God as a punishment for Israel's disobedience and dissatisfaction with the Lord Himself.

When Solomon died and his sons fought to succeed him, driving Israel into a four-hundred year civil war, Solomon's wicked son, Rehoboam, increased Israel's burdens, particularly taxes. In the Bible high taxes are described as a form of punishment for faithlessness. God uses the burdens of government to chastise His people.

After Rehoboam increased Israel's taxes far above the rate established by his father, Solomon,

> "King Rehoboam sent Adoram, who was in charge of the
> revenue; but all Israel stoned him with stones, and he died.
> Therefore King Rehoboam mounted his chariot in haste to flee
> to Jerusalem" (1 Kings 12:18).

Rehoboam stirred up a tax revolt. Unfortunately in ancient Israel there were no mechanisms for the people to change or effect the laws of government, as we have in this country.

Jesus encouraged no such revolt in Jerusalem that day. By telling the people to pay their taxes, even if they thought them excessively high or unfair, He suggested to them that their tax burden should be received as a chastisement from God. Thus, they needed to submit to God's chastisement, and increase their faithfulness to the Lord as the only acceptable solution to the problem. An increase of faithfulness on the part of God's people will eventually result in an increase of faithfulness among the population generally, and eventually it will spread to the leadership.

This scenario is particularly true in America, where we have a democratic republic. Our leaders represent us—that's the problem! Their values truly reflect the values of the American people. So, in order to make any real spiritual progress in our current situation, we must do all we can to increase the faith of the people at large because that is the pool from which leaders are drawn. It is simply unrealistic to think that those who lead a decadent society will work to reform that society for its spiritual good. Those who float to the top of a pool of decadence do so only because they genuinely represent the pool in which they float.

Don't jump to conclusions. I'm not saying that everyone in American government is decadent. Nor am I saying that America is as bad as it can get. There are still many fine Christians in government, as there are many fine Christians in society. However, decadence and moral corruption are definitely on the rise, and that is not a good sign.

The point I want to make is that our secular, American government will not be able to make any critical difference in the morality of society because that is not the area of responsibility God gave government. All they can do is to punish the increasing numbers of wrong doers. They cannot alter the morality—the hearts, values, and beliefs—of the people. Why not? Because that is an area of church responsibility. Teaching morals, values, and beliefs—changing hearts and minds—is the bailiwick of God's church, which is no more than the collection of God's people. Thus, social morality is the special and unique burden of the church.

That doesn't mean that Christians are free to impose their own values on others. They are not. The government is correct to oppose all such imposition. However, that does not mean that Christians cannot talk about their faith, beliefs, values and morality in the public sphere. Christians must speak of these things. Christians must teach God's way because no one else can.

However, the government must realize that public conversation about God or the Bible does not constitute a moral imposition upon others. Hearts and minds will be changed as they encounter God's Word and God's people, but that does not mean that Christians are imposing their values on others. Christians don't change hearts and minds, only God can do that. Thus, when hearts and minds are truly changed the responsibility does not lie with individual Christians or their churches, but with God Himself. That kind of change cannot and should not be outlawed. That kind of change is the only change that will ultimately make any difference in our precious quality of life.

How can we raise the levels of morality in society? By raising them among ourselves, in our own homes, churches and communities. And how can we do that? By engaging God's Word seriously. By worshiping God with biblical integrity. By sharing Christ, sharing the gospel, teaching the Bible. We must be examples of what we teach. The first step is coming to Christ ourselves. The first step is acknowledging our own sin and seeking forgiveness and reconciliation with the Lord.

50. RESURRECTION

*Then some Sadducees, who say there is no resurrection, came
to Him; and they asked Him, saying: "Teacher, Moses wrote to
us that if a man's brother dies, and leaves his wife behind, and
leaves no children, his brother should take his wife and raise up
offspring for his brother. Now there were seven brothers. The
first took a wife; and dying, he left no offspring. And the second took her, and he died; nor did he leave any offspring. And
the third likewise. So the seven had her and left no offspring.
Last of all the woman died also. Therefore, in the resurrection,
when they rise, whose wife will she be? For all seven had her as
wife." Jesus answered and said to them, "Are you not therefore
mistaken, because you do not know the Scriptures nor the
power of God? For when they rise from the dead, they neither
marry nor are given in marriage, but are like angels in heaven.
But concerning the dead, that they rise, have you not read in
the book of Moses, in the burning bush passage, how God
spoke to him, saying, 'I am the God of Abraham, the God of
Isaac, and the God of Jacob'? He is not the God of the dead, but
the God of the living. You are therefore greatly mistaken."*
                                                —Mark 12:18-27

Mark reminds us that the Sadducees rejected the biblical teaching of the resurrection. While it is true that Jesus had not yet
been resurrected so God's definitive statement regarding it
had not yet been written, it is also true that the Old Testament teaches
the resurrection sufficiently that they should have believed it. The Pharisees taught it. Whether they actually believed it or not, at least they
taught that Scripture proclaimed it to be true. Again, remember that the
Pharisees were the conservatives of the past and the Sadducees were ancient liberals.

Just as the Pharisees had tried to trip Jesus up with the question
about paying taxes to a pagan state, but failed, so now the Sadducees
came to trip Jesus up with a question about heaven. Like the Pharisees

before them they thought that they had a watertight argument by which they would be able to condemn Jesus no matter how He answered.

The point of the law that concerned them is found in Deuteronomy 25:5,

> "If brothers dwell together, and one of them dies and has no son, the widow of the dead man shall not be married to a stranger outside the family; her husband's brother shall go in to her, take her as his wife, and perform the duty of a husband's brother to her."

In order to increase the difficulty of the problem the Sadducees invented a situation in which this scenario played itself out seven times in the same family. Seven times the husbands die and each time another brother takes the woman as his own wife.

The first thing we should notice is the unlikelihood of this scenario in real life. It is an extrapolation from reality that suggests the world of fantasy and speculation in which the Sadducees operated. To bring such a speculative concern to Jesus suggested that they did not have a firm grasp on reality, much less on the Bible. This was Jesus' first response to them.

> "Are you not therefore mistaken, because you do not know the Scriptures nor the power of God?" (v. 24).

The first thing that Jesus noticed about them was their lack of biblical knowledge, which fed their lack of knowledge about God. Because they didn't understand Scripture they didn't understand God, so their question itself was absurd from a biblical perspective. We must be careful not to pass over this point too quickly. One of the keys to understanding Scripture is to realize, admit, and confess our own ignorance. Until we genuinely acknowledge our own ignorance, we tend to use Scripture to proof-text or prove the validity of our own values, insights, and understanding. We believe what we believe, and then seek to establish it by finding Scripture that agrees with us. Dare I say that most people engage Scripture in this manner. I know because I did it myself for years and years.

But by the grace of God something happens to undo or undermine our trust and belief in our own thoughts and dreams. That, by the way, often involves a horrendous internal struggle as we face our own failures, follies, and foibles. This process of conviction disturbs us to the core as God shakes our deepest personal foundations in order to show us our weaknesses and demonstrate His strength. It comes as an intrusion into our tidy world of self-made values and preconceptions—usually by the means of gospel preaching. Whether we read it or hear it, its source is outside of us. God's perspective does not reside within, but breaks into human consciousness from without.

The mistake the Sadducees made was to project an earthly concern upon a heavenly situation. Their mistake was to think that what was valued on earth would be valued in heaven. Marriage was the foundation of the church, and the church was the foundation of society. The values of the family fed the values of the church, which in turn fed the values of society. It was true then just as it is true today. So, in speaking of marriage and family values, they thought they were speaking about the bedrock values of heaven as well.

While it is true that family bonds will be acknowledged and respected in heaven, family bonds will not play the same role they play on earth. More important than family bonds will be our covenantal bond with the Lord Himself. Our bodies will be changed,

> "flesh and blood cannot inherit the kingdom of God; nor does corruption inherit incorruption" (1 Corinthians 15:50).

The concerns of flesh and blood, marital relations, and bearing children will be different in heaven than it is on earth. We don't know how it will be different, just that it will be.

Consequently, the Sadducees erred by thinking that they knew more than they actually knew. They thought that they knew what they were talking about, when in fact they were ignorant of Scripture. Had they known Scripture better they would never have posed such a question, nor would they have sought to trip Jesus up in order to accuse Him.

We see the same errors today as people speculate about the end-times and the second coming of Christ. All kinds of wild speculations and predictions are being made, and have been made for centuries. In my liberal seminary training I was taught to read Scripture through the lens of current events, to have the Scripture in one hand and the newspaper in the other. It was an effort to make Scripture relevant. Little did I know at the time how that study method is able to twist Scripture into anything anyone wants it to mean.

That Bible study method is so close to the truth that it tends to be confused with the truth. But the better method for Bible study is to read current events through the lens of Scripture. The correct methodology involves an inversion of one's perspective. To use current events to help us understand Scripture turns Bible study into pure speculation. Rather, the Bible is intended to help us understand current events. Rather than spinning our understanding of Scripture based upon our knowledge of current events, we need to shape our understanding of current events based upon our knowledge of Scripture. Scripture helps us understand the world, the world does not help us understand Scripture.

In the same way the Sadducees based their understanding of Scripture upon their knowledge of the world, where they should have based their understanding of the world upon their knowledge of Scripture. If it sounds like I am just playing with words, you don't yet understand this crucial issue. Either I have failed in my communication, or you have failed in your understanding, or both. But if you do understand what I'm talking about, you recognize the difference between God-centered and man-centered Christianity.

Jesus explained the truth about resurrection by citing Exodus 3:6, where God said to Moses from the burning bush,

> "I am the God of your father—the God of Abraham, the God of Isaac, and the God of Jacob."

The fact that the bush burned but was not consumed pointed to the eternal, enduring nature of God. God's identity as the God of Abraham, Isaac, and Jacob pointed to the ongoing existence of these three men, who were father, son, and grandson—all long passed from this earthly scene. They were dead, yet alive in the Lord. God said, "I am," He used the present tense. Abraham, Isaac, and Jacob continue to love and serve the Lord, though they have long passed from the scene.

That's not the whole story of the resurrection, but it is an important part of it. God revealed enough of the truth of the resurrection to Moses and the prophets that the Sadducees should have believed in it. But they failed to believe because they failed to know Scripture. Did they study it? Yes, they did, but study of Scripture is not enough. Jesus said,

> "I am the good shepherd; and I know My sheep, and am known by My own" (John 10:14).

The Sadducees did not understand Jesus because they were not His sheep. They could not hear His voice because they did not have the Holy Spirit to guide them. And they did not have the Holy Spirit because they turned their backs to Scripture. They did not know it.

What about you? Do you give yourself to the study of Scripture? Can you hear the voice of the Shepherd? Have you responded to His voice? Are you living according to God's Word?

51. ALL YOUR HEART

Then one of the scribes came, and having heard them reason-
ing together, perceiving that He had answered them well,
asked Him, "Which is the first commandment of all?" Jesus an-
swered him, "The first of all the commandments is: 'Hear, O Is-
rael, the LORD our God, the LORD is one. 'And you shall love the
LORD your God with all your heart, with all your soul, with all
your mind, and with all your strength.' This is the first com-
mandment. And the second, like it, is this: 'You shall love your
neighbor as yourself.' There is no other commandment greater
than these." So the scribe said to Him, "Well said, Teacher. You
have spoken the truth, for there is one God, and there is no
other but He. And to love Him with all the heart, with all the
understanding, with all the soul, and with all the strength, and
to love one's neighbor as oneself, is more than all the whole
burnt offerings and sacrifices." Now when Jesus saw that he an-
swered wisely, He said to him, "You are not far from the king-
dom of God." But after that no one dared question Him.

—Mark 12:28-34

Finally one of the scribes came to Jesus to pose a question. This was the third time the enemies of Jesus tried to catch Him up in His own words. Scribes were what we call lawyers. Interestingly, these enemies of Jesus actually performed a great service for His church. They brought difficult questions and issues to Jesus, hoping to trap Him in some way. But what actually happened was the Lord clarified some major issues for the church. God used what had been intended for evil purposes for the good of His church.

This particular scribe was impressed by the quality of the arguments that Jesus used. He had heard Jesus "reasoning" with His opponents, and "answer(ing) them well" (v. 28). His observation and the fact that Mark called attention to it suggest that reason (logic) provides common ground between worldliness and godliness. Reason is understood and respected by both perspectives. While reason alone is not enough to convince unbelievers, it is important to understand that all the teachings of the Bible are reasonable.

The issue that the scribe brought to Jesus concerned the most important of the Commandments. There had been much discussion and difference of opinion among the scribes, Pharisees, and Sadducees. This particular scribe may have believed that resolution of the matter was impossible, and brought it to Jesus in an attempt to entrap Him, as had the others. Or, perhaps he thought that he had the definitive answer in the matter, and sought to instruct Jesus. Or, it may have been that this particular scribe thought himself to be a genuine seeker who sought clarification regarding this matter.

Jesus answered the scribe with Scripture. We must note that even Jesus did not rely upon reason alone, but upon Scripture supported by reason. *According to Scripture,* said Jesus, *God's primacy is the first principle.*

> "The first of all the commandments is: 'Hear, O Israel, the LORD our God, the LORD is one'" (v. 29).

God is supreme, first above all others. Everything is subsumed under God's primacy. God's primacy, then, logically necessitates man's complete love and submission to the will of God. If God is the most important thing, then we must give our undivided love and attention to God.

> "And you shall love the LORD your God with all your heart, with all your soul, with all your mind, and with all your strength" (v. 30).

Scripture employs the words heart, soul, mind, and strength to describe the ideal commitment to God. The Greek word for *heart* (*kardia*) denotes the center of all physical and spiritual life.

The word for *soul* (*psuche*) describes the seat of the feelings, desires, affections, and aversions. The human soul suggests the human will in that people tend to do what they like or want, and tend to avoid what they don't like or don't want. In other words, we must desire to love and serve God. The desire must be our own.

The word for *mind* is *dianoia*, which refers to our understanding and imagination. Our thoughts, including our hopes and dreams, must be centered and consumed with God and His Word. This teaching flies in the face of the modern effort to maintain a balanced life. The effort to live a balanced life wants no one particular concern to override all others.

However, Scripture teaches that Christians should be totally devoted to God. We tend to call such people extremists. But Jesus called them faithful. Scripture has no place for balancing competing values and concerns, but seeks to ground the faithful in the values and concerns of God and His Word.

Ischus, translated as *strength*, points to one's ability, force, and might. Whatever power we may have, says the Scripture, should be devoted to the service of God. All of our strength and ability, force and might should be used in the service of God.

This is a tall order for anyone. Loving and serving God in this way cannot be a minor concern. We cannot do this without aggressively employing all our resources to accomplish it. This is no minor undertaking, not a Sunday only religion. Christians cannot be weekend warriors for God. Christians are called to complete and total devotion to the Lord. Christians in every age have blurred this teaching. Yet, inasmuch as we fail to understand and engage it, we fail in our calling as Christians.

In the light of Scripture, the Second Commandment results logically from the first. "You shall love your neighbor as yourself" (v. 31). All of the energy, love, and commitment that we are to have for God must be expressed as love and concern for others. This does not mean that we can become Christians by loving our neighbors. We cannot. In fact, the truth is that we cannot really love them unless and until we are Christian. In other words, real love and commitment to God produces real love and concern for others. But it doesn't work the other way: love and concern for others do not necessarily result in love and commitment to God.

The scribe who brought this question to Jesus responded as if he had a deep understanding of this issue. He acknowledged that Jesus had "spoken the truth" (v. 31). He acknowledged the supremacy of God's primacy, that God is first above all. However, his repetition of Scripture's command was inaccurate. He said that we are to love God with all our heart, understanding, soul, and strength, where Scripture said heart, soul, mind, and strength. The difference involves the two words *understanding* and *mind*. The scribe used the word *sunesis* where Jesus used *dianoia*.

Is the difference important? It amounts to what we would call head-knowledge versus heart-knowledge. Sometimes we say that there is a difference between knowing about Christ and knowing Christ personally. One involves a familiarity with the language of the Bible, the other involves a commitment to the Person of Christ. These two things should never be separated, of course. But the truth is that people often separate them. On the one hand we see an intellectual faith without passion, and on the other we see a passionate faith without intelligence. Scripture binds them together to reveal a faith that is both intelligent and passionate—not one or the other, but both.

This scribe seems to have had only a head-knowledge of God. In fact, the story demonstrates how far a person can understand spiritual truths and still be lost. This man knew of the primacy of God and of God's demand for personal commitment to love the Lord with all one's heart, soul, and strength. He was even familiar with the prophets and their insistence that

> "love(ing) one's neighbor as oneself, is more than all the whole
> burnt offerings and sacrifices" (v. 33).

His words are so right and so true. He evidences nearly every mark of a regenerate Christian.

But something was missing. Jesus noted that this scribe was "not far from the kingdom of God" (v. 34). Not far from it, but not in it either. The implication was that he was not on the path of salvation, but had fallen on the wayside. He was close, but not on the path. The literary implication suggests that the scribe had received the Word on the wayside (*hodos*). Jesus suggested that he had a wayside faith. Earlier Jesus had described such Christians.

> "And these are the ones by the wayside where the word is sown.
> When they hear, Satan comes immediately and takes away the
> word that was sown in their hearts" (Mark 4:15).

Jesus had now answered several very difficult questions that had been brought to him. Lawyers and theologians from both the conservative and liberal factions of the day had tried to trip Him up, to no avail. The best minds of the day had been unable to poke any holes in Jesus' testimony or theology. At this point no one was left who "dared question Him" (v. 34).

The faith, testimony, and theology that Jesus taught had been sufficient to dispel all doubts and questions to the contrary. As it was for them, so it is for us yet today. Jesus' faith, testimony, and theology provide sufficient instruction for His people. Have you applied yourselves to them? Do you understand the Lord in these matters? Have you trusted yourself to Him

"with all your heart, with all your soul, with all your mind, and
with all your strength" (Mark 12:30)?

Do you find joy in the truth of God's Word? Do you love your neighbor as yourself? Do you put others before yourself?

As we settle these matters with the Lord, our lives will grow in grace. Peace, happiness, contentment, fulfillment, etc. come as God's blessings to those who find peace in God's Word. We are called to be established in God's Word, to make peace with the Lord first, and then to find peace with all of God's people on that basis. It all begins by conforming our minds to Scripture, by understanding the truth of God's Word. This effort should dominate the lives of God's people because for them there is no greater joy or satisfaction.

52. When Less is More

Then Jesus answered and said, while He taught in the temple,
"How is it that the scribes say that the Christ is the Son of
David? For David himself said by the Holy Spirit: 'The Lord
said to my Lord, "Sit at My right hand, Till I make Your ene-
mies Your footstool."' Therefore David himself calls Him
'Lord'; how is He then his Son? And the common people heard
Him gladly. Then He said to them in His teaching, 'Beware of
the scribes, who desire to go around in long robes, love greet-
ings in the marketplaces, the best seats in the synagogues, and
the best places at feasts, who devour widows' houses, and for a
pretense make long prayers. These will receive greater con-
demnation.'" Now Jesus sat opposite the treasury and saw how
the people put money into the treasury. And many who were
rich put in much. Then one poor widow came and threw in
two mites, which make a quadrans. So He called His disciples
to Himself and said to them, "Assuredly, I say to you that this
poor widow has put in more than all those who have given to
the treasury; for they all put in out of their abundance, but she
out of her poverty put in all that she had, her whole livelihood."
—Mark 12:35-44

Having answered all the questions that people brought to Him, Jesus now turned His attention to teaching what He wanted to teach. He had dealt with the concerns of the people—even His enemies, and now turned to His concerns. Because the enemies of the Lord had been the ones asking the questions at this point, He now asked a question of them. However, the question He asked was not directed only at God's enemies, but was presented in mixed company. The question was intended to confound the godless and to comfort the godly.

> "Then Jesus answered and said, while He taught in the temple,
> 'How is it that the scribes say that the Christ is the Son of
> David?'" (v. 35).

There are two questions implicit here. First, how can Christ be the Son of David? And second, how can the faithless scribes make such a claim? Jesus referred to David who

> "himself said by the Holy Spirit: 'The LORD said to my Lord, 'Sit at My right hand, Till I make Your enemies Your footstool.' Therefore David himself calls Him 'Lord'; how is He then his Son?" (vs. 36-37).

How can a father call a son "Lord?"

Of the several issues involved in the Lord's question, the most important involves the reversal of values brought by God's kingdom. Jesus said to His disciples

> "If anyone desires to be first, he shall be last of all and servant of all" (Mark 9:35).

Later He spoke about the relationship between wealth and salvation and said that "many who are first will be last, and the last first" (Mark 10:31). The coming of the kingdom, which is equivalent to the conversion of salvation or repentance—which means to turn around or change one's mind about something—brings a reversal of values as God's values begin to take precedence above the values of the world.

The issue of this reversal of values pertains to the role of Jesus Christ in Jewish history. When Jesus appeared on the scene (and still today) the Jews considered David to be their greatest king. David was the model king. His leadership provided the high-water mark in the Israelite monarchy. He was the greatest of the greats. Yet, the traditional Old Testament understanding of Psalm 110, which Jesus quoted here, was that David himself anticipated another king who would be much greater than himself. Psalm 110 provided clear evidence that David anticipated Christ. In that anticipation, David acknowledged that the anticipated king who would come some day in the future was his Lord.

Thus the greatness of the Davidic kingdom paled in significance to the coming of Jesus Christ. What was considered to that point in Jewish history to have been great, suddenly became much less important in the light of Christ's presence. We see here that Jesus made reference to this reversal of values, this role reversal wherein the lesser becomes greater and the greater lesser. Jesus pointed out the fact that those who had faith in Christ had already made that conversion of perspective, whereas those who did not have faith had not.

Thus, the Scribes and Pharisees struggled to make sense of Jesus' words. They didn't understand or believe that Jesus was superior to

David. That was the rub! They probably realized that David had anticipated the coming of Messiah in Psalm 110, but they failed to identify Jesus with the one David anticipated. On the one hand they claimed to be
faithful, and on the other they denied the chief object of faith—Christ
Himself.

But before we judge them too quickly, we must realize that we
would have performed no better than they. Most of us would have failed
to recognize Jesus as Messiah had we lived in that day. It is only by the
grace of God, the dispensation of the Holy Spirit, and the testimony of
the Scripture—now complete in its witness to Jesus Christ as Messiah—
that we today are able to make a faith claim with any integrity. Understanding Christ as Messiah is much easier in our day because we have
the completed Scripture to guide us. God's grace has been manifest
much more broadly and generously during this Christian Era. And for
that we praise the Lord!

Notice the conclusion of verse 37, "And the common people heard
Him gladly." While the lawyers and theologians of both the right and
the left failed to properly understand Jesus, the ordinary people—not all
of the ordinary people, of course, but those whom God had called to Jesus—heard Him without discomfort.

Mark continues, "Then He said to them in His teaching…" (v. 38).
Who was Mark talking about? Whom does "them" refer to? It refers to
the common people. Jesus turned from the scholars and academics to
talk to the common people. And what did He say to them?

> "Beware of the scribes, who desire to go around in long robes,
> love greetings in the marketplaces, the best seats in the
> synagogues, and the best places at feasts, who devour widows'
> houses, and for a pretense make long prayers. These will receive
> greater condemnation" (vs. 38-40).

Jesus warned the people about their own religious leaders.

He said that those who would be least likely to understand and follow the gospel of grace would be those with a vested interest in maintaining their own leadership positions during a time of change or revival. Check it out for yourself, those in church leadership prior to any
revival period are not those in leadership afterward. Revival or renewal
implies a significant change of both values and practices. That's what revival is!

Revival only comes to that which is dead. The word (*revival*) means
to live again. Revival and renewal return Christians to biblical values
and practices because such values and practices have been abandoned.

They come to churches that are spiritually dead. And the values and practices of the dead differ from the values and practices of the living. As the values and practices change in the power of revival, so the leaders change. Again, the allusion is to the reversal of values that is associated with repentance and conversion.

To illustrate this reversal Mark employs the story of the Widow's Mite. The story begins by telling us that Jesus went to the Temple to watch the contribution process. The story illustrates the reversal of values that is part and parcel of repentance and conversion. Further illustrating that reversal we find that Jesus took up a position "opposite the treasury" (v. 41). The KJV reads that He "sat over against the treasury...."

Though I don't want to make too much of it, I believe that it is important to note the position Jesus took. The Pharisees were on one side with the treasury, Jesus was on the other "over against" it. Where the prestige of money is valued by the worldly, the Godly value something else much more than money. What the Godly value is the lesson of the story.

Those who were wealthy put a lot of money into the treasury. This was not surprising and should be expected. Jesus paid little attention to it. But when a "poor widow came and threw in two mites, which make a quadrans" (v. 42), Jesus made an object lesson of it. This poor widow valued something that the others did not—or at least she valued it more than the others. Jesus said that

> "this poor widow has put in more than all those who have given
> to the treasury; for they all put in out of their abundance, but she
> out of her poverty" (vs. 43-44).

What did He mean? A quantitative answers suggests that the percentage of her gift compared to all she owned was much higher than those who gave more money but less a percentage of their total worth. Her gift represented ninety or a hundred percent of her financial worth, where the others represented only ten or twenty percent of theirs. Jesus, unlike the Pharisees, was not concerned about the amount of the gift. His interest was what the gift represented.

When we say that Adam was the federal head of humanity, we mean that he represented humanity in the covenant with God. Adam was the human representative who entered into covenant with God. And Adam's fall was then a representative fall. His fallen state represented humanity's fallen state. When we say that Christ is the second

Adam we mean that Christ has taken Adam's place as the human representative as regards God's covenant. Through Christ's shed blood God has entered into a New Covenant with Christ's people. Christ is the New Covenant representative. Maybe that's why He was so interested in what this widow's gift represented.

And what did it represent? It represented her love for God. Though her means were small, her love for the Lord was great. Whereas in contrast, all the others had great means, but their love for the Lord represented by their gifts was meager. What did Jesus say was the First Commandment?

> "And you shall love the LORD your God with all your heart, with all your soul, with all your mind, and with all your strength" (v. 30).

Not some, but all. Not ten or twenty percent, but a hundred percent.

What the world thinks important—wealth and big gifts, Jesus disregards. He is not opposed to wealth per se, but it is simply not important to Him. Loving the Lord, whether you have a lot or a little, that's the important thing—much more important than anything else.

The story of the widow's mite provides a fitting conclusion to chapter twelve. The wicked vine dressers didn't love the Lord. The Pharisees, concerned about paying taxes didn't love the Lord. The Sadducees, struggling with the resurrection, didn't love the Lord. The Scribes, arguing about the most important commandment didn't love the Lord. But King David loved the Lord and anticipated the coming of Christ. And the poor widow exemplified that love by contributing all she had to the cause of Christ.

How much do you love the Lord? Money is not the measure because it is so relative. Rather, the measure is found in our response to Jesus—heart, soul, mind, and strength. If we concentrate on these things, we won't have to worry about the money. Whatever God has provided will be sufficient.

53. ROAD SIGNS

Then as He went out of the temple, one of His disciples said to Him, "Teacher, see what manner of stones and what buildings are here!" And Jesus answered and said to him, "Do you see these great buildings? Not one stone shall be left upon another, that shall not be thrown down." Now as He sat on the Mount of Olives opposite the temple, Peter, James, John, and Andrew asked Him privately, "Tell us, when will these things be? And what will be the sign when all these things will be fulfilled?" And Jesus, answering them, began to say: "Take heed that no one deceives you. "For many will come in My name, saying, 'I am He,' and will deceive many. But when you hear of wars and rumors of wars, do not be troubled; for such things must happen, but the end is not yet. For nation will rise against nation, and kingdom against kingdom. And there will be earthquakes in various places, and there will be famines and troubles. These are the beginnings of sorrows. But watch out for yourselves, for they will deliver you up to councils, and you will be beaten in the synagogues. You will be brought before rulers and kings for My sake, for a testimony to them. And the gospel must first be preached to all the nations. But when they arrest you and deliver you up, do not worry beforehand, or premeditate what you will speak. But whatever is given you in that hour, speak that; for it is not you who speak, but the Holy Spirit. Now brother will betray brother to death, and a father his child; and children will rise up against parents and cause them to be put to death. And you will be hated by all for My name's sake. But he who endures to the end shall be saved."   —Mark 13:1-13

The disciples, having understood that the values of Jesus opposed the values of the treasury (Mark 12:41), they began to see that the gospel was opposed to materialism, including materialism supported by the Temple. Realizing that the values of the kingdom inverted the values of the world, they called Jesus' attention to the obvious massive power and apparent reality of the materialism of the world He seemed to oppose. The Old Testament world revolved around the Temple. The Pharisees and Sadducees controlled the Temple, and the Temple set the values of the whole society.

> "Teacher, see what manner of stones and what buildings are
> here" (v. 1)!

The stones used to build the Temple were extremely large. Perhaps you have seen pictures of the Wailing Wall, the only piece of the ancient Temple still standing. Moving such stones even by today's technological standards would be quite difficult. Or perhaps the disciples called Jesus' attention to the two main pillars of the Temple, which were eighteen feet in diameter, making the same point.

The disciples were shocked to learn that their spiritual leader was opposed to the Temple and what it had become under the leadership of the Pharisees and Sadducees. It was like thinking that Jesus is opposed to America, baseball, and apple pie. Opposing the dominant values of any society is like cursing the wind. What fool would think that he can effect storm patterns by hollering at them. Yet, Jesus had already demonstrated His control over nature. I can imagine that Jesus spit His answer at them.

> "Do you see these great buildings? Not one stone shall be left
> upon another, that shall not be thrown down" (v. 2).

His point was that God was greater than the stones of the Temple. Men think that they are so great because they can move a couple of rocks around the playground. Because people are so filled with pride, believing in the ultimate power of their own knowledge and society, Jesus began to put human knowledge and power in perspective. *The greatness of the Temple will not withstand the Word of God,* He said. The Temple itself had become an idol, so God would remove it from history.

The disciples were impressed by Jesus' description of the power of God. If God could tear down the Temple and build another in three days, as Jesus said in the next chapter (Mark 14:58), then God was truly a power to be reckoned with. *When will all these things happen?* they asked.

Yes, said Jesus, *God is a power to be reckoned with.* And He began to tell them about ever greater acts of God that would soon befall not only Israel, but the whole world. Verse 3 tells us that Jesus then took up a position "on the Mount of Olives opposite the Temple."

When will these things happen, Lord? "And what will be the sign when all these things will be fulfilled?" (v. 4). The disciples wanted to know when this process would begin and when it would end. They knew that Jesus was talking about the day of the Lord. Jeremiah had prophesied about it.

> "For this is the day of the Lord GOD of hosts, A day of vengeance, That He may avenge Himself on His adversaries. The sword shall devour; It shall be satiated and made drunk with their blood" (Jeremiah 46:10).

Jesus' answer provides one of the most distressing soliloquies in Scripture. He cites three things that will happen: great deceit, wars, and natural disasters. Furthermore, He said that these things will produce trouble and sorrow, and that they "must happen." These were not potential scenarios that would occur if people didn't straighten up and fly right. These were not possible consequences of disobedience. Rather, said Jesus, "such things *must happen*" (v. 7—italics added)! These things are not optional, but would unfold as part of God's salvation plan. If you don't find this a bit distressing, then you haven't understood what Jesus said. I'm not telling you this, Jesus is.

But these cataclysmic events were not to happen in order to punish the wicked, though that would be a consequence of them. Rather, these things would happen in order to bring faithful Christians "before rulers and kings for (Jesus') sake, for a testimony to them" (v. 9). God's purpose here and in all that He has done is to preach the gospel to all the nations (v. 10).

God's plan has always employed the three R's—ruin, regeneration, and repentance. First, people must realize the ruin that sin has made of their lives. Then, they must receive the Holy Spirit, who alone can bring about repentance and new life in Christ. God knows that people will not listen to Him until they are compelled to do so. Isn't that the way it really is? People generally don't turn to the Lord until they find themselves in a predicament that they cannot control. Most people turn to the Lord only in the midst or aftermath of a crisis. This doesn't have anything to do with free will. I'm not saying that God compels faithfulness. Rather, I'm only making an observation about human nature. Most people turn to the Lord only when the circumstances of their lives are beyond their own control. Illnesses, accidents, or tragedies of some sort bring people to call on the name of the Lord. Think about your own conversion, was it not like this? Every conversion doesn't happen this way, but most do.

In the same way God's salvation plan will bring all of His people to call upon His name, to turn to Him for salvation. Those who are saved before the end of the world will be used by the Lord to preach and witness the gospel of His grace and mercy. Some will be preachers, others will be witnesses in their communities, at home and on the job, among their friends, and among God's enemies.

We don't need to invent an evangelism strategy. Rather, we must participate in God's evangelism strategy. God will bring about the circumstances in our personal lives in which we will be able to testify to the promises of God. Some will be brought before rulers and kings, others before friends and neighbors, but all will have the opportunity and the responsibility to testify about Jesus Christ. That is God's purpose and plan.

Yet, we don't need to worry. We don't need to worry about our salvation, nor about our lives because God is in control. God is all-powerful, all-knowing, and sovereign. We don't need to worry about our evangelism plan. God will provide the circumstances, the people, and the words we need to speak. In other words, evangelism is best carried out in a natural way, in ordinary circumstances. We don't need a canned approach. We don't need strategies. We don't need programs.

But that doesn't mean that we have no role or responsibility for evangelism. God works through means. He uses His people to carry out His plan. Thus we need to be willing vessels. We do need to be willing to follow God's lead. We need to be responsive to God's guidance. We need to live and speak our faith in all that we do. The best evangelism is a by-product of faithfulness. Faithfulness is God's evangelism strategy. We must be faithful in our thoughts, faithful in our words, faithful in our actions. God does not call His people to sit around and do nothing, but to be faithful in all they do, and to do everything out of love and service to Him.

It is difficult to read God's road signs without wondering where we are in history. Are these the end times? I don't know. I don't really think it makes much difference for Christians. If you are trying to wait until the last moment to give yourself to Jesus, then you might be concerned. But if your life already belongs to Christ, it won't make much difference in what you think, say, or do. God's plan is the same whether Jesus returns in a week or another thousand years.

Nonetheless, Jesus gave three road signs to help us determine our place in history. Deception, war, and natural disaster are the signs. There are certainly an abundance of natural disasters, but I don't know if there has been an increase or not. As the population grows, such disasters will have a greater effect on more people because large numbers of people live in increasingly diverse places. Perhaps that's what Jesus meant.

War has been a regular staple of history. If you don't know this, you really should read up on it. I understand that the twentieth century has been the most war-torn century in history. Does that mean the twentieth century is the terminal century? Not necessarily. It could get a lot worse. America is presently engaged in a war in Bosnia. But it doesn't affect most of us very much. Indeed, it could get much worse.

When looking for historic signposts, the first thing that Jesus cautioned was, "Take heed that no one deceives you" (v. 5). Apparently, the greatest concern regarding the signs of the times is deception. People are deceived when they believe something that is not true. In other words, Jesus said that the first concern regarding the signs of the times is knowing the proper way to read the signs. If you don't know how to read them, the signs themselves will be of no help. Or if you misread them, they will be a hindrance rather than a help.

Knowing the truth is our only safeguard. When federal agents are trained to recognize counterfeit currency, they are taught how to recognize the real thing. Recognizing the varying marks of counterfeit currency is much too confusing. So, agents are taught to recognize the genuine article. Anything that varies from the real thing is counterfeit. So it is with the gospel. To keep from the deception ourselves we must study to know God's truth in its most original and fundamental aspects. We must know not only God's road signs, but His landmarks as well.

Surely we must receive the salvation provided by Christ's atonement. However, such reception is not the high-water mark of faithfulness. Such reception provides the beginning not the fulfillment of faithfulness. Receiving Christ is not the end of the journey, but only the beginning.

54. TRIBULATION

"So when you see the 'abomination of desolation,' spoken of by Daniel the prophet, standing where it ought not" (let the reader understand), "then let those who are in Judea flee to the mountains. Let him who is on the housetop not go down into the house, nor enter to take anything out of his house. And let him who is in the field not go back to get his clothes. But woe to those who are pregnant and to those who are nursing babies in those days! And pray that your flight may not be in winter. For in those days there will be tribulation, such as has not been since the beginning of the creation which God created until this time, nor ever shall be. And unless the Lord had shortened those days, no flesh would be saved; but for the elect's sake, whom He chose, He shortened the days. Then if anyone says to you, 'Look, here is the Christ!' or, 'Look, He is there!' do not believe it. For false christs and false prophets will rise and show signs and wonders to deceive, if possible, even the elect. But take heed; see, I have told you all things beforehand. But in those days, after that tribulation, the sun will be darkened, and the moon will not give its light; the stars of heaven will fall, and the powers in the heavens will be shaken. Then they will see the Son of Man coming in the clouds with great power and glory. And then He will send His angels, and gather together His elect from the four winds, from the farthest part of earth to the farthest part of heaven." —Mark 13:14-27

Mark 13 and the corresponding chapters in the other gospels are among the most disputed sections in all of Scripture. Behind these disputes are vying perspectives and theologies, as well as the genuine mystery of the unfolding end-times. Jesus' prophecy builds upon the prophecy of Daniel, so it behooves us to be familiar with Daniel's prophecy before we examine how Jesus has expanded, corrected, or clarified it. The "abomination of desolation" is referred to in Daniel 9:27, 11:31, and 12:11.

The ninth chapter of Daniel deals with Daniel's vision of the seventy-weeks. That vision predicted the destruction of Jerusalem and the coming of Messiah. Rather than getting bogged down in the disputes about the dating of the book of Daniel, and whether Daniel's vision applied to Jerusalem's destruction in 597 B.C. by the Assyrians or in A.D. 70 by the Romans, or has yet to see its fulfillment, we will look for the principles of God's involvement in history.

Generally speaking, Daniel's seventy-weeks vision prefigured a distinction between the Old Testament administration of Temple sacrifices and laws and the New Testament administration in which Temple sacrifices were abandoned by the grace of God through the propitiation of Christ's atonement on the cross. This, of course, can only be said by reading historical meaning back into Daniel's vision. We do this with the understanding that the Old Testament is made clearer by the advent of Christ, and by the guidance of Paul, who said that the events of the Old Testament had become examples for us, that we might learn from them (1 Corinthians 10:6).

Daniel's vision also confirms that the transition between the Testaments and the comings of Messiah would involve cataclysms of both nature and history. Fulfillment tells us that an end would come to the daily Temple sacrifices. That prophecy was fulfilled by the various destructions of Jerusalem and by the advent of Christ.

Finally, the allusion to the "abomination of desolation" in Daniel 12 ends with the encouragement that God's people will find rest and fulfillment by enduring in the faith until the end of time.

> "And from the time that the daily sacrifice is taken away, and the
> abomination of desolation is set up, there shall be *one thousand
> two hundred and ninety days*. Blessed is he who waits, and
> comes to the *one thousand three hundred and thirty-five days*"
> (Daniel 12:11–12—italics added)

—forty-five days longer. God's blessing is promised to those who endure beyond the "abomination of desolation." Thus, the faithful are encouraged to persevere all the various tribulations that will precede the end of time.

The question of whether there are many abominations of desolation or only one hinges on our understanding of Antichrist. Is there only one Antichrist, or are there many? The second century Church Father, Origen, described Antichrist as generically one, but composed of many species. He went on to say that there is a generic unity in falsehood, though there are many different types of errors. The Greek word *an-*

tichristos literally means "against Christ." Thus, all who are against Christ are antichrists in the biblical sense of the word. To be in error in your understanding about Christ is to be against the true Christ, as well.

In verse 14 Jesus said, in essence, that when His people were able to see the "abomination of desolation" spoken of by Daniel and great cataclysms in nature and history, they should flee for their lives. When abomination and desolation are observed by ordinary people, they can be assured that they are living in the midst of God's judgment. Thus, the faithful should separate themselves from the bulk of society for their own protection. Jesus recommends fleeing to the mountains without stopping to gather up your belongings.

The sense of it is that disaster is imminent, and no time should be wasted in departure.

> "In those days," *said Jesus,* "there will be tribulation, such as has not been since the beginning of the creation which God created until this time, nor ever shall be" (v. 19).

One of the interpretive difficulties here is knowing whether Jesus was referring to the destruction of Jerusalem in A.D. 70 or the end of the world at the close of time.

The premillennialists believe that Jesus was talking about the end of the world, where the postmillennialists believe that Jesus was talking about the imminent destruction of Jerusalem. The amillennialists believe that Jesus was teaching a principle regarding the fulfillment of God's covenant. That covenant (Deuteronomy 28) promised blessings for obedience and cursings for disobedience. Thus, here we find an application of this principle from the lips of Jesus regarding the disobedience of the covenant and God's subsequent judgment. The disobedience, of course, pertained to the crucifixion of Christ, which was part and parcel of Jesus' prediction of His death on the cross.

Jesus said that God's judgment against a rebellious humanity who would not receive His Son began with the destruction of Jerusalem and has continued throughout history. That is to say, the great tribulation that Jesus alluded to began with His death on the cross and will continue until His return in glory.

The Greek word for *tribulation* is *thlipsis*, which indicates the pressure that occurs from, for instance, pressing grapes to make wine. It involves a gathering and squeezing. *Thlipsis* would be used to describe the action of wringing out laundry—squeezing, pressing, forcing the water out. Indeed, the whole of Western history has involved an ongoing pressing out of God's people toward the fulfillment of the fullness of Christ's coming. The allusion suggests Christ's return in that His coming will not be complete until He returns in glory to hand over the rebellious but subdued kingdom of earth to His Father in heaven (1 Corinthians 15:24).

Verse 20 provides an important key to understanding this section of Scripture.

> "And unless the Lord had shortened those days, no flesh would
> be saved; but for the elect's sake, whom He chose, He shortened
> the days."

Here we find two suggestions. First, that without Jesus' intervention, no one would ever be saved. And second, that Jesus' intervention on behalf of the elect shortened the period of time required for the fulfillment of God's worldwide salvation plan. In other words, the advent of Christ is responsible for bringing the period of tribulation to a head. Again, the period of tribulation is the time between Jesus' death and His return in glory. Jesus has hastened the tribulation by entering into history. Consequently, Jesus has quickened or intensified the pressure of persecution for the sake of His elect.

Next, Jesus warned that false christs, false prophets, and false teachers would

> "rise and show signs and wonders to deceive, if possible, even the
> elect" (v. 22).

The Lord Himself confirmed that His people would need to know the difference between truth and falsehood because both would compete for their attention and commitment. He already said that many would be deceived during the last days, the days of tribulation (Mark 13:6). Now He declares that even the elect will be tempted to believe falsely.

Notice that Jesus presupposes the biblical teaching on election. I don't want to get sidetracked by that discussion because it takes us away from the primary thrust of the passage. However, it is important to note that Jesus uses the term in a way that suggests that He believes it to be true. What is truly distressing here is that Christ admits that even the elect may be deceived for a time, though the Lord will persevere in the truth with them in the end.

The application of this truth is that no individual is able to keep from being deceived through his own power and resources. Every person is susceptible to self-deception and the duplicity of Satan. Therefore, the faithful must rely upon the power of God to save them. We cannot save ourselves. Knowing that fact in advance, we can spare ourselves the effort and the heartache of self-reliance.

Finally, said Jesus, at the close of the period of tribulation, *when the cataclysms of nature and history are so overwhelming that everyone can see them, then the Son of Man will come in power and glory.* He refers to the fact that His Second Coming will be the terminal event in the tribulation period. Thus, He Himself defined the tribulation as that period between His death and His return in glory.

When Jesus returns in glory the elect will be gathered from all over the earth and from all over heaven. He alludes to the fact that many saints will have died and gone to heaven, yet they will be gathered together when He comes in glory.

Will you be part of this gathering? Will Christ account you faithful when He returns? The days are hastening by. The time to make peace with the Lord is upon us. For He says:

> "now is the accepted time; behold, now is the day of salvation" (2 Corinthians 6:2).

55. Watch

Now learn this parable from the fig tree: When its branch has already become tender, and puts forth leaves, you know that summer is near. So you also, when you see these things happening, know that it is near—at the doors! Assuredly, I say to you, this generation will by no means pass away till all these things take place. Heaven and earth will pass away, but My words will by no means pass away. But of that day and hour no one knows, not even the angels in heaven, nor the Son, but only the Father. Take heed, watch and pray; for you do not know when the time is. It is like a man going to a far country, who left his house and gave authority to his servants, and to each his work, and commanded the doorkeeper to watch. Watch therefore, for you do not know when the master of the house is coming—in the evening, at midnight, at the crowing of the rooster, or in the morning—lest, coming suddenly, he find you sleeping. And what I say to you, I say to all: Watch!

—Mark 13:28-37

Do you believe that Christ will return personally in power and glory? I do. I'm eager for the Lord to come and set things right. The world is in such a mess, and it seems that every time we human beings try to straighten it out it only gets worse. I suppose that we should expect things to be that way because the nature of sin is such that it effects everything that we think and do.

Jesus reminds us of the parable of the fig tree, the story of God's glory passing from Israel because Israel neither recognized the Lord of Glory, Jesus Christ, nor manifested the fruits of repentance. The fig tree blooms in the late Spring, giving evidence of the approach of Summer. Summer for the fig tree is a time of ripening in the hot sun and of harvest. With Summer comes the brightest light and the hottest heat. Here the reference is to the light of Christ having come into the world to hasten the harvest of souls according to God's plan, and to the heat of persecution which Christ said that He came to intensify.

Jesus has been teaching His people how to recognize the signs of the times, how to understand history from a Christian perspective. Christ's advent into the world signaled the beginning of the end. Christ would usher in great cataclysms of nature and history—earthquakes, famines, troubles, and sorrows (v. 8). He also said that the "abomination of desolation" (v. 14) and Christ's return "in the clouds" (v. 26) would be apparent to every Christian as signs of the end.

In addition to these signs, His allusion to the fig tree suggests that there would also be a crop of gospel fruit ripe for the harvest. Though the withered fig tree (Israel) of Mark 11:12-14 would shrivel and die, a harvest of gospel fruit would be produced by another tree. Like Israel, it would be a tree of God's own choosing—none other than the Church of Jesus Christ.

Verse 30 has provided much difficulty.

> "Assuredly, I say to you, this generation will by no means pass away till all these things take place."

Scholars have interpreted it every which way, trying to force it into service in one or another biblical scheme. What did Jesus mean by "generation?" What did He mean by "pass away?" Did He really mean that "all" these things would happen? Etc.

It seems that the plain meaning of the verse best serves the postmillennialists who understand that this prophecy was fulfilled with the destruction of Jerusalem in A.D. 70. There we see great cataclysms of nature and history—an earthquake tore the Temple curtain, the administration of Temple sacrifices and services passed away, the outpouring of the Holy Spirit at Pentecost resulted in a great gospel harvest, etc. These events were experienced by the generation living when He did through the events surrounding the fall of Jerusalem in A.D. 68-70.

Furthermore, the preservation of the New Testament has provided a fulfillment of sorts for Jesus admonition that

> "Heaven and earth will pass away, but (His) words will by no means pass away" (v. 31).

Obviously, heaven and earth have not passed away yet, but neither have His words. Thus, this prophecy is in the process of fulfillment in that the words of Jesus have survived two thousand years. Again, the sense of the thing is that His prophecies are in the process of fulfillment. They have been fulfilled, yet their fulfillment is not yet complete.

Jesus' prophecy that heaven and earth would pass away, but His
Word would not echoes God's teaching in the Old Testament.

> "Of old You laid the foundation of the earth, And the heavens
> are the work of Your hands. They will perish, but You will
> endure; Yes, they will all grow old like a garment; Like a cloak
> You will change them, And they will be changed. But You are
> the same, And Your years will have no end" (Psalm 102:25-27).

Isaiah said the same thing,

> "Lift up your eyes to the heavens, And look on the earth beneath.
> For the heavens will vanish away like smoke, The earth will
> grow old like a garment, And those who dwell in it will die in
> like manner; But My salvation will be forever, And My
> righteousness will not be abolished" (Isaiah 51:6).

The practical application of this is that God's people will thrive unto
salvation only by tenaciously clinging to God's Word. Everything else
can—and will—change over time! Everything else is negotiable. But
God's Word is the "Rock of our salvation" (Psalm 95:1).

What do we mean when we say that we believe God's Word, or
that we believe the Bible consisting of the Old and New Testament, to
be the only inspired, inerrant, infallible, authoritative Word of God
written? Do we mean that we treasure the Bible in our hearts and live
however we want? Not at all. To believe the Bible means not only that
you believe its stories and teachings to be true, but that the Bible serves
in the most fundamental way as your personal guide for living and for
worship. God goes to great pains to teach His people how He is to be
worshiped and how to organize His churches.

To believe in the Bible means that whatever Christians do—acting
personally as moral agents or worshiping corporately as God's people—
must have precedent in Scripture. Our worship, our morality, our actions and behaviors, our families and church structures must find justification in and conformity to Scripture. If we are to enact God's will in
our lives, then we must do what God wills. And the only sure place we
can discover God's will is Scripture. If we aren't living according to biblical principles, personally, as families, and corporately as a church, then
we don't really believe the Bible because to believe it means to live it—
not perfectly, of course, but as best as we are able with the help of the
Holy Spirit.

To aim at less than that is to fail to believe the Bible. If we know
that Scripture teaches that we should not lie or cheat or gossip and we

lie or cheat or gossip anyway, then our actions betray our real convictions. It greatly behooves liars and cheaters to say that they don't lie or cheat. But it is their actions that reveal their true beliefs (or lack of commitments).

So, we can be assured that Jesus will return in glory and judgment because He said He would, and the Lord doesn't lie or make mistakes. He will return! And people would like to know when He will return so they can get ready. Don't you clean the house before company comes over? Don't you like to know when someone is coming to dinner, so you can make sure that there is enough? We all do. It's quite natural.

But Jesus didn't say when He was coming back, only that He would most certainly come back. Though He never said when He would return, He did say two things about the time of His return. He said that He would come unexpectedly (1 Thessalonians 5:2, 2 Peter 3:10), that

> "no one knows, not even the angels in heaven, nor the Son, but only the Father" (v. 32).

Secondly, be ready. The reason that we are not to know when the Lord will return is to keep us alert.

> "Take heed, watch and pray; for you do not know when the time is" (v. 33).

Did your parents ever leave you home alone when you were young? Did they ever go out to a party or a meeting or something, and leave you without a babysitter or anyone to watch over you when you were old enough to know better but too young to resist? If you knew that your parents wouldn't be home until a certain time, you would be more tempted to do something that they would not approve of, knowing that you could clean up the mess or get back before them so they wouldn't know anything about it.

Like the immoral wife in Proverbs 7 whose husband was away on a long journey and would not be home until "the appointed day" (Proverbs 7:20). She figured she was free to sin because she knew that her husband always came home when he said he would, never early, never late. Aren't sinners like that? While the cat's away, the mice will play. That's why Jesus didn't tell us when He would be back. He wants us to be in perpetual readiness, to be on guard against sin all of the time, not just when we expect Him back. That's what being a Christian is all about—being ready to meet Jesus face-to-face on a moment's notice.

We should always be doing what Jesus would approve of, so when He surprises us He will find us engaged in His work.

Today, we find a plethora of literature speculating on the immanent return of Christ as a mark of the millennium. And that's fine inasmuch as it serves to help people prepare for His return. But there are two things that bother me about that literature.

First, Christ Himself told us that no one knows the day, which suggests that such speculation is futile at best. If Jesus said that no one knows, then how can these modern "prophets" be so sure? Yet, it's true that Jesus also said that we are to read the signs to know the times. However, if we are to have any real understanding of the signs and the times, we must know history, particularly church history. To fail to understand history is to be

> "tossed to and fro and carried about with every wind of doctrine" (Ephesians 4:14).

Second, Scripture tells us that the mark of a true prophet is whether the prophecies come true (Jeremiah 23:23-28). If they do not come true, then he is a false prophet and at least is not to be listened to any more. The track record for unfulfilled Messianic and millennial prophecies is horrible. Yet, the same authors continue to sell millions of books. Here the fault is not so much with those who write the books—though they must share the blame, but the real problem is with the Christian community that continues to buy and read their books as if history itself has not proven them wrong.

Yet, having read much of that literature myself, I understand that it is exciting and passionate, much more exciting than a simple life lived in obedience to Christ. But by living quiet lives in obedience to the Lord, whether Christ returns this afternoon or not for another thousand years, His people will be ready.

What about you? Are you ready?

56. ANOINTED

After two days it was the Passover and the Feast of Unleavened Bread. And the chief priests and the scribes sought how they might take Him by trickery and put Him to death. But they said, "Not during the feast, lest there be an uproar of the people." And being in Bethany at the house of Simon the leper, as He sat at the table, a woman came having an alabaster flask of very costly oil of spikenard. Then she broke the flask and poured it on His head. But there were some who were indignant among themselves, and said, "Why was this fragrant oil wasted? For it might have been sold for more than three hundred denarii and given to the poor." And they criticized her sharply. But Jesus said, "Let her alone. Why do you trouble her? She has done a good work for Me. "For you have the poor with you always, and whenever you wish you may do them good; but Me you do not have always. She has done what she could. She has come beforehand to anoint My body for burial. Assuredly, I say to you, wherever this gospel is preached in the whole world, what this woman has done will also be told as a memorial to her." Then Judas Iscariot, one of the twelve, went to the chief priests to betray Him to them. And when they heard it, they were glad, and promised to give him money. So he sought how he might conveniently betray Him.

—Mark 14:1-11

The enemies of the gospel had done everything they could to dissuade, interrupt, or derail the ministry of Jesus. In their frustration with their own inability to impede the progress of God's Word, they decided to eliminate Him. They planned to "take Him by trickery" (v. 1) and deceit—the only tools they knew—and murder Him quietly and unobtrusively, without calling public attention to their deeds. They planned to simply sweep Him from the stage.

But God's providence frustrated their every plan. While they had planned to eliminate Jesus quietly, away from public purview, apart from the Passover celebration that would be in full swing just two days

from the hatching of their plot, God decided otherwise. Jesus was crucified at the very height of Passover, with a public trial before the gover-
nor, on a hill for all to see. God even uses the plans of the wicked to accomplish His purposes. There is no one like this God in power and wisdom!

Jesus was in the village of Bethany (the house of dates or of fruitfulness), not Bethsaida (the house of fruitlessness). Mark also tells us that He
was at the house of Simon the leper. Not much is known about Simon.
He may have been the father of Martha, Mary, and Lazarus. If it was important to know who he was, Mark would have told us more.

Mark did mention that he had leprosy. In those days before modern
science and medicine leprosy was understood to be a generic sort of
body rot that was highly contagious. This detail of the story is very significant. In those days no one in their right mind would associate with a
leper. Because of the supposed contagion of leprosy it was thought that
to touch a leper or to touch anything that a leper touched would likely
spread the disease. Yet, there was Jesus eating at the home of a leper!

The scene suggests tremendous compassion for and identification
with those who suffer. Jesus' mere presence at Simon's house speaks volumes about His love and concern for the dregs of society. Nothing
could keep the Lord from sharing with and caring for those who suffered.

It was there, at Simon's house that a woman came and anointed Jesus' head with costly oil. Why would she do such a thing? She did it as
an act of worship. Anointing conveyed the sense of the presence of
God's Holy Spirit. The anointing suggested that God's Spirit had greatly
blessed Jesus, and that He was in some sense chosen by God. The Old
Testament practice of anointing was related to the coronation of kings.

Part of this woman's act of worship involved making a costly sacrifice as an expression of her love and commitment to the glory of God.
That's what real worship is. It's not simply listening to a lecture about
the Bible. Real worship involves costly sacrifices of time, talent, and
treasure—not for the public demonstration of your love and commitment (that's what the Pharisees did), but in response to God's grace that
issues from genuine love and thanksgiving for the Lord. Real worship
occurs in one's personal relationship with God. It is an attitude, but
more than an attitude. It is an act, but more than an act. It is a commitment, but more than a commitment. It is like trying to explain your love
for your wife and children.

So, this woman worshiped Jesus by making a sacrifice of costly oil, but some were indignant and thought, What a waste! What they said was that the resources used for worship were wasted resources, that those resources could have been put to better use, a more practical use. If nothing else they could have been used to feed the poor. Those who were indignant toward this woman for what she did, revealed the fact that they did not properly value worship. They were pragmatists, unconcerned with the value of worship. They thought that there were more important things to do than to worship Jesus. So, "they criticized her sharply" (v. 5).

But Jesus came to her defense. "Why do you trouble her?" (v. 6). Why indeed? "Why do the nations rage?" (Psalm 2:1) Why were some of the disciples so concerned with this woman? What had she done that deserved their ire? Jesus said that His faithful saints would have trouble in the world, but have you ever wondered why they should have such trouble? Wherever Christians express true commitment for the cause of Christ they are met with envy, jealousy, malice, and ignorance.

People don't like God's sovereignty. They don't like the fact that God is above our limited understanding of the law, that He can do whatever He wants whenever He chooses. They don't like God's grace or the fact that God can save whoever He chooses. People want salvation to be fair. People think that everyone should have an equal opportunity to go to heaven. If entrance into heaven is not based upon equal opportunity, then they don't want anything to do with it.

Why? Well, if it is based on equal opportunity, then those who claim heaven actually make a claim of superiority. If salvation comes through equal opportunity, then those who claim it claim superior effort. If it is equally available to all, and some are not saved, then the reason they are not saved is that they did not apply themselves sufficiently. But that is not what the Bible teaches. When salvation is understood to be a matter of equal opportunity, then it becomes a matter of works-righteousness. It becomes a matter of applying one's self sufficiently in order to attain it.

But salvation is not simply a possibility or an opportunity. It is a certainty. God will not fail to save all of His people. The only real question is, Am I one? Are *you* one? We all must answer that question one way or the other.

Jesus said that

> "wherever this gospel is preached in the whole world, what this woman has done will also be told as a memorial to her" (v. 9).

Wow! Whatever this woman did must have been pretty important to Jesus. So, what did she do? She worshiped the Lord Jesus Christ with a costly sacrifice. She revealed her heart—her love for the Lord—by the way that she worshiped Him. She demonstrated her love for Christ in a real, tangible way, and by doing that she identified herself as belonging to God. She had been saved from the ravages of hell and she knew it. Her sacrifice was offered in grateful thankfulness for her salvation wrought in Christ. She answered the question, not with words, but with her life. She offered all that she had in worship of the Lord.

Our lives are to be similar expressions of living faithfulness evidenced by costly sacrifices given in grateful thankfulness. When you can do that, you will be sure of your salvation. The Rich Young Ruler couldn't. The Pharisees couldn't. Many can't, but can you?

Judas appears to be the primary person who objected to what he thought to be a frivolous waste of resources. Judas was the treasurer, the one charged with stewardship of the disciple's money. It is not coincidental that an excessive concern for money and material undermines the value of worship. The Bible teaches that worship of the Lord needs to be the number one priority for God's people. No expense was spared for the construction of the Temple, nor did God spare any expense regarding the purchase of His people by the blood of His Son. Jesus Himself paid the highest price possible to redeem the elect.

Following the biblical model, then, we too must be willing to offer all, and especially the best part of our time, talent, and treasure in the worship of our Lord Jesus Christ. The biblical tithe is described as

> "firstfruits… the best of the oil, all the best of the new wine and
> the grain" (Numbers 18:12),

and "without blemish" (Exodus 12:5). In other words, our worship of the Lord, what we offer in response to salvation must be the best of what we have. We are forbidden to offer leftovers to the Lord. His cut, if you will, must be off the top. Anything less than the best we have—and that does not mean that we must have the best of everything, but simply the best of what we have—must be offered, sacrificed to God. To do less than that is to reveal to the Lord that we do not value Him above all else.

In essence, that is what Judas said when he criticized the woman who anointed Christ with such costly oil. Long before Judas betrayed the Lord to the chief priests he had betrayed Christ in his heart. This anointing of Christ was nothing but an example that Judas' betrayal of

Christ had already been made in his heart. Judas' betrayal was not simply the selling of Christ to the chief priests for thirty pieces of silver. His be-trayal was the failure to properly worship the Lord in the first place. Ju-das' values were still worldly, still materialistic. He was a disciple in the inner circle, but had never really been converted. His dastardly deed with the chief priests was simply an expression of his lack of conversion.

At that point Judas himself saw that Jesus' values were different than his own. And he, of course, thought himself to be right and Jesus wrong. So he began to consider "how he might conveniently betray Him" (v. 11). The betrayal of Jesus Christ usually happens because of the conflict between godly worship and practical values, the conflict be-tween what people see as the most practical, efficient use of their limited resources and God's demand for proper worship through costly sacrifice.

We need not limit our understanding of this issue to money. A proper tithe involves time, talent, and treasure. Money is only a third of the concern. Are you willing to give God the time He requires? Too many people consider reading to be a waste of time. Others consider reading the Bible or biblical history, or theology (which is nothing else than the study of God) to be a low priority. Maybe not in what they say, but certainly in what they practice. We may say that we believe these things to be important, but if we don't do them ourselves our actions betray our real convictions. Too many people consider the church to be too insignificant a concern in which to invest their skills and abilities.

Worship is not just what we do on Sundays. Real worship involves our entire lives. Real worship is putting God first in all that we do and say. Real worship occurs in that intimate relationship between Christ and His people.

57. Is It Me?

Now on the first day of Unleavened Bread, when they killed the Passover lamb, His disciples said to Him, "Where do You want us to go and prepare, that You may eat the Passover?" And He sent out two of His disciples and said to them, "Go into the city, and a man will meet you carrying a pitcher of water; follow him. Wherever he goes in, say to the master of the house, 'The Teacher says, "Where is the guest room in which I may eat the Passover with My disciples?"' Then he will show you a large upper room, furnished and prepared; there make ready for us." So His disciples went out, and came into the city, and found it just as He had said to them; and they prepared the Passover. In the evening He came with the twelve. Now as they sat and ate, Jesus said, "Assuredly, I say to you, one of you who eats with Me will betray Me." And they began to be sorrowful, and to say to Him one by one, "Is it I?" And another said, "Is it I?" He answered and said to them, "It is one of the twelve, who dips with Me in the dish. The Son of Man indeed goes just as it is written of Him, but woe to that man by whom the Son of Man is betrayed! It would have been good for that man if he had never been born." —Mark 14:12-21

Passover had arrived.. The disciples asked Jesus where He would celebrate the feast. This Passover would be like no other. Jesus needed privacy in order to do what He needed to do with the disciples. It was

> "the first day of Unleavened Bread, when they killed the Passover lamb" (v. 12)

He sent two of them (Peter and John) into Jerusalem to find a man who carried water. Such a man would not be difficult to spot because carrying water was the work of women and children. A man who carried water was a man without any women or children. Without women or children, his house would not likely be filled with family and friends for the Passover feast. In other words, such a man 1) had a house, 2) had no women to work it, and 3) would have available space.

> "His disciples went out, and came into the city, and found it just
> as He had said to them; and they prepared the Passover" (v. 16).

Passover, like all Jewish holidays, began at sunset. Thus, Jesus came in the evening and gathered with the twelve disciples. At this point in Mark's story Jesus had predicted His death and resurrection a couple of times, but no one had understood Him—nor could they have.

John told us that Jesus disciples had been arguing about who was the greatest disciple as the Passover meal was to begin. With no women or servants around, Jesus

> "took a towel and girded Himself. After that, He poured water
> into a basin and began to wash the disciples' feet, and to wipe
> them with the towel with which He was girded" (John 13:4-5).

Mark mentions no such event, but then again Mark wasn't there. However, John's story of the betrayal is linked to the foot washing. John recorded the words of Jesus following the event.

> "So when He had washed their feet, taken His garments, and sat
> down again, He said to them, 'Do you know what I have done to
> you? You call me Teacher and Lord, and you say well, for so I
> am. If I then, your Lord and Teacher, have washed your feet, you
> also ought to wash one another's feet. For I have given you an
> example, that you should do as I have done to you. Most
> assuredly, I say to you, a servant is not greater than his master;
> nor is he who is sent greater than he who sent him. If you know
> these things, blessed are you if you do them. I do not speak
> concerning all of you. I know whom I have chosen; but that the
> Scripture may be fulfilled, 'He who eats bread with Me has lifted
> up his heel against Me.' Now I tell you before it comes, that
> when it does come to pass, you may believe that I am He. Most
> assuredly, I say to you, he who receives whomever I send
> receives Me; and he who receives Me receives Him who sent
> Me.' When Jesus had said these things, He was troubled in spirit,
> and testified and said, 'Most assuredly, I say to you, one of you
> will betray Me.' Then the disciples looked at one another,
> perplexed about whom He spoke" (John 13:12-22).

Jesus said several important things here. First He said that all of His disciples were called to service. Secondly, He said that God's blessings don't come from knowing this, but from actually doing it. Thirdly, He said that He was not speaking to all of the twelve disciples.

> "I do not speak concerning all of you. I know whom I have chosen" (John 13:18).

Not all of the disciples would be saved. We know that Judas was ultimately lost.

From God's perspective Judas was lost because he had never been slated for salvation. From man's perspective Judas was lost because he rejected Christ. These are not different insights, nor are they contradictory. We might be tempted to ask, *Am I slated for salvation?* But the better question is, *Have I rejected Christ?* Judas' betrayal of Christ for thirty pieces of silver was not the first indication that he had rejected Christ. Jesus had known it all along. Judas never really believed. Jesus simply revealed that fact to the disciples in advance to encourage their belief that He really is who He says He is.

John 13:20 then established lines of authority for Jesus' disciples.

> "He who receives whomever I send receives Me; and he who receives Me receives Him who sent Me."

God is received through Christ, and Christ is received through whomever Christ sends. Sometimes it is difficult for us to know exactly who Christ has sent to whom. There is much struggle in the New Testament between true and false apostles. Paul was adamant that there were many people who claimed to be apostles, whom Paul was certain that Christ had not sent. If you are not familiar with these issues read Jude and the letters to Peter.

This issue concerns pastoral qualifications. Are there pastoral qualifications? We believe there are. People differ about the particulars of those qualifications, and I don't want to get into that. Simply note that there are qualifications for pastoral office, just as there are qualifications for elders and deacons. There are even qualifications for church membership. For instance, all Christians must believe that they are saved by the blood of Christ for service through Christ, and manifest some evidence of the reality of their belief.

Revisit John 13:20, "he who receives whomever I send receives Me." Surely every church believes that Christ has sent (called) its particular pastor to serve that particular church! In other words, if Christ has indeed called a pastor to serve a particular church, then for the members to reject that pastor is to reject Christ. Jesus had said the same thing earlier, "whoever will not receive you nor hear you (gospel preachers), when you depart from there, shake off the dust under your feet as a testimony against them. Assuredly, I say to you, it will be more tolerable for Sodom and Gomorrah in the day of judgment than for that city!" (Mark 6:11).

Christ's ambassadors carry Christ's authority—not the authority to do whatever they themselves want, but the authority to administer or carry out God's will. Where do we find God's will perfectly expressed? In His Word, the Bible. Thus, His ambassadors simply carry out His orders as found in Scripture. Does this make the pastor superior to his congregation? Not at all! Christian leadership is servant leadership.

Christians are called into Christian service.

"Jesus called them to Himself and said, 'You know that the rulers of the Gentiles lord it over them, and those who are great exercise authority over them. Yet it shall not be so among you; but whoever desires to become great among you, let him be your servant. And whoever desires to be first among you, let him be your slave—just as the Son of Man did not come to be served, but to serve, and to give His life a ransom for many.'" (Matthew 20:25-28).

Gospel authority is not a mark or function of superiority but of responsibility. Having authority does not make a person better than anyone else. Yet, people—even people in the church—don't yet understand this issue. In order to properly exercise biblical authority, one must himself be under authority. Authority is nothing more than a proper chain of command. God, of course, is author of all things and, therefore, sits at the top of the chain of command as the author of history. God then grants authority to those who are able to respond to Him appropriately. The word *responsibility* means the ability to respond.

However, the proper response to God is humility and repentance, not pride and vanity. Thus, God gives authority to the humble and repentant to engage in service to Him. God's authority is not about rights or equality. It's not about superiority or having a "place at the table." It's not about human freedom and self-fulfillment. It's about humility and repentance. It's about obedience to Scripture—loving God and loving your neighbor as yourself. It's about submission to God's Word.

Judas failed to understand this. Judas sought to use Jesus as a means to accomplish his own purposes. Judas was in it for what he could get for himself, not for what he could give of himself. Judas never really understood the gospel of Christ, though he was himself an apostle of the highest order. Judas betrayed Christ by failing to understand the gospel.

Yet, the Lord used Judas' failure. All Christians are called to the bar of judgment to determine if they have betrayed Christ like Judas did. All Christians are called to inquire whether they really believe and understand the gospel, the Lord, and the Bible, or whether they simply believe what they themselves choose to believe. It's easy to say that we believe the Bible. But if we don't act like we believe it, we probably don't. It's easy to say that we understand God's Word. But are we really manifesting the fruits of the Spirit?—

> "love, joy, peace, long-suffering, kindness, goodness, faithfulness, gentleness, self-control" (Galatians 5:22).

What about *you*? Do you really believe the Bible? Do you understand it from God's perspective? Or just from your own? Are you living in obedience to Scripture? Have you properly submitted to God's authority?

58. LORD'S SUPPER

And as they were eating, Jesus took bread, blessed and broke it,
and gave it to them and said, "Take, eat; this is My body." Then
He took the cup, and when He had given thanks He gave it to
them, and they all drank from it. And He said to them, "This is
My blood of the new covenant, which is shed for many. As-
suredly, I say to you, I will no longer drink of the fruit of the
vine until that day when I drink it new in the kingdom of
God." And when they had sung a hymn, they went out to the
Mount of Olives. —Mark 14:22-26

I t is important to understand that Jesus instituted the Lord's Supper in the midst of His teaching on the nature of Christian authority, leadership, and servanthood. And it is important to note that His teaching on these very things led to His betrayal and abandonment. All of the gospel writers concur about this important fact.

In the Upper Room Jesus washed His disciples' feet as a symbol of the reversal of values brought by the gospel of grace. The disciples had been arguing about who would be the greatest in the kingdom of God, and were shocked to hear the reversal of values—that the greatest would be the least, that the Master performed the duties of the servant. Peter refused to let Jesus wash his feet. Peter thought that Jesus was wrong about this great reversal of values. Finally Peter submitted, but he did so under protest. Judas, while it appears that he submitted to the outward form of the ceremony, hardened his heart against the Lord and His gospel of free grace.

Paul found the same kind of difficulties in the church at Corinth. 1 Corinthians 11 begins with Paul's teaching on the symbols of Christian authority. 1 Corinthians 11 is not a commentary on first century fashions regarding heads, hair, and hats. Not at all! Rather 1 Corinthians 11 is Paul's teaching about the practice and symbols of Christian authority in the home and by extension in the church.

Paul began by calling Christians to imitate him because he was imitating Christ. In other words, what Paul said and did carried the authority of Christ. Here Paul identified himself as standing in the teaching and tradition of the Lord Himself.

Paul then moved to an explanation that the gospel brings a reversal of values. The natural order—the order of nature—is subservient to the order of Christ. Paul lists a hierarchy of gospel authority—God, Christ, man, woman, in that order. God is the supreme authority. As Christ submitted to God, so man is to submit to Christ, and woman to man. Thus, an order of submission is set for all humanity. Like it or not, that is the traditional order of Christian authority. Remember that Christian authority is not to be lorded over others, but is to be understood as submission and service to our "higher" authority. Christ submitted to God. Paul submitted to Christ. Similarly, in imitation of Paul, men should submit to Christ, and women to their husbands or fathers.

Every king had a crown and scepter, the symbols of kingly authority. Paul taught that Christ also had His symbols of authority. Because Christ reigns in the hearts of His people and in their relationships with one another, His symbols of authority were both individual and corporate. As a king wears a crown to symbolize his personal authority, so Christians are to wear the whole armor of God, spoken of in Ephesians 6. But that is not what Paul is talking about here.

A king also carried a scepter, a fancy staff or stick that represented his authority among his subjects in his kingdom. The authority of the king brought order and peace to his kingdom. Similarly, Paul taught that there were symbols of Christian authority, symbols of Christian order and peace in the church. These symbols had to do with heads, hair, and hats.

The word *head* still signifies the one to whom others submit in authority, i.e., the head of a company, the head of a government, etc. The physical heads of men were to be uncovered to symbolize their submission to Christ. When a man comes "hat-in-hand" with his head uncovered, he symbolizes his humility and subjection. This gesture of humility was particularly appropriate during prayer and worship. Thus, men remove their hats when coming into the church to symbolize their submission to Christ.

Women, on the other hand, were to cover their heads during prayer and worship. Why the difference? Because in the order of Christian authority—God, Christ, man, woman—women were not in submission to Christ directly, but were to be in submission to Christ through their faithful husbands. A husband was to represent—to teach and adjudicate—Christ's authority in the home, among his family, among his wife and children. The husband, then, was responsible for teaching and maintaining Christian authority in his home. He was to teach the Bible to his wife and children, and thereby to grow in his own faith. You know that the teacher always learns more than the student, don't you?

This was the essential pattern or structure of authority in the early church. This was the tradition that Paul called Christians to imitate (1 Corinthians 11:1-2). Every Christian was to be in submission to an authority. Christian authority was not to be understood as an authority over others, but as an authority under which each individual stood in service. Our eyes are to be on Christ, not upon each other.

Was this pattern of authority operative at Corinth? No. The church was disordered. Bickering had led to conflicts, schisms, and divisions. Into this environment of dissension Paul brought the proper institution of the Lord's Supper as the solution to the abandonment of Christian authority that was causing problems at Corinth. But how does the Lord's Supper institutionalize Christian authority, or promote biblical order in the church?

The symbolism of the Lord's Supper points to God's covenant with His people. The covenant is the contractual agreement that determines and orders the relationship between God and His people. The Old Testament covenant was symbolized by the ritual use of blood, to include the practice of circumcision. Various animals were sacrificed and their blood was sprinkled about to signify God's forgiveness. If a person committed a particular sin, he would take a particular animal to the temple to be sacrificed as an act of contrition and atonement. Similarly, male infants were circumcised so that they would carry a mark of the covenant. It was a way to call the individual to remember God's covenant all his life.

In a similar way the blood of Christ on the cross serves as an act of contrition and atonement, not for His sin, but for ours. Thus, as Christians feed on the body and blood of Christ by receiving the Lord's Supper, they symbolize their submission to Christ and to the New Covenant, written in His blood for the remission of sin.

The order of the Lord's Supper should reflect Christ's order for the church, which is based upon His order for the family. The Lord's Supper is a symbolic celebration (but not merely so) of God's authority and Christ's submission, which then provided His atonement, the basis of Christian salvation. Christian men honor God's authority by coming to Him hat-in-hand, in humility and submission. Christian women honor

God's authority by honoring their husband's authority, by standing-by-her-man, symbolized by the wearing of a head cover.

Jesus brought a similar order when He fed the masses. There He gave thanks and blessed the food, giving it to the disciples for distribution. Similarly, the pastor gives thanks for the elements and the deacons distribute them. To carry the symbolism further, the deacons should then give the elements to the men—husbands and fathers, who in turn distribute them to their own families. This then unifies the symbolism between the order of the family and the order of the church. Christ orders the relationships between human beings. Christ's order is, of course, to love one another. Jesus gave a

> "new commandment… that you love one another; as I have
> loved you, that you also love one another" (John 13:34).

But we should not think of the Lord's Supper as some kind of magical rite. There is no spiritual power in bread and wine. Rather, this sacrament derives its power from God's Word, God's covenant. It symbolizes the reception or rejection of the salvation bought by the blood of Christ. Those who receive it open themselves to the blessings of the covenant. And those who reject it open themselves to the curses of the covenant (Deuteronomy 28). But the symbol is only real is there is a reality to it.[11]

Consequently, Paul calls whoever "eats this bread or drinks this cup of the Lord" to examine themselves, to examine their own hearts and determine whether they are living in proper submission to Christ and His church. Are you dressed in the full armor of God (Ephesians 6)? Is your household ordered so that your family and their relationships with each other bring glory to God? When these things are in proper order, we can be sure of receiving God's blessings. If our intention is to get our lives and our families in God's order, then we will grow as we work to establish it.

But when things are not in order, when someone

> "eats and drinks in an unworthy manner (he) eats and drinks
> judgment to himself" (1 Corinthians 11:29)

because he has not properly understood and practiced the order that Christ has established for His body. The failure to properly discern the Lord's body—the church—results in weakness and sickness among God's

---

11 See: *The True Mystery of The Mystical Presence*, Phillip A Ross, John
     Williamson Nevin, Pilgrim Platform, Marietta, Ohio, 2011.

people. Paul said that if we would discipline ourselves, get our own lives, our homes, and our churches in order—in God's order, then the Lord would not have to discipline us. Paul said that repeated failure to conform to God's order will eventually bring God's judgment.

When the children in a family have a squabble, it is better for them to settle it themselves, rather than wait for dad to come home and settle it for them. The proper administration of the Lord's Supper is a means of grace, a way of encouraging God's will in our personal lives, our families, and our churches.

Those who receive the Lord's Supper will receive either God's blessings or God's curses. Thus, Paul warns those who receive it, to receive it worthily or properly, lest it contribute to the hardening of their own hearts.

59. I Will Not

Then Jesus said to them, "All of you will be made to stumble
because of Me this night, for it is written: 'I will strike the
Shepherd, And the sheep will be scattered.' But after I have
been raised, I will go before you to Galilee." Peter said to Him,
"Even if all are made to stumble, yet I will not be." Jesus said to
him, "Assuredly, I say to you that today, even this night, before
the rooster crows twice, you will deny Me three times." But he
spoke more vehemently, "If I have to die with You, I will not
deny You!" And they all said likewise. Then they came to a
place which was named Gethsemane; and He said to His disci-
ples, "Sit here while I pray." And He took Peter, James, and
John with Him, and He began to be troubled and deeply dis-
tressed. Then He said to them, "My soul is exceedingly sorrow-
ful, even to death. Stay here and watch." He went a little far-
ther, and fell on the ground, and prayed that if it were possible,
the hour might pass from Him. And He said, "Abba, Father, all
things are possible for You. Take this cup away from Me; nev-
ertheless, not what I will, but what You will." Then He came
and found them sleeping, and said to Peter, "Simon, are you
sleeping? Could you not watch one hour? Watch and pray, lest
you enter into temptation. The spirit indeed is willing, but the
flesh is weak." Again He went away and prayed, and spoke the
same words. And when He returned, He found them asleep
again, for their eyes were heavy; and they did not know what
to answer Him. Then He came the third time and said to them,
"Are you still sleeping and resting? It is enough! The hour has
come; behold, the Son of Man is being betrayed into the hands
of sinners. Rise, let us be going. See, My betrayer is at hand."
—Mark 14:27-42

Having instituted the Lord's Supper, Jesus took His disciples out
to the Mount of Olives to pray. On the way He told them that
they all would "be made to stumble" (v. 27) because of Him,
because of His ministry, His teaching and preaching, and His salvation

message. What Jesus meant here was that all Christians will at some point in their lives stumble on the gospel of Jesus Christ. The Greek word is *skandalizo*, which literally means *scandalize*. To scandalize the gospel means to speak evil of it without regard for its truth.

What He means is that no one is born a Christian, that every Christian must be converted from the natural, human perspective. What He means is that God's perspective—that of objective truth and perfect holiness—is so foreign, so different than the natural, subjective experience of human beings that the orthodox understanding of God—His Word, His Scripture, His perspective—sets up a conflict between God's Word and human experience. What He means is that in our natural human state, prior to conversion, we have no regard for God's objective truth.

God's Word opposes knowledge based on human experience. The teaching of the virgin birth, various biblical miracles, Christ's resurrection, and so forth are antithetical to human experience. The teaching of Scripture and particularly the ministry of Jesus generates a conflict between God's infinite wisdom and our limited human knowledge. That conflict must be resolved. That conflict results in our trust of either God and His Word or our trust in our own human experience and understanding. We must either believe God's Word or our own unsaved, unconverted experience. God's Word brings a dilemma, an inner conflict of faith and belief that must be resolved one way or another. This is the crisis of faith that every Christian must face and resolve without rejecting any of God's Word.

Of course, once a person is saved and converted these two perspectives begin to work together in the process of sanctification or spiritual growth. However, real spiritual growth is impossible until one has emerged from that central crisis of conversion. In other words, everyone who comes to any genuine understanding of Christianity will at some point "stumble" on Christ—on His preaching and teaching, His miracles, His virgin birth or resurrection, etc.

But Peter, not having been converted yet, did not believe that *he* would stumble as the Lord said he would. Even if everyone else stumbles, he said, *I* will not. Even if it costs me my life, I will not deny you. "And they all said likewise" (v. 31).

Jesus said they would stumble, they said they would not. Faith or belief is trusting God's Word, even when it does not fit with our own experience. Being faithful is trusting God beyond what we understand, beyond what we have experienced. Trusting beyond what you know is childlike faith. Peter and all the disciples repudiated the Lord and bragged that they would not stumble, even if everyone else did. These words of Peter and the apostles, though they sound faithful and pious, were filled with pride and self-confidence. Jesus said, *You will.* They said, *We will not!*

The disciples were guilty of what may be called spiritual pride. They knew that Jesus was the Messiah. They had walked and talked with the Lord for a couple of years at this point. They had heard Him preach, sat under His teaching, and witnessed His miracles. They had decided to follow Him, and in fact had been following Him. Yet, here we find them self-centered, self-reliant, and pridefully boasting about their superior commitment and spiritual maturity.

Peter said he would not fall away or deny Jesus, even if it cost him his life. Peter was convinced that he would be true! But Jesus, knowing Peter better than he knew himself, told him otherwise.

> "Assuredly, I say to you that today, even this night, before the rooster crows twice, you will deny Me three times" (v. 30).

It is easy to imagine Peter going off in a huff, mumbling to himself that Jesus was wrong about this.

The scene in the Garden at Gethsemane serves to illustrate the degree to which Jesus was right and Peter wrong. Going into the garden, Jesus left most of the disciples in one place and took Peter, James, and John to another to pray. Shortly thereafter, Jesus "began to be *troubled and deeply distressed*" (v. 33—italics added).

Mark used similar words only twice before. Once when they saw Jesus walking on the water (Mark 6:50), and once when Jesus told them not to be troubled by "wars and rumors of wars" (Mark 13:7). These words (*tarasso* and *throeo*) indicate the kind of trouble that produces tears and weeping. We can best understand them to express a kind of fear or grief that is overwhelmed by tears. Mark used a different word when he described Jesus as being troubled in the garden. *Ademoneo* conveys a deep depression. As if depression were not enough, Mark added the word *ekthambeo*, which suggests terror and amazement. Jesus became deeply depressed as God's way of suffering and death opened before Him. He became thoroughly astounded and amazed as He contemplated the wonders and the ways of God's sovereignty.

We can share in the Lord's wonder and amazement as we face the wonder of God's salvation plan ourselves. The eternal lives of sinners purchased by the death of One not guilty of sin. The righteousness of Christ applied to the unrighteous. Righteousness exchanged for sin, sin for righteousness—all accomplished by God Himself for the sake of the undeserving. What a wonder, this God, this salvation!

The disciples—Peter, James, and John—simply could not deal with such a wonder. As Jesus prayed and wrestled with the implications of God's plan of salvation, the disciples slept. Their awareness could not embrace this salvation. They couldn't deal with it. Jesus only wanted them to "watch" (v. 34), to be aware of what was happening as His own human nature submitted to the will of God. He wanted them to understand that all human beings—Himself included—must yield their own desires and understandings to those of God. He wanted them to witness Him yield to the Lord.

Jesus knew that "all things are possible for (God)," so He asked God to "take this cup away," to find some other way than the cross. In His human nature He did not want to submit to suffering and death on the cross. He didn't want to, but He did it anyway. He was not forced or coerced, but went willingly. "Nevertheless, not what I will, but what You will" (v. 36). These may be the most important words in Scripture because they describe the heart of Christian discipleship. Christians are called to restrain their own thoughts and desires and submit themselves to God's thoughts and desires.

Peter and all of Christ's disciples fail in this regard when they boast of their own strength and commitment. No matter how great our own strength and commitment are, they will fail to overcome Satan. Our puny efforts pail in comparison to Satan's. We are out-numbered, out-manned, out-gunned, out-smarted, out-strategized, and out-foxed. Satan is stronger, smarter, and richer that we are. We cannot defeat him, neither in our own strength, nor in our own flesh. But Christ can! And will! And already has! Yet, the struggle rages.

Peter provides an example of the struggle and a lesson about God's mercy. He couldn't stay awake for an hour. He demonstrated the weakness of the flesh as he slept.

> "Simon, are you sleeping? Could you not watch one hour? …
> The spirit indeed is willing, but the flesh is weak" (vs. 37-38).

He called Peter to watch and pray, but came back later only to find him "still sleeping" (v. 41).

Because we know that Peter failed and was forgiven, we know that God is exceedingly merciful. We see that even the best Christians are weak. We see that they stumble in their faith and their commitment to God. We see that they sometimes sleep through the most important parts of life. Yet, God saves them. If Peter could stumble and choke on the gospel of grace and deny the Lord as he did and still be saved, then so can you and I. When God calls people to faithfulness, He calls them for good. He calls them for keeps.

But how can we tell the difference between the reality of God's call and the fantasy of our own imaginations? We know that whatever God begins He finishes, whoever God calls, He does not fail to bring into the kingdom. But how can we be sure of God's call upon our own hearts?

In a nutshell, God Himself must convince us, and He does so by converting our beliefs and our behavior to conform to His Word. As we talk the talk and walk the walk, we become more and more personally convinced of God's call upon our own lives. We must believe as Scripture teaches, but we must also live as the Lord would have us live—as best as we are able under the guidance and power of the Holy Spirit. It happens in the midst of our personal relationship with Christ. He knows when our intentions are right, and He knows when they are wrong.

It is not the pastor's job to convince people that they are right about what they believe, about their salvation. Rather, the pastor's job is to call everyone to receive the grace and mercy of God's salvation, and to challenge those who respond to actually be the Christians that God has called them to be.

Do you know God's Word? Do you know God's grace and His law? Has God called you to salvation? Are you living up to His expectations—not mine or anyone else's, but His?

60. Forsaken

*And immediately, while He was still speaking, Judas, one of the
twelve, with a great multitude with swords and clubs, came
from the chief priests and the scribes and the elders. Now His
betrayer had given them a signal, saying, "Whomever I kiss, He
is the One; seize Him and lead Him away safely." As soon as
He had come, immediately he went up to Him and said to
Him, "Rabbi, Rabbi!" and kissed Him. Then they laid their
hands on Him and took Him. And one of those who stood by
drew his sword and struck the servant of the high priest, and
cut off his ear. Then Jesus answered and said to them, "Have
you come out, as against a robber, with swords and clubs to
take Me? "I was daily with you in the temple teaching, and you
did not seize Me. But the Scriptures must be fulfilled." Then
they all forsook Him and fled. Now a certain young man followed Him, having a linen cloth thrown around his naked
body. And the young men laid hold of him, and he left the
linen cloth and fled from them naked.* —Mark 14:43-52

Jesus had prayed in the garden that the Lord take this cup of suffering
from Him. The Lord is not a masochist, He did not cherish the idea
of suffering and death. But He was committed to doing God's will,
no matter what the cost—"not what I will, but what You will" (v. 36).
Jesus would do whatever was needed to fulfill God's plan of salvation.

God answered His prayer by interrupting it. "While He was still
speaking" (v. 43), while He was engaged in prayer with the disciples, He
was interrupted by Judas and his band of soldiers. It was more of a mob
than a police unit. A great multitude with swords and clubs approached,
like a bunch of vigilantes they were ready to take the Lord by force.

How little the enemies of the Lord understand Him or His kingdom. The nature of spiritual reality is hidden from those who have
turned away from Christ. Their understanding is not illumined by
the light of Christ. Thus, their relationships do not reflect the au-

thority of Christ, nor their lives the fruits of the Spirit. Nowhere in this passage do we see

> "love, joy, peace, patience, kindness, goodness, faithfulness, gentleness, (or) self-control" (Galatians 5:22-23)

—except in Jesus.

Judas greeted Jesus with a kiss, not as an act of respect or love, but as an act of betrayal. Judas pretended to love the Lord, pretended a relationship of love and respect. It was not until after the deed had been done that Judas began to see his own betrayal of the Lord. In the midst of it he was oblivious to his own hardened heart. He had convinced himself that he loved the Lord, convinced himself that he was committed to the cause of God. Only as the events of his betrayal unfolded was he able to see that the object of his love and commitment was not the Lord God, but an image, an imitation that was a product of his own heart and mind.

The zealous are so often so caught up in their own passion that they cannot or will not entertain any thought that is not in conformity with what they already believe. However, we are not able to think God's thoughts without His help.

> "My thoughts are not your thoughts, Nor are your ways My ways," says the LORD. (Isaiah 55:8).

Before we can begin to be aware of God's thoughts, God's perspective, God's truth, we must realize that there is a profound difference between our own natural, human thinking and the revelation of God. The limitations of human thought cannot reach the limitless bounds of God's thought.

An understanding of God is not constructed by piecing together various elements of history, philosophy, theology, etc. God's truth is not a matter of picking and choosing various elements from the smörgåsbord of world religions, or even from the assortment of Christian denominations. While God's truth is revealed everywhere in nature and history, it is particularly manifest in the pages of Scripture. Nowhere else has God provided such a comprehensive and systematic self-revelation. Thus, it behooves us to learn about Him from His Book.

As they "laid their hands on (Jesus)" (v. 46) one of the Lord's defenders reacted in the flesh. Peter drew his sword to defend Jesus. In the scuffle that ensued, he cut off the ear of one of the servants of the high priest. Imagine the scene. Jesus was praying in the garden when a mob came with swords and clubs to arrest Him. When Judas identified Jesus with a kiss of betrayal, the mob lurched forward to capture Him. In a moment of fear Peter reacted instinctively, drew his sword and engage the mob, cutting off the ear of his assailant.

There is nothing untrue in any of this. However, it is interesting that it was an ear that was damaged. The result of the rash response of this follower of the Lord interfered with the hearing of an assailant. The behavior of the guy who acted on his own to defend the Lord actually caused the person he attacked to be less able to hear the Lord. It may be a bit of a stretch, or too much an allegory, but there is some truth in it. When we try to defend God apart from His Word, we may be more part of the problem than the solution.

Luke, of course, reported that as soon as the ear had been cut off "Jesus...touched his ear and healed him" (Luke 22:51). Again, there is no reason to doubt the truth of this detail. And no reason not to extend the allegory. Just as the rash action of one of Jesus' disciples interfered with a man's ability to hear the Lord, so the Lord Himself restored both the man's ear and his hearing. Thus, the extended allegory suggests that it is not the action (or lack of action) on the part of Christians that causes or impedes the hearing of the gospel. Rather, it is the Lord who makes Himself known by bestowing the gift of faith through the power and presence of the Holy Spirit. Accordingly, Christians are not responsible to make others hear the Lord, neither can they scuttle God's salvation plan by their impetuosity—or by their apathy. God will accomplish what He set out to accomplish, as He intends to accomplish it.

John identified Peter as the one who drew the sword and cut off Malchus' ear (John 18:10). Peter had been the leader of the disciples. Brash and bold, he often opened his mouth before he thought about what he would say. Peter always reacted instinctively. Here he instinctively defended Jesus the only way he knew how. He drew his sword and engaged the enemy. John didn't record the healing. Rather, Jesus reprimanded Peter's rash action. Jesus said to Peter,

> "Put your sword into the sheath. Shall I not drink the cup which
> My Father has given Me?" (John 18:11).

Right or wrong, the disciples often followed Peter. When Peter said he was willing to die for Jesus, the other disciples responded in agreement. But here Jesus stopped Peter from defending Him. At that point Peter surely didn't know what to do. Having drawn his sword he was liable to be arrested. In confusion he fled, as did the others.

Here we see again that all of Jesus' disciples must renounce the ways of the flesh, the thoughts of the flesh, and the weapons of the flesh. Peter and the disciples were stripped bare of their every reaction and response. God's plan of atonement cannot be accomplished by worldly means. Rather, all of God's people must surrender to God's will, as did Jesus, come what may.

We must be careful because the words that Jesus spoke at this point provide an opportunity for speculation. Who was Jesus talking to? And who fled? Verse 48 seems to suggest that He spoke to the mob. But He may also have been speaking by implication to those disciples who thought they could defend Him with worldly weapons. The gist of what He said here is that the mob had no idea who He was, if they thought that their weapons would be effective against Him. The kingdom of God cannot be brought about by the sword, nor can the sword hinder its coming.

In verse 49 Jesus told them about the real battlefield, and their inability to stop Him there. He said,

> "I was daily with you in the temple teaching, and you did not seize Me."

Nothing was done as He taught daily in the temple, pouring out the grace of God into the hearts of His people. Nothing was done to impede the progress of the kingdom there because no one could do anything about it. There the providence of God kept Jesus safe from His enemies.

The latter part of verse 49 goes on to tell us why Jesus was protected as He taught in the temple, and why He would now surrender to the mob at Gethsemane—because "the Scriptures must be fulfilled." The purpose of Christ's ministry was the fulfilling of Scripture. Thus, His teaching must be disseminated, and He must die on the cross. There was a time for Him to teach, and a time for Him to die on the cross. God provided for all of these things to happen in order to complete His great salvation plan.

At this point Jesus was perfectly aware that God's plan included His suffering and death on the cross, even though He had prayed for some other way. As a military commander might initially question the validity of sending troops on a sacrifice mission, Jesus sought an alternative. However, once the alternatives were explored and rejected, the commander must submit to the battle plan with full cooperation and allegiance to the cause. Similarly, Jesus willingly committed Himself to God's atonement plan.

Verse 50 tells us that "they all forsook Him and fled." It is instructive to ask who forsook Him and fled. To forsake a person or cause one must first have had some commitment to it. You cannot forsake what you do not support. Consequently, when Mark said that "all" had forsaken the Lord and fled he did not mean all the mob, but rather all those who had committed themselves to Christ. At that point they all reneged on their commitment. That would include all the disciples and whatever believers there may have been in the mob. All those who had once trusted Christ, all who had pledged allegiance to Him, all who believed on their own power "forsook Him and fled" (v. 50).

We learn that there was a half-dressed young man who had followed the excitement stirred up by the mob. He must have been roused unexpectedly and followed in his bed clothes. In addition, he must have exhibited some sympathy for Jesus or exhibited some disagreement about the behavior of the mob. Mark tells us that some of the young men, presumably part of the mob, for some unspecified reason "laid hold" (v. 51) of this young man. They undoubtedly wanted to arrest him as an accomplice.

Thus, we see that there were some people in this crowd who were willing to follow Jesus, but who were also unprepared. Mark tells us that this young man was half-dressed. That is, he was ill-prepared for the events and challenges of discipleship. In order to flee, this young man abandoned his "linen cloth" (v. 52) or bathrobe or whatever it was. They undoubtedly grabbed him by the clothes he had on, so he simply ran away "naked," in his underwear.

This event suggests several points. First, there were other believers in the crowd. Second, those believers like all the believers Jesus encountered were unprepared for real discipleship. They were unwilling and unable to follow Jesus. And third, the reality of the cross as God's way of salvation rendered all believers, all disciples helpless and naked. The reality of the cross as God's instrument of atonement firmly established our inability to save ourselves. Even more, it established the human inability to willingly cooperate with God.

Of course, Christians do cooperate with God once they have been saved. Only when you have been converted to God's perspective, only having turned away from sin and submitted to God's salvation plan are Christians willing to be used by the Lord. But prior to conversion, prior to our surrender to God, people are not interested in cooperating with the Lord, nor are they able to help. Paul said,

"For by grace you have been saved through faith, and that not of yourselves; it is the gift of God, not of works, lest anyone should boast" (Ephesians 2:8-9).

Faith is not something that we are able to work up in our own strength. It is a gift. Faith is the gift of grace. We all stand helpless and naked before the Lord. We will either be clothed in Christ's righteousness or none, because we have none ourselves. We cannot earn it. We cannot make it happen for ourselves or for anyone else. We can only receive what the Lord has given.

61. Are You?

And they led Jesus away to the high priest; and with him were
assembled all the chief priests, the elders, and the scribes. But
Peter followed Him at a distance, right into the courtyard of
the high priest. And he sat with the servants and warmed him-
self at the fire. Now the chief priests and all the council sought
testimony against Jesus to put Him to death, but found none.
For many bore false witness against Him, but their testimonies
did not agree. Then some rose up and bore false witness against
Him, saying, "We heard Him say, 'I will destroy this temple
made with hands, and within three days I will build another
made without hands.'" But not even then did their testimony
agree. And the high priest stood up in the midst and asked Je-
sus, saying, "Do You answer nothing? What is it these men tes-
tify against You?" But He kept silent and answered nothing.
Again the high priest asked Him, saying to Him, "Are You the
Christ, the Son of the Blessed?" Jesus said, "I am. And you will
see the Son of Man sitting at the right hand of the Power, and
coming with the clouds of heaven." Then the high priest tore
his clothes and said, "What further need do we have of wit-
nesses? "You have heard the blasphemy! What do you think?"
And they all condemned Him to be deserving of death. Then
some began to spit on Him, and to blindfold Him, and to beat
Him, and to say to Him, "Prophesy!" And the officers struck
Him with the palms of their hands. —Mark 14:53-65

As they took Jesus to the high priest for questioning, Peter followed. It had been Peter who cut off the servant's ear, and it
had been Peter whom Jesus reprimanded for attempting to defend Him. The disciples had pledged themselves to follow Jesus even to
the death. Then in the garden Jesus forbade them from defending Him.
In confusion they all fled, not knowing what to do.

The lesson of the garden taught that true discipleship must strip all
Christians of their natural desires and responses. Our human efforts to
respond and/or follow the Lord are tainted with human sin. They origi-

nate in the human heart, and are filled with the freight of the human heart. Jeremiah rightly described the human heart as

> "deceitful above all things, And desperately wicked; Who can know it?" (Jeremiah 17:9).

You would think that Peter had learned this lesson by now. But he hadn't. Peter followed his heart again. He seems to have had a kind of romantic understanding and/or love of Jesus. So, he followed those who had taken Jesus right into the back yard of the Lord's chief enemy. Mark said that Peter followed Jesus "right into the *courtyard of the high priest*" (v. 54—emphasis added). The implication is that Peter had followed the captured Lamb right into the lion's den, which is a dangerous place to be!

Not only did Peter go right into the courtyard of the high priest, but he revealed himself in the light of the fire among the high priest's employees. Obviously, Peter had no idea of the danger he was in. Peter had previously pulled out his sword and cut off the ear of one of the high priest's servants, and now he waltzes into the high priest's backyard, and steps into the light of the fire. Peter was like a tragedy looking for a place to happen.

No doubt, Peter strained to hear what was happening inside. A kangaroo court was in session.

> "The chief priests and all the council sought testimony against Jesus to put Him to death, but found none" (v. 55).

False witnesses offered various false testimonies, but a case could not be made because the details of the accusations didn't add up.

Then someone tried to accuse Jesus of insurrection against the temple.

> "We heard Him say, 'I will destroy this temple made with hands, and within three days I will build another made without hands.' But not even then did their testimony agree" (vs. 58-59).

Accusations were flying right and left. Tension filled the air and emotions were high. The high priest couldn't believe that Jesus did not defend Himself. It was as if Jesus was not concerned about the accusations or the mock trial. Finally,

> "the high priest asked Him, saying to Him, 'Are You the Christ, the Son of the Blessed?'" (v. 61).

The question is important and instructive. Neither the question nor the priests challenged the fact that the Messiah was divine, that the Christ—whenever He would come—was the very Son of God. Christ's divinity was not at issue. The sticking point was whether or not Jesus of Nazareth was the Christ. They didn't doubt the reality of God's Messiah, or that God had promised to send Him, or the fact of His divinity.

But they were categorically unable to believe that God would send the Messiah in their time, or that He would be such a person as Jesus. They could not consider it because it was not what they expected. Almighty God, dressed as a beggar, standing before them as a common criminal? Unthinkable! The high priest and his Pharisees, like Peter and the disciples, and the people who had followed Jesus around the country side, were bound and blinded by their own expectations regarding Jesus. They were all constitutionally in and of themselves unable to understand who He really was or to respond to Him appropriately.

Yet, the high priest of Israel asked Jesus who He was. *Are you the Christ?* I wish we could hear the tone of the high priest's voice. Was he taunting Jesus? Was he sarcastic? Or incensed? Was there any hint of honest inquiry?

Jesus responded emphatically, "I am." There was no doubt or hesitation on His part. He simply acknowledged the fact of the matter. But that is not all He said.

> "And you will see the Son of Man sitting at the right hand of the Power, and coming with the clouds of heaven" (v. 62).

By identifying with the Person of God, Jesus claimed that the divine power that directed both nature and history was His to wield, and that through Him God would accomplish a feat no less spectacular or meaningful than the Exodus itself. Jesus' identification as the Son of Man established Him as the New Adam, the new federal head of humanity. Jesus was not merely the Son of God. In other words, Christ's divinity was not merely an abstract concept of His perfection, but His divinity was inextricably intertwined with His humanity. Jesus indeed was fully human, but not merely so. In His humanity He represented humanity as Adam before Him had. Where the sin of Adam resulted in the Fall of humanity, so the sinlessness of Christ would result in humanity's salvation through the atonement by Jesus Christ.

Scripture uses the phrase "right hand" to indicate the source of honor and authority. Mark used the word *dunamis*, which has been translated as *power* and means ability. Power is the ability to get things done. It requires the authority and competence to make things happen.

When Jesus said that He would be "sitting at the right hand of power" (v. 62) He claimed omnipotence for Himself as the Son of Man, the second Adam or federal head of humanity. Jesus acted here not in the capacity of his personhood as a man of Nazareth. Rather, He acted in the capacity of His office as the federal head of humanity.

The distinction between person and office is difficult for many people. When someone acts as an individual person he has certain responsibilities and rights. But when someone acts as an office holder in society he has different responsibilities and rights. Office holders do not represent themselves when they act or make decisions. The high priest himself was such an office holder. In fact, he represented the highest office of the Old Testament state of Israel. Caiaphas knew about the distinction between person and office. He had to deal with it regularly. Caiaphas also knew the process by which he had acquired the office of high priest.

And who did this young whipper-snapper from Nazareth think he was! Who made Him so important as to think that He sat at the right hand of power!

You see, Caiaphas did not recognize that the authority of God superseded his own authority as high priest. Or another way to say it is that Caiaphas thought that he as high priest was the mouthpiece of God, and that God would not act apart from him as high priest.

Little did he realize that he was right! God had not acted apart from the high priest, but used the power and authority of the high priest to condemn Jesus in order to accomplish the atonement. The wonder and beauty of God's sovereignty and providence is amazing!

Not only did Jesus claim the authority and power of God, but He predicted the accomplishment of God's salvation plan in His reference to "the clouds of heaven" (v. 62). The Greek word used for *cloud* (*nephele*) indicates a particular and definite cloud. It was not the general word (*nephos*) for ordinary clouds in the sky. The reference was not to ordinary clouds, but to a particular cloud, or kind of cloud. And the particular cloud referred to in Scripture was the cloud that led the Israelites in the wilderness by day (Exodus 13:21). The implication was that the Son of Man was operating under the leadership of the cloud of Yahweh.

Caiaphas knew exactly what Jesus meant. He did not require any explanations or interpretations. Enough, he cried! "You have heard the blasphemy!" (v. 64). Caiaphas had no doubt that Jesus had committed blasphemy against the office of the high priest. What Caiaphas didn't realize was that humanity's sin had enthroned Man in the place of God through the office of the high priest. Caiaphas failed to understand that his own office as high priest was limited by the authority and power of God.

Turning to the others Caiaphas asked,

> "'What do you think?' And they all condemned Him to be deserving of death" (v. 64).

The fault did not belong to Caiaphas alone, but as he asked his associates he gave them the opportunity to agree with Jesus or with himself. By agreeing with Caiaphas they confirmed the fact that the entire priestly structure had made the same error as its leader. They all placed the power and authority of Man, represented by the high priest, over the power and authority of God, represented by Jesus.

We can see it so clearly in the struggle between Jesus and Caiaphas, or between Jesus and the Pharisees. It is more difficult to see in and among ourselves, in our own time, in our own society. Yet, sin remains sin. The basic character or patterns of sin haven't changed. Nor have the basic character or habits of men and women. The struggle today is the same as it was then. It is the same struggle that brought about Adam's fall from grace. It is the struggle for ascendancy between the power and authority of humanity and the power and authority of God.

When we make our own rules regarding the nature and structure of Christ's church, we side with the Pharisees. When we think that church officers are supposed to represent various factions and groups within the church, we have assumed the authority of the people of the church over the authority of God or God's Word. Church officers are not to represent the thoughts and opinions of various groups and factions in the church. Rather, church officers are to represent or epitomize the thoughts and opinions of God in the church. Those who represent groups and factions cannot represent God because God is above all groups and factions.

Similarly, when we consider that all interpretations of the Bible are equally valid, we side with the liberal Sadducees. The only biblical interpretation that counts is Jesus' interpretation. Various human interpretations and understandings of Scripture are not all equally valid, but are equally invalid. God's people must acquire His perspective and abandon their own—no matter what their current office or station in life.

When the Pharisees, Sadducees, and scribes who had been in Caiaphas' house for the proceedings of the kangaroo court heard the truth

of Jesus and agreed with the response of Caiaphas, they exploded in out-
rage. God's truth had offended their human pride.

> "Some began to spit on Him, and to blindfold Him, and to beat
> Him, and to say to Him, 'Prophesy!' And the officers struck Him
> with the palms of their hands" (v. 65).

62. Think About It

Now as Peter was below in the courtyard, one of the servant girls of the high priest came. And when she saw Peter warming himself, she looked at him and said, "You also were with Jesus of Nazareth." But he denied it, saying, "I neither know nor understand what you are saying." And he went out on the porch, and a rooster crowed. And the servant girl saw him again, and began to say to those who stood by, "This is one of them." But he denied it again. And a little later those who stood by said to Peter again, "Surely you are one of them; for you are a Galilean, and your speech shows it." Then he began to curse and swear, "I do not know this Man of whom you speak!" A second time the rooster crowed. Then Peter called to mind the word that Jesus had said to him, "Before the rooster crows twice, you will deny Me three times." And when he thought about it, he wept. —Mark 14:66-72

The story of Peter in the courtyard is very simple to understand. Peter, who had been so willing to defend Jesus to the death— and who had tried, but was stopped by Jesus Himself, now lies when confronted with the truth. It is not insignificant that Peter was challenged by a young servant girl to either stand by the truth or deny it.

The Greek word *arneomai* means to speak falsely. The girl asked him about his relationship with Jesus and he denied it. By doing so Peter attempted to avoid the responsibility associated with that relationship. We are all aware of Cassie Bernall, the girl who was shot at Columbine High School in Denver, Colorado (1999), when she responded positively that she believed in God. There are responsibilities related to faithfulness that cannot be denied without serious consequences. Christians are called to speak the truth in faithfulness, and to let the chips fall as they may.

Peter was afraid of how the chips might fall if he acknowledged his relationship with Jesus at that particular moment, so he lied. He abdicated his responsibility as a disciple. Christians are responsible to always

speak God's truth no matter what it might cost them to do so. The scene
is reminiscent of Adam and Eve in the garden.

There are several things that we should notice about Adam's situation in the garden of Eden. Genesis 2:15-18 reads,

> "Then the LORD God took the man and put him in the garden of
> Eden to tend and keep it. And the LORD God commanded the
> man, saying, 'Of every tree of the garden you may freely eat; but
> of the tree of the knowledge of good and evil you shall not eat,
> for in the day that you eat of it you shall surely die.' (Only then)
> the LORD God said, 'It is not good that man should be alone; I
> will make him a helper comparable to him.'"

Notice that God entrusted the law or the keeping of His Word to
Adam before Eve was created. In other words, Adam was personally responsible to God for obedience to God's Word. Notice that God did not
give Eve the prohibition about eating from the tree of the knowledge of
good and evil. He gave it to Adam. It was then Adam's responsibility to
pass it along to Eve.

In Genesis 3 we see that the serpent spoke, not to Adam but to Eve.

> "Now the serpent was more cunning than any beast of the field
> which the LORD God had made. And he said to the woman, 'Has
> God indeed said, "You shall not eat of every tree of the
> garden"?'" (Genesis 3:1).

We know the story well. The serpent convinced Eve that God's Word
to Adam was inaccurate. He convinced her that God was wrong about
the consequences of sin, "You will not surely die" (Genesis 3:4). Eve ate
of the fruit and baked up a delicious forbidden fruit pie for Adam.

We can imagine Adam coming to dinner that evening to be greeted
by his dear wife and helper, Eve, who had prepared a sumptuous dinner
and special dessert for him. These things are hard to resist. Scripture isn't
clear whether or not Eve told him before hand that he was eating forbidden fruit pie. And it really doesn't matter because either way Adam
abdicated his responsibility either to instruct Eve sufficiently about
God's prohibition, or to confront her with her disobedience. Thus, the
root of the sin—the responsibility—lay with Adam because God had personally given him the prohibition.

When the Lord confronted Adam about his disobedience, he
avoided responsibility by blaming Eve, and Eve blamed the serpent. We
know the story, but the point is that at the heart of the Fall was the de-

nial of man's personal relationship with and responsibility to God, to His Word, and to His authority. God makes the rules, we don't.

Peter's denial of Christ in the garden that night was cut from the same cloth as Adam's sin in the garden of Eden. Confronted by the servant girl, Peter denied his relationship with and responsibility to Jesus Christ as his personal Lord and Savior. To demonstrate that Peter's denial was willing and intentional, the Lord caused it to happen three times, just as Jesus had predicted. Each time the denial became more vehement, adding an oath and even swearing about it. Thus Peter broke the third commandment,

> "You shall not take the name of the LORD your God in vain"
> (Exodus 20:7), and the ninth, "You shall not bear false witness
> against your neighbor" (Exodus 20:16).

Why was Peter subjected to all this? Why did the Lord go to so much trouble with Peter? Peter brought it on himself. Proverbs 14:14 reads, "The backslider in heart will be filled with his own ways." Jeremiah had said the same thing,

> "Your own wickedness will correct you, And your backsliddings
> will rebuke you. Know therefore and see that it is an evil and
> bitter thing That you have forsaken the LORD your God, And the
> fear of Me is not in you," (Jeremiah 2:19).

Just a little while earlier Peter and the disciples thought that they were doing pretty well. They thought that they had been faithful disciples. They had been with Jesus for some time, and had witnessed many miracles and healings. They had the privilege of His personal instruction. They had received the keys to the kingdom, the Lord's Supper had been instituted among them. In fact, if you remember, some of them had been arguing about their positions of privilege in the kingdom. They had pledged themselves to follow Jesus no matter what, even if it resulted in their deaths. They were adamant about being His disciples.

But in spite of all of this, the disciples—here represented by Peter— had denied the Lord. They had all denied Him, and Peter was the spokesman. Peter's denial in the garden wasn't just a slip of the tongue. It wasn't an isolated incident in the midst of a life of faithfulness. Rather, Peter's denial in the garden was the epitome of his discipleship up to that time. Peter's denial didn't just happen in the high priests courtyard. Rather, what happened that night was the logical conclusion of Peter's lifelong denial of God, which included the time he had spent with Jesus in ministry, teaching, and particularly the vain commitment he had made to follow Christ to the death.

The disciples, and particularly Peter, had failed to properly acknowledge or honor Jesus even though they had pledged obedience to Him. How could the disciples have been so close to the Lord and yet so far from Him? Understanding this is absolutely fundamental to our own discipleship, to our own personal relationship with Christ, to our own salvation. Peter had been so full of himself, full of his own thoughts and ideas, his own likes and dislikes that there was no room in his heart, his mind, for Christ, for Christ's thoughts and ideas, Christ's likes and dislikes.

Because of this Peter's commitment was really a commitment to himself, not to Jesus Christ. Peter's commitment to Christ was only an extension of himself. It was a commitment to his own spiritual strength, to his own human ability to be faithful as he understood faithfulness. And it stood in the way of a real relationship with Jesus Christ that was founded and grounded on God's strength and Christ's ability to faithfully bring about the salvation of humanity. As long as Peter was able to be a faithful disciple in his own strength and commitment, he did not need Christ. If he could do it himself, he didn't need Christ's atonement. God in His infinite wisdom and mercy went to great lengths to point this out to Peter and to Peter's posterity, Christ's church.

Paul had written to the Corinthians that everything in the Old Testament had

> "happened ... as examples, and ... were written for our admonition, upon whom the ends of the ages have come. Therefore let him who thinks he stands take heed lest he fall. No temptation has overtaken you except such as is common to man; but God is faithful, who will not allow you to be tempted beyond what you are able, but with the temptation will also make the way of escape, that you may be able to bear it." (1 Corinthians 10:11-13).

Paul was looking at the Old Testament, but we can also look at the New because what was true for Paul is also true for us today. God's truth does not change. Peter's example was for *our* benefit. Peter's folly was set forth clearly in Scripture so that *we* might learn from his example. Peter's sin, Peter's denial was not unique, but is the most common folly known to Man. People who do not understand Peter's sin, people who are not in personal repentance for the same sin themselves cannot truly know Jesus Christ—not savingly.

Adam blamed Eve. Eve blamed the serpent. Who do you blame for your irresponsibility? Maybe some particular individuals or group of people? The lesson that Peter learned when the cock crowed was that there was no one to blame but himself. When Nathan accused David of adultery with Bathsheba, he cried, "Thou art the man!" (2 Samuel 12:7). David wept in sorrow and guilt because he knew it was true.

After Peter had witnessed his own denial of Christ, not once but three times, only then did it occur to him that he himself was responsible for repeatedly denying the Lord. Each time he was asked about his relationship with Jesus and each time he denied it. He had no one else to blame. As this fact became more and more clear to him, he found himself increasingly frustrated and angry. Thus, each denial became increasingly vociferous.

So it is with all of us. Whenever people are finally cornered by the convicting power of God's Word, and they realize that the blame for their guilt lies squarely upon their own shoulders, they respond in frustration and anger. That is the critical moment of conversion. Will they accept their own sinfulness and receive the forgiving grace of God? Or will they maintain their own innocence and finally blame God, or God's Word, or God's representative, or God's people?

The point of Peter's denial is that he thought that he was already there, already walking with the Lord, already a faithful disciple. He didn't realize that from God's perspective he had missed it by a country mile. Up to that point he didn't realize that he had been using Jesus and God to justify himself, just like the Pharisees and Sadducees and scribes had done. The issue that remained for Peter was, Could he now receive the justification that Jesus would provide through His atonement on the cross? Or would he hold on to his own futile attempts to justify himself?

Peter's denial was not a unique incident in the history of Christianity. It was not an isolated event in an otherwise faithful life of a believer. Rather, Peter's denial is a clear expression of the sinfulness of Man in the face of a holy God. The lesson of Peter's denial is that no one is exempt from the effects of the Fall and its sin, no one. Not those in the highest ranks of religious organizations, nor a lowly country bumpkin who heartily embraced the very Messiah of God Himself.

63. STIRRING UP THE CROWD

Immediately, in the morning, the chief priests held a consulta-
tion with the elders and scribes and the whole council; and they
bound Jesus, led Him away, and delivered Him to Pilate. Then
Pilate asked Him, "Are You the King of the Jews?" He an-
swered and said to him, "It is as you say." And the chief priests
accused Him of many things, but He answered nothing. Then
Pilate asked Him again, saying, "Do You answer nothing? See
how many things they testify against You!" But Jesus still an-
swered nothing, so that Pilate marveled. Now at the feast he
was accustomed to releasing one prisoner to them, whomever
they requested. And there was one named Barabbas, who was
chained with his fellow rebels; they had committed murder in
the rebellion. Then the multitude, crying aloud, began to ask
him to do just as he had always done for them. But Pilate an-
swered them, saying, "Do you want me to release to you the
King of the Jews?" For he knew that the chief priests had
handed Him over because of envy. But the chief priests stirred
up the crowd, so that he should rather release Barabbas to them.
Pilate answered and said to them again, "What then do you
want me to do with Him whom you call the King of the Jews?"
So they cried out again, "Crucify Him!" Then Pilate said to
them, "Why, what evil has He done?" But they cried out all the
more, "Crucify Him!" So Pilate, wanting to gratify the crowd,
released Barabbas to them; and he delivered Jesus, after he had
scourged Him, to be crucified.   —Mark 15:1-15

First thing in the morning those who had interrogated Jesus took Him to Pilate. No doubt having been instructed by the high priest, Pilate asked, "Are You the King of the Jews? (v. 2). John tells us that Jesus tried to explain the nature of His kingdom to Pilate.

> "My kingdom is not of this world. If My kingdom were of this world, My servants would fight, so that I should not be delivered

to the Jews; but now My kingdom is not from here" (John 18:36).

But Pilate wasn't interested in the spiritual nature of Christ's kingdom. He pressed to the point. "Are You a king then?" (John 18:37). Having qualified the nature of His kingdom, Jesus said that indeed He was.

It's funny how people get a certain idea in their mind and then proceed to interpret everything in terms of that one idea. The high priest had been intent on making some serious charge against Jesus. He had, no doubt, settled on this idea that Jesus could be prosecuted on the charge of political insurrection. Nothing else mattered except this one point, Are you a king? If He answered *yes*, He was in conflict with Rome. If He said *no*, His followers would abandon Him.

God, in His amazing providence, used this situation to establish in a court of law that Jesus was crucified for claiming to be the King of the Jews. Later, Pilate would order that charge to be placed on His cross in three languages. The highest court in the land believed Jesus' claim and crucified Him for it. But that gets ahead of the story.

That was not the only accusation against Jesus. There were many. But Jesus ignored them. He didn't say a word about them. Pilate marveled at His grace under fire. Jesus had answered the only charge that mattered, and would not even acknowledge the false accusations. Everyone knew they were false. There was no point in discussing anything about them.

The poise that Jesus maintained during that scene issued from His meekness. To be meek is to be obedient to God, to trust in God's provision. To be meek is not to be mousy, but to be humble. It is not an inferiority complex, but is submissive to God's Word. The meek have no desire for attention, but quietly and obediently live lives of Christian service. Such people will inherit the earth.

The fact that Pilate was accustomed to releasing a prisoner during certain festivals was a sure sign of his corruption and contempt for law and justice. To release a guilty person was a flagrant abuse of justice by any standard. Why would Pilate do such a thing? To establish that his own personal power was greater than the Roman justice system. Roman law was formidable. Roman law held the Roman empire together, and here Pilate put himself above the law that he was supposed to uphold. It was the wicked deed of a corrupt politician.

Yet, Pilate was not completely insensitive to the issues of justice. The high priest had brought him a man who really wasn't guilty, and requested the death sentence. Pilate had no reason to execute Jesus. So perhaps he thought he could establish his own innocence regarding Jesus by putting the final judgment in the hands of the people. He may even have thought that he was giving Jesus a pretty good chance, because no one doubted Barabbas' guilt.

Again, God's providence allowed the innocent to take the place of the guilty on the cross. This chance opportunity provided by Pilate perfectly demonstrated the logic of Christ's atonement—His suffering for our sin, our guilt for His innocence.

Verse 10 tells us that the chief priests envied Jesus. The Greek word, *phthonos*, literally means *corruption*. The dictionary defines *envy* as a feeling of discontent and resentment aroused by and in conjunction with desire for the possessions or qualities of another. They were jealous of something that Jesus had—spiritual authority.

Remember that Jesus taught "as one having authority, and not as the scribes" (Mark 1:22). Jesus' authority had been disputed from the beginning of His ministry to the end. "By what authority are You doing these things?" (Mark 11:28) they had demanded. Jesus tied His answer to the baptism of John and asked if they recognized John's authority to baptize. They wouldn't answer that question, so Jesus told them nothing about His own authority.

If there is one issue that gets people into trouble, it is authority. When someone tangles with the authorities, it means trouble. Ignoring or disregarding the legal authority of the state will surely land a person in trouble. And so will ignoring or disregarding God's law, God's authority. That was the issue. John baptized by God's authority, just as Jesus had preached and healed by it. The difficulty for the priests and lawyers was that God's authority was not equivalent with the authority of the temple (or the state). The problem was that the temple (or the state) did not recognize the fullness of God's authority.

Authority in the church is a function of Scripture. As evangelical Protestants we stake our lives on the authority of Scripture. Our lives, our families, our churches, are to honor and respect God's authority by obedience to Scripture. That obedience should then permeate all of the structures of our society. All Christian authority is authority in submission. To be a Christian, first and foremost, is to live in submission to God's Word.

The priesthood of all believers does not mean that every Christian is supposed to be a pastor. Rather, it means two things: 1) that Christians don't need clergy to mediate God's grace, and 2) that every Christian is called to service. The Greek word *diakonos* means servant. The first deacons were called to be table waiters. Thus, servanthood requires an attitude of servitude or meekness. A good servant does not call the shots or make the decisions, but defers to his or her master (overseer). For Christians, that master is Jesus Christ, who is also known as God's Word, and His representatives. All Christian authority rests upon Scripture, and all Christians must defer to the authority of Scripture in all they think and do.

Scripture does not grant all authority to any one individual, office, or institution, but distributes God's authority within and among the various elements of human society, i.e., families, churches, governments. Biblical authority requires certain relationships among and between these various elements that honor the Bible itself as the basis for human society. Thus, Scripture should be the highest authority for all Christians because it determines the nature and extent of these various relationships. God has determined how these different relationships can best function in the world.

The leaders of Israel erred when they assumed more authority than Scripture (the Old Testament) had given them. They had ingratiated themselves into positions of power, and were intent, not on serving the Lord, but on maintaining their own power. Thus, Jesus was a threat to them because His truth was greater than their power. His truth threatened their positions of prominence. They envied Him, envied His authority.

So "the chief priests stirred up the crowd" (v. 11) in order to influence the decision between Jesus and Barabbas. They didn't have the spiritual authority to challenge Jesus—and they knew it. So they "stirred up the crowd." The Greek word is *anaseio,* and is composed of two words that literally mean *go into* and *agitate.* The KJV reads "moved the people." They did what they could to turn popular opinion against Jesus.

One of Satan's most effective weapons has always been the tongue. James said,

> "if you have bitter envy and self-seeking in your hearts, do not
> boast and lie against the truth. This wisdom does not descend
> from above, but is earthly, sensual, demonic. For where envy and
> self-seeking exist, confusion and every evil thing are there"
> (James 3:14-16).

Slanderous accusations and gossip are the primary means that Satan uses.

There was a recent shooting at a Jewish daycare center in Los An-
geles. The shooter seems to believe that he was doing the world a favor
by killing Jews. No doubt, his hatred of Jews goes back to the question,
Who killed Jesus? Scripture is pretty clear that the temple leaders manipulated both the Roman authorities and the populace to act against Jesus.
But the real culprit is not a who but a what, not a particular group of
people but a particular attitude. Envy, malice, hatred, slander, gossip, rebellion against God's authority—these are the things that killed Jesus.
And these are the very things that Christians are called to put an end to.

> Now the works of the flesh are evident, which are: adultery,
> fornication, uncleanness, lewdness, idolatry, sorcery, hatred,
> contentions, jealousies, outbursts of wrath, selfish ambitions,
> dissensions, heresies, envy, murders, drunkenness, revelries, and
> the like; of which I tell you beforehand, just as I also told you in
> time past, that those who practice such things will not inherit the
> kingdom of God. But the fruit of the Spirit is love, joy, peace,
> longsuffering, kindness, goodness, faithfulness, gentleness, self-
> control. Against such there is no law. And those who are Christ's
> have crucified the flesh with its passions and desires. If we live in
> the Spirit, let us also walk in the Spirit. Let us not become
> conceited, provoking one another, envying one another
> (Galatians 5:19-26).

The high priests were successful in their effort to work up the
crowd against Jesus. Hate and discord are easy to stir up. The more difficult challenge is to sow peace and harmony. Notice Pilate's attitude, his
response to the crowd. "So Pilate, wanting to *gratify* the crowd…" (v.
15—italics added). Pilate wanted to do what the people wanted. He
didn't really care about Jesus or Barabbas. He didn't care about truth or
justice. Either decision would be fine with him. Pilate would do whatever the majority of the people wanted him to do. By appealing to the
people he could maintain his position of authority in their eyes. He
could say that he just went along with what the people wanted to do.
He had no commitment to Jesus, no commitment to God's truth. He
just wanted to do the most expedient, most practical, most effective
thing he could to solve the immediate problem. He was a consummate
politician, a man without principles, a man who followed the polls to
preserve his position.

Who killed Jesus? The crowd did. They made the final decision.
They tipped the scales. Going along with the crowd means death to Jesus because following Jesus is not a matter of popularity but of principle.

Popularity and Christian principles are diametrically opposed to one another. Christians can never just "go along to get along." Rather, Christians must live their lives according to biblical principles. There are no shortcuts. There are no substitutes. To do anything less amounts to denying Jesus Christ and renouncing the faith.

64. SEE AND BELIEVE

*Then the soldiers led Him away into the hall called Praetorium,
and they called together the whole garrison. And they clothed
Him with purple; and they twisted a crown of thorns, put it on
His head, and began to salute Him, "Hail, King of the Jews!"
Then they struck Him on the head with a reed and spat on
Him; and bowing the knee, they worshiped Him. And when
they had mocked Him, they took the purple off Him, put His
own clothes on Him, and led Him out to crucify Him. Then
they compelled a certain man, Simon a Cyrenian, the father of
Alexander and Rufus, as he was coming out of the country and
passing by, to bear His cross. And they brought Him to the
place Golgotha, which is translated, Place of a Skull. Then they
gave Him wine mingled with myrrh to drink, but He did not
take it. And when they crucified Him, they divided His garments, casting lots for them to determine what every man
should take. Now it was the third hour, and they crucified
Him. And the inscription of His accusation was written above:
THE KING OF THE JEWS. With Him they also crucified
two robbers, one on His right and the other on His left. So the
Scripture was fulfilled which says, "And He was numbered with
the transgressors." And those who passed by blasphemed Him,
wagging their heads and saying, "Aha! You who destroy the
temple and build it in three days, "save Yourself, and come
down from the cross!" Likewise the chief priests also, mocking
among themselves with the scribes, said, "He saved others;
Himself He cannot save. "Let the Christ, the King of Israel, de-
scend now from the cross, that we may see and believe." Even
those who were crucified with Him reviled Him.*
—Mark 15:16-32

Convicted and abandoned, Jesus was turned over to the soldiers.
Having watched Jesus' trial, they mocked Him. They ridiculed
Him—made Him appear to be ridiculous. Charged with insur-
rection, they dressed Him like a king, with a purple robe and a crown of

thorns. Little did they realize that as they freely chose to deride the King of heaven, they fulfilled prophecy. Isaiah 50:6 prophesied that He would be beaten and whipped. Their very thoughts and actions against Christ had been predestined before time itself. But they were not aware of it. At this point they were not acting as soldiers under orders, but were expressing themselves freely.

Having beat Him and spat upon Him, they bowed their knees and "worshiped Him" (v. 19). I'm sure that you have heard that Satan is not an original thinker, but is, rather, a skilled counterfeiter. Satan is a pretender, a liar whose purpose is deceit and confusion. Thus, when we see that the soldiers "worshiped" Jesus, we know that their worship was not genuine but false. They pretended to worship and honor Him. In doing so they were not only making fun of Jesus, but were making fun of all who would actually worship Him.

Because soldiers act under orders or under authority, and because contempt amounts to a disregard of authority, their thoughts and actions toward Jesus perfectly exemplify the hatred and spite of the world for the authority of the Lord. A Jesus who leaves people free to embrace Him or not, to receive Him or not, is a Jesus crafted by Satan. It is a Jesus without divine authority. A Jesus you can choose is a Jesus you can refuse. If we can choose to obey God's authority, we can choose to refuse it. And an authority that we can refuse to obey is no real authority at all.

For instance, the state has the authority to tax its people. But if the people can refuse to pay taxes, then the government does not really have the authority to tax them. But in fact we are not free to ignore the authority of the state. Nor are we free to ignore God's authority. Oh, we can refuse to pay taxes, or we can refuse the grace of Christ's atonement, but we are not so free that we can escape the consequences of our refusal. God's authority, like that of the government, cannot be ignored. We will comply with it one way or another. And so it was with the soldiers. They mocked the authority of Christ only by submitting to the authority of Scripture. They fulfilled biblical prophecy concerning Christ.

Crucifixion was a punishment invented by the Persians and adopted by the Romans, who used it mainly against rebellious slaves and insurrectionists. The fact that Jesus was crucified stands as a witness to the charge against Him. Insurrection is the act of rebelling against an established authority. Was Jesus an insurrectionist? Did He not come to establish an authority other than the established authority of either the temple or Rome?

No, Jesus was not an insurrectionist. He did not come to usurp the existing authorities. He came to establish them. He submitted Himself to the judgment of the high priest and to the punishment of Rome. However, He did come to correct a mistaken understanding about the nature of authority itself. The high priests believed themselves to be the greatest authority in Israel, and Rome believed itself to be the highest authority in the world. Both were mistaken. The high priests do not establish religious authority, nor can civil government establish its own authority.

We must remember that the theocracy of the Old Testament had failed. It simply could not be established because of the sinfulness of humanity. Similarly, no civil government has ever been able to establish its own authority. The effort to do so is called fascism. It, too, has failed many times in history. Both of these misunderstandings of the nature of authority make the same error. They invert the authority that God established at creation. God stands at the apex of all authority—not the church, not the state. The church does not establish the authority of God. Rather, God established the authority of the church. This distinction is at the heart of the difference between Roman Catholicism and Reformed Protestantism. Nor does the state establish the authority of God, but God established the authority of the state.

Simon was then enlisted to carry Jesus' cross—not because he chose to do so, but because he was "compelled" (v. 21) to do so. Simon provided a perfect example of Christian discipleship. Jesus said,

> "Whoever desires to come after Me, let him deny himself, and take up his cross, and follow Me" (Mark 8:34).

In fact, as we saw earlier that particular verse is the crux—the fulcrum or hinge—around which the gospel of Mark is organized. One of the main themes of the gospel of Mark is the necessity of self-denial for Christian discipleship.

Jesus died on Golgatha. Golgatha, or Place of the Skull (v. 22) symbolizes Christ's headship. Christ is the head of the church, and the atonement required His death, which occurred on Golgatha. Nothing is more important than the atonement of Christ. And only Jesus, the Son of God, could accomplish it. The atonement was dependent upon Christ's headship. And it applies only to the body for whom Christ is the head.

Those who crucified Jesus offered Him "wine mingled with myrrh to drink" (v. 23) to ease His personal pain. Myrrh has a very bitter taste. The bitter drink symbolizes the world's attempt to ease the personal pain and suffering of genuine discipleship. Jesus refused it, just as all disciples refuse the bitter assistance of worldly counsel, whose primary purpose is to insulate people from the atonement of Christ.

When the soldiers cast lots for Jesus' garments they accomplished two things. First, they again demonstrated that their actions were under the sovereign authority of the prophecies of God. Psalm 22:18 prophesied the division of the Lord's garments and the casting of lots for them. Secondly, it established that the soldiers themselves believed in the doctrine of contingency—that God was not sovereign, but that things happened by chance. They believed that chance not God ruled the universe. Their very actions of dividing and casting lots for the Lord's garments proved God's sovereignty because by doing so they fulfilled Scripture. Yet they themselves refused to believe that God was sovereign.

If any one thing established the great reversal of values (the conversion of His people) that Jesus came to inaugurate, it is the atonement, His death on the cross. How could such an awful thing bring about so much good for the kingdom? Because it wasn't what it seemed to be. It seemed to be Jesus' greatest failure, but it was His greatest success. It seemed to be the end of everything for Him and His band of disciples, but it was the beginning of the greatest cultural advancement the world has ever known. So often Jesus taught the disciples that things were not what they seemed to be. Why? Because sin has corrupted human understanding. If sin is real, then we are all affected by it. And for the most part we don't realize how it affects us.

Verse 28 brings us to a Bible translation difficulty. Unless you are reading the King James (or New King James) Version, verse 28 is listed as a footnote. Three of the earliest existing manuscripts don't have it, but the rest of the nearly five thousand Greek manuscripts extant do. But whether your Bible has it or not, the meaning of the verse is certainly implied by verse 27. Luke 22:37 also quotes this prophecy from Isaiah 53:12. Verse 28 establishes two things: 1) it was another indication that Jesus' crucifixion was the fulfillment of Scripture, and 2) that things were not what they seemed to be.

The atonement of Christ required the most severe punishment because Jesus had to pay the penalty for the worst sins. If the atonement was to be effective for the worst sinners it had to include the worst punishment. Were Jesus to suffer less, His atonement would be less effective.

Thus, Jesus was accounted as a transgressor in order to atone for transgressors. On the one hand we don't want to see the Lord of glory numbered among transgressors. But on the other, we want His atonement to
apply to all of His people. Thus, there is more to lose by omitting the
verse (or relegating it to a footnote) than by including it in the text.

The crowd that cast the deciding vote to crucify Jesus now passed
by wagging their heads and saying, "save Yourself, and come down
from the cross!" (v. 30). They ridiculed His prophecy that He would destroy the temple and rebuild it in three days. They not only mocked the
Lord's ability to accomplish such a feat, but they mocked the very purpose for which Jesus came. That purpose being to fulfill the Old Testament administration and inaugurate the New, to fulfill Old Testament
prophecy and to establish His church on the earth.

Jesus hung on the cross as the representative of human sin. He did
not die for His own sin, but for the sins of His people. At that moment
Jesus was in the full flower of His humanity, and therefore, at that point
to save Himself would symbolize humanity saving itself. That, however,
is not the gospel of Jesus Christ. Man as humanity is not able to save
himself, and the suggestion that he can flows from the very lips of Satan.
Self-salvation is the lie that deceives the multitudes in every age.

Furthermore, the invitation to "come down from the cross" (v. 30)
was an invitation to nullify the effectiveness of the atonement. The
atonement required His suffering and death on the cross. To come
down would break the power of the atonement to satisfy God's demand
for justice on behalf of the elect. Thus, to come down from the cross
would empty salvation of its meaning and effectiveness. Jesus could not
save Himself and come down from the cross, not because He didn't have
the power or ability to do so, but because doing so would require Him
to disobey God. It was Satan who called Him to come down, and obedience to Satan would require disobedience to God.

The chief priests then joined in the ridicule. The priests and the
lawyers joked among themselves,

> "He saved others; Himself He cannot save. Let the Christ, the
> King of Israel, descend now from the cross, that we may see and
> believe" (vs. 31-32).

Several important things are revealed in their words. They acknowledged that He had saved others. They were probably referring to those
He had healed, and we must remember that salvation was often part of
their healing.

They also recognized that Jesus could not save Himself and be true to God. They were theologically astute enough to know that self-salvation was no salvation at all. Consequently, they called for a miracle. Jesus had been known for working miracles, so they called Him to perform a saving miracle for them to see. Like so many misguided people they thought that seeing a miracle would make them believe in His Messiahship. They thought that faith could be produced by seeing a miracle.

We see the same thing today. People flock to see the various so-called miracles of the Virgin Mary. They think that if they see a statue weep or a heavenly image of Mary it will eliminate all their doubts and produce the faith they seek. We also see people running off to Toronto or Brownsville (Florida) to be caught up in the miraculous signs and wonders of revival in the hope of seeing and believing. It is no different than the crowds who followed Jesus seeking miracles and healings from Him.

However, the overwhelming testimony of Mark is that faith does not work that way. The faithful do not believe because they see, rather they see because they believe. Witnessing miracles has never saved anyone! Miracles do not save, they only increase one's preexisting faith or lack of faith. When believers witness miracles their faith is confirmed. But when nonbelievers witness miracles their hearts are hardened. Pharaoh witnessed many miracles, but was not saved. Rather, each succeeding miracle only further hardened his heart against God and His people.

Thomas was one who didn't believe in the miracle of resurrection until he saw it himself. When Jesus finally confronted him with the facts, Thomas confessed his belief. Thomas' faith was genuine, but it was not characteristic of ordinary Christian faith. Jesus said to him,

> "because you have seen Me, you have believed. Blessed are those
> who have not seen and yet have believed"(John 20:29).

Thus, Jesus confirmed that the ordinary experience of the faithful did not require or include seeing miracles.

Ordinary salvation comes by faith alone in Christ alone through Scripture alone. What are *you* looking for?

65. Forsaken Again

Now when the sixth hour had come, there was darkness over the whole land until the ninth hour. And at the ninth hour Jesus cried out with a loud voice, saying, "Eloi, Eloi, lama sabachthani" which is translated, "My God, My God, why have You forsaken Me?" Some of those who stood by, when they heard that, said, "Look, He is calling for Elijah!" Then someone ran and filled a sponge full of sour wine, put it on a reed, and offered it to Him to drink, saying, "Let Him alone; let us see if Elijah will come to take Him down." And Jesus cried out with a loud voice, and breathed His last. Then the veil of the temple was torn in two from top to bottom. So when the centurion, who stood opposite Him, saw that He cried out like this and breathed His last, he said, "Truly this Man was the Son of God!" There were also women looking on from afar, among whom were Mary Magdalene, Mary the mother of James the Less and of Joses, and Salome, who also followed Him and ministered to Him when He was in Galilee, and many other women who came up with Him to Jerusalem. —Mark 15:33-41

The gospels tell us that as Jesus hung on the cross "there was darkness over the whole land until the ninth hour" (v. 33). In all probability there was a solar eclipse that plunged Jerusalem into a twilight of dreary darkness. Eclipses produce a weird darkness that is neither dawn nor dusk. The shadows and the light are unlike anything else. Yet, an eclipse is neither magical nor mystical.

Scripture often has many layers of interwoven meaning. So, we must inquire about the symbolism of the darkness that came upon the land during the hour of Jesus' death. The Greek word for *darkness, skotos,* means not only an absence of sunlight, but it also carries the metaphorical sense of darkened eyesight or blindness. Metaphorically, it implies an ignorance of both divine decrees and human duties, and an accompanying ungodliness and immorality that leads to a consequent misery in hell. Matthew used the word to set the context for the coming of Christ: "The people which sat in darkness (*skotos*) have seen a great light" (Matthew 4:16).

Thus, the darkness that covered the land was not merely a three-hour event, but was metaphorically about the context of the ministry of Jesus. Jesus had come into a land of darkness during a time of darkness, preaching, teaching, and ministering God's grace. Jesus' ministry was aimed at a people who had lost sight of God's will, God's way, and God's Word. In the midst of that darkness, Jesus cried, "*Eloi, Eloi, lama sabachthani?*" (v. 34). Scripture leaves these words untranslated in their original Aramaic. It is important that we understand that Jesus spoke these words in Aramaic. Why?

First of all the language of Aram was the language of the people who lived in the high country northeast of Palestine on the plane between the Euphrates and the Tigris rivers. We know that region today as the fertile crescent valley, the birthplace of human civilization itself. Jesus spoke the language of the people who lived in the land of the beginning. It was also the language of the common people of Palestine.

The words comprise the first line of Psalm 22, which describes the suffering, praise, and posterity of the Messiah. By quoting this verse Jesus indicated that He was the Messiah suffering in the fulfillment of Scripture.

But when the people nearby heard Him they said, "Look, He is calling for Elijah!" (v. 35). But He never mentioned Elijah, which means that the people either misheard Him or misunderstood Him. There was Jesus hanging on the cross, about to expire, when He called attention to the fact that the very suffering that He was enduring was the fulfillment of Scripture, and those who heard Him didn't understand what He was talking about. It was as if He was speaking a foreign language! Alas, most of the Lord's preaching and teaching may as well have been in a foreign language because the people were not conversant in the language of God, the language of Scripture.

He wasn't calling for Elijah. Rather, the reference to the man who thought He was calling for Elijah brings attention to a man blinded by his own eschatological expectations. This man was looking for a Messiah in the likeness of Elijah. The popular expectation was that the Messiah would call down fire upon the false prophets of Ba'al (2 Kings 1:10), and return the throne of Israel to a position of political prestige and power. The Old Testament expectations of the Jews blinded the people of Jerusalem to the truth of God in Christ that hung on the cross before their very eyes.

Jesus had refused the narcotic of worldly counsel earlier (v. 23), but once again someone—one who was among those who didn't understand what Jesus was talking about

> "ran and filled a sponge full of sour wine, put it on a reed, and offered it to Him to drink" (v. 36).

This may have been well-intentioned, but in reality it was not a helpful thing to do. The mixture of vinegar and myrrh, though narcotic in effect once swallowed, would have caused a choking or gagging reflex that would shoot tremendous pain through the tortured body that hung on the cross.

Worldly people often want to help the Lord, but failing to understand God's will, God's way, and God's Word, their help only makes things worse. The counsel of the world cannot accomplish or even assist the purposes of God, except in a negative way—like the worldly actions of Judas who betrayed Jesus, whose betrayal brought Jesus to the cross. Judas' actions did fulfill God's purpose in a roundabout way, but only by his own faithless disobedience. Judas is not one whose life and actions can be imitated by faithful disciples.

The one who tried to give Jesus a drink—like the chief priests and the lawyers—then demanded a miracle from the Lord of glory. "Let Him alone; let us see if Elijah will come to take Him down" (v. 36). Stuck in his own eschatalogical expectation, he would not help Jesus, but insisted that his own expectation about Elijah be miraculously fulfilled before *his* own eyes. A man hung nailed to a cross before him, and he wanted to prove his own understanding of the end times.

Eschatology is the study of the end times. Today we know it mostly in its classic forms: premillennialism, postmillennialism, and amillennialism. As important as such discussions can be, to refuse to help a dying man in order to prove that you are right about your eschatology is sheer madness. But that's what this guy seems to have done!

And at that point, "Jesus cried out with a loud voice, and breathed His last" (v. 37). The Greek word for *cried out* here is interesting. *Aphiemi* literally means to send away, or to pardon. It is also translated "to let go" and "to leave behind." But it also carries the sense of forgiveness, as if Jesus' last words were words of forgiveness. More than likely He cried them out to the man who's help was less than helpful, or to the man who was so stuck in his own end times vision that he would allow someone to die in front of him to prove a point, or to the men who had no idea of what Jesus was talking about. Yet, in spite of it all Jesus' last word conveyed forgiveness.

When one of the centurions who had been assigned to guard Jesus on the cross saw what had happened, that Jesus' last breath brought a word of forgiveness, he said, "Truly this Man was the Son of God!" (v. 39). The centurion confessed three things about Jesus: 1) Jesus' faithfulness to the last, 2) the fact that Jesus actually died, and 3) Jesus' divinity as the Son of God.

Again the timing is critical. At the very moment that Jesus died "the veil of the temple was torn in two from top to bottom" (v. 38). The veil of the tabernacle hung between the holy place and the most holy place that only the high priest could enter (Exodus 26:31-35). When the Temple was built a partition wall was added that separated these two rooms. The veil concealed two swinging doors, which were supposed to have been always open. The high priest then lifted the veil when he entered into the sanctuary on the day of Atonement. Thus, the veil is intimately tied to atonement.

The tearing of the veil from the top indicated that it had been torn from above by the Lord Himself. The tear originated on God's side of the veil. The theological understanding of this event is that the veil was not just torn, but torn down, opened or removed. Jesus, as the High Priest Himself symbolically (mystically) entered the holy of holies as the sacrifice of atonement for the sins of God's people. The removal of that veil, then, for those who have eyes to see revealed that Jesus as High Priest had sacrificed Himself as the Lamb of God for the atonement of the sins of His people.

Then there were the women. The women played such a significant role in the story of the life, ministry, death, and resurrection of Jesus. Old Testament women were often depicted as a temptation and snare—think of Eve offering the fruit to Adam, of Sarah offering Hagar to Abraham, of Rebecca, Rachel, Delilah, Bathsheba, Jezebel. These are stories of temptation and sin. But in the New Testament we often find that women are mentioned as a help and comfort to the cause of Christ. Elizabeth, the Marys, Martha, Dorcas, Lydia, Phoebe are all cases in point.

Yet, it must be understood that these feminine examples of faithfulness are not important because they were women, but because they were faithful. Salvation in Christ knows no distinction between male and female, slave or free, Jew or Gentile. In Christ there is salvation for all of God's people, and a place of service for each.

Mark mentioned Mary Magdalene, Mary the mother of James, and Salome. John tells us that from the cross Jesus charged the beloved disciple to care for His mother (John 19:26-27), so Jesus' mother was there—as well as many others. Many of these women had "followed Him and ministered to Him when He was in Galilee" (v. 41). The Greek word is *diakoneo* and means served, attended, like a domestic servant or slave. It means to wait upon, like a waitress waits a table. They provided for Jesus' needs during His earthly ministry—food, shelter, probably clothing, etc.

These women served as examples for us all about what it means to be a Christian. Every Christian is to be a minister or servant in this sense. The women were always around, always helping as best they could—cleaning, preparing, fixing, fussing. Around the cross the women were the last to leave, and the first ones to return in the morning. The work of ministry is much like the work of a midwife—cleaning, preparing, holding hands, setting up chairs, wiping up messes, etc. Ministry is not glamorous work. Most of the time it is the thankless and endless drudgery of serving and helping those who struggle under the pain of labor. Ministry is not glory but humility, not prestige but insignificance, not popularity but faithfulness.

Jesus said that ministry would require a humble attitude of generosity and selflessness, and a heart for serving others. It is the purpose of such ministers to help with the ministry of Christ's church. Furthermore, women were not to simply remain in the background fixing and fussing, but as Jesus called Martha to cease all her *diakoneo* and join Mary at His feet to learn the gospel, He calls all disciples to first learn and then to apply the gospel to themselves (Luke 10:38-42).

As Jesus hung on the cross, He was abandoned by all. Peter's valiant attempt to defend Him in the garden had been chastised by the Lord Himself. After that Peter and the disciples didn't know what to do. All of their expectations about the Messiah had been shattered by Jesus. Thus, the disciples had been scattered and broken. A few women wailed and waited to attend His corpse. As He suffered and bore the sins of the world, even God Himself turned His back. That was the price that had to be paid.

66. Go, Tell

Now when the Sabbath was past, Mary Magdalene, Mary the mother of James, and Salome bought spices, that they might come and anoint Him. Very early in the morning, on the first day of the week, they came to the tomb when the sun had risen. And they said among themselves, "Who will roll away the stone from the door of the tomb for us?" But when they looked up, they saw that the stone had been rolled away—for it was very large. And entering the tomb, they saw a young man clothed in a long white robe sitting on the right side; and they were alarmed. But he said to them, "Do not be alarmed. You seek Jesus of Nazareth, who was crucified. He is risen! He is not here. See the place where they laid Him. But go, tell His disciples—and Peter—that He is going before you into Galilee; there you will see Him, as He said to you." So they went out quickly and fled from the tomb, for they trembled and were amazed. And they said nothing to anyone, for they were afraid.

—Mark 16:1-8

Jesus' final week in Jerusalem ended unceremoniously as the Lord's highest achievement culminated in His crucifixion, death, and burial. Taken from His instrument of torture, He lay all night in the cold, dark tomb of Joseph of Arimathea. He had been taken down from the cross after He died on Good Friday, so that His body would not offend the sensitivities of the Saturday Sabbath. The Sabbath, as you remember, begins at sunset on Friday evening and lasts until sunset on Saturday evening. First light Sunday morning was the earliest that the women could get to Jesus to anoint His body for burial.

Three women ventured out, Mary Magdalene, Mary the mother of James, and Salome. Mary Magdalene had been possessed by a legion of demons (Mark 16:9). Being listed first among the women she served as a kind of representative of those upon whom God would shed His grace. She had been a particularly vile sinner before she was saved. She was the lowest of the low, a woman, a sinner, sexually and morally corrupted, unclean. Yet, she had been saved, and had come to Jesus for service.

357

They came knowing that the stone blocked entry to the tomb. They discussed among themselves about who they could get to roll it aside. But when they got there they saw that the stone had already been moved. There is no mention of the guards placed by Pilate. They may have been frightened off by the earthquake or the angels. Or they may have been there. We don't know.

Entering the tomb, the women "saw a young man clothed in a long white robe" (v. 5). In Revelation 6:11 we learn that Christian martyrs were clothed in white robes in heaven. It is, no doubt, a reference to the robe of Christ's righteousness. Though the man was young, he was fully a man, and clothed in the righteousness of Christ.

Was it a vision or an apparition, a dream, or a ghost? There is no indication that what the women saw was anything but real. Thus, "they were *alarmed*" (v. 5—italics added). The Greek word means amazed, astounded, and terrified.

Imagine the shock of seeing a dead person get up. There was a story several months ago about a person who revived while in the morgue. Apparently he just got up from where he was lying. The person who witnessed it died of a heart attack. One up, one down. The point is that seeing someone who is supposedly dead get up is a shocking experience.

The young man told them not to be alarmed. Right!

He knew that the women had come seeking Jesus, and that Jesus had been crucified, and that He had risen from the dead. He then invited them to see for themselves that He was not there. The young man told them the gospel of Jesus Christ in one verse.

> "Do not be alarmed. You seek Jesus of Nazareth, who was crucified. He is risen!" (v. 6).

He spoke of four elements of gospel truth.

First, don't be afraid. Christians are called to overcome or transcend their fears. "There is no fear in love; but perfect love casts out fear" (1 John 4:18). In Christ there is nothing to be afraid of. Nothing is more secure than the love of Christ. Nothing is more powerful than the power of God. In Christ, in God, in salvation there is nothing to fear.

Second, Christians seek Jesus. They desire Him. They crave Him. But theirs is not a desperate craving as if they are addicted to something that they do not possess. Rather, Christians seek to know Jesus more fully. They have tasted the goodness of the Lord and crave to know and to experience Him more fully. Thus, Christians eagerly engage in worship, Bible study, and prayer. They can't wait to learn more, to sing more, to pray more, to fellowship more. This kind of seeking is the essence of faithfulness.

Third, the hinge or key to salvation is the fact of Jesus' crucifixion. Christians must come to the point that they can see the most unjust action the world has ever known—the crucifixion of the Son of God—in a positive light. Jesus' death, as awful and horrible as it was, served as the propitiation for the sins of God's people. The death of Christ satisfied the justice of God—not for Jesus' sake, but for God's. Here we see that the story of humanity's sin and desperate need of salvation, coupled with the story of the death of Christ is indeed the most positive story the world has ever known—positive because His death is the means of eternal life.

For Christians the preaching of sin and human depravity, coupled with the death and resurrection of Christ is "the aroma of life leading to life" (2 Corinthians 2:16). Proverbs tells us that

> "A satisfied soul loathes the honeycomb, But to a hungry soul
> every bitter thing is sweet" (Proverbs 27:7).

While well-fed children find that they don't like this or that at the dinner table, hungry children delight in what others consider to be the most awful things. Similarly, in the light of Christ the doctrines of sin, depravity, and damnation are understood as undeniable evidences of God's grace and mercy. We deserve death, yet He gives us life. Those who don't understand their own willing complicity in sin and depravity cannot appreciate the gift of salvation. The better you understand that you don't deserve it, the better you understand God's amazing grace.

The fourth element of the gospel of Jesus Christ is that "He is risen" (v. 6). While Christ's crucifixion provided the necessary punishment for our sin, satisfying the justice of God, His resurrection provided the foundation upon which salvation is received—faith. "Christ suffered for us in the flesh" (1 Peter 4:1), He took on our sins that we may take on His righteousness. He took on our guilt that we may take on His forgiveness. His suffering and death is the historic event that fulfills the promises of God's justice.

His resurrection then is the historic event that fulfills the promises of God's mercy. His crucifixion was for God's sake, His resurrection was for our sake. His resurrection must be taken on faith. There is no proof, only an empty tomb and the testimony of witnesses.

Verse 7, the following verse, provides us with the first response to the gospel of Jesus Christ.

> "But go, tell His disciples—and Peter—that He is going before you into Galilee; there you will see Him, as He said to you." (v. 7).

As obedience is the fruit of the gospel, the disciples are told to go and tell what they have seen, what they trust to be true. They are commanded to share the gospel as an act of obedience, which helps to establish the reality of the gospel in their own lives. Sharing the gospel requires that you believe and understand it enough to say something about it. Your sharing the gospel is evidence that you believe it.

Who are they to tell? The disciples. The women, including Mary Magdalene who represents the greatest of sinners in that she had been possessed by a legion of demons, were to tell the disciples—not the world, not the unchurched, not the heathen, but the *disciples*. Peter in particular was singled out because he represented the failure and depravity of the disciples, having denied Jesus three times.

The gospel was to be shared from Mary Magdalene to Peter. Thus the gospel moved not just from one sinner to another, but from a worldly perspective it moved from the lowest of the low—a woman, heathen sinner, probably divorced, sexually impure and unclean, yet saved—to the highest representative, the leader of the disciples. The women were to share the gospel with the disciples. Mary was to share the gospel with Peter.

Jesus would send the disciples out into the world soon enough, but first the gospel must be received by His disciples. His own disciples must become the body of Christ before they go out to the world. They must first be filled with the power of the Holy Spirit (Acts 1:8), only then would they be able to fulfill the Great Commission. Before they could posses the insight, wisdom, courage, resolve, etc. to go out and make disciples, they would need the discernment, wisdom, strength, commitment, etc. of the Holy Spirit. Before any church can engage in faithful outreach, the people of the church need the unity of the Spirit. They need to be on the same page, pulling in the same direction. Otherwise their witness to those they try to reach will be a witness of confusion and disorder.

Jesus brought His disciples to a progressive realization of the truth of all that He had taught them. He brought them along step by step, as their own abilities and sensitivities would allow them. The women were told of His resurrection. They were then told to tell the disciples. But they were weak and afraid. They were confused and distressed by all that had happened.

"So they went out quickly and fled from the tomb, for they trembled and were amazed. And they said nothing to anyone, for they were afraid" (v. 8).

They didn't know what to say. They didn't think that anyone would believe them.

67. Still Didn't Believe

Now when He rose early on the first day of the week, He appeared first to Mary Magdalene, out of whom He had cast seven demons. She went and told those who had been with Him, as they mourned and wept. And when they heard that He was alive and had been seen by her, they did not believe. After that, He appeared in another form to two of them as they walked and went into the country. And they went and told it to the rest, but they did not believe them either. Later He appeared to the eleven as they sat at the table; and He rebuked their unbelief and hardness of heart, because they did not believe those who had seen Him after He had risen. And He said to them, "Go into all the world and preach the gospel to every creature. He who believes and is baptized will be saved; but he who does not believe will be condemned." —Mark 16:9-16

In order to keep us from becoming overly discouraged by the ministry of Jesus, we now jump to the end of His last week in Jerusalem to see the end of the story. The first disciples did not have the benefit of Scripture to know the whole story as we do. Thus, we should not be too quick to judge them for their disbelief. We would have done no differently had we been in their shoes. Nonetheless, it is essential that we keep the fact of their disbelief in our minds because it plays a significant role in the story of Jesus.

Mary Magdalene had been a particularly vile sinner, having had a legion of demons cast out of her when she was saved. That detail suggests the degree of her sin and possession by evil forces. Mary Magdalene was among the last to see Jesus on the cross and among the first to arrive at the empty tomb. Such commitment in both life and death suggests the depth of her love for the Lord.

Verse 9 tells us that Jesus "appeared first to Mary Magdalene." This is a significant detail because it shows the importance of love and commitment to Jesus. He first showed Himself to one who loved Him dearly and was committed to Him in life and in death. This fact should speak volumes to us about the appropriate response to Jesus. He honored Mary

Magdalene—among the most vile of sinners—above all others because of her love for Him.

True love does not depend upon who we are. It does not depend upon our personal successes or failures. Marriage is the highest expression of genuine love between people. Listen to the wedding vows:

> I, (name), take you, (name), to be my wedded wife/husband, to
> have and to hold, from this day forward, for better, for worse, for
> richer, for poorer, in sickness and in health, to love and to
> cherish, till death do us part, according to God's holy ordinance, I
> pledge you my faith.

The old English word was *troth*, I pledge you my troth. Troth means both trust and truth. The pledge involves both trusting and being trustworthy. It means giving and receiving the truth.

The love between husbands and wives does not depend on performance. One's success or failure doesn't matter, wealth or poverty makes no difference, health or illness cannot interfere with marital love. Marital love serves God's purposes. It is good for us as well, but only secondarily. God brings it into existence and sustains it. I'm not suggesting that Mary Magdalene was married to Jesus, but that the character of Mary's love is best understood in those terms. It was true love in the best sense. In light of this fact we ought to emulate Mary by committing ourselves to that kind of true love for the Lord.

Scripture itself describes the church as the bride of Christ (Revelation 21:2). In fact, it seems that only those who evidenced this kind of love were able to "see" the resurrected Jesus. Even today, we can only see the Lord as we love Him. He reveals Himself in Scripture, but not everyone can see Him—only those who truly love Him. And, of course, that love is not something that we can work up in our own strength or faithfulness, but it is given to us as a gift of grace.

At first Mary and the other women were afraid and "said nothing to anyone" (v. 8). But having seen Jesus—which was the evidence of her love for Him and His gift of grace to her—she then "went and told" the others, who were still in mourning, still weeping, still broken, still in disbelief. The death of Jesus had utterly destroyed their hopes and dreams. And that is as it should be. As long as we are caught up in our own hopes and dreams, we cannot see Jesus—not as He is in reality, not as Lord and Savior.

We have seen this truth again and again in our study of Mark's gospel. The disciples themselves have been unable to "see" or understand Jesus throughout His ministry to this point. They had glimpses of Him now and then. They thought they understood Him, but most of His ministry was aimed at disabusing them of their own preconceptions and misperceptions, weaning them of their own hopes and dreams regarding Him.

We see the same disillusioning scenario played out in many marriages. Young people often have a lot of preconceptions regarding marriage—questions about who and what a wife or husband is supposed to be. Couples don't really learn the truth about each other until those false hopes and dreams have crashed and burned. And that is an ordinary part of marriage. It's not an excuse for divorce, it's an opportunity for people to move beyond the self-centeredness of loving their own hopes and dreams as they project them onto their spouse.

The same dynamic plays out in personal, spiritual growth as the Lord brings people to the end of their own thoughts and understandings, to the end of their own hopes and dreams about who and what Jesus is. In fact, it is only when people are finally disabused of their own hopes and dreams, their own thoughts and understandings that they can begin to see Jesus and Scripture as they really are. Most of the time our own preconceptions shape and determine what we think we know. Only by overcoming our preconceptions can the Lord finally share His thoughts with us.

> "For My thoughts are not your thoughts, Nor are your ways My ways," says the Lord. "For as the heavens are higher than the earth, So are My ways higher than your ways, And My thoughts than your thoughts" (Isaiah 55:8-9).

Mary Magdalene was finally ready to see Jesus because her preconceptions—her hopes and dreams—had died on the cross. The cross had humbled her because it had taken away any hopes that she may have had about trying to have a relationship with Jesus that issued from or even supported her own hopes and/or expectations. Her human relationship with Jesus was taken from her by His death.

But when the resurrected Jesus appeared to her that relationship was given back to her, but not on her terms—on His. That relationship was then given to her as a pure gift of grace. She could not establish it. She could not sustain it. Only on those conditions does Jesus reveal Himself to His people.

The difficulty is that this kind of relationship is completely foreign to us. It runs counter to everything we think we know. It requires, not the fulfillment of our hopes and dreams but the death of our hopes and dreams. Out of that death, then, the hopes and dreams of Jesus Christ can inhabit our thoughts. Out of the death of the old man, comes the birth of the new. However, the birth of the new man cannot happen until the death of the old.

> "Most assuredly" said Jesus, "unless a grain of wheat falls into the ground and dies, it remains alone; but if it dies, it produces much grain" (John 12:24).

Mary went and told the mourning disciples that their tears and sorrows were foolish and unnecessary because Jesus was alive. She had seen Him. How did they respond to her witness? She shared her faith with them, but they didn't believe her. Remember, these were God's elect! He had called them and sanctified them, yet they rejected her story and therefore Christ's resurrection. They still didn't believe. Why not? Why didn't they believe? Why don't so many of the people we share our faith with believe? Why doesn't it work? What's missing?

> "After that, He appeared in another form to two of them as they walked and went into the country" (v. 12).

He didn't identify Himself, nor did they recognize Him. But He drew them into conversation about His crucifixion and death. They, too, told all they knew. They, too, shared the story of Jesus—what they knew of it. Luke 24:21 tells us that they were "hoping that (Jesus) was going to redeem Israel." They too had been filled with their own hopes and dreams regarding Jesus. They were close to the truth, yet they missed it by a mile.

Jesus would redeem Israel, but not in the way that they thought, and not the Israel they thought. They thought that He was going to be a political redeemer of the Old Testament nation of Israel. They didn't know—and couldn't know in themselves—that He was the spiritual redeemer of a New Israel. But He explained it all to them,

> "beginning at Moses and all the Prophets, He expounded to them in all the Scriptures the things concerning Himself" (Luke 24:27).

He told them everything. He showed them everything.

In that story the two disciples did not recognize Jesus until

> "He sat at the table with them, (and) He took bread, blessed and broke it, and gave it to them. Then their eyes were opened and they knew Him." But as soon as they recognized Him, "He vanished from their sight" (Luke 24:30-31).

The whole purpose of His resurrection appearances was to make Himself known to His disciples. Jesus wants His people to know Him intimately. We are to know Jesus as a man knows his wife—intimately, deeply, personally. We are to know all about Jesus, personally and up close.

Mark left the story of Jesus' Emmaus appearance with the two disciples coming back and telling the others about their experience. And what happened as these disciples shared their personal faith with the others? No one believed them either. Again and again, Mark hammers this recurring theme of misunderstanding and unbelief.

Surely, if those who experienced Jesus first hand had difficulty believing, there is no reason to think that it would be easy for anyone. In fact, belief in Christ's resurrection is completely impossible except for one thing. No one can believe in His resurrection or in the gospel unless and until the Lord Himself sends the Holy Spirit to change his heart and mind.

That is the whole point of Mark's gospel. We can't do it! It's impossible unless the Lord does it for us. We cannot change anyone else's mind. We can't even change our own minds. Only Christ Himself can do that. Only Christ can convert and renew us. It's not what *we* do, it's what *He* does that makes the critical difference. It's all about grace.

But that does not mean that we should sit around and do nothing because it's all up to God and not us. Rather, knowing that it's all up to God, and that God has sent His Holy Spirit to inhabit the hearts and minds of His people, we should do what we can, knowing that what God does through His people cannot be stopped. And God works mostly through His people. The fact that God is the source of Christian energy and accomplishment is not an excuse to sit back and let God do it Himself. Rather, it is a goad of encouragement to know that God will use our measly efforts to accomplish great things.

Scripture Index

Alphabetical Index

295, 298, 300, 307, 309,
310, 312, 319, 322, 324,
327, 330, 335, 339, 341,
342, 344, 346, 348, 349,
350, 351, 360, 361, 362,
365
benefit......35, 46, 47, 52, 81,
103, 122, 135, 196, 207,
226, 227, 264, 338, 362
Bernall, Cassie.................335
Bethany..........253, 256, 304
Bethpage.................253, 254
Bethsaida........................304
bewilderment...................16
Bible study 47, 80, 101, 116,
121, 167, 224, 229, 275,
358
biblical values..2, 34, 74, 75,
285
blasphemy...31, 32, 71, 112,
332
blasphemy against the Spirit
.....................................72
bless...................................51
blessing....46, 47, 49, 51, 71,
79, 82, 83, 94, 106, 109,
134, 145, 149, 152, 156,
170, 228, 229, 230, 262,
264, 282, 294, 295, 309,
316
blood...55, 76, 99, 100, 101,
104, 107, 109, 142, 149,
150, 183, 186, 231, 275,
287, 290, 306, 310, 315
born again.....116, 151, 183,
204, 205
Bosnia............................292
bread..22, 63, 132, 134, 147,
160, 174, 175, 176, 309,
316, 365
bribe...........................34, 269
broken 37, 55, 149, 181, 225,
356, 363
Caanan....................243, 246
Caesarea Philippi;.............96
Caiaphas.........................332
Calvary.....................71, 181
Calvin................19, 76, 212
candidates for baptism....261
Capernaum....12, 27, 29, 30,

141, 142
casting lots.......................349
casting out26, 212, 213, 214,
229
centurion.........106, 164, 355
chain of command.........311
charismatic 16, 114, 149, 152
checkbook.......................236
child3, 6, 21, 51, 69, 94, 104,
110, 116, 117, 154, 156,
160, 162, 164, 166, 202,
203, 209, 211, 217, 228,
229, 230, 231, 234, 260,
267, 269, 275, 308, 315,
317, 359
childlike faith..................319
choice..........48, 58, 117, 267
chosen people..................148
Christ alone 43, 55, 107, 116,
199, 204, 205, 221, 245,
247, 256, 351
Christ's return..........296, 299
Christian education...43, 116
Christians are weak........321
church fellowship..............75
church membership 261, 310
Church officers........215, 333
circumcision..........2, 42, 315
clean.....................15, 27, 161
cleansing of the Temple. 249
coddled and spoon-fed...161
coincidence.....................245
colt 254
come unexpectedly.........301
comfort......9, 10, 48, 79, 84,
103, 114, 115, 283, 355
command 19, 110, 121, 138,
171, 204, 220, 224, 251,
265, 280, 311
commercial opportunities
.....................................249
common sense.................269
communicated by touch.107
compassion....52, 55, 61, 77,
116, 118, 131, 165, 170,
304
complain..............15, 72, 116
condemnation.....53, 72, 73,
214, 285
conditions.......8, 69, 79, 101,

364
Confederate Soldier........242
confess.....3, 13, 52, 93, 128,
129, 156, 162, 168, 186,
187, 190, 194, 245, 260,
261, 274, 351, 355
confront...96, 147, 175, 335,
336, 351
conscience.........27, 126, 127
conservatives...54, 128, 268,
269, 273
consistent.....................81, 96
contemporary church...101,
261
contempt.........117, 341, 347
contingent.................47, 349
contradict..18, 19, 120, 187,
214, 218, 310
control.3, 88, 117, 164, 165,
229, 230, 252, 264, 289,
290, 291, 312, 324
conversion2, 8, 35, 214, 215,
226, 284, 286, 291, 307,
319, 327, 339, 349
convulsed..................16, 204
corban......................150, 151
corrupt37, 99, 154, 161, 210,
215, 236, 272, 275, 341,
342, 349, 357
costly oil...........................305
coterminous.........................4
counseling.................43, 160
counterfeit..............292, 347
covenant2, 41, 42, 126, 223,
224, 225, 226, 275, 286,
295, 315
creation...25, 172, 224, 225,
295, 348
crisis.................221, 290, 319
cross...17, 26, 36, 41, 49, 56,
69, 71, 76, 111, 122,
134, 145, 172, 173, 181,
183, 190, 191, 194, 195,
197, 198, 199, 206, 208,
221, 231, 234, 235, 239,
242, 245, 255, 258, 267,
294, 295, 315, 321, 326,
327, 339, 341, 342, 348,
349, 350, 352, 353, 354,
356, 357, 362, 364